Global Transformations in Media and Communication Research - A Palgrave and IAMCR Series

Series Editors

Marjan de Bruin
HARP, Mona Campus
The University of the West Indies
Mona, Jamaica

Claudia Padovani
SPGI
University of Padova
Padova, Italy

The International Association for Media and Communications Research (IAMCR) has been, for over 50 years, a focal point and unique platform for academic debate and discussion on a variety of topics and issues generated by its many thematic Sections and Working groups (see http://iamcr.org/) This new series specifically links to the intellectual capital of the IAMCR and offers more systematic and comprehensive opportunities for the publication of key research and debates. It will provide a forum for collective knowledge production and exchange through trans-disciplinary contributions. In the current phase of globalizing processes and increasing interactions, the series will provide a space to rethink those very categories of space and place, time and geography through which communication studies has evolved, thus contributing to identifying and refining concepts, theories and methods with which to explore the diverse realities of communication in a changing world. Its central aim is to provide a platform for knowledge exchange from different geo-cultural contexts. Books in the series will contribute diverse and plural perspectives on communication developments including from outside the Anglo-speaking world which is much needed in today's globalized world in order to make sense of the complexities and intercultural challenges communication studies are facing.

More information about this series at
http://www.palgrave.com/gp/series/15018

Adrian Athique • Vibodh Parthasarathi
Editors

Platform Capitalism in India

palgrave
macmillan

Editors
Adrian Athique
Institute for Advanced Studies Humanities
University of Queensland
St Lucia, QLD, Australia

Vibodh Parthasarathi
Centre for Culture Media and Governance
Jamia Millia Islamia
New Delhi, India

Global Transformations in Media and Communication Research - A Palgrave and IAMCR Series
ISBN 978-3-030-44562-1 ISBN 978-3-030-44563-8 (eBook)
https://doi.org/10.1007/978-3-030-44563-8

Cover Illustration: Alex Robinson / gettyimages
Cover design: eStudioCalamar

This Palgrave Macmillan imprint is published by the registered company Springer Nature Switzerland AG.
The registered company address is: Gewerbestrasse 11, 6330 Cham, Switzerland

This book is dedicated to Professor Tom O'Regan,
his unmatched grasp of ontology
and a fierce mind.

Contents

Notes on Contributors

Hrishikesh Arvikar is pursuing his PhD on Early Cinema in Bombay Presidency—its developments, progressions and delineations—at the School of Communication and Arts, University of Queensland. He has a filmmaking diploma from Xavier Institute of Communications (XIC), Mumbai. He later pursued his MPhil at Jawaharlal Nehru University (JNU), New Delhi. His dissertation, titled *The Cinema of Prabhat—Histories, Aesthetics, and Politics* (School of Arts and Aesthetics, JNU), dealt with questions of film practice, territoriality and studio space in Western India in the late colonial period. He has published papers for local, regional and international journals, including one on the political economy of Prabhat studio published in *Widescreen*. He is writing a monograph, two film scripts and a web series.

Adrian Athique is principal research fellow in Cultural Studies at the University of Queensland. Adrian is the author of *The Multiplex in India* (2010, with Douglas Hill), *Indian Media: Global Approaches* (2012), *Digital Media and Society* (2013) and *Transnational Audiences: Media Reception at a Global Scale* (2016). He has also edited volumes on *The Indian Media Economy* (2 Vols., 2018, with Vibodh Parthasarathi and S.V. Srinivas) and *Digital Transactions in Asia* (2019, with Emma Baulch), and is co-editor of the journal *Media International Australia* and the Oxford University Press series *Media Dynamics in South Asia*. Adrian is collaborating with Shishir K. Jha, Pradip Thomas,

Vigneswara Ilavarasan and Scott Fitzgerald on the SPARC project *Platform Economies in Digital India: Assessing Implementation, Impact, Infrastructure and Aptitude*.

Philippe Bouquillion is Professor of Communication at the University Sorbonne Paris Nord and a researcher at the Laboratory of Excellence *Cultural Industries and Artistic Creation* and at the Laboratory of Information and Communication Sciences. His work focuses on cultural and creative industries and especially on the issues of concentration and financialization, transnationalization and the transformations of public policies in cultural and creative industries. His most recent research deals with audiovisual digital platforms in Europe and India. He has managed several research contracts, including contracts commissioned by the French Ministry of Culture and Communication and the National Research Agency.

Scott Fitzgerald is a senior lecturer and discipline lead (People, Culture and Organizations) in the School of Management at Curtin University in Western Australia. His research interests cover the networked media economy, cultural industry corporations and cultural work, as well as public services (especially education) and new public management. He is working on the Government of India SPARC project *Platform Economies in Digital India: Assessing Implementation, Impact, Infrastructure and Aptitude* as part of a research team led by Shishir K. Jha and Adrian Athique. Scott is also an active member of IAMCR and the South Asian Studies Association of Australia, which kindly funded the presentation and workshop of many of the papers included in this book at Curtin University in July 2019.

M. Shuaib Mohamed Haneef is an assistant professor in the Department of Electronic Media and Mass Communication, Pondicherry University, India. His areas of interest include digital media and culture, specifically focusing on interactivity and agency, digital journalism, algorithms and digital media, and digital media and affect studies. He has published on materiality of dress in digital media, art, protest and affect in digital media, Deleuzian reading of music as well as digital art and so on. He also edits an online open-access journal *Communication and Culture Review*.

Christine Ithurbide holds a PhD in Geography from Paris Diderot University, is a postdoctoral researcher with the Laboratory of Information and Communication Sciences (LabSIC) at Paris 13 University and an associated member with the Centre de Sciences Humaines, New Delhi. Her researches focus on cultural industries, economy and labour in India in the context of globalization. Since 2017, she coordinates (with Philippe Bouquillion) the research programme *Cultural Industries in India: Digital, Platforms and Regulation* at LabEx ICCA and studies the deployment of digital technology and the reconfigurations of music and film spaces, industries and economy, especially in Mumbai.

Arpan Kumar Kar is an associate professor in the Department of Management Studies, Indian Institute of Technology Delhi. His research interests are in the domain of e-business, social media, e-governance, data analytics and technology management. He has published over 75 articles in reputed journals and is the managing editor of *Global Journal of e-Business & Knowledge Management* and associate editor of *Global Journal of Flexible Systems Management*. He has previously worked for the Indian Institute of Management (IIM) Rohtak, IBM Research Laboratory and Cognizant Business Consulting. Professor Kar has received multiple awards and recognitions for his research from reputed organizations like the Association of Indian Management Schools, Tata Consultancy Services, Project Management Institute and IIM Rohtak.

Aquil Ahmad Khan is a full-time research scholar at the Department of Electronic Media and Mass Communication, Pondicherry University. His research interest includes political economy and digital journalism. He has presented papers at national and international conferences. His doctoral research seeks to understand digital labour in select digital native news websites in India.

Akshaya Kumar is Assistant Professor of Sociology at the School of Humanities and Social Sciences, Indian Institute of Technology Indore. His first monograph, *Provincializing Bollywood: Bhojpuri Cinema in the Comparative Media Crucible*, is to be published under the *Media Dynamics in South Asia* series of Oxford University Press. His interests include the questions of capital, genre, stardom, provinciality and language in Indian media, informal economies and platform capitalism. His essays have appeared in *Postmodern Culture*, *Social Text*, *Media Industries Journal*, *Television and New Media* and various other journals.

Vibodh Parthasarathi maintains a multidisciplinary interest in media policy, creative industries and media history, his most recent work being the co-edited double-volume *The Indian Media Economy* (2018). An associate professor at Jamia Millia Islamia, he has been visiting scholar at KU Leuven, the University of Queensland, the Indian Institute of Technology Bombay and the University of Helsinki, besides ongoing affiliations at CMDS, Central European University and SASNET, Lund University. He is a winner of numerous international grants, including from the Ford Foundation, Canada's IDRC, Social Science Research Council, HIVOS and India New Zealand Education Council, besides those from India's University Grants Commission and ICSSR. Parthasarathi has been invited in editorial advisory roles at Massachusetts Institute of Technology Press and Oxford University Press, at the *Journal of Communication* and *Global Media and Communication* and at the public intellectual platform *The Conversation*. Presently he serves on the board of the *Centre for Internet and Society* (Bangalore) and on the executive council of *The Media Foundation* (New Delhi). His recent work has been exploring the dynamics of digitalization unfolding in various sites of the Indian media, including in newspapers, journalism, broadcasting and cable distribution. He is working on a book on media regulation in the longue durée in modern India.

Amit Rai is Reader in Creative Industries and Arts Organisation and the programme director of the MA Creative Industries and Arts Organisation at Queen Mary University of London. He has previously taught at Stanford, the New School for Social Research, Lorton Maximum Security Prison, Georgetown University, the Tata Institute of Social Sciences (Mumbai) and the Florida State University. Amit is the author of *Rule of Sympathy: Race, Sentiment, and Power, 1750–1860* (Palgrave, 2002), *Untimely Bollywood: Globalisation and India's New Media Assemblage* (2009) and *Jugaad Time: Ecologies of Everyday Hacking in India* (2019), and has also written numerous articles for journals throughout the world.

Usha Rodrigues is Senior Lecturer in Communication, with expertise in journalism practice and scholarship, at Deakin University in Melbourne, Australia. She is the co-author of three books, including two significant works, *Indian Media in a Globalised World* (2010) and *Indian News Media: From Observer to Participant* (2015). Usha has also undertaken several studies in journalism, social media and political communication, diversity and the media, globalization and new media technologies' impact on journalism practice and citizen and community media enterprise. Presently, she is investigating representation of the #MeToo movement in the mainstream media and racism in fake news circulated on various media platforms.

Pawan Singh holds a PhD in Communication from the University of California San Diego. From 2016 to 2019, he was a New Generation Network Scholar in Contemporary Histories at Deakin University and the Australia India Institute. His work on digital identity and privacy rights in the Indian context has been funded by the Toyota Foundation Award for 'exploring new values for society' and the Digital Identity Research Initiative fieldwork grant from the Indian School of Business during 2018–2019. His manuscript addresses the adjudication of privacy as a fundamental right in India in relation to biometric identity, bodily autonomy and governance.

Pradip Thomas is an associate professor at the School of Communication and Arts, University of Queensland. A previous vice-president of the International Association of Media and Communications Research, his work focuses on communication and social change, communication rights, political economy of communications, religion and media. He is the author and editor of several books on the media in India, including *Strong Religion, Zealous Media: Christian Fundamentalism and Communication in India* (2008), *Political Economy of Communications in India: The Good, The Bad and The Ugly* (2010), *Negotiating Communication Rights: Case Studies from India* (2011), *Digital India: Understanding Information, Communication and Social Change* (2012), *Empire and Post-Empire Telecommunications in India: A History* (2019) and *The Politics of Digital India: Between Local Compulsions and External Pressures* (2019).

Ishita Tiwary is a Horizon postdoctoral fellow at the Mel Hoppenheim School of Cinema, Concordia University. Her research interests include video cultures, media infrastructures, contraband media practices and media aesthetics in South Asia. Her work has been published in *Bioscope: South Asian Screen Studies*, *Post Script: Essays in Film and Humanities* and *Marg: Journal of Indian Art*, amongst others.

Ravinder Kumar Verma is a PhD student at the Department of Management Studies, Indian Institute of Technology (IIT) Delhi. His doctoral topic is related to the digital economy in India. He also has research interests in e-governance, ICT4D and development studies. Prior to joining IIT Delhi, Ravinder completed an MPhil in Planning and Development at the Indian Institute of Technology Bombay. He also holds a degree in Science from Gujarat University and an MBA with distinction from SCDL.

P. Vigneswara Ilavarasan is a professor in the Department of Management Studies, Indian Institute of Technology (IIT) Delhi. His specific research interests are information and communication technologies and development (ICTD), Indian IT industry and social media. Professor Ilavrasan has been a recipient of the Outstanding Young Faculty Fellowship Award at IIT Delhi and Prof. M.N. Srinivas Memorial Prize of the Indian Sociological Society. He has held research grants from IDRC (Canada), the Government of India, Oxford Analytica (UK), IPTS (European Commission) and IdeaCorp (the Philippines). Previously, he has taught at Pondicherry Central University and the Indian Institute of Management Rohtak.

List of Tables

CHAPTER 1

Platform Economy and Platformization

Adrian Athique and Vibodh Parthasarathi

In this book, we begin to interrogate the phenomenon of India's expanding platform economy in terms of both rationale and process, linking a series of empirical inquiries to a critical analysis of the prevailing logics of 'platform capitalism' and 'platformization'. This approach reflects our view that platforms are market systems rather than simply technical systems and explores the consequent need to situate their evolution in India both contextually and historically. In this respect, we diverge from an understanding of platforms as novel forms of firm emerging unheralded from the affordances of data mining and mobile technologies. In developing a markets-based approach towards the platform economy, we attempt to outline the key motivating tendencies playing out across the interlocking domains of commerce, technology, sociability and logistics. In doing

A. Athique (✉)
Institute for Advanced Studies Humanities, University of Queensland,
St Lucia, QLD, Australia
e-mail: a.athique@uq.edu.au

V. Parthasarathi
Centre for Culture Media and Governance, Jamia Millia Islamia,
New Delhi, India
e-mail: vibodhp@yahoo.com

A. Athique, V. Parthasarathi (eds.), *Platform Capitalism in India*,
Global Transformations in Media and Communication Research - A
Palgrave and IAMCR Series,
https://doi.org/10.1007/978-3-030-44563-8_1

so, this collection of chapters seeks to establish a set of analytical markers more precisely attuned to the cultural dynamics and path dependencies shaping digital marketplaces in India. In undertaking this task, the contributors to this volume offer a range of perspectives, articulated across different disciplines and different sites of the platform economy. Collectively, we situate 'platform capitalism' as a phenomenon emerging from the extension and convergence of long-term tendencies in media markets, state policy and the central pursuit of a technocratic solution to India's development goals, paying attention to the widespread and multitudinous issues arising from those endeavours. Critically, each of the authors argues in their own way for a substantially *sui generis* approach to understanding platform capitalism in India.

Successive governments over the past two decades have staked a significant stock of their political capital on the 'global positioning' of India as a digital power (Thomas 2012). Since 2015, the Government of India has made strenuous efforts to facilitate the infrastructure necessary for realizing the vision of the 'Digital India' programme, with universal access to online services and a fully integrated data infrastructure. The high rhetoric of 'Digital India' is founded upon the biometric architecture of the Aadhaar platform, the world's largest and most ambitious 'mechanism of legibility' (Cohen 2017). Riding over the country's vast telecom and other digital networks, Aadhaar underpins the further policy ambitions of the 'India Stack' and the realization of a transactional economy (Aiyar 2017; India Stack 2020). Joining the international race to harness 'smart' technologies for sustainable cities and renewing economic growth via the 'fourth industrial revolution', the incumbent government has assiduously courted Silicon Valley giants on securing technology transfers, while forging systemic partnerships with domestic conglomerates to provide the necessary investments in fibre networks and data centres (see Thomas 2019). The present era of Digital India, then, is quite different in temper from the heyday of liberalization between 1991 and 2008. As the key interest in incubating the platform economy, the state functions as an orchestrator and an instrument in shaping market norms, while also being a seller of bandwidth and a procurer of infrastructural development (see Parthasarathi and Athique 2020). This ethos reflects international trends in the emerging formulation of post-globalization politics and a digital economy increasingly dominated by national champions closely linked to state sponsorship and backed by accommodating policies intended to harness the benefits of automation, digitization and various avatars of artificial intelligence.

Of itself, the $17 billion Digital India programme has become feasible only because the mobile telecoms boom in the 2000s brought major business houses into a commanding position in the overall economy of media and communications. The entry of Reliance Industries Limited (India's largest diversified industrial conglomerate) into the mobile data sector in 2016, via its Reliance Jio subsidiary, has accelerated consolidation in mobile telecoms to the point where only three operators remain (Hill and Athique 2018; Curwen 2018). For their part, the global tech giants have proved receptive to the wider ambitions of Digital India, precisely because its core initiatives are intended to deliver the necessary ecosystem for a vast platform economy centred upon digital goods and services. Failed efforts by Facebook in 2016 to set up proprietary systems via their Free Basics initiative have not prevented India from becoming the largest user base for this platform globally (as it now is also for Facebook's affiliate, WhatsApp). Google dominates the digital advertising market in India as a near monopoly, and the predominance of Indian music content on YouTube has led to their acquisition of legacy domestic rights holders, such as T-Series. The tussle between Amazon and Walmart for a controlling stake in India's e-commerce markets through the latter's purchase in 2018 of FlipKart, the largest domestic ecommerce enterprise was followed by the announcement in 2019 that India would be a test bed for Facebook's Libra currency experiment. Since then, the tie-up announced between Reliance and Microsoft in developing a vast network of data centres reflects a common adherence to the populist mantra that 'data is the new oil'.

At the shopfront, a host of domestic entrepreneurs have been developing digital start-ups and platform brands across a broad range of marketplaces and services. Indian platforms such as Ola, FlipKart and PayTM have attracted multiple rounds of funding, initially from ambitious 'technology-banks' elsewhere in Asia (such as Ali Baba, Softbank and Mediatek) and, more recently, from major US players (such as Amazon, Walmart and Microsoft). Notwithstanding competition from the global giants, India's plentiful start-ups must also contend with the consequences of domestic conglomerates moving into content and service provision as a means of driving their own expansion in data infrastructure. This is epitomized by Reliance launching its Jio mobile network, along with Jio TV and Jio Music (Mukherjee 2019). One feature of this expanding cornucopia of platform offerings is their exuberant promotional ethos, reflected in a vast network of brand tie-ups, cross-platform cashbacks and novel forms of credit that can be accumulated and spent across the digital economy.

Thus, for the verified users of Digital India, the burgeoning suite of platforms provides not only novel logistical opportunities and channels of communication, but also an expansive range of tangible and intangible commodities. These enticements rest upon various types of cross-subsidization, both between platforms and from the deeper pockets of the communication layer that supports the system. As we begin to comprehend the increasing mobility and monetization of both content and users across this interlinked ecology of platforms, we are increasingly prompted to consider the consequences of digital consolidation for the everyday transactions of commerce, culture and politics across India.

Whilst the emerging research on mobile platforms has tended to take a single firm or single product approach, there is an imperative to undertake a more holistic approach that accounts for the systemic integration intrinsic to the design and execution of the platform economy. Such an undertaking goes beyond mapping synergies and subsidies, data exchanges and algorithmic interoperability, or of the datafication and behavioural traits of consumers. Rather, it requires us to grasp something of the underlying impulse that drives this larger design: a platform ethos that might be captured by Appadurai's consideration of the 'spirit of calculation' in our times, or by the political economy of Srnicek, who describes the advent of platforms as indicating the emergence of a novel form of 'platform capitalism' (Appadurai 2012; Srnicek 2017). Such analytical explanations of the fundamentals of platform economy are reference points addressed throughout this volume, most directly in the first part and in a number of specific contexts in subsequent chapters. As scholars, we are also compelled to consider the social and cultural forces and mores that are being dis-embedded and re-organized by the platform economy in India. The focus of the leading platform operators on remediating economies that already exist, and which by their nature are deeply embedded in the currents of everyday life, necessarily inflects our understanding of the potentials and implications of a Digital India.

It is also a point of significance that the sectors and activities being refashioned under platform capitalism are overwhelmingly sectors previously located in the informal economy. The era of platforms marks an expansion of the frontiers of the formal economy, meditating its integration with the informal economy and thereby affecting a greater intimacy with everyday life. Rather than simply celebrating disruption for its own sake (given such a condition is hardly novel for modern India), it is important to apply a critical lens to the promise and potentials of the platform economy. In the first place, we need to understand how platform logics may or may not be applicable to India's cultures, economy and society, or more specifically, applicable to certain parts of it and not to others. We also have to be aware that the stakes are high. The present focus of investments in data centres, smart cities, digital transactions and 5G networks is taking place precisely at a moment when the Indian economy, like others globally, is experiencing a slowdown in consumption, investment and industrial output. After three decades of tangible growth, tax receipts and employment are also tapering off. The international economic outlook for 2020 is uncertain at best, and the informal sector has been in a particular state of crisis since 2016. There is no escaping the fact that the offerings of the platform economy, so heavily based around discretionary spending and the convenience of delivery, are heavily disposed towards urban and middle class consumers. The purported benefits for a large and distressed rural sector, and for an equally large segment of the urban population on marginal incomes, have been widely touted but are yet to be realized.

The remediation of public sector programmes operates as the central strategy, intended to be underwritten by efficiency gains from automation and taxes collected from smartphone spenders in urban India. This mode of redistribution, notwithstanding the massive infrastructure costs that will be required for some years to come, constitutes a great leap of faith in the transformative power of the digital. For this reason, the contributors to this volume have been asked to consider both the ethos of platform capitalism and its rendering in contexts particular to India. At the same time, we have also been prompted to go beyond the description of socio-economic phenomena, however distinctive, in order to identify the antecedents of the platform economy in the domains and exemplars under analysis. In that sense, our impetus is to challenge the persistent novelty of digital aspiration and to clearly identify the trajectories that we now see converging in the present socio-technical interface. To put that more simply, the platform economy did not emerge fully formed from the most widely held smartphone in a single decade. Rather, it was preconceived and predisposed by a series of long term evolutions in informatics, commerce, governance and popular culture over the course of a century. Consequently, we need to understand the emergence of platforms in historical terms and to understand platform structures and businesses as constituting actions rather than objects of analysis. As with the governing mentalities of development in India past and present, 'platformization', as the verb form of 'platform', compels an analytical emphasis on process (Parthasarathi 2018; Nieborg and Helmond 2019; Zhang 2020).

Platformization as a Verb

In terms of technological processes, platformization can be understood in a number of ways: in terms of interoperability, hyperconnectivity, individual addressability and algorithmic automation. As a configuration of media, a more general tendency of platformization can be traced via the effective convergence between the domains of mediation and communication. Consequently, the sensory melding of media content and interpersonal communication is a vital process within the aesthetics of platforms. In more functional terms, mobile phones have converged the enabling and entertainment functions of media, rapidly breaking down distinctions between public mediation, commercial logistics and interpersonal communication. In this context, we have to consider whether we should maintain a distinction between the platformization of an Indian *media economy* (i.e. the convergence between a set of content-producing industries with particular social, cultural and commercial logics) and platformization via the increasingly *mediated economy* of India (where an apparatus of information technologies converges logistical processes, monetary exchanges and political action) (see Athique 2018, pp. 2–3). This distinction is especially important in setting the boundaries of where media and communications research should begin and end in the era of platforms. In a larger sense, as the complexity of media systems increases, a mediated economy becomes substantially more dependent upon the parallel expansion of the media economy and vice versa. Here, we can say with some confidence that one major trajectory of platformization is to bring these two communication domains within a single process. In turn, as the dominant social mediums of contemporary society, the interrelated development of the mobile phone and the Internet implies large-scale re-orderings of sociability and social relations as economic processes.

Platformization is, of course, a global tendency, which usefully reminds us that the worldwide reach of the Internet remains as radical as its qualities of interactivity and simultaneity. Consequently, the combination of global expansion and procedural platformization compels us to consider a vast complex of transnational trade flows entailing e-commerce, cross-border wallets and online video. For instance, although Netflix makes products from various countries available in many other countries, the overall pattern of distribution advantages US-origin products (Aguiar and Waldfogel 2017). At the same time, supposedly global platforms such as Netflix tend to gather different meanings and orientations across different jurisdictions and cultures (Lobato 2019a). Scholars record users in India having similar understandings of gratification derived from, say Airbnb, with users in other national cultures (Brochado et al. 2017). Yet, even a cursory look at the actual operations of Airbnb in India indicates important disjunctures with universal rationales for such 'sharing economies'. Despite the stark geopolitical disparities of the digital economy, the global dynamics of platformization require more than an 'indigenization' argument, as both Airbnb and Uber have come to be swiftly integrated into pre-existing practices of service provision in India, both formal and informal. Such adaptation is by no means unidirectional, as we must also be attentive to Indian platforms that are operating outside the country's geography (see, e.g., Lobato 2019b). Websites of leading news outlets in India garner over a third of their viewers from abroad, the cab service platform Ola operates in Australia and the UK, as does hotel booking platform OYO in China and Southeast Asia. Thus, the interlacing and extension of the Indian economy beyond its sovereign jurisdiction is also fundamental to platformization as process.

Within India, platformization 'as a verb' allows us to locate and explicate the platform economy via the evolution of certain structures, institutions, settings and norms (such as the census, the bourses, union ministries, urban master plans, conglomerates and party political structures). This undeniably complex field of precedents provides the basis for a more discerning understanding of longer term tendencies that have shaped the present pursuit of a platform economy in India. Here, the tendencies of platformization can been identified across various processes: the inexorable pressures of massification, the mechanization of information, the automation of industrial processes, the globalization of service economies, the formalization of social exchanges, the exploitation of mediatized sociability and the interdependency of public and private marketplaces. It is through a complex aggregation and simultaneity of all these trajectories that platformization emerges as a novel mechanism to organize and reformulate markets in India, where digitization is energetically touted in government ads as 'the solution to all problems'. Accordingly, the various contributors to this volume begin to consider how the universal ethos of 'platformization' has become operative across different domains. Before proceeding to those accounts, we will briefly consider indicators of platformization across four vectors: (1) the extension of the existing media economy through new commodity platforms, (2) the expansion of the mediated economy to new adopters and sectors through distribution platforms, (3) the formalization of social economies through their enclosure within exchange platforms and (4) the platformization of state functions and governance of platforms.

Platformization in the Media Economy

Platformization, as a means of fashioning communication within a set of channels, with attendant feedback loops and sets of secondary markets for information and influence, is an economic logic that has evolved from the particular characteristics of media. One of the most significant antecedents of platformization is television, with its longstanding investments in the identification, enumeration and behavioural understandings of its audience (Balnaves and O'Regan 2011). The commercial evolution of television through branded channels, subscription models, encrypted signals and dual product markets centred on advertising revenues clearly predisposes the logics of the platform era. In India, the platformization of television emerged out of the cable sector, largely informal, and the de-regulation of broadcasting in the early 1990s. In the 2010s, the re-regulation and digitalization of cable networks furthered the platformization of television via proprietary set top boxes, encrypted signal flows, the bundling of TV content and on-demand, often exclusive, programming. Thus, arguably, the institution of multi-sided markets for content and market data became formalized in the Indian media economy via cable TV. The legal privileges of platform status were also first claimed in this industry. The earliest satellite-based PayTV services in India referred to themselves in policy deliberations as 'platforms', emphasizing their distinction as services not merely relaying signals of broadcasters but also offering their own interfaces and suites of programming. Subsequently, the mandatory digitalization of the distribution chain for cable-based Pay TV services facilitated a convergence with the telecoms sector that, in turn, brought about standardization in network infrastructures, signal flows and retail price-points (Parthasarathi et al. 2016).

The formalization of the trade in TV signals in such a manner fundamentally re-organized TV as a commercial and viewing experience. Platformization marked a significant shift in the regime of legibility (i.e.

identifying/enumerating audiences), with the monopoly of third-party, 'independent' ratings agencies giving way to TV distributors, armed with their ability to harvest not just a sample but the complete universe of audience-preferences. Thus, in television, a technological convergence enabled the incorporation of erstwhile market mediators within the proprietary domain of platforms. In parallel, television provided the foundations for the co-location of content, advertising and material retail systems. Here, cable distributors such as DEN, through a JV partnership with Snapdeal, launched a cable TV channel aiming to leverage its footprint of 13 million homes in 200 cities as a marketplace for merchandise. A raft of web-based TV and OTT video services also entered the market, including offerings from transnational broadcasters such Murdoch-owned STAR and Sony. Platformizing their content catalogues (through HotStar and SonyLIV, respectively) is a strategy that reflects a significant shift of audiences from conventional to mobile TV. In the last three years, the number of OTT operations in India has increased to around 30, with local broadcaster-owned platforms, telecom operators and global players like Netflix and Amazon Primer all entering the market with advertisement (AVOD) and subscription video on demand (SVOD) services (see Fitzgerald 2019). These developments emerge from the convergence of the television sector with other sectors, especially between content-based media industries and the telecoms sector via internet-enabled services.

In market terms, the platformization of the television medium via OTT formats has emerged in the context of a rapidly expanding but simultaneously fragmenting audience. Online music platforms such as Saavn are similarly diversifying content and consolidating ownership in the popular music market (see Booth 2017). The reshaping of movie distribution via OTT platforms, and their bundling with telecoms services, has encapsulated the home cinema market. Outside the home, the majority of 'standalone' cinema halls have been platformized through the technical standards imposed by E cinema and D cinema platforms, now firmly consolidated under UFO Moviez. In conceiving their 'platform' offerings, editors and management at Indian newspapers have negotiated various forms of risk, especially those around editorial control (brand attribution, context, onward journey), data (access to individual-level information about users) and the monetization of audiences as they compete for a shrinking share of advertising in India's digital space. As a counterpoint, a vociferous space of independent journalism has utilized the carriage provided by platforms such as YouTube and Facebook to sustain an idealistic critique of scrutiny and dissent. Here, the refugees of serious journalism rub shoulders with immensely popular channels marking the boisterous expansion of folk and regional cultures. In an era of public communication centred upon the handset, the production and circulation of news in India has been entirely transformed (Jeffrey and Doron 2013; Sundaram 2017). Across all these domains we are witnessing the subsumption of the erstwhile 'media industries' under the imperium of providers of digital infrastructure.

Platformization in the Mediated Economy

Underlying processes of communication, datafication and algorithmic reproduction are driving the platformization of the wider economy in India. At an obvious and basic level, platformization constitutes a technological precondition for a mediated economy where digital systems operate as carriers of logistical services to a vast range of markets. At the point of sale, the central infrastructure is mobile phone networks, whose proprietary platforms underwrite and determine access to digital technologies. The critical function of mobile telecoms, as the enabler of a mass Internet in India, and their steady consolidation under three big houses has been central to the creation of a viable market for platform services. The vast resources need to implement and under-write wireless coverage in India via the private sector has led inexorably to a sector dominated by India's largest business houses and their foreign counterparts. The convergence of telecoms and Internet in a rapidly expanding global data economy also convenes a similar set of actors on the client side, with Tata, Amazon and Google all holding key components of the data infrastructure, both nationally and internationally. Tendencies towards enclosure in the mobile market have been manifested through 'walled gardens' that lock in users via contracts and the lure of added-value services and special offers. However, given that the bulk of India's mobile users rely on sachetized prepaid vouchers and often have only intermittent access to power and network, there are critically important differentiations in the digital experience amongst users from different social strata, reflected in terms of the platform services that they are able to access, utilize and pay for.

The vast overall increases in connectivity, datafication and data generation in the mobile domain necessarily converge with the particular platform logics of the software industries. Here, the trajectories of platformization can be traced back through the history of commercial computing, with key moments being the intellectual property stand-off between India and IBM in the 1970s, the rise of commercial software in personal computers and the entrenchment of proprietary operating systems during the 1980s and 1990s. More recently, these tendencies have been playing out in the mobile platform wars between Samsung and Apple, Android and OS. It is significant that the private sector in India remains almost entirely dependent upon these major international software platforms. This platform dependency has clearly structured the much-vaunted development of the Indian software industry, with its long-standing and far-reaching relationships with Silicon Valley (D'Costa and Sridharan 2004). In the public sector, by contrast, India has made substantive investments in domestic software platforms intended to enable the logistical functions of state enterprises and services. Nonetheless, at the level of network infrastructure, it is the private sector (specifically, Reliance, Tata and Adani) that is making the capital investments in fibre, data centres and cellular coverage. Similarly, it is private-sector platforms that provide the mobile user interface, with many of these platforms being owned and/or carried by the network owners. In this sandwich, public sector software initiatives are clearly intended to piggy back on private and 'public-private' infrastructure, while the public sector infrastructure initiatives face mixed fortunes. It appears they are either being left to starve under the ambit of divestment (such as BSNL, the country's largest wired-line telephone network) or condemned to a slow and chequered roll-out (as with the high-speed broadband network Bharat-Net).

The divergent fortunes of private and public sector infrastructure indicate that the platformization of infrastructure is an underlying process determining the techno-organizational backbone of Digital India. The putative gains derived from platformization of the entire economy are associated with step changes in logistics. In this utopian form, platformization becomes applicable to each and every aspect of the material environment, tracking public transportation, health and security and enabling seamless consumption linked to unique individuals across space and time. Yet in India, the pronouncement of funding for a hundred technologically enhanced 'smart cities' in 2019 has already dwindled to a much lower target of five, with the flagship development of a new state capital in Andhra Pradesh repeatedly reformulated and yet to get underway, despite the acquisition of swathes of agricultural land. As has been the case elsewhere, the automation of urban logistics is proceeding via more piecemeal developments in pre-existing urban spaces. Here, the rapid growth of smartphone-enabled ride hailing platforms (RHPs) has been the most visible and popular innovation. The offerings of Uber and its indigenous competitor, Ola, has transformed the transport economies of Indian cities in terms of availability and pricing, even though it has yet to make any significant contribution to reducing horrendous levels of traffic congestion and pollution. This literal choking of urban India has itself provided an impetus in demand for food delivery platforms like Zomato and Swiggy, and for the overall growth in online shopping.

Perhaps the highest profile intervention of the digital in the wider economy was the arbitrary demonetization of 80% of India's cash supply on 8 November 2016. The coerced expansion of digital money platforms such as PayTM was part and parcel of the conscious disruption of the world's largest cash economy (Ghosh et al. 2017; Athique 2019). Since 2016, the range and availability of payment platforms, mobile wallets and Fintech companies has increased dramatically. Digital payments by various means have become widely accepted in metropolitan India, and platform providers are expanding into a broader range of financial services. The various interests in what is, effectively, the platformization of money have been strongly supported by the government as a systemic intervention that will increase tax collections, reduce criminality and curb the influence of black money across the economy (Reddy 2017). The sanctioned 'cashless India' initiative is also being prioritized because digital transactions are functionally intrinsic to boosting the platform economy in India. Here, mobile money services offer the means by which platform business models become cost efficient and, to a significant extent, financialized. The newly minted status of platforms as financial entities becomes almost inevitable once they become the banking channel for substantial money exchanges between users (as, for example, with the aggregation of daily transport fares by RHPs in a populous city like New Delhi). Digital monies, in this larger sense, operate simultaneously as logistics, resources and commodities in the platform economy, interacting with and under-writing the network infrastructure (see Athique and Baulch 2019).

Platformization of the Social

Thus far, we have traced platformization through developments in the channelling and logistics of economic processes. At this point, it is useful to turn to the human dimensions of those changes. It is worth noting at the outset that the primary resources of the platform economy are fundamentally social and cultural in nature. The dis-embedding and re-embedding of symbolic and social exchanges in commodity forms has always been a central feature of media economies (See Athique, Parthasarathi and Srinivas 2018a, b). This cycle of extraction has been tremendously accelerated by the explosion of social media networks in India. Through the popularity of Facebook, WhatsApp, Twitter and Instagram our interactions with family, friends and strangers are commodified via the panoply of data packs, data points and targeted advertising. Shaped by the compulsive affordances of public sharing, our competitive pursuit of personal publics is quantified in fine detail by the page views, click trails, recommendations and likes that have emerged as effective currencies of social capital. The substantive point is that the monetization of various forms of user data impels the simultaneous integration of platform logics within the nooks and corners of everyday speech (Athique 2020). In aggregate, this dynamic has been highly visible in the day-to-day conduct of the electoral circus in India, where aspirant parliamentarians compete frantically for attention and bandwidth through live interventions in public discourse and debate. At the village level, a similar dynamic plays out through the cellular affordances of WhatsApp, with increasingly tragic consequences around incidences of incitement and violence via the circulation of false and unverified news.

These incidents and their public reactions are emerging as an unintended consequence of the orchestrated commercialization of sociability itself, where 'clickbait' has been an explicit tendency of platformization in India as much as elsewhere. At an equally embedded level, we have seen a rapid expansion in the platformization and commodification of religious practices via websites, podcasts and e commerce. Here, platformization has been enabled by the increasingly mediatized milieu around all religions and the social infrastructure created by networks of devotees, volunteers and patrons (see Chakrabarti 2012; Thomas 2018). We can also see the antecedents of platformization in the mediatization of marriage brokerages. In the mid-1990s, the match making website Shaadi.com was an early example of digital platformization, linking local cultural practices and social preferences with new processes of sorting, selecting and 'consumer' experience (Parthasarathi 2018a). As of now, the sociability afforded by such 'relationship' platforms are being complemented, and sometimes challenged, by social media networks and location-based mobile-dating applications such as Tinder, TrulyMadly and OkCupid. Rudimentary industry surveys suggest that Indian dating apps will gain in popularity as they offer more choice, more profile information and opportunities to meet potential partners and connect online, thereby boosting the $40 billion marriage business in India. In both domains, we can see how platformization is bringing legibility to very substantial areas of financial exchange that have not previously been considered within economic accounting. Nonetheless, matrimony and religion are big business in India, and both rely on network effects that make them prime sites for platformization (in this vector, of sociability itself).

The mining of social data and speech, and the automation of social economies, goes hand in hand with the wider encroachment of Digital India into the country's large informal sector. Traditionally, this sector has employed some 85% of the workforce, but contributed very little to state revenues. It has been reckoned to be as large as the formal sector in terms of turnover, and therefore the aggregation of informal activities is an obvious objective for platform start-ups. In this domain, the imperatives of platforms are both similar to and distinct from their inspirations in the US. There, the 'sharing economy' paradigm is mobilized upon the pursuit of spare capacity in private hands (Sundararajan 2016). In India, the capture of informal businesses within online brokerages is harnessing central capacity within the economy, with the intent of capturing rents and, perhaps, making those sectors both legible and more efficient. In both cases, we could see this strategic pursuit of social resources as a capitalism of last resort, spurred on by falling state revenues and declining profitability in the industrial economy. The 'sharing' tag is largely redundant in India, where it is extremely unlikely that an Uber driver is anything other than a regular taxi driver employed under different (and often precarious) conditions. Similarly, Airbnb in India is dominated by listings for registered guesthouses and private apartment lets, since the complexities of caste, diet and local conventions around visitors and communal 'decency' make the freeform rental of spare rooms to complete strangers a problematic proposition. Rather, the central drive of 'sharing' services in urban India has been the platformization of domestic spaces and informal labour, from drivers to cooks, security guards and household servants.

Platformization and Governance

Although e-governance is only one of the nine pillars of the government's 'Digital India' initiative, the implementation of e-governance platforms clearly reflects the perennial imperative to simply manage the vast and disparate population of the country (GoI 2018). At the core is *Aadhaar*, designed to digitally identify the entire population, thereby providing new capacity for the state and a new transactional relationship with citizens (Shukla 2010). Following the administratively aggressive and judicially fraught implementation of the world's largest and most ambitious citizen identification project, the subsequent platformization of government functions has been touted as the means by which corruption and pilferage will be driven out of the welfare system (Aiyar 2017). As with 'cashless India', a rhetorical drive towards 'purification' has been enacted through the digitization of citizen registrations and enforcement. In this endeavour, the Indian government has developed a close working relationship with Silicon Valley, positioning India as a vast laboratory for the implementation of digital society. At the same time, the government has facilitated the rise of its own national champions, frequently by sidestepping its own laws and regulatory bodies. This close cohabitation with the digital sector, both at home and abroad, raises critical questions around the state's role as the watchdog and arbiter of data privacy, competition and spectrum licensing in the platform economy. The critical issue is that, in such circumstances, the governance of platforms is not easily separated from the platformization of governance itself. Consequently, platformization raises regulatory challenges for the state, while simultaneously becoming central to its administrative ambitions.

In both private and public sectors, platforms connecting service providers, with each other and with consumers, are often discordant with the principles, and indeed the letter, of regulations. On the government side, it remains unclear which components of the platform economy fall into the regulatory ambit of various ministries and regulatory bodies, and there are legitimate concerns whether existing principles of governance can be applied to the digital platform economy as it expands across numerous sectors. At the international level, there is a corresponding set of challenges around international bodies, jurisdictions and domicile that requires concerted action by sovereign states in what is an increasingly febrile international system. It is clear that implementing robust forms of governance in the platform economy is a pressing issue, not least because platforms themselves are effectively acting as forms and sites of governance in their own domains. For our purposes, we can therefore identify that a further trajectory of platformization is the shift from territorial governance, within a jurisdiction with elected representatives, to functional governance on/by the platform itself (see Parthasarathi 2018b). The former tends to defer governance issues to 'community accountability' on the part of users or, arguably, more insidious forms like content moderation by outsourced employees. The latter plays out through forms of distributed intervention of through forms of self-regulation. In their own ways, both of these carry risks associated with the 'logic of opacity' in platform regulation (Roberts 2018).

In public sector services, the government of India has embraced platform models in the name of efficiency gains. These are assumed to flow from simultaneous data exchanges across departments, the elimination of corruption and duplication, and the lowering of the number of employees, real estate and resources used to conduct state functions. Automation in this domain also suggests that the state is seeking, via technological means, to operate transactions with (often unruly) citizens at a more convenient distance. This certainly seems to be particularly the case for welfare systems like PDS, which are a matter of life and death for millions of people in India (see Mishra 2019). Community policing is increasingly operationalized through social media monitoring and interventions via Facebook and WhatsApp (Sundaram 2017). Internet shutdowns have become a normalized mode of collective punishment, more notoriously in the case of Jammu and Kashmir after the dissolution of its special constitutional status in 2019. In recent years, the allocation of digital identities has become a mechanism for exclusion as much as inclusion, creating millions of stateless people through both system errors and political fiat. India's model of e-governance has thus shown itself to be arbitrary and unaccountable. The shouldering of the costs of such interventions by the private sector inexorably leads to the dispersal of state sovereign functions, as in the increasing outsourcing of surveillance and financial systems to private players. A cogent example is the free flows of user transaction data between platform operators and state agencies, along with the securitization of public data from the citizenry. Consequently, we can argue that the implicit transfer of sovereign rights, if not sovereign privilege, to the private sector is a central tendency of platformization.

Critical Approaches to Platforms

Having explored something of the complexity of India's platform economy as a set of interlocking social and economic processes, and having identified some of the vectors of platformization, we can now open the floor for discussion. We are both pleased and honoured to have the opportunity to curate a series of highly original contributions that range across different themes, topics and sites of research. Each of the chapters that follow provides thoughtful insights on the ethos, particularities and trajectories of platform capitalism in India. In Part I of the volume Adrian Athique, Scott Fitzgerald and Akshaya Kumar interrogate the concept of platform capitalism in an Indian context. In Part II, Ishita Tiwary, Christine Ithurbide and Phillipe Bourquillon illustrate the dynamics of platform businesses in the media sector. Ravinder Kumar Verma, Vigneswara Ilavarasan, Arpan Kumar Kar, M. Shuaib Mohamed Haneef and Aquil Ahmad Khan then direct our attention to the lived experience of platform labour. In Part IV, Pawan Singh, Usha Rodrigues and Hrishikesh Arvikar explore the political manifestations of the platform economy. This turn to the social domain is further enhanced by insightful accounts of the cultural aspects of platformization, with contributions from Akshaya Kumar, Pradip Thomas and Amit Rai. Naturally the scale of the task means that there are many more platforms that deserve attention, and our understanding of the vectors of platformization will be further enhanced as research in the field progresses. In that respect, we hope that the generous contributions made here will provide useful stimulus for researchers, in India and elsewhere, as we collectively explore the era of platforms.

References

Aguiar, L., & Waldfogel, J. (2017). Netflix: Global Hegemon or Facilitator of Frictionless Digital Trade? *Journal of Cultural Economics, 42*(3), 419–445.

Aiyar, S. (2017). *Aadhaar: The Biometric History of India's 12-Digit Revolution.* Delhi: Westland.

Appadurai, A. (2012). The Spirit of Calculation. *The Cambridge Journal of Anthropology, 30*(1), 3–17.

Athique, A. (2018). Media Development to Media Economy. In A. Athique, V. Parthasarathi, & S. V. Srinivas (Eds.), *The Indian Media Economy Vol 1: Industrial Dynamics and Cultural Adaptation* (pp. 1–21). New Delhi: Oxford University Press.

Athique, A. (2019). A Great Leap of Faith: The Cashless Agenda in Digital India. *New Media and Society., 21*(8), 1697–1713.

Athique, A. (2020). Integrated Commodities in the Digital Economy. *Media, Culture & Society, 42*(4), 554–570.

Athique, A., & Baulch, E. (Eds.). (2019). *Digital Transactions in Asia: Economic, Social and Informational Processes.* New York: Routledge.

Athique, A., Parthasarathi, V., & Srinivas, S. V. (2018a). *The Indian Media Economy Vol 1: Industrial Dynamics and Cultural Adaptation.* New Delhi: Oxford University Press.

Athique, A., Parthasarathi, V., & Srinivas, S. V. (2018b). *The Indian Media Economy Vol 2: Market Dynamics and Social Transactions*. New Delhi: Oxford University Press.

Balnaves, M., & O'Regan, T. (2011). *Rating the Audience*. London: Bloomsbury Academic.

Booth, G. D. (2017). A Long Tail in the Digital Age: Music Commerce and the Mobile Platform in India. *Asian Music, 48*(1), 85–113.

Brochado, A., Troilo, M., & Shah, A. (2017). Airbnb Customer Experience: Evidence of Convergence Across Three Countries. *Annals of Tourism Research, 63*, 210–212.

Chakrabarti, S. (2012). The Avatars of Baba Ramdev: The Politics, Economics, and Contradictions of an Indian Televangelist. In P. Thomas & P. Lee (Eds.), *Global and Local Televangelism*. London: Palgrave Macmillan Limited.

Cohen, J. E. (2017). Law for the Platform Economy. *University of California Davis Law Review, 51*(2017), 131–204.

Curwen, P. (2018). Reliance Jio Forces the Indian Mobile Market to Restructure. *Digital Policy, Regulation and Governance, 20*(1), 99–102.

D'Costa, A., & Sridharan, E. (Eds.). (2004). *India in the Global Software Industry*. New Delhi: Macmillan India.

Fitzgerald, S. (2019). Over the Top Video Services in India: Media Imperialism after Globalization. *Media Industries Journal, 6*(2).

Ghosh, J., Chandrasekhar, C. P. & Patnaik, P. (2017). *Demonetisation Decoded: A Critique of India's Demonetisation Experiment*. New Dehli: Routledge.

Government of India. (2018). 'Digital India', Ministry of Electronics & Information Technology, Government of India. Retrieved February 22, 2020, from http://www.digitalindia.gov.in/.

Hill, D., & Athique, A. (2018). The Role of Off Shore Financial Centres in Indian Telecoms. In A. Athique, V. Parthasarathi, & S. V. Srinivas (Eds.), *The Indian Media Economy—Volume 1: Industrial Dynamics and Cultural Adaptation* (pp. 66–92). New Delhi: Oxford University Press.

India Stack. (2020). India Stack. Retrieved February 22, 2020, from https://www.indiastack.org/.

Jeffrey, R., & Doron, A. (2013). *Cell Phone Nation*. Delhi: Hachette India.

Lobato, R. (2019a). *Netflix Nations: The Geography of Digital Distribution*. New York: New York University Press.

Lobato, R. (2019b). The OTT TV Box as a Diasporic Media Platform. *Media Industries Journal, 6*(2), 133–150.

Mishra, R. (2019). The Two Faces of the Digital State: A Tale of Tweets and Foods. In A. Athique & E. Baulch (Eds.), *Digital Transactions in Asia*. New York: Routledge.

Mukherjee, R. (2019). Jio Sparks Disruption 2.0: Infrastructural Imaginaries and Platform Ecosystems in 'Digital India'. *Media, Culture & Society, 41*(2), 175–95.

Nieborg, D., & Helmond, A. (2019). The Political Economy of Facebook's Platformization in the Mobile Ecosystem: Facebook Messenger as a Platform Instance. *Media, Culture and Society, 41*(2), 196–218.

Parthasarathi, V. (2018a). *Verbing Platforms: Iterative Notes on Platformization in India*. Paper presented at Platforms Seminar, MSH Nord, Paris, September 2018.

Parthasarathi, V. (2018b). Between Strategic Intent and Considered Silence: Regulatory Contours of the TV Business. In A. Athique, V. Parthasarathi, & S. V. Srinivas (Eds.), *The Indian Media Economy, Volume 1: Industrial Dynamics and Cultural Adaptation* (pp. 144–166). New Delhi: Oxford University Press.

Parthasarathi, V., Amanullah, A., & Koshy, S. (2016). Digitalization as Formalization: A View from Below. *International Journal of Digital Television, 7*(2), 155–171.

Parthasarathi, V., & Athique, A. (2020). Market Matters: Interdependencies in the Indian Media Economy. *Media, Culture & Society, 42*(3), 431–448.

Reddy, C. R. (2017). *Demonetization and Black Money*. Hyderabad: Orient Blackswan.

Roberts, S. (2018). Digital Detritus: 'Error' and the Logic of Opacity in Social Media Content Moderation. *First Monday, 23*(3–5). Retrieved June 26, 2018, from http://firstmonday.org/ojs/index.php/fm/article/view/8283/6649.

Shukla, R. (2010). Reimagining Citizenship: Debating India's Unique Identification Scheme. *Economic and Political Weekly, XLV*(2), 31–36.

Srnicek, N. (2017). *Platform Capitalism*. Cambridge: Polity.

Sundaram, R. (2017). Paper presented at 'Digital Transactions in Asia', Queensland University of Technology, Brisbane, Circulation Takes Command?: The Sensory Infrastructure of the Mobile Phone, August 2017.

Sundararajan, A. (2016). *The Sharing Economy: The End of Employment and the Rise of Crowd-Based Capitalism*. Cambridge, MA: MIT Press.

Thomas, P. (2012). *Digital India: Understanding Information, Communication and Social Change*. New Delhi: Sage.

Thomas, P. (2018). Religion, Communication and Political Economy in India: The Case of Gospel for Asia. In A. Athique, V. Parthasarthi, & S. V. Srinivas (Eds.), *The Indian Media Economy, Vol. 1: Industrial Dynamics and Cultural Adaptation*. New Delhi: Oxford University Press.

Thomas, P. (2019). *The Politics of Digital India*. New Delhi: Oxford University Press.

Zhang, L. (2020). When Platform Capitalism Meets Petty Captialism in China: Alibaba and an Integrated Approach to Platformization. *International Journal of Communication, 14*(2020), 114–134.

PART I

Platform Capitalism

CHAPTER 2

Digital Emporiums: Evolutionary Pathways to Platform Capitalism

Adrian Athique

Emporia Redux

In Janpath, a major thoroughfare at the heart of Lutyen's New Delhi, stands a series of state-operated emporiums offering goods from across India. In a concretization of the political and economic relationships of the 1970s, the row of emporiums offering wares from specific Indian states sits across the road from the towering structure of the All India Central Cottage Industries Emporium. As reminders of the heyday of the command economy era under Indira Gandhi, Delhi's handicraft emporiums continue to offer customers a consciously curated array of goods, enclosed within a tightly regulated space where the inefficiencies and hassles of everyday exchange are negated by the standardization of both prices and goods under the aegis of the state. They also deliver. A reminder of the rational promises of a receding era, these emporia in turn reference the retail emporiums that appeared in global metropoles at the end of the

A. Athique (✉)
Institute for Advanced Studies Humanities, University of Queensland,
St Lucia, QLD, Australia
e-mail: a.athique@uq.edu.au

A. Athique, V. Parthasarathi (eds.), *Platform Capitalism in India*,
Global Transformations in Media and Communication Research - A
Palgrave and IAMCR Series,
https://doi.org/10.1007/978-3-030-44563-8_2

nineteenth century, heralding the era of the urban department store. Beyond its historical resonance as a grandiose sensory-retail experience, I propose that the emporium might serve us well as both a metaphor and a structural analogy for India's emerging 'platform economy', through its component qualities and their attendant vectors:

1. The emporium pioneered a multi-product retail space with disparate supply chains, thereby marking the historical co-evolution of the colonial bazaar and global trade.
2. The emporium materialized the enclosure of goods and services under a branded banner, thereby reflecting the commanding logics of aggregation and enclosure evident in platform business models.
3. The emporium showcased the diversity of product origins, cultural markets and social transactions being captured, thereby foreshadowing the dynamics of discovery in the platform economy.
4. The emporium responded to the densification and machination of urban life, thereby occupying a central position around which transport, entertainment and service economies were organized.
5. The emporium evolved into the modern department stores, which introduced the system of cashless transactions that enable platform businesses in the present era.
6. The emporium referenced the capacity of privatized markets to determine both products and subjects, thereby echoing the foundation of modern India on the commercial sovereignty of the Company Raj.

Amidst the discourses of novelty and disruption circulating in both public and private sector offices regarding the disruptive effects of Digital India, this more evolutionary perspective allows us to situate 'platform capitalism' as a phenomenon emerging from the extension and convergence of long-term tendencies in media markets. It also implies a substantially *sui generis* approach to platform capitalism in India, on the basis that platform economies tend to 'platformize' existing market exchanges rather than fashion new objects of exchange. As Julie Cohen puts it: 'platforms do not enter or expand markets; they replace (and rematerialize) them' (Cohen 2017). For this reason, I have argued that internet-enabled platforms are perhaps best understood as attempts to constitute a transactional layer over and above existing markets and social relations (see Athique and Baulch 2019). In a structural sense, it is clear that the major platforms are seeking to establish proprietary markets, or 'ecosystems', within the commercial geography of India. Such ambitions are, of course, quite familiar and consistent with India's economic history. Equally, while the rapid 'platformization' of peer-to-peer exchanges may well be novel in devices, scope and form, the multi-sided market logics of platform businesses clearly extend tendencies long evident in media economies (See Athique et al. 2018a, b). Due to the intrinsically embedded nature of mediation, the substantive point of novelty may well be the protocols through which digital platforms are seeking to channel India's informal and social economies (see Kumar 2019; Rai 2019).

Digital Emporiums

We can develop the structural analogy of the emporium by demonstrating the continuation of its major vectors in the evolution of India's platform economy. The most obvious examples of the multi-product marketplace are in e-commerce, including the Amazon-inspired FlipKart platform, and Amazon itself in its Indian manifestation. Beyond the virtualization of the everyday marketplace, the mutual constitution of retail and service platforms brings together goods, labour and cultures from across India, as the state emporiums once did, but now recasts the retail space across the larger pan-Indian space previously offered up as a metropolitan fantasy. Where the consumer was once configured as a benevolent bureaucrat or international tourist, the all-India market array is now configured for the benefit of the urban middle class consumers mobilized through three decades of liberalization (see Varma 1998; Srivastava 2014). As Pradip Thomas has noted, the looming enclosure of India's vast middle class of small-scale producers and retailers within the online retail space has been figured as both an economic and a political threat by influential components within the ruling Bharatiya Janata Party (BJP) (Thomas 2019a). At the same time, Indian retailers have proved adept in marketing their own goods worldwide through global platform outlets, while the Government of India has moved somewhat erratically between regulatory protection for local producers and regulatory loopholes allowing WalMart and Amazon to establish a duopoly in the servicing of online distribution (Thomas 2019b). This statutory equivalence stems not only from overlapping and outmoded ministerial jurisdictions, but directly from the Government of India's reliance on technology companies to provide the pipes and platforms necessary for realizing its 'Digital India' vision of aggregated and automated governance (Mukherjee 2019).

The orientation of platforms offering services (such as food, taxis, domestic labour) and the offering of platforms selling goods (with their multiple tie-up offers for film tickets, virtual cashback and coffee vouchers) indicate marketing logics that firmly position customers within an urban leisure economy (see Athique and Hill 2010; Brosius 2012). Nonetheless, like the erstwhile colonial bazaar described by Ray, Bannerjee and others, the wider platform ecology brings a proliferation of communities and cultures into contact via open platforms such as WhatsApp and YouTube (See Bannerjee 1989; Chakrabarty 1991; Ray 1995; Parthasarathi and Athique 2019). In the latter case, intensely local popular cultures across India have established channels alongside the exotica of foreign content that lures urban elites to Netflix (Lobato 2019). As meeting points for so many vernaculars of culture and commerce, the User Generated Content (UGC) platforms are unruly spaces where the sensorial spectrum of the digital breaks through the logics of aggregation in all directions (Srinivas 2017). At the back end, the new market regimes for platform labour (i.e. for cooks, drivers, guards and maids) instituted by service platforms like Zomato, Ola and UrbanClap link them directly into the stratified layers of India's informal economy. In doing so, the complex relationships between improvisational and marginal spaces of the digital and the affordances of automated consumers armed with smartphones are remediating power and precarity through new forms of algorithmic discipline. A gig economy is, of course, nothing new to India's expansive pool of marginal and migrant labour, but the rating of their daily fortunes by digital brands threatens to make these entities curators of the informal sector in much the same fashion that state emporia were once the curators of village handicrafts.

Platforms operationalize machine logics of efficiency and control and, like emporiums before them, they furnish a distinct set of transactional logics. Automation is deployed to increase the scale, scope, speed and volume of transactions, and an important element of this is the centralization of money exchanges (Athique 2019a). A key component of the architecture of emporiums was their central payments space, and mobile payment systems occupy this critical space within the ecology of platforms. Thus, we also have to understand the emporium and the platform as vast mechanisms for handling money. The aggregation of cash fosters market power and the ability to carry loss-leaders, paving the way for regimes of brand loyalty embedded in the expansion of consumer credit. In the Indian context, where the vast bulk of petty exchanges have operated in the informal and untaxed sector, the imposition of central accounting regimes also constitutes an overarching 'mechanism of legibility' that scrutinizes even the smallest symptom of leakage. The production of transaction records is itself central to the business of governance, and the capacity of mobile payment systems to provide integrated individualized transaction records makes them intrinsic to the nervous system of the state. No one doubts that the near simultaneous launch of mobile money platforms such as PayTM in 2015 and the shock demonetization of the cash supply in 2016 were conjoint processes (Athique 2019b). State patronage for a 'cashless India' is reciprocated by the sharing of transaction data, where PayTM records facilitate revenue collection and the security profiling of citizens in Kashmir and elsewhere.

The Metaphors of Platform Capitalism

The structural analogy of the emporium is useful, then, for situating the digital 'disruption' of India within a longer evolution of retail and control regimes. By contrast, taking the 'digital emporium' as a metaphor allows us to de-naturalize the hegemonic metaphors of 'platform capitalism'. In the colonial metropoles, the emporium was in its day an unabashed metaphor for the expansive conquests of global trade, bringing an expansive range of material and ethnological goods from the far flung corners of empire. This etymology was echoed in India's state emporiums of the 1970s, where the diverse products of India's villages economies were aggregated at the federal centre. Then, as now, imperial instincts were driving a centrifugal impulse, as Delhi worked to rationalize and subdue India's federal patchwork. Thus, in both cases, the shared etymology between emporium and imperium unabashedly highlights the intertwined logics of market integration and territorial commerce. By contrast, the modern-day metaphors associated with the platform economy are wilfully evasive. To begin with, the metaphor of 'cloud computing' provided a non-threatening overlay to the worldwide harvest of information, arguably the greatest power grab in human history (Athique 2013). The accompanying metaphor of the platform, as Tarleton Gillespie argued, infers a non-threatening neutrality and a multi-faceted good (Gillespie 2010). At one level, the platform is a quasi-technical catchall for an operating environment, carriage system or a piece of infrastructure. The Web

2.0 era dovetailed this usage with the parallel notion of an 'advertising platform', where the platform serves as a vehicle for influence and profit. The liberal notion of an 'open platform' softens the edges of this convergence by invoking democratic connotations of meritocratic ambition, free speech and equal competition (ibid.).

'Technology companies' have thus reliably deployed the metaphor of the 'open platform' to defend themselves against responsibility for the content and consequences of the digital services that they operate. In turn, the critical response to the expanding concentration of platform power has extended the metaphor as coinage of its own critique. As a proponent of the recent analytical concept of 'platform capitalism', Nick Srnicek characterizes the new affordances of 'platform capitalism' that that digital platforms have brought into being. As he puts it:

> Platforms, in sum, are a new sort of firm: they are characterized by providing the infrastructure to mediate between different user groups, by displaying monopoly tendencies driven by network effects, by employing cross-subsidisation to draw in different user groups and by having a designed core architecture that that governs the interaction possibilities … all of these characteristics make platforms key business models for extracting and controlling data … they are an extractive apparatus for data. (Srnicek 2017: 48)

By this formulation, the technological metaphors (core architecture, interaction possibilities) converge with capitalist tendencies (monopoly, cross-subsidization) in order to multiply and monetize 'network effects'. The underlying goal is to enclose and maximize 'data extraction' from the user base. As such, the platform inculcates novel logics predicated upon the boosting of data-based discovery. Amidst the furore surrounding the ethical wants of data mining and the tech-topic proposition of algorithmic culture, it is certainly hard to avoid the extractive logics that now pervade our digital experience (see Gago and Mezzadra 2017). With the expansion of 'platforms' such as Google and Facebook, we have all become acutely aware of the fact that platforms design and exercise their protocols in order to harvest and analyse data (Fisher and Mehozay 2019). Whether big or small, aggregators or niche, platforms engage in 'alchemical processes' intended to realize surplus value from user data (Athique 2018). This commodification of user data takes many forms, from traditional 'market intelligence' to behavioural interventions and the rejuvenated numerology through which predictive analysis proffers computerized modes of divination (ibid.: 62). In the wake of the Cambridge Analytica scandal, our attention has been further drawn to the commercial and political imperatives under which platforms, state bodies and political actors join hands in exchanging the benefits of these data 'resources'. It would be naïve to expect otherwise in India, and the role of digital platform strategies in the 2014 and 2019 elections has not escaped the attention of political observers (Goel 2018; Rodrigues 2020).

The critical discourse on platforms piles up the metaphors, through extensive combinations of business argot and Marxist terminology. That is, 'platforms' constitute the primary apparatus for 'mining' the social domain, acquiring and retaining multitudinous users in order to 'accumulate' quanta of data and realize value. This highly symbolized 'value chain' is taken by Srnicek to be the defining logic of 'platform capitalism' (2017: 48). Nonetheless, beyond the imperatives of accumulation, the 'shop-fronts' of the various high-profile platforms 'brands' also work hard to articulate distinctive service offerings. With these apparent affordances in mind, Srnicek offers a basic typology of contemporary platforms, where he identifies:

> Advertising platforms … which extract information on users, undertake a labour of analysis, and then use the products of that process to sell ad space … Cloud platforms … which own the hardware and software of digital-dependent businesses and are renting them out … Industrial platforms … which build the hardware and software necessary to transform traditional manufacturing into internet-connected processes … Product platforms … that generate revenue by using other platforms to turn a traditional good into a service and by collecting rent … Lean platforms … which attempt to reduce their ownership of assets to a minimum and to profit by reducing costs. (Srnicek 2017, pp. 49–50)

On the face of it (or rather, the screen), we could readily apply this model to the Indian case, whereby: Google and the online editions of *The Hindu* could both be categorized as 'advertising platforms', TataSky could be positioned as a 'cloud platform', Infosys becomes a provider of 'industrial platforms', e-commerce operations like FlipKart and digital film companies such as UFO Moviez would all be 'product platforms', whereas labour-outsourcing operations such as Ola (taxis) and OYO (hotels) can be lumped together as 'lean platforms'. This sorting seems neat enough, being a typology based upon 'what does the firm do?'. By taking this approach. Srincek's typology attempts to account both for different sources of profits and for the different products and services platforms offer to their users. In practice, however, this neatness is arbitrary, since these various categories do not constitute any definite series. Consequently, various platforms either operate across or simply fall into multiple categories and, equally critically, there is evidence to suggest that the various platforms are functionally and, often, financially dependent upon each other. That is, the market systems constituted within platform models are, like all markets within a true economy, significantly dependent upon their interaction with other markets (and thereby other platforms).

This interdependence between product markets, which Srnicek refers to as 'cross-subsidization', is by no means particular to the digital economy. As with the 'monopoly tendencies' of communication, it has been a distinctive feature of media markets for at least a century, in India as much as elsewhere. Within this larger whole, platforms can only be partially understood as 'firms', 'brands', 'portals' or 'shopfront' businesses. These elements are primarily indicative of the ownership, functionality and retail interface of platforms, which tend to differ in each case. The wider attempt to institute platform ecosystems necessarily interacts with existing modalities of social exchange. Alongside media platforms driven by content (whether professionally or user-generated), the platform economy encompasses expanding infrastructure of digital finance, along with aggregating informal markets for 'services' (such as drivers, guest houses, home security and deliveries) as well as grey economies (such as second hand markets and content piracy) (see Punathambekar and Mohan 2019). What we are seeing first hand in social media platforms is the simultaneous processes through which everyday interaction, sociability and democracy are being integrated within this wider transactional architecture. Thus, the fundamental commonality between all digital platforms is their systematic formalization of peer-to-peer exchanges within a rules-based system. Consequently, their primary characteristics are those of a marketplace, not a firm.

Market Automata

Across the platform economy as a whole, we see some useful exemplars of the increasing number of market exchanges being aggregated within portals that allow value capture at the transactional level (through data, certainly, but more explicitly through commissions and subscriptions). One of these would be the commissions taken by the hotel booking platform OYO, another would be the capacity to offer money storage in mobile wallets to underpin banking services and micro-finance. E-commerce is, by its very nature, a vast clearing house. These market offerings are attractive because of their capacity to furnish zero-level entry barriers to participants. As part of the bargain, platforms out-source transactional costs to participants, enforce arbitrary terms and conditions and enclose buyers and sellers within a proprietary system. At the operational level, the role of a market 'mediator' of peer-to-peer exchanges (as opposed to an owner, buyer or seller within the relevant market) allows for the 'lean' existence of internet portals and their opportunistic location for tax purposes. The programmatic and proprietary logics of these businesses suggest that, somewhat unlike earlier media industries, the institutional logic of a platform is not the organization of any productive process per se, but rather the design and population of an automated market system.

Approaching platforms as a set of transactional markets rather than as types of firms encourages some different thinking on 'platform capitalism'. Not least, it prompts us to reconsider the 'stack' of infrastructure as being, simultaneously, a stack of markets and a stack of technologies (Bratton 2016). In each phase of development, it has been the commercial potentials of the public internet that have been paramount to the extension of the system, with each additional layer of functionality adding purposefully to the impetus towards commodification. In the 1990s, value was extracted from the communication layer, through the sale of hardware, software subscriptions, data packs and other forms of access rents. In the 2000s, additional value was being extracted from the distribution layer, through content subscriptions, pay-per-view offerings, user-generated content and the bulk of the world's advertising revenues. In the 2010s, further value is being extracted from various forms of piece work, user tracking, data mining and the aggregation of commissions exercised over peer-to-peer exchanges. This is the transactional layer where platform businesses operate. It is too narrow, therefore, to explicate platforms as simply data collection companies operating in the guise of service providers. There is a much higher order of integration in play across these layers, where each platform integrates multiple products in simultaneous transaction (Athique 2019c). While platform logics should by no means be seen as an 'outcome' of the so-called Web 2.0 era, it is at the present technical level that the mass individuation and interoperability of digital systems has allowed platforms to realize opportunities for synchronizing large sets of marketplaces in real time.

Platforms extract different forms of rent from online transactions (whether this is social communication, peer-to-peer selling or labour exchanges). As digital manifestations of certain 'market ideals', platforms are designed to profit from 'optimal pricing' and to multiply 'friction-free capitalism' amongst users who are simultaneously producers and consumers (Gates 1995). They are protected from both buyers and sellers by virtue of safe harbour clauses enshrined in (or, as in the Indian case, derived from) the Digital Millennium Copyright Act. By such means, platforms seek to locate themselves in the transactional layer of the digital economy, not simply to benefit from a 'lean' operating model, but to avoid being regulated as businesses within the markets they are seeking to encapsulate. If Netflix is not a broadcaster, PayTM is not a bank, NaMo TV is not a news channel and Amazon is not a retailer, they avoid any regulatory norms save their own, thereby acquiring a sovereign advantage in the relevant market. Platforms thus claim the right to operate as essentially privatized markets, under a branded entity that sets its own regulatory norms. As I indicated at the outset, this form of commercial extra-territoriality is hardly unknown to India, nor is the consequent capacity of such players to furnish multiple products and multi-sided markets. The arrival of the Californian East India Companies has been coterminous with the evolution of similar entitles, both within India and across the Asian region (such as Softbank, Alibaba and Reliance Jio).

Although these various ambitions for market monopoly seem clear enough, we should be wary of schematizing another seemingly tidy structural form as an autonomous reality. In practice, the real analytical benefit of a markets-based approach is that it allows us to uncover a great deal of untidiness in India's platform economy. At present, there are around 150 million regular users of broadband in India, which is only 13% of the population, and even this level of access is typically intermittent and unstable. The infrastructural layer is fundamentally uneven in terms of coverage, capacity and access (between metro and rural, between West and East, between rich neighbourhoods and poor ones). Even for the one sixth of the population that has regular access, irregular electricity supplies, lack of fixed connections and the limitations of mobile spectrum all serve to ensure an intermittent digital environment (Thomas 2012). Deficiencies in power and speed impede platforms that distribute digital goods, whereas for platforms that seek to facilitate materialized markets, additional infrastructural lacks come into play, not least in road transport. In India, e-commerce operators have been forced to invest in their own distribution infrastructure and to employ a vast host of couriers for delivery. With only half of the population captured within the banking system, and the majority still preferring to avoid debit cards, India's e-commerce operations are forced to handle a lot of cash, thereby increasing the cost and complexity of their operations. The attempt to overcome this barrier, and to supercharge the platform economy, through the 'surgical strike' of demonetization was an economic debacle which demonstrated the dangers of trying to constitute a platform economy by fiat, without due regard for material constraints (see Reddy 2017).

For any realist, India's distribution layer clearly suffers from geographical, temporal and monetary bottlenecks that should logically impede the expansion of the online market. Nonetheless, India's platform economy continues to expand in the face of such obstacles precisely because labour is incredibly cheap. It is nearly always cheaper than any reliable form of automation. In India, platforms can rely on a labour surplus to 'absorb' infrastructure bottlenecks. This fact alone undermines a central rationale for platform economies in the industrialized world (as per Srnicek and Williams 2016; Ford 2016). Thus, in the Indian context, the major opportunities for platforms lie not in outsourcing labour costs, but in capturing large sectors of economic activity that previously operated in the informal economy. Guest houses, street food, rickshaws, drivers and guards—these are all largely disaggregated cash-based sectors. Their aggregation within platforms constitutes a private sector 'mechanism of legibility', intent upon simultaneously formalizing these markets and bringing them with the ambit of transactional records (Maurer 2012). In this respect, the rent capture of informal markets echoes the recession economics of 'the developed world, where the implicit reliance of platforms on a social surplus that absorbs production costs is euphemized by the utopian deceit of a 'sharing economy' (as per Sundararajan 2016). In India, however, this sector is far larger and constitutes central rather than surplus capacity (see Rai 2019). In a country where low prices and subsistence wages have always been normative, the transactional costs of the digital must be borne by the petty traders that constitute the majority of the lower middle classes. For the platform operators, far smaller profit margins are offset by the sheer numbers involved. It is evident, then, that aggregation of population, not capital, is the guiding principle of platform economy.

Evolutionary Processes

The evolution of 'the stack', as a conjoint commercial and technological apparatus, is one obvious genealogy of the platform economy. It is hardly surprising, therefore, that this pathway dominates our discussion of digital capitalism (see McAfee and Brynjolfsson 2017; McChesney 2013). Without doubt, we must account for the ways in which platforms and novel 'technology banks' operate as capital interests in the transactional layer of the platform economy. However, it may be equally critical to understand their institutional function, which is market integration. With their penchant for 'nudging' their users, the ethos and ethics of platforms have emerged from pathways laid down by the marketing profession that guided consumption in the latter half of the twentieth century. Similarly, as Ramon Lobato observes, we still have to consider a player like Netflix not only within the overarching ecology of platforms but also within the *longue durée* of the business and usages of television (Lobato 2019). Rather than reading 'affordances' off the screen, we need to 'restore intention' to our understanding of the seemingly inexorable technological and financial trajectories within the platform economy (as per Williams 1974). At this point, then, I will attempt to canvas four critical evolutionary pathways that have determined the evolution of platforms: media convergence (between interpersonal and social communication), guided consumption (via market information and audience manipulation), conglomeration (driven by logistical interoperability) and market automation (via the equivalence of data and money exchange).

From the perspective of user experience, the most obvious evolutionary process is that of convergence between the domains of interpersonal, logistical and social communication. These domains were long separated by a division of functions enforced by state regulation, thereby guaranteeing neutral logistical functions in the commercial domain and a degree of horizontal (if not vertical) privacy in the domains of personal communication. The convergence of these different usages of media within personalized media devices, along with the wholesale transfer of network operations to the private sector, led unquestionably to a new sensory environment where the flows of personal, political and commercial information became inextricably mingled. It is the consequences of this process that has driven the popularity of platforms like WhatsApp in India, along with their tragic interaction with village vigilantism, fake news and electoral politics across the breadth of the country. The converged flows and cellular architecture of such platforms has invigorated the multitude of vernacular public spheres in rural India, bringing these previously informal domains into the digital domain. As much as this has been an exemplar for micro-profits in the developing world, it hasn't been a pretty sight, prompting both WhatsApp and the Government of India to disavow responsibility for the consequences of platform architectures in the hinterlands (Sundaram 2017).

The evolving role of the audience in an interactive media apparatus is another critical evolutionary pathway of the platform economy. It has long been recognized that the goods and services, assets and values operative across media processes are necessarily different from the nineteenth-century model of extraction, labour, manufacture and sale that has dominated our understanding of 'industries' (see Lash and Urry 1994). Media producers must garner audiences for what are largely experiential products (whether there content is expressive or informative in intent). Thus, the production of audiences is always a persuasive process. In turn, the generation of audience mass provides the basis for communication systems to facilitate wider process of persuasion. As Dallas Smythe noted long ago, media producers are implicated not only in the production of their own advertisement but also in the sale of the audience commodity itself (Smythe 1977). Media industries therefore played a central role in the wider project of 'guided consumption' that was taken up as an alternative to 'planned production' in the mass economies of the twentieth century. As a consequence, they were able to generate not only a market for influence but also a wealth of market information about consumers which, in turn, generated its own customers (Lazarsfeld 1941). In an era of individual addressability, platforms converge these functions within a single automated process. Thus, while platforms may seek to fashion an enclosed marketplace (a 'one-stop shop') via their 'user experience', on the server side they operate multi-sided markets for numerous clients for market information and social data.

The primacy of user data in the platform economy runs in parallel with the longer term evolution of economic planning. In the Indian context, this process is often seen as being marked by the institution of the planning commission in 1950, followed by the rupture of 'liberalization' in 1991 and the turn away from industrial planning and towards a consumer-led economy. The major distinction between planning and guiding, often confused with ideological trappings, is simply between producing what people need and giving people what they want. Since both require mediation, this tends in practice to devolve to a choice between giving people what they are told that they need (say, Aadhaar) and giving people what they are told to want (say, Amazon). Both are top-down processes and this is why media platforms like YouTube have been associated with a novel liberation of media content production from the hands of media corporations to the putative benefit of small producers and the general public (notably by Burgess and Green 2009; Cunningham and Craig 2016). However, it is highly significant in the Indian case that there were scarcely any such media corporations twenty years ago. In fact, there has, over the 'liberalization' period, been a clear evolution towards conglomeration via the application of digital technologies (Booth 2017). The Indian media economy over the past twenty years has seen private capital taking over the communication domains of the state and subsequently 'formalizing' previously disorganized sectors of media business, before moving on to 'platformize' other markets for goods and services. In part, the concentration of platform power has occurred because the shift to the digital has come with extremely high infrastructure costs, which only a handful of private interests can bear, and in part because the internal logics of a platform ecology necessitate a high degree of interoperability and mobility across platforms.

Another important point of distinction in the Indian case is that all three layers of the platform economy are being built simultaneously and, in the most part, under-written by the same actors. Consequently, the interests of platform businesses are effectively attuned to the interests of India's telecoms networks, which is primarily in driving network expansion and increasing data traffic. Similarly, it is not by chance that financial entities are major investors in the platform sector. The guiding ethos of FinTech is to ensure that every peer-to-peer transaction generates a commission or deposit. Whereas early proponents of digital technologies emphasized their potentials for reducing transaction costs, the era of platforms has deliberately inverted this logic, precisely because platform businesses make their money on each transaction. This fosters a novel equivalence between airtime, user data, commissions and digital finance in the platform economy, and thereby signifies the financialization of the social domain on a vast scale (see Maurer 2015). Fundamentally, the primary motivation of platforms as aggregators of peer-to-peer exchanges is to enhance and widen the number, depth and range of transactions in play. In that respect, the conceptual evolution of computerized markets from the 1970s onwards, implemented incrementally from the bourses in the 1980s down to previously informal sectors in the 2010s is a neglected, but obviously central, evolutionary pathway. One apparent consequence of these four converging genealogies is that the major interests behind the platform economy are relatively content agnostic. They do not particularly care if the data being circulated is Aamir Khan, *Comicstaan*, fascist memes or video calls from a particularly intrusive aunty as long as transactions of time, data and money are being captured.

Bundling India

From the nineteenth-century bazaar to the twentieth-century emporium and the twenty-first-century platform, India has inspired the sovereign ambitions of companies seeking to diversify their products, build their own transport systems, mint their own coin, write their own laws, collect their own taxes and determine the rights of producers and consumers. The unavoidable example in the Indian context is not Mark Zuckerberg's Facebook, but India's Reliance. The ever-expanding integration of goods and services under the Reliance flag certainly seems redolent of the imperial commerce of the nineteenth century. Diversification over a thirty-year period from textiles into oil refining, power generation, financial services, telecoms, media and entertainment, grocery stores and mobile apps and banking has created a multi-product retail space of astounding proportions. In 2015, it was Mukesh Amabani who orchestrated vast levels of investment by Reliance Industries Limited (RIL) into upgrading India's digital infrastructure, some $42 billion according to Rahul Mukherjee (2019: 176). This was accompanied by the launch of Reliance Jio, which provided mobile subscribers with free call plans and data plans far below market costs (Curwen 2018). The vast loss-leader of free Jio services and its cheap handsets have captured hundreds of millions of users, thereby creating the user base for a raft of Jio platform services, including JioMoney, JioChat and JioTV (ibid.: 177). Within the space of two years, Reliance Jio has been able to integrate what Rahul Mukherjee calls the 'pipes and platforms' of Digital India, easily securing its ambition to become the provider of 5G networks in India (2019).

The Reliance brand now encloses goods, services and markets across the breadth of India, allowing for the aggregation of economic, social and political transactions across all major sectors of the economy, including defence. This sweeping set of interests underpins Reliance's emergence as a 'national champion' and provides the heft for its working partnerships with transnational capital, expressed in its recently announced alliance with Microsoft and the aim of becoming 'India's Huwei'. Despite protestations from competitors and regulators, including the Comptroller and Auditor General (CAG), this vast acquisition of market power has been actively supported by the Government of India, for whom the partnerships inherent in realizing the infrastructure of Digital India are far more important than the norms of market regulation. The unique capacity of Reliance to operate at scale at the All-India level makes it a natural partner for developing India's platform economy. From powering homes and vehicles to laying down fibre networks, Reliance now occupies a central position around which transport, entertainment and service economies are being reorganized, with its financial infrastructure capable of servicing venture capital markets as well as everyday mobile payments on its JioMoney platform. In all these undertakings, RIL is closely aligned with the current Government of India's technologically inspired vision of reshaping the citizenry. From its trademark skyscraper in South Bombay, Reliance thus has a reasonable claim to the status of a modern-day East India Company, a vast conglomerate easily capable of competing with its international counterparts in their attempts to dominate the markets of a Digital India.

Nonetheless, the notion of platform capitalism may not quite capture the full extent of the 'great integration' envisioned through the platform economy model. Such an undertaking requires the market logics of content, of carriage, of service, of labour, of airtime, of user input, of data assets, of convenience, of surveillance, of gratification, of energy and of sociability to become effectively synchronized. This implies there has to be more to platform economies than 'capitalism' alone. Indeed, these market systems may not be capitalist in the modern sense, since the means of participation (i.e. ownership of the market) is far more central than ownership of the means of production (per se) or profit from outputs (as long as sufficient volumes of transactions are being captured). At the very least, since they rely heavily on the simultaneous operation of reciprocity and redistribution across each network of exchange, my sense is that platforms which transact social economies cannot be solely capitalist. India's extensive familial economics remain laden with reciprocal exchanges across all socio-economic classes, and Reliance is no exception to this general rule. Thus, while we could simply consider Reliance as a 'firm' working across Srnicek's typology and beyond, it is in a larger sense part of an historically recurring pursuit of paramountcy over India's market systems. Standing against such ambitions, both domestic and international, is always the questions of what the market will bear, what these vast ambitions will cost and what the polity will succumb to (i.e. aside from free data). Certainly, mediation is more central to day-to-day social and economic processes than ever before, but it becomes increasingly hard to discern anything we could call a media industry as such. If Reliance Jio is producing music and television content primarily to lock customers into its retail, telecoms and data ecosystem, can it be adequately understood as a media firm? Given the scale of its operations, perhaps it might be better considered as an economy in and of itself. That is, as an emporium.

Acknowledgement An earlier version of this chapter was published previously as 'Digital Emporiums: Platform Capitalism in India' in *Media Industries Journal*, 6(2), 2019. I would like to thank the journal reviewers and editors for their comments on the draft copy.

References

Athique, A. (2013). *Digital Media and Society: An Introduction*. Cambridge: Polity.

Athique, A. (2018). The Dynamics and Potentials of Big Data for Audience Research. *Media, Culture and Society, 40*(1), 56–74.

Athique, A. (2019a). Digital Transactions in Asia. In A. Athique & E. Baulch (Eds.), *Digital Transactions in Asia: Social, Economic and Informational Processes* (pp. 1–22). New York: Routledge.

Athique, A. (2019b). A Great Leap of Faith: The Cashless Agenda in Digital India. *New Media & Society, 21*(8), 1697–1713.

Athique, A. (2019c). Integrated Commodities in the Digital Economy. *Media, Culture and Society*. Online first. 0163443719853495.

Athique, A., & Baulch, E. (Eds.). (2019). *Digital Transactions in Asia: Economic, Social and Informational Processes*. New York: Routledge.

Athique, A., & Hill, D. (2010). *The Multiplex in India: A Cultural Economy of Urban Leisure*. New York: Routledge.

Athique, A., Parthasarathi, V., & Srinivas, S. V. (2018a). *The Indian Media Economy Vol 1: Industrial Dynamics and Cultural Adaptation*. New Delhi: Oxford University Press.

Athique, A., Parthasarathi, V., & Srinivas, S. V. (2018b). *The Indian Media Economy Vol 2: Market Dynamics and Social Transactions*. New Delhi: Oxford University Press.

Bannerjee, S. (1989). *The Parlour and the Streets: Elite and Popular Culture in Nineteenth-Century Calcutta*. Calcutta: Seagull.

Booth, G. D. (2017). A Long Tail in the Digital Age: Music Commerce and the Mobile Platform in India. *Asian Music, 48*(1), 85–113.

Bratton, B. H. (2016). *The Stack: On Software and Sovereignty*. Cambridge, MA: MIT press.
Brosius, C. (2012). *India's Middle Class: New Forms of Urban Leisure, Consumption and Prosperity*. Delhi: Routledge India.
Burgess, J., & Green, J. (2009). *You Tube: Online Video and Participatory Culture*. Cambridge: Polity.
Chakrabarty, D. (1991). Open Space/Public Place: Garbage, Modernity and India. *South Asia: Journal of South Asian Studies, 14*(1), 15–31.
Cohen, J. E. (2017). *Law for the Platform Economy. U.C. Davis Law Review* (p. 51).
Cunningham, S., & Craig, D. (2016). Online Entertainment: A New Wave of Media Globalization? *International Journal of Communication, 10*, 5409–5425.
Curwen, P. (2018). Reliance Jio Forces the Indian Mobile Market to Restructure. *Digital Policy, Regulation and Governance, 20*(1), 99–102.
Fisher, E., & Mehozay, Y. (2019). How Algorithms See their Audience: Media Epistemes and the Changing Conception of the Individual. *Media, Culture and Society*. 0163443719831598.
Ford, M. (2016). *The Rise of the Robots: Technology and the Threat of Mass Unemployment*. New York: Basic Books.
Gago, V., & Mezzadra, S. (2017). A Critique of the Extractive Operations of Capital: Toward an Expanded Concept of Extractivism. *Rethinking Marxism, 29*(4), 574–591.
Gates, B. (1995). *The Road Ahead*. London and New York: Penguin.
Gillespie, T. (2010). The Politics of Platforms. *New Media & Society, 12*(3), 347–364.
Goel, V. (2018). In India, Facebook's WhatsApp Plays a Central Role in Elections. *New York Times*, 14 May.
Kumar, A. (2019). Informality in the Time of Platformization. *Media Industries Journal, 6*(2).
Lash, S., & Urry, J. (1994). *Economies of Signs and Space*. London: Sage.
Lazarsfeld, P. F. (1941). Remarks on Administrative and Critical Communications Research. *Studies in Philosophy and Social Science, 9*, 2–16.
Lobato, R. (2019). *Netflix Nations: The Geography of Digital Distribution*. New York: New York University Press.
Maurer, B. (2012). Mobile Money, Communication and Consumption in the Mobile Payments Space. *Journal of Development Studies, 48*(5), 589–604.
Maurer, B. (2015). *How Would You Like to Pay? How Technology Is Changing the Future of Money*. Durham, NC: Duke University Press.
McAfee, A., & Brynjolfsson, E. (2017). *Machine, Platform, Crowd: Harnessing Our Digital Future*. WW Norton & Company.
McChesney, R. W. (2013). *Digital Disconnect: How Capitalism is Turning the Internet Against Democracy*. New York: The New Press.

Mukherjee, R. (2019). Jio Sparks Disruption 2.0: Infrastructural Imaginaries and Platform Ecosystems in 'Digital India'. *Media, Culture and Society, 41*(2), 175–195.

Parthasarathi, V., & Athique, A. (2019). Market Matters: Interdependencies in the Indian Media Economy. *Media, Culture and Society*. Online first. https://doi.org/10.1177/0163443719853495

Punathambekar, A., & Mohan, S. (Eds.). (2019). *Global Digital Cultures: Perspectives from South Asia*. Ann Arbor: University of Michigan Press.

Rai, A. S. (2019). *Jugaad Time: Ecologies of Everyday Hacking in India*. Chicago: Duke University Press.

Ray, R. K. (1995). Asian Capital in the Age of European Domination: The Rise of the Bazaar, 1800–1914. *Modern Asian Studies, 29*(3), 449–554.

Reddy, C. R. (2017). *Demonetization and Black Money*. Hyderabad: Orient Blackswan.

Rodrigues, Usha (2020). Political Communication on Social Media Platforms. In A. Athique & V. Parthasarathi (Eds.), *Platform Capitalism in India*. Basingstoke: Palgrave.

Smythe, D. (1977). Communications: Blindspot of Western Marxism. *Canadian Journal of Political and Society Theory, 1*(3), 1–28.

Srinivas, S. V. (2017). Politics in the Age of YouTube: Degraded Images and Small Screen Revolutions. In J. Neves & B. Sarkar (Eds.), *Asian Video Cultures: In the Penumbra of the Global* (pp. 217–239). Durham, NC: Duke University Press.

Srivastava, S. (2014). *Entangled Urbanism: Slum, Gated Community and Shopping Mall in Delhi and Gurgaon*. New Delhi: Oxford University Press.

Srnicek, N. (2017). *Platform Capitalism*. Cambridge: Polity.

Srnicek, N., & Williams, A. (2016). *Inventing the Future: Postcapitalism and a World Without Work*. London: Verso.

Sundaram, R. (2017). Circulation Takes Command? The Sensory Infrastructure of the Mobile Phone. Paper presented at *Digital Transactions in Asia*, Queensland University of Technology, 8–10 August 2017.

Sundararajan, A. (2016). *The Sharing Economy: The End of Employment and the Rise of Crowd-Based Capitalism*. Cambridge, MA: MIT Press.

Thomas, P. N. (2012). *Digital India: Understanding Information, Communication and Social change*. New Delhi: Sage.

Thomas, P. N. (2019a). Infrastructure and Platform Anxieties in India. In A. Athique & E. Baulch (Eds.), *Digital Transactions in Asia: Economic, Social and Informational Processes* (pp. 44–62). New York: Routledge.

Thomas, P. N. (2019b). *The Politics of Digital India*. New Delhi: Oxford University Press.

Varma, P. K. (1998). *The Great Indian Middle Class*. New Delhi: Penguin.

Williams, R. (1974). *Television: Technology and Cultural Form*. London: Collins.

CHAPTER 3

The Networked Media Economy and the Indian Gilded Age

Scott Fitzgerald

The rapid and conspicuous growth of the networked media economy in India, comprising of network infrastructure, content industries and online media, has been boosted over the last decade by the rapid digitisation of production, distribution and consumption. This development has aligned the increasingly networked media economy with the broader vector of 'platform economics', in which maximum data extraction is key. Arguments about how this data should be controlled, and more specifically concerns about the regulation of so-called cross-border data flows, have been expressed through different analogies. Mukesh Ambani, chairman, managing director and largest shareholder of Reliance Industries Limited (RIL), has recently argued that

> India's data must be controlled and owned by Indian people—and not by corporates, especially global corporations. For India to succeed in this data-driven revolution, we will have to migrate the control and ownership of

S. Fitzgerald (✉)
Curtin University, Bentley, WA, Australia
e-mail: s.fitzgerald@curtin.edu.au

A. Athique, V. Parthasarathi (eds.), *Platform Capitalism in India*, Global Transformations in Media and Communication Research - A Palgrave and IAMCR Series,
https://doi.org/10.1007/978-3-030-44563-8_3

> Indian data back to India—in other words, Indian wealth back to every Indian ... we have to collectively launch a new movement against data colonisation. In this new world, data is the new oil. And data is the new wealth. (Economic Times 2019)

In response, Facebook's Vice-President for Global Affairs and Communications, Sir Nick Clegg, sought to challenge this view by saying:

> There are many in India and around the world who regard data as the new oil—and that, like oil, having a great reserve of it held within your national boundaries, will lead to sure-fire prosperity. But this analogy is mistaken.... Data isn't oil—a finite commodity to be owned and traded ... a better liquid to liken it to is water, with the global Internet like a great border-less ocean of currents and tides. (The Telegraph 2019)

These contrasting perspectives underscore Athique's earlier observation that, rather than control over content and message, the geopolitics of information in the digital era are primarily centred upon control over the data infrastructure and data harvest (2016, p. 53; see also Schiller 2014). Thus, in its *Digital Economy Report 2019*, the UN Conference on Trade and Development (UNCTAD) notes: "while it is important that data be allowed to flow easily in order to harness the benefits of the digital economy, it is equally important to ensure that the associated gains are shared in a fair manner by the actors and countries involved in the value creation process" (UNCTAD 2019, p. 92). Despite the exponential growth of data production and use, UNCTAD observes that developing countries confront the "increasing dominance of global digital platforms and their control of data, as well as their capacity to create and capture the ensuing value" (ibid.). UNCTAD highlights the dominance of seven 'super platforms': Microsoft, Apple, Amazon, Google, Facebook, Tencent and Alibaba. The UN body therefore calls for national development strategies to "enhance domestic capacities to 'refine' the data" and ensure that local firms can upgrade their position within data value chains so as to avoid the "emergence of a new kind of international dependency pattern, with developing countries having to rely mainly on global digital platforms based in the United States or China" (UNCTAD 2019, p. 99).

The UNCTAD report focuses primarily upon inequalities and power imbalances confronting developing countries. Yet, the expansion of the networked media economy in India over the last two decades has taken place within a domestic economy that has seen inequality deepen dramatically. Wealth held by India's billionaires increased by almost ten times over the last decade, including an astounding leap of 36% in 2017 (the year following the surprise demonetisation of India's cash economy). This widening gap has fostered claims that we are witnessing an 'Indian Gilded Age' (Oxfam India 2018; Chancel and Piketty 2017). Given Mukesh Ambani's status as (by far) India's wealthiest individual, his claim that a countermovement against 'data colonisation' from large US-based firms will return the "control and ownership of Indian data and wealth back to every Indian" should compel some critical questions about the line between public good and private wealth when it comes to assessing the strategic imperatives of India's home-grown digital platforms and technology companies.

In taking up this enquiry, this chapter is divided into five major points of discussion. Firstly, the notion of an 'Indian Gilded Age', premised on the proportional wealth and influence of Indian billionaires, is discussed with reference to the historical relationship between the state and capital in India. Secondly, given debates over new forms of economic dependency arising from the power of digital platforms, a Braudelian model of global capitalism is explored in the context of the networked media economy. The third point of discussion examines the consolidation of India's domestic telecommunications and communications conglomerates, which increasingly influence the operations of the far smaller cultural and media industries. The fourth point of discussion is the financialisation of the networked media economy and distinctive characteristics of capital interests in the Indian context. This naturally segues into the fifth point, which returns to the role of the state as the regulator and champion of capital in the platform economy. The chapter concludes by questioning the limitations of a world systems approach, which can be, and often is, marshalled to support the interests of dominant nationally based companies.

The Rise of Indian Billionaires and the Gilded Age

For the past decade, academics, politicians and commentators have suggested that Indian capitalism is beginning to resemble the 'Gilded Age' in the United States (e.g. Sinha and Varshney 2011; Gandhi and Walton 2012). A comparison with late-nineteenth-century American 'robber barons' has emerged in response to the rapid expansion of a cohort of Indian billionaires (exemplified by figures such as such as Mukesh Ambani,

Gautam Adani and Lakshmi Mittal). A number of measures further encourage the comparison between contemporary India and America's Gilded Age. First of all, the wealth of India's billionaire's as a percentage of GDP is seen as unusually high for a relatively poor country (Crabtree 2018). Secondly, they are also numerous, with the number of Indian billionaires estimated between 106 and 118 in 2018, ranking India third globally behind China and the United States (UBS/PwC 2017). Thirdly, following the pattern set by the American robber barons, Walton suggests that over half of the wealth accrued by India's billionaires between 1996 and 2013 comes from what he describes as 'rent-thick' sectors (sectors with high levels of extractive rents derived from links to the state) (2017). Rather than productivity-enhancing Schumpeterian rents, these actors appear to achieve returns well above those of 'fully competitive markets', assumedly via political patronage, preferential access to state-controlled resources and monopolistic market power. Consequently, Walton uses the same methodology as *The Economist*'s list of 'crony-capitalism' industries (The Economist 2014).

This dynamic in the Indian economy reflects, in part, the enduring remnants of the state-capitalism and licensing regime pursued after 1947 as a 'unique Indian business model' (Khatri and Ojha 2016; Varma et al. 2016). In this model, a core business competence was establishing relationships of patronage and mutual support with politicians and state bureaucrats as a means of gaining access to resources (Gupta 2017). While the size of corporations and the power of the capitalist class in India has clearly grown in the wake of economic liberalisation since the 1990s, clientelism, cronyism and corruption still permeate India's state-capital relationships. Crabtree observes that during the liberalisation period: "public resources were being gifted to industrialists in increasingly vast quantities … allowing them to rake in outsized and undeserved profits" (2018, p. 63). Rather than being wound back, as Chandra points out, state patronage relations expanded into new areas of the economy through the creation of new regulations, control of access to previously reserved sectors of inputs such as credit, coal or 2G spectrum allocation (2015).

As Walton notes, while the American Gilded Age was characterised by a lack of regulations, the so-called Indian Gilded Age has unfolded in a space of extensive legal and regulatory capacity, albeit one characterised by weak and/or accommodating regulatory practice (2017). Indian civil servants and governments retain "considerable discretionary power over various aspects of the policy process" that shape and codify state-capital relationships (Murali 2019, p.47). While the enforcement of laws covering corrupt corporate activities have often been weak or absent, Chandra has argued that patronage relations, which "exploit and expand the discretion available within the law, rather than breaking it outright" are becoming more common (2015, p. 47). Thus, while patronage "certainly provide ample opportunities for rent-seeking on both sides, state officials may also be motivated by business-friendly notions of 'development', and business owners may also cultivate relationships with state officials as a necessary evil to get work done in an ambiguous environment" (ibid.). This gives rise to what could be seen as another key aspect of an 'Indian business model', a response to what Sinha argues is the Janus-faced nature of the Indian state, which pursues *both* development and patronage, a situation that "allows business actors to infiltrate multiple arenas and access points across institutions of democracy, public institutions, and regulatory bodies" (2019, p. 51).

As well as being India's largest and most profitable firm, Reliance Industries Limited (RIL) is commonly, as Caussat notes, "portrayed as the quintessential crony capitalism group in India" (2017, p. 210). Echoing Walton's point about the preponderate role of extractive rents rather than innovation in the development of Indian corporations, Mazumdar remarks that Reliance's

> movement to the top of the corporate hierarchy in India … was based on so little of what could be considered as expressions of *industrial entrepreneurship*. The only two related elements that can be identified as the key to separating Reliance from others … were its exceptional success in gaining from the regulatory regime and in mobilizing financing. (2017, p. 20)

Having achieved unmatched cash flows from vertical integration in polyester textiles, petrochemicals and petroleum, Reliance moved in the early 2000s "to grab … a 'once in a lifetime opportunity' to lay down and own the knowledge economy's equivalent of the railway and thus become the 'carrier's carrier'" for India's digital economy (McDonald 2010, p. 303). The import of Reliance's larger investment strategy became evident in late 2015, when its subsidiary, Reliance Jio, entered into the mobile telecom market via a loss-leading provision of mobile data. This prompted substantial industry consolidation, as smaller firms rapidly exited or merged with other firms, with Reliance Jio quickly emerging as the third largest telecoms operator. As the largest Indian firm by revenue, market capitalisation and profit, across all economic sectors, it is necessary to underline the relative size of RIL compared to its competitors in the networked media economy. RIL has been able invested more than US$30 billion in digital infrastructure, "the most expensive new venture of its kind by any global company" (Mundy 2019). Over the past decade, the centre of gravity in the media and entertainment sector in India has moved inexorably towards sectors where online provision, data use and data extraction are most pronounced. By 2021, online media is expected to overtake print as the second largest media segment, behind television (FICCI-E&Y 2019). This development has propelled Reliance further into the sector through its existing interests in film and radio and through now ventures in OTT video and streaming music services (see Fitzgerald 2019).

Reliance, like other telecom service providers (TSPs), bundles digital content services with data plans to gain a competitive edge and boost the volume, collection and sale of data. FICCI-E&Y suggests that Indian TSPs paid between INR 3.5 and 4 billion (US$49–56 million) in 2018 for content syndication rights, a figure predicted to reach INR 8–10 billion (US$112–140 million) by 2021 when a predicted 375 million subscribers will be accessing bundled content (2019, pp. 120, 127). The development of India's networked media economy has also been marked by the growing presence of the seven global 'super platforms' identified by UNCTAD (2019). Critical analyses of global platform corporations have equated their operational ethos with the privileges of gilded age capitalism (Zuboff 2019; Wu 2018). In the Indian context, these platforms and their domestic competitors have been making comparable demands for self-regulation, based on either the 'evolutionary laws of business' or 'network effects'. Essentially, these are strategic attempts to limit the encroachment of democracy on their business operations by developing partnerships with state institutions. Growing fears of a form of international digital dependency in India, as exemplified by the UNCTAD report, has opened a new chapter in the dynamic between patronage and development in capital-state relations: one, as we will see, that favours the further rise of Reliance.

Braudelian Approaches to Media and Cultural Industries

Given that the rise of global digital platforms is apparently linked with the emergence of a super-wealthy strata and new forms of international dependency, some scholars have drawn upon the work of Fernand Braudel, whose account of the changing structure of capitalism can be applied to recent developments in the networked media economy. Bouquillion, in particular, argues that the subsumption of communication and culture industries into the capitalist realm has been deepened by processes of digitalisation and platformisation in the twenty-first century (2007, 2008). Bouquillion draws on Braudel in order to refute the model of a naturally competitive market, since it fails to explain the development pathways of the networked media economy. For his part, Braudel regarded the competitive market model as only ever being an ideal type, premised upon the interaction of a great number of actors via the mechanisms of supply and demand (i.e. a self-balancing market based on exchange between 'price-takers'). Braudel's contrasting description of capitalism considered its operations to be inherently non-competitive in a manner which made capitalism categorically distinct from the market economy.

Braudel's influence has been strongest in the body of work known as World-Systems theory, but is also clearly evident in Armand Mattelart's work on dependency and communication (Mattelart 1978, 1994). More recently, Sousa has used Braudelian notions of time to discuss social change and new information and communication technologies (2006). It is the interpretation of Braudel's model of capitalism developed by world-systems theory that Bouquillion emphasises (as per Wallerstein 1991). Here there is preponderance to understanding the world economic system in terms of dependency upon elite, and largely Western, capital interests. In communications research this approach has often been adopted in parallel with notions of cultural dependency imposed upon the developing worlds by Western media systems. Outside of communications research, Giovanni Arrighi emerged as probably the leading advocate of a Braudelian legacy in political economy (1994, 2001, 2007). Arrighi identified three claims that he considers central to Braudel's contribution to our understanding of historical capitalism:

The first is that the essential feature of historical capitalism over its longue durée, that is, over its entire lifetime, has been its "flexibility" and "eclecticism" rather than the concrete forms it assumed at different places and at different times. The second claim is that, world-historically, the financial rather than the commercial or industrial arenas has been the real home of capitalism. And the third is that the identification with states rather than markets is what has enabled capitalism to triumph in the modern era. (2001, p. 111)

It is Braudel's basic conception of the evolving operations of capitalism within a stratified global economy that unites the arguments of Arrighi and Bouquillion. It also clearly resonates with the three-tier model of India media markets posited recently by Parthasarathi and Athique (2019). According to Braudel's conception, capitalism occupies the top layer of a three-tiered structure, differentiated on the basis of a 'hierarchy of exchanges' (Braudel 1977, 1982). Thus, we have three relatively distinct 'spheres of circulation' guided by their own socio-temporal logics: the non-economy of material life, the market economy and the sphere of capitalism. The age-old routines and rituals of material life form the base of the two other tiers. Yet, for Braudel, this vast lower layer of material existence largely remains outside the formal logics of economic exchange (1982, p. 21). It is the manner in which these logics play out in the upper two tiers that marks the distinction between the market economy and capitalism. As Arrighi summarises:

In Braudel's conception, capitalism is 'the top layer' of the world of trade. It consists of those individuals, networks, and organizations that systematically appropriate the largest profits, regardless of the particular nature of the activities (financial, commercial, industrial, or agricultural) in which they are involved. Braudel distinguishes this layer from the lower layer of 'market economy', which consists of participants in buying and selling activities whose rewards are more or less proportionate to the costs and risks. (2007, p. 267)

Braudel juxtaposes the market economy (where the 'wheels of commerce' are greased by "equal terms between traders (pure, perfect competition), transparency, symmetry of information") with the intentionally opaque zone of capitalism (where regularity and transparency are absent and risk, and hence speculation, predominates) (Boltanski and Chiapelle

2005, p. 5). In Braudel's terminology, capitalism constitutes *contre-marchés* or anti-markets (1982). Political power is the crucial mechanism in Braudelian capitalism, because it allows capitalists to operate above the market economy. Braudel equates the sphere of capitalism with "giant corporations, big business, buccaneering raids, boardroom knavery, and other practices and institutions made possible by monopoly power" (Haskell and Teichgraeber 1996, p. 16). According to Braudel, capitalism is a world, or rather worlds (*économie monde*), of monopolies (see Taylor 2000). At this level, commands replace price as the main mechanism of coordinating economic activity. The power configurations within anti-markets give each monopoly a unique logic. This is why identification with states is central to the success of capitalists, since state support is typically a critical element of anti-market power. The businesses of media are also particularly suited to generating anti-market power, which bestows media corporations with substantial economic and political leverage.

Bouquillion argues that existing and emerging factors have combined to move media industries away from any semblance of operating according to the ideal type of the competitive market (2007, pp. 175–176). Fundamentally, there appears to be a basic incompatibility between the socio-economic specificities of the networked media economy and the idealised movements of the competitive market advocated by orthodox economics. Bouquillion is not alone in making this point. Bouquillion argues that Braudel's model of capitalism accords with the three broad features of today's networked media economy. First, changes in the industrial structures of these industries associated with financialisation and concentration. These changes underwrite corporate internationalisation and, in turn, militate against competition through their incorporation within what Amin has referred to as 'oligopoly-finance capitalism' (2008). Second, changes in the commodities produced by networked media economy firms, in particular because of the introduction of new methods of financing and monetising the production and distribution of content. Third, the re-working of media regulation and wider competition policies through processes of liberalisation, which began in advanced capitalist nation states, has unleashed the forces of capitalism rather than encouraged market imperatives. In this context, state authorities endeavour to legitimatise and facilitate the incorporation of the networked media economy within an anti-market domain.

Consolidation in India's Network Media Economy

Bhattacharjee and Agrawal track the emerging oligopolistic nature of the Indian media sector from 2004–2011, noting even at this stage the growing size and influence of Reliance and Sun Networks in the telecommunications sector (2018). Their analysis has limitations, however, because it does not fully address the central implication: that distribution operates as "the key *locus of power and profit*" in media economies (Garnham 2000, pp. 161–162). As power aggregates vertically within a network media economy, we can see some forms of competition decrease. Thus: "Content providers, while not small, are significantly more competitive, and are facing a less competitive provider market in the essential service of distribution. This imbalance leads to rent extraction by the less competitive segment" (Noam 2016, p. 1345). As is already evident in three crucial areas of distribution in the Indian media network economy (TV distribution, mobile telephony and broadband internet), this is a capital intensive segment of the value chain that tends towards concentration and reduced competition. In turn, control over distribution presents opportunities for creating bottlenecks and reinforcing market power (see Fitzgerald 2015). As Evans and Donders have noted, the ability to bundle broadband, voice and subscription television offers network operators "significant advantage vis-à-vis satellite operators and streaming platforms" (2018, p. 32). They operate as the internet's gatekeepers, dictate the terms of access and means to connect to consumers. In an era of broadband network infrastructure, network owners "virtually control the new distribution channel of the new television industry and have bottleneck power" (ibid., p. 72).

The consolidation of telecommunications is probably the most critical area where a battle for market power has been fought over the past two decades. A policy shift in 2001 removed the state monopoly over the telecommunications sector, attracting both foreign direct investment and a host of private operators interested in developing India's mobile telecoms market (Mukherji 2008). By 2010, competition between 15 major players drove the expansion of coverage and the reduction of charges and tariffs, making India the world's second-largest telecom market. In the same year, Mukesh Ambani's RIL emerged as the only successful bidder for pan-Indian 4G wireless spectrum (it achieved this by acquiring the broadband services provider Infotel Broadband Services Limited immediately after its successful bid) (Pendakur 2013). Mukherjee posits that Reliance was then able to use regulatory loopholes to corner the 4G market, in part because state agencies "deliberately" allowed Reliance "to untie regulatory knots because that was the best policy to guarantee the spread of Indian telecom revolution" (2019, p. 182).

Using a 2013 license conversion process for converting internet service providers into full service operators, Reliance launched its Reliance Jio subsidiary in 2015 and, in 2016, instigated a price war that forced competitors to match Jio's loss-making deals on data, causing a rapid decline in revenues and substantial industry consolidation (Thakurta and Ghatak 2016). Jio thereby emerged as the third largest operator with 340 million subscribers. Smaller firms merged with other firms or exited (TTSL, Telenor, MTS). Ironically, Reliance Communications (RComm) owned by Mukesh Ambani's brother Anil, previously the second-largest TSP in 2010, was forced into bankruptcy. In 2018, the Indian state regulators approved the purchase of the third-biggest TSP, Idea, by the largest player, Vodafone, in a deal that gave Vodafone a majority stake (45.1%) in the combined entity with the Aditya Birla Group holding a 26% stake. By the end of 2019, Jio had become the second-largest operator and is currently only 50 million subscribers behind Vodafone (Fitch Solutions Group 2019).

A similar trajectory has been seen in television, where the Cable Television Networks (Regulation) Amendment Bill 2011 prompted consolidation of the cable and satellite segments of India's network infrastructure. High capital expenditure requirements on set-top boxes and back-end infrastructure came at a time when broadcasters were facing new competition from over-the-top platforms made possible by cheaper internet rates and subsidised through bundled service packages offered by the major telecom operators, Vodafone, Airtel and Reliance Jio. Subsequently, the number of direct-to-home (DTH) platforms has reduced from 7 to 5. In 2017, the Essel Group (owner of Zee Entertainment and Dish TV) acquired a controlling stake in the satellite firm Videocon D2H in order to consolidate its position through acquisitions of regional MSOs. But, by 2019, mounting debt pressures compelled Essel to combine its satellite operations with Airtel Digital. The deal between Airtel and Dish TV can also be seen as a response to the continuing expansion of Reliance Jio (Laghate 2018). In October 2018, Reliance acquired controlling stakes in India's two largest cable TV and broadband companies (a 51.3% stake in Hathway Cable & Datacom and a 66% stake in DEN Networks).

These acquisitions were part of Reliance's larger goal to create a fibre-to-the-home (FTTH) broadband service called JioGigaFiber (Ramachandran 2018; Pandey 2019a). After the acquisitions of Hathway and Den, Reliance now controls 24 million cable-connected homes of these two companies across 750 cities, around 35% of the estimated cable user base of 70 million. As Parthasarathi and Srinivas note, these acquisitions have created effective cable monopolies in some regions (2019). Nonetheless, while this may be a substantial holding in the cable television market, it is only one piece of Reliance's strategy of expanding market share in the network economy through a so-called triple play of mobile phones, TV distribution and home broadband. The media strategy is, in turn, subservient to the larger aim of developing the underlying network, where Reliance's interests as an infrastructure business converge with its newfound interest in data storage and mining. Thus, in announcing the JioGigaFiber project at Reliance's AGM, Mukesh Ambani emphasised this would be the world's largest greenfield fixed-line broadband rollout, with a simultaneous launch in 1100 cities across India and a total of 1600 cities connected (Pandey 2019b).

Financialisation 'with Indian Characteristics'

Financialisation in India's media sector, via both domestic and imported sources, has been prompted in a large part by the massive capital investment costs associated with the development of digital and data infrastructures. From a Braudelian perspective, financialisation deepens the integration of the networked media economy with the non-competitive plane of anti-market capitalism. Three processes can be distinguished as part of this shift. First, through financialisation, companies and industries become objects of speculation. Second, financialisation engenders a reorganisation of industry structures, by enforcing an equivalence between market concentration and financial capacity. For Bouquillion, it is these developments associated with media cross-ownership, increasing market dominance and vertical integration that are fundamentally detrimental to processes of competition (2008). Anti-competitive practices allow corporations to dominate their markets, take advantage of their customers and manage the lavatory nature of valorisation through preferential modes of financing. Thirdly, through financialisation, the networked media economy comes under the wider influence of the global financial sphere. All three processes entrench the hierarchies of the economic world (*économie monde*) within culture and communication.

Bouquillion's work deploys Wallerstein's notion of a concentric model of influence and exploitation, figured by core, semi periphery and periphery, with Anglo-American institutions at the centre of the financial web (1991). The manner in which corporations interact with finance in India, however, raise important questions about the purported centrality of Anglo-American finance in a Braudelian analysis. Khatri and Ojha highlight three elements that define how financial relations have operated in the post-liberalisation period (2016). First, the 'business group' remains an enduring institutional characteristic of Indian capitalist enterprise (Caussat 2017; Mazumdar 2011). Here, family-controlled conglomerates remain the typical unit of decision-making and dense corporate networks based on business group, family and caste remain evident. Second, banks do not play the same coordinating role as in other economies (Naudet and Dubost 2016). Indian corporate businesses rely on political connections to facilitate financing from public sector banks. Third, Indian corporate businesses display a "cavalier attitude toward loan repayment because they have very little of their own capital" at stake (Khatri and Ojha 2016, p. 64). The private wealth of family conglomerates is well protected by fraudulent accounting practices and tax loopholes, while the financial reliance of businesses on the state banking sector has led to the overhang of non-performing assets (NPAs) on the ledgers of state banks (Mukhopadhyay 2018).

Public banks typically take on private sector losses but are, in turn, recapitalised by the state, especially when it comes to what are regarded as priority areas. In that respect, the digital sectors have been heavily favoured, even though the costs of digitisation and infrastructure upgrades have been very high. Even with the public sector backstop, Reliance Jio's entry into the market came at a time when debt levels were already affecting the major players in this sector. The Reliance ADA Group led by Anil Ambani, as the parent of RComm, was forced into bankruptcy and taken to court by the Ericsson group for non-payments of debt (Kurup 2019a; Shrivastava 2018). Another major player in the network infrastructure space, the Essel Group faced similar problems and was forced to seek buyers of its assets. Vodafone Idea may have to exit the market, due to rulings that impose significantly higher government dues on data traffic. For the previous two decades, the controlling shareholders (often called 'promoters') in large business businesses could expect sympathetic treatment from their lenders, typically state banks. A seismic change came in 2016, when the government approved the formation of the National Company Law Tribunal (NCLT) and passed the Insolvency Bankruptcy Code (IBC), both of these initiatives being enacted in response to the dire state of bank lending as corporate loan defaults reached drastic levels.

The IBC determines that a defaulting company's boards and management can be removed and assets put up for sale. As banks scaled back their lending, heavily indebted groups turned their attention to the long- stagnant corporate bond market, mutual funds and non-bank institutions. The Reserve Bank of India put a limit on bank exposure to individual groups. Financial institutions now have greater confidence in getting their investments back and crucially they have begun to secure loans against the promoter's personal shares in listed companies. Following bond defaults of IL&FS, a big infrastructure group, in 2018, weaker promoters found it harder to renew debt financing and mutual funds began to sell shares when a decline in value challenged their claims on the debt. This forced some promoters, notably Essel Group's Subhash Chandra to sell off parts of their empires to pay back creditors with a claim on their personal shares. These forced sales reflect a shift in balance in a system long typified by passive investors and toothless banks.

In this new context, private equity firms inevitably become larger players, as buyout firms fill the void for companies cut off from bank lending or the corporate bond market (Wilson 2019). There are also new opportunities for the strong, as billionaire family businesses increasingly conducting private market transactions via private equity firms (UBS/PwC 2017). The value of private equity deals in India hit a peak in 2019, with the largest private equity deal ever in India, a US$ 3.66 billion investment by Canadian firm Brookfield Infrastructure Partners in one of Reliance's network infrastructure investment trusts which controls 170,000 telecom towers (Kurup 2019b). Reliance had previously signed another deal to raise US$14 billion through the sale of a 20% stake in RIL's refining and petrochemicals business to Saudi Aramco. With the new 5G spectrum auction scheduled for the 2019 financial year, one commentator noted that "this is grave news for RIL's competitors, whose resources now look even more scarce in comparison to the conglomerate" (Philipose 2019). Thus, it is by no means clear that the larger players in India's networked media economy have passed under the domination of the global financial sphere and are driven by "the drum beat of Wall Street, quarterly returns and the stock price" (Garnham 2004, p. 99).

Data Protection and the Search for National Champions

Institutions of the state are equally crucial to Braudel's explanation of capitalist anti-market dynamics, given their capacity to organise oligopolistic competition and guarantee the international hierarchy of capitalist interests. In India, both before and after independence, the state has played a critical role in enforcing domestic monopolies and oligopolies, while periodically tilting the balance between national and international capital interests. The most recent example, in 2018, is a series of regulations and policy statements on data localisation that are intended to constitute parts of a new Data Protection Framework. In April 2018, the Reserve Bank of India directed payment firms to store data locally. In July 2018, the Personal Data Protection Bill 2018 mandated that an active copy of personal data records be stored in India. In December 2018, new e-commerce rules prevented foreign companies from selling products in India from their own affiliated companies, causing the likes of Amazon and Walmart to significantly restructure their operations. Separately, a draft report from a panel working on cloud-computing policy recommended that data currently kept in the cloud be stored in India. In February 2019, the Data Protection Framework was more firmly enunciated in the E-Commerce Policy draft, which also seeks to regulate cross border data flows and mandates that after a three-year period all data generated in India, via social media, search engines and e-commerce, must be stored in India. Effectively, this furthered the proposition enunciated in the Government's earlier Electronic Commerce 2018 consultation paper that Indian data should be "stored exclusively in India" (DPIIT 2018, p. 6; cf. Goel 2018, 2019).

Beyond a broad shift to data localisation as the key element of the Data Protection Framework, the Draft National E-Commerce Policy posits a substantially different perspective from the Personal Data Protection Bill and the TRAI recommendations on *Privacy, Security and Ownership of the Data in the Telecom Sector* released in July 2018 (MEITY 2018; TRAI 2018). While also acknowledging that individuals are the right holders of their data, there is a an important shift in the E-Commerce Policy, which states: "The data of a country, therefore, is best thought of a collective resource, a national asset, that the government holds in trust, but rights to which can be permitted. The analogy of a mine of natural resource or spectrum works here" (DPIIT 2019, p. 14). It proposes viewing data as a property owned by the state and commercially licensed to those who seek to mine it for the purposes of "maximizing growth and for delivering the greatest benefits to all sections of society". The policy further states that the "the presence of 'network effects' means that … Digital capital (granting data the status of 'capital' at par with financial capital of a corporation) has come to be reckoned as one that matters no less than intellectual property or industrial capital (funds)" (DPIIT 2019, p. 6).

The Draft National E-Commerce Policy and consultation paper notes that "just a handful of companies have managed to dominate the digital economy" and its purpose was to boost "the domestic digital economy to find its rightful place with dominant and potentially non-competitive global players" (DPIIT, 2019 p. 15; DPIIT, 2018, p. 2). Previously, in July 2018, India's representatives at the WTO complained that developed and dominant countries, such the United States and China, were attempting to instigate international rules on e-commerce in a manner that would harm domestic interests in India. Reflecting the perceived need for a robust Indian response, the secretary of India's Telecommunications Department, Aruna Sundararajan, announced in January 2019 that a private meeting that the Indian government, having noted the success of China's internet giants, Alibaba and Tencent would introduce a so-called national champion policy to promote the success of domestic companies. The *Wall Street Journal* later reported that the intent was to promote Indian companies in ways that allow them "to become global champions" (Purnell and Roy 2019). In practice, all the changes suggested in the Data Protection Framework and the wider push to create a national champion are mostly likely to favour Reliance. As one Indian consultant noted: "We're witnessing the evolution of a big digital player … It looks like Jio is emerging as a national champion" (Findlay 2019; Purnell and Roy 2019).

There is a striking overlap in the wording and imagery used by the Department for Promotion of Industry and Internal Trade in the draft policy on Indian National E-Commerce and the mantra that equates 'data as the new oil' being expounded by Reliance. This is not entirely surprising in itself, given the prominent role that Reliance executives played in the formulation of the new draft bill, and their obvious benefit from legislation that requires data created by users in India from e-commerce platforms, social media and search engines be "stored exclusively in India" (Sen 2018). Reliance has vigorously lobbied to have laws enacted that would lead to data localisation, and the company also made this position clear in its submission to the TRAI's *Privacy, Security and Ownership of the*

Data in the Telecom Sector consultation, once again calling for data localisation, specifically in relation to Over-The-Top (OTT) operations. Analysts have concluded that "if the ecommerce draft in its current form gets enshrined as law, Jio will have a huge edge over others" (Sen 2018). In e-commerce specifically, Reliance Retail already boasts 10,000 stores across the country and is the largest organised retail chain by revenue in the country. It is currently ranked the fifth-fastest growing retail company in the world by Deloitte.

Mukesh Ambani has made it clear that he plans to use the Reliance Jio network to turn RIL's retail arm into an e-commerce platform. Unlike international competitors such as Amazon, Reliance will be permitted to operate an ecosystem model, in which it can sell its own inventory and simultaneously act as the e-market operator. This model of operation will not be available to Walmart-Flipkart and Amazon, unless they substantially restructure their operations through investments in locally based infrastructure and procurement. In order to house data locally, both companies would have to use local data centres, which would be costly and deprive their operations of the advantage of possessing a mature architecture. Furthermore, the requirement to house data in India will open up access to digital advertising on both platforms for Reliance. A Merrill Lynch report concludes that this alone could benefit RIL by US$1–2.5 billion per annum (IANS 2019). Meanwhile, Reliance has announced further investments in five tech companies, specialising in services ranging from logistics to voice technology, all of which support the central goal of integrating the group's burgeoning "digital initiatives".

Localising Platform Capitalism

The expansion of the digital economy and growing heft of large platform operators from the United States and China, and now possibly India, through the 'national champion' model, underscores many of the concerns raised UNCTAD about unequal power relations in global data value chains. An increasing digital dependency prompted by the market domination of the seven 'super platforms' aligns well with a Braudelian framework that views capitalism as a system of power built on a global scale. As Bouquillion argues, Braudel's approach is in accord with other theorists such as Schumpeter and Galbraith who argue that the power of large institutions over market dynamics invalidates neoclassical economists' claims that capitalism can be equated with the ideal-type conception of the market (2007, pp. 173–174). There are, however, fundamental theoretical questions about Braudel's proposed divide between a 'fully competitive market economy' and a private anti-competitive realm of capitalism (see, e.g., Howard 1985). For one thing, it runs counter to classical political economy's notion of 'real competition', in which positions of monopoly and rent-extraction provide the basis of ongoing competition (Shaikh 2016). From another perspective, it can be seen to infer that the market economy 'below capitalism' is somehow characterised by transparency, equal exchange and equilibrium. As Parthasarathi and Athique's analysis of the meso-level 'market of operations' in the Indian media economy makes abundantly clear, the regional and cultural affinities, political connections and power imbalances that mark the development of network infrastructure at the local level invalidate any such notion of perfect competition stabilising below the elite domain of capital interests (2019).

There are also crucial domestic characteristics that an approach based on Braudel and inter-national dependency models tends to elide. If capitalism is too narrowly defined by production for profit in a world system of exchange, in which countries in the periphery are "exploited" for the benefit of the core, then the internal power relations that characterise the development of the digital economy within a complex society such as India can end up being understated, or even overlooked entirely. Equally, dependency and world systems approaches to media and communication can be easily manipulated through nationalist discourses in situations where state interests and 'business-friendly development' are so often substitutable. Indeed, recent shifts across the world towards various forms of state-sponsored 'collective data ownership', which clearly benefit domestic state-capital alliances, can be too readily justified by making ominous references to the 'imperialism' of the seven super-platforms emanating from the United States and China. Given India's considerable scale and diversity, its highly concentrated capital distribution, uneven economic geography, lingering feudal social structures and the close relationships between political actors and family-held business empires, we should remain attentive to the fact that core-periphery issues have to be understood as being as much internal as external factors. In that respect, the greater utility in a Braudelian analysis may be found in its application beyond the concerns of world systems theory, where it could offer some fresh insights into the co-evolution of 'crony capitalism' and networked media economies.

References

Amin, S. (2008). 'Market Economy' or Oligopoly-Finance Capitalism? *Monthly Review, 59*(11), 51–61.

Arrighi, G. (1994). *The Long Twentieth Century*. London: Verso.

Arrighi, G. (2001). Braudel, Capitalism and the New Economic Sociology. *Review, XXIV*(1), 107–123.

Arrighi, G. (2007). States, Markets, and Capitalism, East and West. *Positions: East Asia Cultures Critique, 15*(2), 251–284.

Athique, A. (2016). *Transnational Audiences*. Cambridge: Polity Press.

Bhattacharjee, A., & Agrawal, A. (2018). Mapping the Power of Major Media Companies in India. *Economic and Political Weekly, 53*(29), 48–57.

Boltanski, L., & Chiapello, E. (2005). *The New Spirit of Capitalism*. London: Verso.

Bouquillion, P. (2007). Les Industries De La Culture, De L'information El De La Communication Dans Le Capitalisme. In P. Bouquillion & Y. Combes (Eds.), *Les Industries De La Culture Et De La Communication En Mutation*. Paris: L'Harmatthan.

Bouquillion, P. (2008). *Les Industries De La Culture Et De La Commmunication: Les Strategies Du Capitalisme*. Grenoble: PUG.

Braudel, F. (1977). *Afterthoughts on Material Civilization and Capitalism*. Baltimore: Johns Hopkins University Press.

Braudel, F. (1982). *Civilization and Capitalism, 15th-18th Century. Vol. 2 The wheels of commerce*. London: Collins.

Caussat, P. (2017). Competing for Public Acquaintances: The Case of the Reliance Group in India. In C. Rowley & M. Marie dela Rama (Eds.), *The Changing Face of Corruption in the Asia Pacific: Current Perspectives and Future Challenges*. Elsevier Science.

Chancel, L., & Piketty, T. (2017). *Indian Income Inequality 1922–2014: From British Raj to Billionnaire Raj*. CEPR Discussion Paper No. DP12409.

Chandra, K. (2015). The New Indian State: The Relocation of Patronage in the Post-Liberalisation Economy. *Economic and Political Weekly, 50*(41), 46–58.

Crabtree, J. (2018). *The Billionaire Raj: A Journey through India's New Gilded Age*. London: Oneworld Publications.

Department for Promotion of Industry and Internal Trade (DPIIT). (2018). *Electronic Commerce in India: Draft National Policy Framework*. New Delhi: Government of India.

Department for Promotion of Industry and Internal Trade (DPIIT). (2019). *Draft E-Commerce Policy*. New Delhi: Government of India.

Economic Times. (2019). Indian Data Must be Owned by Locals: Ambani Companies Pursuit of Profit. *The Economic Times*, 19 January.

Evans, T., & Donders, K. (2018). *Platform Power and Policy in Transforming Television Markets*. Cham: Palgrave Macmillan.

Federation of Indian Chambers of Commerce and Industry and Ernst & Young (FICCI-E&Y). (2019). *A Billion Screens of Opportunity*. New Delhi: Ernst & Young.

Findlay, S. (2019). India's War on Foreign Tech Creates Opportunity for Reliance. *Financial Times*, 6 March.

Fitch Solutions Group. (2019). *India Telecommunications Report—Q4 2019*. London: Fitch Solutions Group Limited.

Fitzgerald, S. (2015). Structure of the Cultural Industries—Global Corporation to SMEs. In K. Oakley & J. O'Connor (Eds.), *The Routledge Companion to the Cultural Industries*. London: Routledge.

Fitzgerald, S. (2019). Over-the-top (OTT) Video Services in India: Media Imperialism after Globalization. *Media Industries Journal, 6*(2).

Gandhi, A., & Walton, M. (2012). Where Do India's Billionaires Get Their Wealth? *Economic and Political Weekly, 47*(40), 10–14.

Garnham, N. (2000). The Media as Cultural Industries. In *Emancipation, the Media, and Modernity: Arguments About the Media and Social Theory* (pp. 39–62). Oxford: Oxford University Press.

Garnham, N. (2004). Class Analysis and the Information Society as Mode of Production. *Javnost/The Public, 11*(3), 93–104.

Goel, V. (2018). India Pushes Back against Tech 'Colonization' by Internet Giants. *New York Times*, 3 September.

Goel, V. (2019). India Proposes Chinese-Style Internet Censorship. *New York Times*, 14 February.

Gupta, C. D. (2017). *State and Capital in Independent India: From Dirigisme to Neoliberalism*. London: School of Oriental and African Studies, University of London.

Haskell, T. L., & Teichgraeber, R. F. (1996). *The Culture of the Market: Historical Essays*. Cambridge: Cambridge University Press..

Howard, M. C. (1985). Fernand Braudel on Capitalism: A Theoretical Analysis. *Historical Reflections / Réflexions Historiques, 12*(3), 469–483.

Indo-Asian News Service (IANS). (2019). RIL to Gain from Personal Data Laws: Merrill Lynch. *Business Standard*, 27 March.

Khatri, N., & Ojha, A. K. (2016). Indian Economic Philosophy and Crony Capitalism. In N. Khatri, K. Abhoy, & A. K. Ojha (Eds.), *Crony Capitalism in India* (pp. 61–85). London: Palgrave Macmillan.

Kurup, R (2019a). Reliance Communications Goes Belly up, to Move Nclt. *Hindu Business Line*, 1 February.

Kurup, R. (2019b). Reliance Jio Transfers Fibre, Tower Units to Investment Trusts. *Business Line*, 3 April.

Laghate, G. (2018). Reliance to Buy Majority Stakes in Den Networks, Hathway Cable for Rs 5,230 Crore. *Economic Times*, 18 October.

Mattelart, A. (1978). The Nature of Communications Practice in a Dependent Society. *Latin American Perspectives, 5*(1), 13–34.

Mattelart, A. (1994). *Mapping World Communication.* Trans. Susan Emanuel and James A. Cohen. Minneapolis and London: University of Minnesota Press.

Mazumdar, S. (2011). *Continuity and Change in Indian Capitalism.* Munich Personal RePEc Archive. Retrieved August 26, 2019, from https://mpra.ub.uni-muenchen.de/38907/.

Mazumdar, S. (2017). From "Outsider" to Insider: The Case of Reliance. *South Asia Multidisciplinary Academic Journal, 15*, 1–27.

McDonald, H. (2010). *Mahabharata in Polyester.* Sydney: New South.

Ministry of Electronics and Information Technology (MEITY). (2018). *The Personal Data Protection Bill.* New Delhi: Government of India.

Mukherjee, R. (2019). Jio Sparks Disruption 2.0: Infrastructural Imaginaries and Platform Ecosystems in 'Digital India'. *Media, Culture and Society, 41*(2), 016344371881838.

Mukherji, R. (2008). The Politics of Telecommunications Regulation: State–Industry Alliance Favouring Foreign Investment in India. *The Journal of Development Studies, 44*(10), 1405–1423.

Mukhopadhyay, A. (2018). *Finding Innovative Solutions to India's NPA Woes.* New Delhi: Observer Research Foundation (ORF).

Mundy, S. (2019). Mukesh Ambani Sets out to Dominate Digital India. *Financial Times*, 30 May.

Murali, K. (2019). Economic Liberalization and the Structural Power of Business. In C. Jaffrelot, A. Kohli, & K. Murali (Eds.), *Business and Politics in India* (pp. 25–49). London: Oxford University Press.

Naudet, J., & Dubost, C. L. (2016). The Indian Exception: The Densification of the Network of Corporate Interlocks and the Specificities of the Indian Business System (2000–2012). *Socio-Economic Review, 15*(2), 405–434.

Noam, E. (Ed.). (2016). *Who Owns the World's Media.* New York: Oxford University.

Oxfam India. (2018). *India Inequality Report 2018: Widening Gaps.* New Delhi: Oxfam India.

Pandey, N. (2019a). Plugging into India's Broadband Revolution. *Mint*, 4 June.

Pandey, N. (2019b). TRAI to Frame Network Testing Rules for Wireline Broadband Operators. *Mint*, 5 June.

Parthasarathi, V., & Athique, A. (2019). Market Matters: Interdependencies in the Indian Media Economy. *Media, Culture and Society.* https://doi.org/10.1177/0163443719853495.

Parthasarathi, V., & Srinivas, A. (2019). Problematic Ownership Patterns: The Evolution of the Television Distribution Networks in India. *Economic and Political Weekly, 54*(12).

Pendakur, M. (2013). Twisting and Turning: India's Telecommunications and Media Industries under the Neoliberal Regime. *International Journal of Media and Cultural Politics, 9*(2), 107–131.

Philipose, M. (2019). Reliance Industries Hits Two Birds with One Stone through Saudi Aramco Deal. *LiveMint*, 12 August.

Purnell, N., & Roy, R.. (2019). Amazon, Facebook and Walmart Need to Watch Their Backs in India. *Wall Street Journal*, 29 January.

Ramachandran, N. (2018). Reliance Industries Spends $712 Million on Cable and Broadband Acquisitions. *Variety*, 19 October.

Schiller, D. (2014). Rosa Luxemburg's Internet? For a Political Economy of State Mobilization and the Movement of Accumulation in Cyberspace. *International Journal of Communication, 8*, 355–375.

Sen, S. (2018). How Reliance Shaped the India First Agenda in the Draft Ecommerce Policy. *Factor Daily*, 7 August. Retrieved August 8, 2018, from https://factordaily.com/how-reliance-shaped-the-india-first-agenda-in-the-draft-ecommerce-policy/.

Shaikh, A. (2016). *Capitalism: Competition, Conflict, Crises*. New York: Oxford University Press.

Shrivastava, B. (2018). The $41 Billion Wealth Gap That Divides the Ambani Brothers. *LiveMint*, 22 October.

Sinha, A. (2019). India's Porous State: Blurred Boundaries and the Evolving Business-State Relationship. In C. Jaffrelot, A. Kohli, & K. Murali (Eds.), *Business and Politics in India* (pp. 50–92). London: Oxford University Press.

Sinha, J., & Varshney, A. (2011). It Is Time for India to Rein in Its Robber Barons. *FT.Com*, 6 January.

Sousa, H. (2006). Information Technologies, Social Change and the Future: The Case of Online Journalism in Portugal. *European Journal of Communication, 21*(3), 373–387.

Taylor, P. J. (2000). World Cities and Territorial States under Conditions of Contemporary Globalization. *Political Geography, 19*, 5–32.

Telecom Regulatory Authority of India (TRAI). (2018). *Recommendations on Privacy, Security and Ownership of the Data in the Telecom Sector*. New Delhi: Telecom Regulatory Authority of India.

Thakurta, P. G., & Ghatak, A. R. (2016). The Immaculate Conception of Reliance Jio. *The Wire*. Retrieved September 17, 2017, from https://thewire.in/tech/the-immaculate-conception-of-reliance-jio.

The Economist. (2014). The New Age of Crony Capitalism; Crony Capitalism. *The Economist*, 15 March.

The Telegraph. (2019). Oil and Data Don't Mix in World of Facebook and Ambani. *The Telegraph*, 13 September.

UBS/PwC. (2017). *New Value Creators Gain Momentum: Billionaires Insights 2017*. Retrieved July 15, 2019, from https://www.pwc.com/gx/en/financial-services/Billionaires%20insights/billionaires-insights-2017.pdf.
UNCTAD. (2019). *Digital Economy Report 2019: Value Creation and Capture: Implications for Developing Countries*. New York: United Nations.
Varma, A., Hu, B., & Bloomquist, L. (2016). Family Oligarchies and Crony Capitalism in India. In N. K. India & A. K. Ojha (Eds.), *Crony Capitalism in* (pp. 159–176). Palgrave Macmillan.
Wallerstein, I. (1991). Braudel on Capitalism, or Everything Upside Down. *The Journal of Modern History, 63*(2), 354–361.
Walton, M. (2017). India's Political Economy: What Can Be Learnt from the US Progressive Era Response to the Gilded Age? Retrieved January 22, 2020, from http://www.michaelwalton.info/wp-content/uploads/2019/03/Walton-gilded-age_Jan2017.pdf.
Wilson, E. (2019). PE Changes the Face of Corporate India. *Euromoney*, 19 March.
Wu, T. (2018). *The Curse of Bigness: Antitrust in the New Gilded Age*. New York: Columbia Global Reports.
Zuboff, S. (2019). *The Age of Surveillance Capitalism: The Fight for a Human Future at the New Frontier of Power*. London: Profile Books.

CHAPTER 4

The Derivative Values of Platform Capitalism

Akshaya Kumar

The recently concluded General Election in India was not only its costliest ever, the overall expense nearly doubled over the previous iteration, in 2014. While the expense has gone up six times since 1998, in about two decades, the jump between the last two iterations is alarming for a number of reasons. Indian economy has been doing rather badly, particularly since the demonetization event, in which the government excluded nearly 86% of its active currency from legal tendering. Since then, there has been a remarkable fall even in official growth numbers. Unemployment is the highest it has been in decades, and small and medium enterprises have been struggling to stay afloat, by all accounts. How do we reconcile with the two contrasting set of graphics, then? While it may have increasingly become a common sense of 'life in capitalism', the paradox of a struggling economy confronted with the loudest, the most self-assured and blatantly self-congratulatory government should be a moment of reckoning. Particularly so, for those of us in media and communication studies who are left befuddled by the extraordinary convergence between advertising-led trajectories of electoral and entertainment platforms. This chapter

A. Kumar (✉)
IIT Indore, Indore, India
e-mail: akshaya.kumar@iiti.ac.in

A. Athique, V. Parthasarathi (eds.), *Platform Capitalism in India*, Global Transformations in Media and Communication Research - A Palgrave and IAMCR Series,
https://doi.org/10.1007/978-3-030-44563-8_4

makes an attempt to unpack a little of this convergence via the political economy of platform capitalism.

There is a growing pile of recent literature which grapples with, and builds upon, the idea that the media audience metadata is hoarded and exchanged across platforms in the new scheme of things. Expectedly, the narrative typically begins with Google's near-monopoly on search engine market enabling target advertising to be embedded across a vast number of platforms. Nonetheless, as Athique notes: 'At one level, the mania for targeted advertising is simply a more sophisticated manifestation of America's rejection of planned production in favour of guided consumption. What is more significant is the multiple vectors of 'market information' coming on stream, and their seamless automated operation' (Athique 2019a). Hoarded data by itself does not qualify as a valuable commodity, as any real authority on data capitalism would promptly remind us. Rather, the value is added by analytics instead. That is why what we are confronted with is not data collection as the primary enterprise, but various manifestations of algorithmic governance. Let us take the example of Netflix. Not only has it been burning capital without charging the subscribers proportionately, its advertising-free content means that Netflix's doors are shut even for the pre-eminent model of platform business—free content traded for attention to merchandise advertorials. While it is not my intention to speculate over Netflix's longer-term viability, one is certainly encouraged to take an off-side view of the phenomena of profitability and market valuations in platform capitalism. Without discounting the *value* of data itself, or of sophisticated analytics (as an entire set of mechanisms for data harvesting, classification and running algorithms over them), I would nonetheless like to concentrate on the lofted discursive inevitability of growth by numbers which is essentially based on the monopolistic urge of digital platforms.

To clarify this point, what I address as monopolistic in this chapter is not necessarily a technical monopoly over the business segment. Instead, my focus is upon the surge of businesses designed to be viable and profitable in the long-term only as monopolies. Invariably, they enter the respective markets with predatory pricing or free services which can turn profitable only if they achieve monopoly control of the market segment in question. To understand why such large quanta of capital are taking that plunge, we must consider how computational capital powerfully reconfigures the attention economy towards mass address, by building predictive systems based on massive chunks of data and proportionate computational ability. Such systems, by breaking down habits, events and phenomena into data-sets, claim to make futures predictable as well as tractable. Given the thirst for inputs, this is precisely where advertising comes into the frame—along with paranoid systems of national security—to harvest data so as to manipulate consumer choices, certainly, but also to engender the field of probabilistic calculus. The power of advertising, as it persists, rests within the subsequent deployment of rhetoric, which may not exhaust its prowess in any singular iteration of influence. Instead, the algorithmic dispersal of rhetoric works best when it spreads as a contagion, as a force unleashed, not merely to stimulate profit, but to catalyse value, unleashing what Athique has called the 'alchemical processes' of the data economy (2018).

The Derivative Rhetoric of Inevitability

One of the catchiest phrases used for the 2019 elections, which was also turned into Twitter hashtags and a music video shared by the official Facebook handle of the Bharatiya Janata Party (BJP), was *Ayega toh Modi hi* [Modi's return is inevitable]. As the song featuring Devang Patel—a long-forgotten singer-actor of yesteryears—illustrates best, the vitality of the phrases lies in its rhetoric of inevitability. It suggests that regardless of all the corruption scandals and political charges of failure labelled against Narendra Modi, the incumbent Prime Minister, he would make a return to the office. I reckon the power of this rhetoric should not be mistaken, since it was creatively citing an entire cycle of public debate over the BJP's diminishing chances in various state elections. The idea hurled at people, therefore, was that you ***know*** this script already. Regardless of all the speculations, there is an inevitability to Modi's triumphal charge and his party's chances are now determined by the destined crowning glory of his iconicity. A close cousin of this rhetoric was the phrase 'If not Modi, then who?' In this way, it was suggest that there is no alternative, hence the inevitability. Indeed, the BJP has strategically turned a parliamentary electoral model into a presidential one, at least for the sake of the public debate. But such a rhetoric also invested a lot of 'value' in one cult figure, implying that while some odds may seem to be against him, the future is already cast in stone, leaving no room for doubt.

Such a forceful hailing of the rhetoric of inevitability has upheld Modi's presumed monopoly over public imagination. The battle, after all, was for that very imagination. The rhetoric of inevitability sought to barricade the bearings of this potentially unwieldy imagination and put it in an enclosure. It sought to claim ownership by making a *derivative* bid for power, I would argue. Derivatives in the market are used to hedge a position or speculate on an asset. They are derived assets, which operate by 'constructing a "virtual" reality composed of relations between qualities that need not correspond to the ways in which those qualities are related in the lived practice of their underlyings' (Arvidsson 2016). Born of key advances in probability theory, derivatives offer a second-order logic of valuation, by enabling the transformation of uncertainties—or intangible assets—into calculable risks (ibid.). Their valuation is anchored by the *fluctuations* of the values of the underlying asset. For derivatives to be lucrative, the discursive landscape of transactions has to be infested with an unpredictable risk-quotient. The derivatives could be based on the speculative frenzy about any risk-laden metric, such as weather (rain data) or currency exchange rates. The higher the risk, the stronger should be the case for entering the derivative markets to hedge one's future against speculations.

To understand the *value* of the rhetoric of inevitability, then, we must take into account the risks it is pitched against. Such a rhetoric provides vital guarantees on the political market of the derivative, which otherwise thrive on the vulnerabilities of the public and the uncertain valuation of their assets. After all, as John Andrews writes, the derivatives anchor conversations across disassembled publics and commodities:

> Derivatives *exploit* risk by disassembling attributes of a commodity and reassembling them into something ad hoc, unfixed, but nonetheless productive. Similarly, publics are increasingly derived from individual identities, special interest groups, or venture philanthropists, creating new attachments and intimacies among numerous aggregates of individuals and groups. The public does not disappear but rather *proliferates*, albeit in a kind of fractured, unpredictable way. (Andrews 2017)

The plank on which the social as well as political logic of derivative is best observed is advertising. In his seminal work on the social logic of the derivative, Randy Martin (2015) suggests that as a financial instrument, the derivative reveals the impossibility of economic knowledge, and is marked by the production of volatility and risk stemming from the attempts to hedge them, and from 'a fracturing of shared values and common norms in the face of a proliferation of means for making sense and creating forms and flows of life'. In a sense then, precisely at the moment when we could and indeed claim to have a better grip on the knowledge of risks, we introduce much more volatility into the system. Martin adds:

> The derivative operates by creating value from nonknowledge of the market but also from the very *contestability of value of commodities*. The result is an ever-increasing excess and noise in which a new social principle emerges: a 'frustration that nothing can be done collides with a conviction that immediate and targeted action can make all the difference, that arbitrage between observed and desired outcomes and leverage of what can be made liquid will create a propitious moment for a salutary context'. (Cited in Andrews 2017)

Bryan and Rafferty argue that derivatives play an anchoring function for capital in a market where, for conventional economists, floating exchange rates did not need an anchor (2006). In this conventional view, the markets would gravitate towards the 'fundamental value'—the notion of an anchor underpinning the neo-classical argument for floating exchange rates since the 1970s (ibid., pp. 268–271). This was, after all, the period during which Keynesian economics, which had sought to socialize risks, was steadily dismantled. It is the gradual erosion of the mythical fundamental value during the dismantling that resulted in the problem of trading financial assets (see Bryan and Rafferty 2005). The financial derivatives were developed by capital as the means to hedge against monetary instability and to provide measures for price certainty in international financial markets. Derivatives are, therefore, products that the market has found profitable to produce, 'to compensate (as it were) for the fact that they don't systematically reflect "fundamentals"' (Bryan and Rafferty 2006, p. 273). The derivative's conversion of nonknowledge into a value also stems from the fact that it has no fundamental value. They are, instead, a new solution to the *problem of value*, addressed in the absence of fundamentals which could make incompatible capitals comparable (Arvidsson 2016).

The next and the most recent step in this direction may be the blockchain technology which comes with the libertarian promise of slipping through all regulatory mechanisms. In a sense, cryptocurrency neoliberalism, which bypasses the monetary control and exchange rates across nation-states, is a key landmark in the triumphal charge of algorithmic governance. For many, it appears to be a value in itself, since it further gravitates towards the idea of uncompromising 'fundamental' valuations.

The valuation, therefore, remains vulnerable to influence management where the intangible assets (such as, popularity indices) can be converted into tangible assets (in effect, when they are modulated from qualitative to quantitative events/commodities). What ties political representation—as a domain of direct address but intangible, unreliable impact—with algorithms of value production in finance capitalism are the digital platforms which make a 'plausible' claim to convert influence into tangible assets via complex modules of probability theory, enacted in concert with the granularity of targeted advertising.

The topography of the digital is rendered legible primarily by the units of the infinite transactions that constitute it. The digital systems record every iteration of such transactions before and after algorithmic processing. In fact, increasingly, digital systems are designed in such a manner that they precipitate and regurgitate more and more of these transactional units (Athique 2019b). Transactions, then, are a way of the digital to appropriate us as users instead of viewers or readers. Such actions are enabled by the landscape of hyperlinks, hashtags, multimedia constellations and complex layouts. The specific orientation of analytics may render the metadata thus generated in preferred ways of legibility for the platforms, but for the users the platforms must offer a whole variety of click baits. Thus, there are two key reasons why these Internet monopolies offer such an invaluable deal to political leadership. First, while an individual liking a Facebook page or following an icon on Twitter may not mean much in terms of conversion to votes, the overall metrics of digital transactions, customisable across a differentially identified user group, engenders robust probability metrics that can be traded further across the digital network, essentially as derivatives. What is effectively traded and synchronized via the network of dubious anchors, then, is not any fundamental value but the calculability of risks (see Ascher 2016).

Indeed, to a large extent, this algorithmic sport with probability metrics is enabled by the unique data/image/code constellations of digital media. Second, slowly but steadily, the Internet monopolies have been hoarding a highly disproportionate share of advertising revenues and concentrated holdings of bandwidth and spectrum, thereby forcing political leadership to consider an alliance of convenience. To this extent, the derivatives of influence do not offer any guarantees. Instead, they offer a second-order agreement to hedge the prevailing risks of nonknowledge in an increasingly uncertain domain. The derivative rhetoric of inevitability promotes itself in this very bracket, where value is produced in a second-order calculus. However fraught the calculus of rhetoric may be, its strength lies in a networked projection—where multiple pieces of an aggregation appear to be in a *probabilistic consensus.* The gap between the first- and second-order calculus is where advertising in general and the rhetoric of inevitability in particular thrive. Particularly so, since advertising offers an ample opportunity to pump capital and manipulate the perception via dubious but substantial claims, accusations and assurances most evident in the explosion of fake news on digital platforms.

To reconnect with where we started, in a first-past-the-post electoral system followed by a multiparty democracy ridden with identitarian fissures of regionality, gender, caste, class and language, the derivative rhetoric of the inevitability of Modi's foretold triumph holds disproportionate derivative value, but not necessarily because of the price of the underlying asset. The role of platforms such as Google, Facebook and WhatsApp needs to be understood in precisely this manner, I would argue. Google's Page Rank and Facebook's News Feed provide us with dubious, but nonetheless valuable, algorithmic guarantees by cutting down on the excess and noise of the Internet. If Google indexes and ranks the Internet for us, Facebook curates our daily feed of social atmospherics, deriving value from our persistent attention to the vortex filtered by computational capital (Beller 2013). WhatsApp, on the other hand, has taken over as a pre-eminent news platform in small-town India (Mullick and Devi 2017). On certain WhatsApp groups operating as ideological-communal enclosures, news appears in the form of an invasive mutant weed. It germinates out of stringer-informant networks, which work for tens of news channels, and a whole variety of print- and/or web-based magazines. However, WhatsApp has become the fastest communication channel to share unverified, alarmist and provocative messages as news, particularly in the form of dubious images and videos. The dubious character of such news draws upon the noisy informality of the medium, which does not promise sophisticated analysis.

WhatsApp news, then, is akin to a libidinal platform on which the public and private come together to create value from another variant of non-knowledge. The political and social scandals, on such a platform, legitimize the 'derivative' rhetorical value of the news since the hidden—although often explicitly added—inscription on such images and videos remains: *mainstream media will never show you this*! The value of such dubious 'news' is thus amplified by the raw brutality of truth embedded in a document which is bound to be diminished, if not set aside, by the various layers of cross-checking and verifications. To that extent, WhatsApp appears to offer a raw and direct interface with the scandalous truths which are filtered out of television channels, primarily because they would be oddly placed in the formal algorithms of the televisual ecosystem. As stated above, then, the contestability of the value of commodities creates a surplus value in the derivative rhetoric, on which entities such as WhatsApp news are mounted. The rhetorical flourish in this derivative market is the embedded advertorial surplus, which offers new values with their own terms of (re)evaluation. The modern polity constituted on the basis of citizenship tethered to the nation-state, otherwise tied to the efficacy of news media, is thus outwitted by a platform economy in which nonknowledge, anchored by rhetorical surpluses and advertorial imperatives, is engaged in the task of value creation.

The Inter-evaluative Dynamic

One of the key features of the platform economy is the *inter-evaluative* dynamic which emerges among a whole variety of users or between, let us say, a driver and a rider. In the former case, users on social media could be engaged to leave an evaluative footprint by liking, sharing, commenting and so on. In the latter case, the driver and the rider could be engaged in a transaction on the reconstructed cartography of the app, on which they would also evaluate the other, while being fully captive to the algorithmic control of the ridesharing company for all the substantial matters. The app, like an electronic voting machine during the elections, only provides the graphic interface of permissible choices. What these inter-evaluative dynamics distract us into believing is that we are secure under the aegis of computational capital, which ranks and effectively regulates civic behaviour, flushing out eccentric and poor retail practices. What such computational utopia pushes into the background are the degrees of debt, unemployment, traffic congestion and unequal class relations which are at the heart of the platform economy (as seen so clearly in the growth of ridesharing apps). We are also led to believe that there is enough investment capital in the market to fuel such debt-ridden growth, without any proportionate promise of profitability.

Nonetheless, the recently unveiled Uber IPO, which came with the Kafkaesque 'warning' that the company may never make a profit. What does Uber promise via a public offering for new stakeholders, then, if not at least the horizon of profitability? I suggest the answer would be privileged access to inexhaustible reserves of capital, ensuring endless growth without any market limitations. What the investors could yet bet on, with some guarantees, is that regardless of its bleeding balance sheet, Uber would never cease to attract more capital to pump more cars on urban streets, more bank loans for car drivers and a climbing mountain of debt. After all, such a mountain would fuel the growth of insurance, automobile manufacturing, auto parts and repairs, petroleum and a number of allied industries such as food delivery, rentals housing and so on, which have gradually altered the character of urban life. The promise of growth is therefore a constant murmur between investible surplus of capital and modern state's developmental mandate. Algorithmic governance through platform capitalism appears to offer a perfect blend to distract us from the failures of the state to provide a fair platform for employment and distribution of wealth. At this very moment, to capture the tragic irony of the state of affairs, the Indian Finance Minister has deployed the millennials' preference for ridesharing apps to set aside a grave ongoing crisis of demand in the automobile sector.

However, whether on account of financial inclusion of the working classes through digital wallets, or the Facebook free basics, or the entertainment-communication hybrid messaging service of WhatsApp, or the generous bandwidth and Internet data offerings of Reliance Jio or the incomparable largesse of Google, platform capitalism has sprung up a new inter-evaluative dynamic between the state and large capital. This is perhaps most evident in the Telecom sector where the public sector giant, Bharat Sanchar Nigam Limited (BSNL), has been gradually hollowed out, even as various chunks of its key assets are handed over to the rival, Reliance Jio. By itself, such a transfer of wealth from public to private assets would qualify for the routines of neoliberalism. In this case, however, Jio offers a unique amalgamation of telecom, high-speed 4G Internet data, digital commerce, media and payment services. It offers WiFi routers, mobile handsets and an entire range of multimedia and digital payment apps to work exclusively on the Jio network, even set-top boxes with direct-to-home (DTH) service and multiplayer online network for gaming with support for many platform controllers. Facilitating the growth, and even monopoly, of strategic players in key segments allows the state to cut down on the excess noise of the market, so as to amplify the derivative value of assurances and guarantees evident in the public endorsement. The vital move here is indeed the repurposing of a hence-renewed value towards advertising.

Modi's grand public endorsement of Paytm, Jio, Facebook, Google and a number of such monopolistic players has of course been a matter of much debate in the popular press. The loudest of such endorsements, which occasioned the grandest possible self-advertisement in return, was after the demonetization. In a memorable full-page advertisement published on 9 November 2016—the morning after the late evening announcement of the catastrophic decision—Modi appeared to endorse PayTM, while on the surface, the latter congratulated Modi for taking 'the boldest decision in the financial history of independent India!'. This double-bill advertisement captures the very essence of an inter-evaluative dynamic, which could make one legitimately wonder which of the two—Modi and PayTM—was getting a larger share of the advertorial mileage. Not only did PayTM, a digital payment service, see a rise of 400–1000% within hours of the announcement, it was by no means unique in such an enthusiastic uptake of what was soon to prove a catastrophic move. A number of e-commerce companies—among them, Freecharge (a digital marketplace for recharging), Zomato (a restaurant listing and food delivery service), Ola and Uber (ridesharing apps) were all quick to endorse the move, congratulate the government and offer digital transactions as a solution to what was effectively reduced to a 'cash problem' (Sankaran 2016). All sorts of local retail vendors and kiosks were forced into the digital wallet economy overnight, even if the digital money would go to bank accounts which, having been rendered inaccessible, did not at all enable them to conduct their own daily transactions.

Athique has discussed these issues in great detail, particularly the rift between the coverage of the event in the international press vis-à-vis the Indian press (2019c). While I have no fundamental disagreement with his reading of the event as a 'two-step process' of Demonetization and Cashless India intended to force India's informal economy into mechanisms of transactional legibility, I would also like to look further into the ways in which such a move was also impelled by the larger push for making intangible assets tangible. The crucial bit remains that monopolistic growth of computational capital built on the mountain of debt procured from investor capital without any horizon of long-term profitability (as with Uber, PayTM etc.) is proving conducive to a particular variant of state-form. The inter-evaluative symbiotics that emerge here may be crucial for all of us. If advertising constitutes the kernel of a double belonging, or an overlapping 'market of interests', for the state as well as computational capital, the surveillance systems hold the other end of the inter-evaluative dynamic (see Parthasarathi and Athique 2019). The tech giants of platform economy provide the sophisticated expertise needed to break down torrents of big data into demographic, psychographic and ideological profile clusters, which have been given an unprecedented valuation in the conduct of contemporary politics. McChesney illustrates in a revealing summary how the political parties have, if anything, raced ahead of the advertising industry in their creative and sinister splintering of the polity:

> You can now acquire comprehensive information about large numbers of people—what their views are, what they're interested in, what sort of appeals to them would be effective and what sort would not. This gives politicians a tremendous amount of power to cherry-pick propagandistic messages successfully and send them to people where it's really going to work… [In 2012, the Obama campaign] used cutting-edge data collection to break down voters, target specific messages to particular groups, etc. … [B]ecause all of the messages were targeted to individual people online, they were not really recognized by news media or the broader political culture… The irony of the 2012 campaign was that it was the first time that the political parties were in front of the advertising people. (2018)

In this key sense, the inter-evaluative dynamic, which emerges as the potentials of platform capitalism, is fundamentally different from mass communication. Since the masses have ceased to exist after the relentless algorithmic scanning of every digital footprint on the network, the fundamental distinction between political campaigns, at least rhetorically built on certain shared principles, and product positioning vis-à-vis individual preferences, has been narrowing down. This requires us to look closer at the advertorial takeover of the media, attention and political communication.

The Dark Side

Obama's 2012 campaign, as McChesney establishes, flipped a balance and unleashed an unstoppable propaganda mechanism. It only took another election cycle for these technologies to 'turn to the dark side: instead of trying to locate and cultivate potential supporters, use the power of this technology to demonize your opponent and undermine support for your opponent'. Infusing poison into the political atmosphere, this has set off the fake news industry, which reaches millions of people with surgical precision, and is not subject to criminal prosecution. Increasingly across the world, the digital technologies are being used to mine and organize data about citizens' political preferences, so as to manipulate or reshape them via clever and dubious campaigns. This is precisely the slot in which WhatsApp sits in India, leading to the witty but derogatory coinage of the term 'WhatsApp University', from where millions acquire their daily dosages of poisonous news, history, biographies, scandals and clarion calls. The BJP is well known to run an entire Information Technology Cell which not only employs an army of paid trolls to heckle commentators all over the Internet, but also produces and circulates 'fake news' routines while obfuscating substantial criticisms of the government and the party. The party, however, does not stop there; it runs a dubious network of foundations, NGOs and private tech companies in deep collusion with government institutions held to ransom by this network.

For example, HuffPost India did a major exposé on Sarvani Foundation which was started to attract female voters and rendered defunct after 2014 elections, then repurposed as the Association for Billion Minds (ABM). Numerous toxic Facebook pages and the campaigns 'Main Bhi Chowkidar', 'Nation with NaMo' and 'Bharat Ke Mann Ki Baat' were launched by ABM, which also 'compiles detailed dossiers on potential candidates from each constituency, prepares poll booth-level political intelligence reports, plots out routes for teams canvassing for votes, runs polling day war-rooms, and designs and manages online propaganda campaigns' (Bansal et al. 2019). Also, the BJP used a private tech company, Sarv Webs Pvt Ltd., to push political propaganda by mass-messaging on WhatsApp, maintaining a huge cache of mobile SIM cards to send messages through multiple registered numbers (Sathe 2019). While Media Studies has always traversed the overlapping edge of political communication and popular culture, the pumping of electoral arena with monopoly capital has begun to merge the two brackets entirely, so as to force us into the domain of advertising proper. Jonathan Beller's suggestion, that 'advertising is an assault weapon … a psycho-economic machine—a key component of the social factory and, as such, an encroachment on the commons' (Beller 2013), seems to account for advertising's true character and its immanent threat. The real subsumption of society by capital, Beller adds, marks 'the conversion of representation itself to advertising' (ibid.). Indeed, when the two appear to merge, advertising no longer remains an allied domain, but encroaches upon all variants of re-presentation. In a creative but insightful formulation, Beller adds:

> Advertising has worked its way into the sign itself and has generated the advertisign. This is not simply the brand but also vectoral language: words in a production channel, the micro-management of desire, the production of new needs, the capturing of the imagination all in order to induce linguistic and behavioral shifts in others is no longer merely the province of advertising but of so-called human interactivity, now become advertisarial through and through. (Beller 2013)

One could indeed recall the television channel, NaMo TV, which surfaced free-to-air just before the start of Lok Sabha polls and was taken off just before the final phase of polling. Featuring in general entertainment and news packages both, the channel presented the most blatant case of political advertising, flouting the rules while the state looked away (The Wire 2019). But it was only one among the many such campaigns—Namo India, an apparel brand mainly known for its Namo kurtas and Namo foods, which earned a lot of media attention when it began delivering food packets to polling booths in the 2019 elections. This curious overlap between random fan activities and party funded advertising amplifies the double-bill advertorial patterns: as opposed to the demonetization-PayTM adverts where Modi appeared to be piggybacking on a digital platform, brands of various hues and sizes have begun to piggyback on the Modi brand. Such cross-promotional excess is not always fine-tuned by algorithmic precision, after all. We can safely conclude that there are different tiers of advertorial excess, which operate simultaneously with varying degrees of precision about the target demographic.

The crucial move in the political arena, one could argue, has to do with its growing intimacy with popular culture in general and reality television in particular. Modi's invariably scripted interviews with self-declared fan-journalists, or Trump's absurd confrontations with journalists and celebrities are staged to be scandalous in a reality television schematic. The audience, both diegetic as well as nondiegetic, are fully aware that there is something about the 'event' which distinguishes it from reality itself. And yet, its variance from the relatively banal and interrogative reality offers a new deal between politics and entertainment. Such a hybrid emerges from our habituation in the atmospherics shared across the media palette (news channels, daily soaps, reality shows), where political communication is reduced to a spectator sport in which sides have already been taken and the staged event showcases the battle (see Kumar 2015; Ohm 2014). McChesney traces these dramatics back to the hollowing out of journalism, due to the sudden withdrawal of advertising revenue:

> The basic problem is that the giant internet companies—especially Facebook and Google—are taking away the advertising money that would've traditionally gone to some newspaper or journalism-producing entity. But Facebook and Google aren't using this money to invest in more journalists or news reporting … The reason has to do with the end of anonymity, the surveillance ability … [W]hat happened with the surveillance model is that no one buys ads on a website … Instead, you go to Google or Facebook or AOL, and you say, 'Hey, I want to reach every American male in this income group between the age of 30 and 34 who might be interested in buying a new car in the next three months', and AOL will locate every one of those men, wherever they are online, and your ad will appear on whatever website they go to, usually straight away … That means the content producers, in this case the news media, don't get a cut anymore. Those advertising dollars used to subsidize most of their work. (McChesney 2018)

The sudden reduction in advertising revenues has drastically reduced the resources required for sustained quality work (O'Regan and Young 2019). In effect, this has substantially reduced the credibility of sincere reportage, reducing it all to opinions and theatrical drama of public disagreements however ill-argued. In absence of a credible journalism that would hold the basis for qualified debate, the door is opened wide 'for a rejection of any news one does not like as 'fake news'. This is Trump's strategy, and it would have been regarded as absurd twenty-five years ago. Now, it finds a population that has no reason to respect news media any more than Trump does (McChesney 2018). Not only does this mean a serious threat to all sorts of trades which traditionally ran advertisements to raise capital, but perhaps more importantly, it means that to establish a near-monopoly in a market segment has become a qualifying criterion to raise capital. It is this debt-monopoly dynamic that constitutes the essence of platform capitalism. As Uber's case best illustrates, raising capital does not require a healthy balance sheet, just as advertising does not require facts. Monopoly constitutes its own self-advertising agency to raise capital, propelled by the derivative rhetoric. Indeed, states may even consolidate 'domestic' monopoly capital to hedge their bets against the multinational counterparts, introducing us to international relations and trade policies, particularly with respect to regional, geopolitical and ideological blocks.

What is important to understand, particularly towards the enmeshing of the vocabulary for political and popular communication, is that celebrities are also a monopolistic construct, who could potentially serve a multimodal function via computational capital. By creatively inducting the political into the popular, politics sets itself up for piggybacking on Internet monopolies' cross-promotional architecture. To unpack this better, I would like us to revisit a phrase which was coined with respect to the insurrectionary tendencies of web-based serials: the membrane of the popular (Kumar 2019). While such a membrane allows a tactile sense of the aggregate popular culture, constituted by the interpenetrations across media platforms and genres, it also collapses some key distinctions between them. For Indian media in particular, but also for media in general, the growing trend to navigate the increasing intimacy across what were autonomous tiers within the media economy is to deploy celebrity icons as the alphabet of popular culture. We are therefore confronted with

> a shift from relatively autonomous media ecosystems of film, television, sports, politics and news to an increasingly contiguous ecosystem characterized by rapid exchanges. The membrane of the popular—a digital layer of media activity where constituents are casually referenced without actually being dealt with—holds the shape of this ecosystem … [T]he bulk of digital media activity participates in this multimodal traffic to reconstitute the popular, for all practical purposes …When this advertorial imperative is expanded and knit into a media constellation, politicians, cricketers, actors, models, journalists or anyone sufficiently famous sit upon [the] flat bench of *celebrity-function*—which I call the membrane of the popular—from where they can be picked, briefly mocked at, and sat right back down. (Kumar 2019)

The instrumentality of a broad celebrity-function for media is significant, particularly how it has begun to suit the political leaders in their campaigns. Across the world, such leaders are beginning to make incisions upon the membrane of the popular, to knit themselves into the promotional artifice so as to route and harvest the consumer traffic already navigating the digital superhighways. Drawing upon the celebrity-function, representation becomes an act of self-promotion, since the self amidst advertorial networks is reconstituted with a keen awareness of the debt its mere existence owes to capital. As *advertisigns* with a relatively stable grammar, holding forth in the midst of free floating risks for capital investments and fluctuating valuations, celebrities emerge as derivative formulations—their second-order valuations are saturated with numbers and indices (box-office figures, endorsement deals' worth, third-party rankings etc.; see Kumar 2018). It is no wonder then that politicians increasingly take their cues from celebrities of various hues, particularly actors, and often try to piggyback on their popularity indices by sharing the spotlight in media events. In such an exercise, the celebrities also offer quasi-monopolies situated on the membrane of the popular, which political leaders like Modi could share the stage with, so as to transform intangible assets into tangible ones—photos and videos running on TV news channels, Twitter, Facebook and WhatsApp, where they could be liked, retweeted, shared and commented upon.

Platform Capitalism as a Derivative Market

This chapter has ventured to grapple with one of the most fascinating contemporary trajectories of platform capitalism, in which apparently incommensurate and incomparable forms of capital are forced into a second-order dialogue via derivative logics. I have showed that political representation in recent times has made vital public confessions to its growing intimacy with Internet monopolies in particular and various quasi-monopolies in general. Not only does the political leadership woo monopoly capital, they are witnessed in an active cross-promotional bid. I have argued that they are brought together by the need to offer a derivative solution to the problem of valuation, by offering to convert intangible assets into tangible ones—a task in which celebrity-function plays a crucial role, for it carries a tangible value soaked in popularity metrics. In many ways, platform capitalism offers the long sought derivative market for campaigners to claim probabilistic value in the high-risk market of politics.

Since derivatives derive their value on account of a future probabilistically extrapolated from the past, the commodities which command extreme trade volumes are the most attracted to play with the resultant projections and probabilities, which could be reliably sold on the market of popular culture. This is where the arena of political and entertainment activity come together, in a perpetual and desperate bid for self-promotion, as both conduits and guzzlers of advertising capital. With respect to Modi and India, while his political rhetoric of Hindu nationalism has been given significant attention, his bid to become a hybrid financial-economic derived asset by mounting monopoly capital is not nearly as well appreciated. It is not my argument that the latter should take precedence, but the creative accounting between the two should be given its due valuation.

On the surface, much of what I have explored in this chapter may appear to be routine neoliberal transactions between public and private assets, where parties depend on corporate funding on the promise that they would hand over due benefits to them from the backdoors of high offices. Subscribing to that implicit continuity for derivative monopolies would however be erroneous, since it would overlook the *publicness* of these transactions—best manifested in PayTM's full-page news chapter advertisement carrying Prime Minister Modi's benevolent image as it inaugurated a sustained spell of monetary doom for billions of Indians in November 2016. The derivative valuations and their monopolistic exchanges depend on the very publicness of social algorithms, which is what allows them to function as the engines for the probabilistic calculus of platform capitalism. If data mining and advertisement are two key components of digital platforms, it is their larger participative mandate—to showcase 'the (digital) people' as formal signatories to the process—that necessitates the aggregation of digital transactions to appear in full public view as source and symbol of sovereign power, thereby allowing the users/citizens/audience to hedge their own portfolios with the 'tangible assets' of popular politics.

References

Andrews, J. (2017). Nonknowledge as Capacity: Randy Martin's *Knowledge LTD* and the Limits of Rationality in the Age of the Derivative. *Social Text Online*. Retrieved March 20, 2020, from https://socialtextjournal.org/nonknowledge-as-capacity-randy-martins-knowledge-ltd-and-the-limits-of-rationality-in-the-age-of-the-derivative/.

Arvidsson, A. (2016). Facebook and finance: on the social logic of the derivative. *Theory, Culture & Society, 33*(6), 3–23.

Ascher, I. (2016). *Portfolio Society: On the Capitalist Mode of Prediction*. Cambridge, MA: MIT Press.

Athique, A. (2018). The Dynamics and Potentials of Big Data for Audience Research. *Media, Culture & Society, 40*(1), 59–74.

Athique, A. (2019a). Integrated Commodities in the Digital Economy. *Media, Culture & Society, 42*(4), 554–570.

Athique, A. (2019b). Digital Transactions in Asia. In A. Athique & E. Baulch (Eds.), *Digital Transactions in Asia: Economic, Social and Informational Processes* (pp. 1–22). New York: Routledge.

Athique, A. (2019c). A Great Leap of Faith: The Cashless Agenda in Digital India. *New Media & Society, 21*(8), 1697–1713.

Bansal, S., Gopal S., Khaira, R., & Sethi, A. (2019). How Modi, Shah Turned a Women's NGO into a Secret Election Propaganda Machine. *HuffPost India*. Retrieved April 4, 2019, from https://www.huffingtonpost.in/entry/how-modi-shah-turned-a-women-s-rights-ngo-into-a-secret-election-propaganda-machine_in_5ca5962ce4b05acba4dc1819.

Beller, J. (2013). Advertisarial Relations and Aesthetics of Survival: Advertising->Advertising. *NECSUS*, 3 June 2020. Retrieved from https://necsus-ejms.org/advertisarial-relations-and-aesthetics-of-survival-advertising-advertisign/.

Beller, J. (2018). The Message is Murder: Substrates of Computational Capital. London: Pluto Press.

Bryan, D., & Rafferty, M. (2005). *Capitalism with Derivatives: A Political Economy of Financial Derivatives, Capital and Class.* London: Palgrave Macmillan.

Bryan, D., & Rafferty, M. (2006). Financial Derivatives: The New Gold? *Competition and Change, 10*(3), 265–282.

Kumar, A. (2015). The Unbearable Liveness of News Television in India. *Television and New Media, 16*(6), 538–556.

Kumar, A. (2018). Media Portfolios after Credit-Scoring: Attention, Prediction and Advertising in Indian Media Networks. *Postmodern Culture, 28*(2). https://doi.org/10.1353/pmc.2018.0014.

Kumar, A. (2019). Insurrectionary Tendencies: The Viral Fever Comedies and Indian Media. In A. Athique & E. Baulch (Eds.), *Digital Transactions in Asia: Economic, Informational, and Social Exchanges* (pp. 192–204). Abingdon: Routledge.

Martin, R. (2015). *Knowledge LTD: Toward a Social Logic of the Derivative.* Philadelphia: Temple University Press.

McChesney, R. (2018). Between Cambridge and Palo Alto. *Catalyst, 2*(1). Retrieved from https://catalyst-journal.com/vol2/no1/between-cambridge-and-palo-alto.

Mullick, D., & Devi, M. (2017, December 1). Group Think: How WhatsApp has Changed News in Small-town India. *Caravan*. Retrieved from https://caravanmagazine.in/reportage/whatsapp-changed-news-small-town-india.

O'Regan, T., & Young, C. (2019). Journalism by Numbers: Trajectories of Growth and Decline of Journalists in the Australian Census 1961–2016. *Media International Australia, 172*(1), 13–32.

Ohm, B. (2014). Contesting Interpretational Authority: Democracy and Fascism in the Indian 'Empowered Public'. *Media International Australia, 152*(1), 119–132.

Parthasarathi, V., & Athique, A. (2019). Market matters: Interdependencies in the Indian Media Economy. *Media, Culture & Society, 42*(3), 431–448.

Sankaran, C. (2016, November 9). PayTM Puts Modi on Ad. Who are the Winners and Losers in the Surgical Strike on Black Money? *DailyO*. Retrieved from https://www.dailyo.in/variety/black-money-rs-500-out-rs-2000-PayTM-ola-uber-ad-modi/story/1/13939.html.

Sathe, G. (2019, April 17). How The BJP Automated Political Propaganda on WhatsApp. *HuffPost India*. Retrieved from https://www.huffingtonpost.in/entry/bjp-automated-political-propaganda-whatsapp-sarv_in_5cb62076e4b082aab08d7f18.

The Wire. (2019, May 20). NaMo TV: It Came, We Saw, It Conquered (the EC). And Now It's Gone. *The Wire*. Retrieved from https://thewire.in/media/as-polls-draw-to-a-close-namo-tv-slips-off-air.

PART II

Platform Businesses

CHAPTER 5

Amazon Prime Video: A Platform Ecosphere

Ishita Tiwary

In the summer of 2018, I found myself hooked to the weekly Amazon Prime Video stand-up comedy competition show *Comicstaan*. I noticed how the interface design influenced my viewing of the show. On the left-hand side, there was a tab titled X-ray, which contained the names of all the contestants and judges appearing on screen before me. In the autumn of 2018, I am renewing my postpaid mobile plan with the telecom giant Vodafone. I am informed that it comes with a free subscription to Amazon Prime Video for a year and I receive text alerts from Vodafone to remind me of my free one-year subscription to Prime Video. Fast forward to the winter of 2018, I am watching a promotional music video on YouTube for the upcoming Bollywood movie *Zero*, the bottom-centre portion of the screen flashes the logo of Amazon Prime, informing me of the availability of the song on Amazon Prime music service.

I begin with this experiential anecdote as it is evocative of Amazon's efforts to establish a platform ecosphere in the Indian media economy. In this chapter, my working definition of ecosphere attempts to address the

I. Tiwary (✉)
Concordia University, Montréal, QC, Canada
e-mail: ishita.tiwary@concordia.ca

A. Athique, V. Parthasarathi (eds.), *Platform Capitalism in India*, Global Transformations in Media and Communication Research - A Palgrave and IAMCR Series,
https://doi.org/10.1007/978-3-030-44563-8_5

ways in which a platform brand integrates its customers within a portfolio of digital goods and services. I will argue that this is where Amazon Prime Video differs from dedicated subscription-video-on-demand (SVOD) platforms, due to the embedding of its video platform within the larger umbrella of services that it offers (specifically its music platform, Alexa assistant and its wider e-commerce operations). This is the strategic approach with which Amazon Prime enters the audiovisual market, not as a television provider per se, but as a seller of video products densely interlinked to multi-sided markets in retail, advertising, music, data and finance. It is the situation of Amazon Prime Video within this platform ecosphere that I will begin to deconstruct in this chapter. To begin with, I will attempt to establish a working definition between various overlapping usages of the terms platform and ecosystem. Firstly, the widespread adoption of the term 'platform' over the past decade has been consciously fashioned from the available cultural vocabulary by apex stakeholders with specific aims. It is carefully massaged in both industry literature and popular discourse in order to affect a particular resonance for particular audiences (Gillespie 2010). Propositions for platform economies 'are efforts not only to sell, convince, persuade, protect, triumph or condemn, but to make claims about what these technologies are and are not, and what should and should not be expected of them' (Berland 2010).

I posit the term ecosphere in recognition of the explicit integration of content streams across a broader multi-product platform that is enabled, but not justified, by the technical ecosystem of digital technologies and mobile phones in particular. Amazon is itself taken as a particular example, since it has been a pioneer of horizontal expansion across products and has, in the process, developed an underlying ecosystem of data centres and services that has itself become a very large component of the digital economy. In this sense, unlike many of the other platforms active in the over-the-top (OTT) video market, Amazon plays a larger strategic role in both ecosystem (infrastructure) and ecosphere (retail market). This makes Amazon a far bigger player than its headline share of the media production sector suggests, a dynamic which not only provides numerous advantages for its component businesses and ventures, but also shapes a set of market strategies in OTT video that are distinct from the traditional logics of media producers, and even from other OTT platform variants such as Netflix. Taking a single-sector approach to the OTT video boom thus far, most studies of SVOD platforms have focused upon the impact of Netflix in the markets of the Global North. This has included detailed discussions around internet-distributed television (IPTV), geo-blocking and content acquirement (see Lobato 2016, 2019; Lotz 2017; Lotz et al. 2018; Wayne 2017). In the case of Amazon Prime Video, however, the provision of media content is only one part of a larger commercial proposition.

In this chapter, I want to think through the emerging Amazon ecosphere in India in terms of its negotiations with the distinctive market conditions in play in India's OTT video market. My opening anecdote predicates this inquiry by demonstrating how the integrative experience of platform ecospheres has already become ubiquitous in everyday life. One therefore gets an everyday and immediate sense of the expansive horizontal integration of a platform such as Amazon Prime Video, through its tie-ins with telecom operators and advertising clients, inter-promotional strategies for content and cross-promotion strategies for their larger suite of platform services. The extent of this inter-linked ecosphere consequently raises immediate and critical questions about where an analysis of Amazon's SVOD service should begin and end. In this chapter, I will sketch the contours of the SVOD market in India, in order to identify the future provocations likely to emerge through the study of SVOD platforms in the global south. I will go on to consider the promotional strategies utilized by Amazon Prime Video in order to enter the Indian market, before proceeding to a brief discussion of the mobile ecosystem upon which SVOD services in India overwhelmingly depend. I will then go on to address Amazon Prime Video's formulation of content acquirement and creation strategies. Finally, I will seek to explicate how Amazon, as a 'global' SVOD platform attempts to 'localize' its ecosphere model as a customer experience in the Indian market.

Integrated Brand Strategies

Amazon Prime Video was launched in the Indian market in December 2016 (Television Post 2018). According to the Financial Express, a mix of direct-to-home (DTH) service providers, international content aggregators and distributors, broadcasters and telecom operators are currently active in the market for online streaming in India (Nath 2017). As of 2018, there are approximately 30 online video streaming platforms that comprise of 90 million active viewers (ibid.). Drawing on their existing advantages in content archive and links to broadcaster and telecoms providers, India-based platforms are the market leaders, with HotStar at 69.4% of market share. Of the global platforms operating in the market,

Netflix has 1.4% of the market share as opposed to Amazon Prime's 5%. It is estimated that, the Indian arms of Amazon Prime Video and other key video streaming platforms spent Rs. 300 crores in 2018 ($41.5 million) on advertising designed to encourage individual viewing as a habit in a market where collective viewing has always been the norm. Ritika Pant's research also notes that the Indian market is governed by acute price sensitivity, which has seen a freemium (free + premium content) model being adopted as the primary strategy for attracting subscribers for online video services (Pant 2019). This is currently the market norm, since local SVOD platforms such as HotStar operate on this model. A recent chapter in the *Hollywood Reporter* has also noted that the most successful platforms in India are those that largely depend on advertisement revenues and hence YouTube (advertiser driven) and HotStar (freemium model) lead the market (Bhushan and Brzeski 2018). For Amazon Prime Video, it raises the question of how to best monetize itself in market primarily driven by the advertisement-funded model.

Thus far, pricing has been a key factor driving SVOD subscription growth in India. Amongst the three major video streaming platforms in India (Amazon Prime Video, HotStar, Netflix), Amazon Prime Video is the cheapest platform to subscribe to amongst the three as is costs Rs. 499 ($7) a year, which works to Rs. 42 ($0.58) a month. In India, non-Prime subscribers will be able to use Amazon Prime at a price of Rs. 129 ($1.79) per month. Amazon offers a number of benefits to its Prime members in India. Prime members get free scheduled delivery, discounted same-day delivery, exclusive deals, unlimited access to video streaming via Prime Video and an ad-free access to playlists via Prime Music. Over time, analysts expect Amazon's local content investments, product integration and tie-ups with local telecom companies to be the key drivers for Amazon Prime Video. At the global level, Michael Wayne observes that Amazon's ability to forge symbiotic relationships and craft their service around well-established TV brand identities must be understood in relation to the company's broader commercial interests. He notes, that Amazon is an e-retailer that uses its SVOD platform to drive customers to its Prime membership program (whose members make more purchases more often than non-members). In that respect, it is significant to note that Amazon Prime's key competitor in the Indian market is not Netflix, but the e-retailer Flipkart (recently acquired by Walmart). We see traces of this larger strategic objective through the pricing strategy described above, but it becomes more evident when one charts the way Amazon has integrated its video service with its other offerings in India (see Wayne 2017). This horizontal integration is pursued though the synchronization of Amazon Prime Video with Amazon's overarching Prime services, with its music platform in particular, and through commercial partnerships with India's telecom giants.

Amazon launched its music streaming service, Amazon Prime Music, February 2018 as a companion to Prime Video. The ad-free music streaming service came with no additional cost to Prime subscribers. Amazon Prime Music inked deals with top-five music labels in the country, including T-Series, Tips Music and Sony Music. Amazon is also actively seeking to integrate its shopping and viewing services and has already added its voice assistant, Alexa, to Prime Video as a tool for users to search and watch content by using voice control. The obvious goal is to integrate Amazon Prime Video and Music and e-retail within the large Amazon ecosphere, where, if you are watching a movie on Prime Video, retail ads for what the character is wearing will automatically appear along with the video. According to Amazon, this new overlay screen will be called 'X-ray' and will appear over whatever you are watching. Vijay Subramanian, head of content for Prime Video India, has stated in an interview:

> Amazon's goal is to make it as easy for the customer to get what she wants. We are always looking to innovate. For example, the new show *Comicstaan* has a skill built into Alexa, where you can ask for a joke from a comedian. We are completely focused on x-ray. We want to populate as that as much as we can to give customers a good customer experience to make their engagement deeper. We will constantly keep adding to the x-ray feature. It is as much a content focus for us as creating content. (Suvarna 2018)

This seamless vertical integration of its shopping, music, voice assistant and video platforms, makes Amazon a unique player in the market, where all the component Amazon platforms are linked in a feedback loop to each other. This synchronization, is intended to foster customers who will subscribe to the entire umbrellas of services. However, this platform ecosphere also has to be tailored locally, taking into account the media infrastructures, taste cultures and regulatory norms that structure Indian media markets. In a context characterized by the rapid and uneven development of digital markets, surveying the state of telecommunication infrastructures in India becomes crucial to understanding the milieu in which the Amazon ecosphere is being designed.

Expanding Infrastructures

Ramon Lobato has noted that SVOD platforms are heavily reliant on telecommunications infrastructure (Lobato 2016). Various internet geographers have also pointed out that infrastructure is vital as to how to experience the internet (Zook 2006; Warf 2013). For streaming video applications that require high download speeds, location is especially important. Lobato cites the example of Netflix which requires 0.5 mbps (megabits per second) and recommends a level of 3.0 mbps. However, in India, the average speed is well below 3.0, effectively putting Netflix out of bounds for most users. Moreover, SVOD streaming services require a credit card account, which constitutes a financial infrastructure requirement that remains out of reach for the majority. Consequently, both access rates and purchasing power are highly stratified in India's digital economy. Despite having half a billion users, only 50 million are enabled to carry out transactions online, a prerequisite for becoming regular customers of big e-players such as Amazon (Sachitanant 2018). Given the socio-economic factors involved, it is also pertinent that the language of the current Amazon user base is predominantly English, since this signifies an elite socio-economic profile. Nonetheless, those left behind in the onset of Web 2.0 due to lack of infrastructure are now entering the internet economy due to the massive growth of mobile-phone ownership (Rashmi 2018). Emerging as a 'mobile-first' market, India is now home to 460 million internet users, second only to China.

According to KPMG, the Indian internet user base is expected to reach 730 million by 2020. Growth will be driven by increasing mobile penetration, faster internet speeds, 4G mobile connectivity and cheaper data charges (KPMG 2018a, b). As per the latest Federation of Indian Chambers of Commerce and Industry (FICCI) Frames Study on the media and entertainment sectors, there are around two million paid digital subscribers across application providers, including video platforms, and 1–1.5 million customers who have moved entirely to digital media (mobile telephony, internet) (FICCI 2018). FICCI expects the number of people using digital platforms is expected to burgeon to four million by 2020 (ibid.). Furthermore, entertainment services are the most accessed services via internet. Almost all telecom service providers now offer mobile data packages for subscribers starting from a minimal price of Rs. 10 or even less. Mobile phones with multimedia capabilities have thus given people from all social strata an unprecedented access to all kinds of media content. Mobile phones have become the preferred viewing device for many Indians mainly due to reasonably priced smart phones, better internet penetration and low mobile data charges. Even basic mobile-phone models come with camera, radio, music player with recording and Bluetooth options. Cost-effective data storage technologies such as micro and mini SD cards have augmented the media capacities of these phones. The availability of mobile packet-data technology has further connected users to the internet at a low cost compared to broadband. This had led to an explosion of content online and the market is steadily opening up to local content production.

According to consultants Media Partners Asia, video content budgets in India topped $4.2 billion. OTT video revenue in India was pegged at Rs. 2019 crore (around $290 million) in 2017 and is expected to reach Rs. 5595 crore (around $776 million) by 2022, helped by the rising adoption of smartphones, smart TVs and other devices (KPMG 2018b) Bandwidth nonetheless remains a major issue as India has one of the lowest broadband speeds in the world, an average of 2 mbps compared to the US average of 11.5 mbps. Data charges have recently fallen due to the launch of Indian telecom major Reliance Jio, backed by India's richest industrialist Mukesh Ambani with an initial $22.5 billion investment. The service had accumulated around 240 million wireless phone users as of August 2018 (TRAI 2018). This expansion of the broadband and DTH infrastructure is linked to the Digital India drive. Digital India is a US $17 billion infrastructure programme intended to usher India into the knowledge-economy era. The vision is to usher in a flow of multilevel transactions that will become the base for commercial, social and citizen engagement. The project entails major public and private investments in national connectivity, infrastructure, smart cities, e-commerce and e-governance. It is an aspirational project that aims to mainstream the transactional economy and for India to become a recognized global power in the digital economy. The Digital India drive is reliant on contribution of private sector firms that are involved in telecommunications, data and internet infrastructure, and a variety of digital platforms. These developments in infrastructure are absolutely crucial to the fortunes of SVOD platforms in India.

A number of scholars have noted that studies of information infrastructures typically point to their similarity and their centrality in shaping the global distribution, production and consumption of goods and services (Dourish and Bell 2011; Gillespie 2010; Parks and Starosielski 2015).

Addressing the Indian case, Pradip Thomas has also observed that over the past decade, the apparent 'privatization' of the internet has run in parallel with the rise platforms whose growth rates are reliant on 'network effects' and 'exemplified by the enormous reach and shaping powers of the big three—Amazon, Google and Facebook—enhanced by their algorithmic dominion over cultures, the idea of the social, political practices, economic futures and their investments in and control over cloud computing practices' (Thomas 2019). Network effects are predicated upon audience capture, which can be clearly seen in India through the sweeping integration of the Amazon platform ecosphere. It is equally obvious that the SVOD scenario in India remains largely dependent on mobile-phone infrastructure, which requires effective working relationships with the dominant telecoms providers. To date, Amazon Prime Video has partnered with telecom service providers BSNL (Bharat Sanchar Nigam Limited) and Vodafone. Vodafone offers its consumers a free Amazon Prime subscription with Vodafone SuperNet 4G plans. In the case of BSNL, customers get free subscription to Amazon Prime Video if they buy BSNL's Rs. 399 ($5.53) postpaid mobile plan or a plan package of Rs. 749 ($10.39) and above. In the *Hindustan Times*, Gaurav Sandhi, Director and Head of Business, Amazon Prime Video, India, stated:

> Prime Video has received an overwhelming response from customers across the length and breadth of the country. We are thrilled that our association with BSNL will expand the reach of Prime Video to an even larger base of customers who can now enjoy premium content on a screen of their choice—be it their mobile device or the television in their living room. (Hindustan Times 2018)

Anupam Srivastava, Chairman and Managing Director, BSNL, chimed in, stating:

> We understand the customer shift towards a highly networked digital ecosystem. Customers today demand freedom and flexibility in shopping and streaming content online. Our collaboration with Amazon India is our commitment to stay ahead of times providing the best to our customers. It provides them access to thousands of Indian and international movies, videos, TV Shows and music on the go. We are confident that our customers can enjoy uninterrupted on-the-go shopping and entertainment benefits with their Amazon Prime membership. (Hindustan Times 2018)

The partnerships with Vodafone and BSNL make it clear that the Amazon ecosphere depends heavily on mobile-phone users for shoring up its subscriber bases, with telecoms providers using the suite of Amazon services as a lure to expand their own subscriptions. Within the Amazon ecosphere itself, SVOD plays a similar role in developing a user base that can be drawn into the broader suite of services. It seems evident, then, that Amazon Prime Video cannot be properly considered as a standalone player in the market for video on demand. Rather, it has to be understood as part of a larger platform ecosphere, where one service cross-subsidizes and create values for other sites of audience commodification.

Populating the Inventory

Having delineated the Amazon ecosphere in a material sense through its hardware infrastructure, I now shift my attention to the domain content creation and its regulation in order to demonstrate how the Amazon ecosphere becomes malleable to market demands. In December, 2016, when Amazon Prime Video entered the Indian market, it brought original shows such as *The Man in the High Castle, Mr. Robot, Transparent, Mozart in the Jungle* and *The Grand Tour*. It also offered an assortment of licensed TV shows in addition to Hollywood and foreign films (Bhushan 2016a). Despite these offerings, it recognized that the Indian market is ruled by local content. According to a KPMG report, Western programming commands a miniscule 0.5% viewership compared to 60% for domestic entertainment on Indian television (FICCI 2017). We have been here before. Jean Chalaby in a classic study of MTV's transition to European markets in the 1980s and 1990s, noticed that 'international' channels were initially oblivious to local market condition and culture (Chalaby 2005). They vastly overestimated the appeal of US-based programming for European audiences and subsequently underwent a process of localization, by hiring multilingual presenters, translations and producing original content for these markets. A similar story played out in India during the television boom of the 1990s and is playing out again through SVOD platform content-creation strategies (see Thussu 2007; Mukherjee 2018).

The consistently strong preference for local content has encouraged international VOD platforms in India to aggressively procure and commission content. Amazon Prime Video has reportedly invested $300 million in producing Indian content, much more than the budgets of most entertainment channels in the country. It has struck content licensing deals with local players such as Dharma Productions and T-Series, garnering exclusive rights to Bollywood and regional movies (see Bhushan 2016a, b; Jarvey and Szalai 2016). It has partnered with most of the top Bollywood production houses in the country to expand its catalogue and commission original series. Notably, Amazon's Prime Video's USP in India is its stand-up comedy specials (Financial Express 2017). In November 2018, a Hindi-language interface was added to Prime Video, allowing Hindi speakers to easily navigate the video platform via desktop and mobile apps, including Android and iOS (Ghosh 2018). It is also producing Telugu-language and Tamil-language originals for South Indian audiences. Amazon brought along what they described as the 'best practices from the US' to support creative partners by providing script consultants, writer's rooms and technical expertise (Bhushan 2018). They see the SVOD local content market in India as a 'fledgling system' (ibid.). One of India's biggest production houses, Eros Entertainment (which has its own SVOD platform), noted that with these moves, Amazon had made itself a tough competitor in the SVOD market (Szalai 2016).

Amazon debuted its first Indian series, the cricket drama *Inside Edge*, in July 2017. Since then, the company has expanded its portfolio with originals like *Breathe*, *Mirzapur*, *Made in Heaven* and other formats, such as the comedy talent hunt *Comicstaan*, the dating show *Hear Me, Love Me*, the Telugu mafia drama *GangStars* and the musical reality show *Harmony*. They also recently announced a new original series *The End* starring Bollywood Megastar Akshay Kumar (Ramachandaran 2019). *Inside Edge* was nominated in the Best Drama Series category of the 2018 International Emmy Awards (Raman 2018). Commenting on *Inside Edge*, Vijay Subramaniam stated:

> *Inside Edge*, at the guts of it, is the drama of politics. The veneer was cricket ... These are things that are relatable. We are not creating this to get somebody in London. We are creating this to make sure that every customer in India loves it. And in that authenticity, comes the global appeal ... [it] all starts with a story and one thing we learnt with our originals is that authenticity counts. The more authentic you are to your stories and the setting, the more likely it is going to be of interest to people who are way outside your radar. Prime Video enables customers to sample content that is of interest to them and give them a customer experience to make it easy to follow content ... adding regional languages to our library is a part of our localisation plan ... In the next six months, you can expect more regional languages. Apart from this, we have started work on originals from Telugu and Tamil.

> It is always a challenge when you are a fan of a particular regional content and are living in another region. Sometimes the films just does not travel. An important part of our quest is to bring the popular, latest films to the customers as quickly as we can. (Ibid.)

With words such as 'authenticity' and 'stand out', Subramaniam is clearly stressing local appeal and foregrounding Amazon's generous investment in creating local content. How should we think of the idea of the local in this context? The idea of the local typically signifies local exhibition, local screenings of national or international cinema and the dialectic of the local versus the global (Toulmin and Loipendinger 2005). Neves and Sarkar, locate the local within ad hoc practices of digital video-making. According to them, with the advent of the digital, the video medium expanded to include 'networked publics and platforms for rapid duplication and sharing (Neves and Sarkar 2017, p. 17). For them, the evolving global video space is now markedly different from the gradual dialectical incorporation of various locals within a homogeneous and universal structure. Penumbral globality would, of necessity, remain partial and contingent, as an emergence that nonetheless 'gestures toward the irrepressibility of local media practices in the face of dominant global norms' (ibid.). Amazon prime video's localization strategy does precisely this, and I seek to illustrate this pandering to the creation of local content and local audiences through a case study of the hit Amazon Prime show *Comicstaan*.

Establishing Product Niches

One of the ways in which Amazon has strategized content production in India is targeting what they deem to be 'special interest areas' for 'young people' (Raman 2018). I will illustrate this by taking the example of Amazon's most successful series, the reality competition *Comicstaan*. The show is about the hunt for the next big stand-up comedian in India. The stand-up comedy scene became popular on Indian television with shows such *The Great Laughter Indian Challenge* and *The Kapil Sharma show*. The emergence of YouTube subsequently led to an explosion of comic content, providing a platform for many budding comics experimenting with political, observational, improv and other forms of comedy. Comedy collectives such as *AIB* (*All India Bakchod*) and *East India Comedy Company* and comedians such as Malika Dua, Aditi Mittal, Biswa Kalyan Rath and Zakir Khan became household names. This encouraged the practice of open mic in urban cities, often hosted by food and beverage venues to attract customers. Many comedians have their own dedicated YouTube channel, Facebook pages and Instagram presence. Comedians such as Vir Das were invited to the American talk show *The Conan O'Brien Show*, and Kenny Sebastien and Abish Matthews performed at the New York Comedy Club (Bose 2017).

This exposure led Amazon and Netflix to offer a platform (to turn a phrase literally) to these comedians to host their specials, since they already had an inbuilt audience in the online sphere. Amazon did it most effectively with *Comicstaan*, which featured seven of India's most prominent comedians—Tanmay Bhat, Kaneez Surka, Kenny Sebastian, Biswa Kalyan Rath, Kanan Gill, Sapan Verma and Naveen Richard as judges/mentors for handpicked contestants from all across India. The format was that every week the contestants would come on stage and perform a different sub-genre of comedy such as topical, sketch and observational comedy amongst others. The would be marked every week based on a four-minute open mic. The marking was distributed 50–50 between the judges and the audience present at the taping. The top five of the ten contestants advanced to the finale. Prior to the unveiling of the trailer, promotions for the show had begun through the judge's social media pages. The marketing campaign also included TV and outdoor campaigns. On digital platforms, it took over the masthead of YouTube. Closer to the launch of the show, viewers noticed that the masthead of India's leading English daily the *Times of India* changed to the *Times of Comicstaan* for a few seconds when visiting the website. Prime Video also integrated its Alexa service, where some of *Comicstaan*'s judges mentored Alexa to be funny. Speaking about *Comicstaan*, Vijay Subramanian, said:

> Comedy is already one of the most watched genres on Amazon Prime Video and customers, across age groups and geographies want to see more. *Comicstaan* will take customers on a hilarious journey alongside some of today's most recognizable comedians, to search for India's next big comedian. Unique, fresh and packed with jokes, the series will make you crack up. The future looks funny indeed! (exchange4media 2018)

Ajay Nair, Chief Operating Officer, of the production company Only Much Louder (OML), stated:

> *Comicstaan* is the exciting next step in our long and fruitful relationship with Amazon. It ties all the best parts of Indian stand-up together into something fresh. Getting the country's top comedians to nurture and mentor new talent is an idea that excited us, and it's been extremely rewarding to see it all come together. (Ibid.)

In its first week, *Comicstaan* became the most watched series on the platform (Farzeen 2018). It is important to note here that all episodes of the series were not available to 'binge watch'. Rather, it followed the conventional television programming model where a new episode was released every Friday. Thus, although Jeanette Steemers has predicted the demise of linear television and scheduled viewing patterns with the internet providing online video streaming platforms like Netflix and Amazon Prime, the case of *Comicstaan* disrupts this narrative (Steemers 2014). *Comicstaan* followed the broadcast model, precisely, in order to get a sense of the audience, monitoring how many people were coming back every week to check out the show on its platform. Like a movie release, the shows were not released on fixed time but on a fixed day. The buzz around *Comicstaan* was discernible: from think pieces of women comedians in India, to the viral circulation of contestants on social media. Since then, the contestants of *Comicstaan* can be seen headlining open mics across the country, and a second season has just concluded on the platform. The show's success has hinged on 'local' conventions of audience-building and capitalizing on the successful stand-up comedy scene in India, rather than the 'global' factor of SVOD disrupting norms of distribution. The case of *Comicstaan* therefore demonstrates that content platforms need to have a grasp of the local market and its demands. This required is further illustrated in the way the Amazon ecosphere has responded to the demands of censorship regulations in the Indian market.

Negotiating Regulation

Complaints levelled at SVOD services in Western countries have tended to revolve around anxieties around media concentration and tax jurisdictions. In Asia, policymakers appear to be far more concerned with asserting content censorship and sovereign jurisdiction over moral standards. As of now, internet-distributed services remain free of government regulation in India and are thus attractive for some audiences because they can offer uncensored English-language programmes. Nonetheless, Pradip Thomas has notes that platform and infrastructure anxieties are being felt by the Government of India, although primarily in areas where state privilege are concerned as opposed to due to the potential consequences for domestic content industries (2019). Thus, SVOD is seen primarily to pose a challenge to the government role in censorship. Consequently, a critical aspect of building a content archive within the Amazon ecosphere is an evolving negotiation of regulatory regimes and programming norms in India. In India, the censorship of films comes under the ambit of the Indian Cinematograph Act. The Indian Cinematograph Act was passed and came into effect in 1920 in British-ruled India. Regional censor boards were constituted in the cities of Madras, Bombay, Lahore and Rangoon and Calcutta. After Independence in 1947, the board was unified under the 1952 Cinematograph Act and reconstituted as the Central Board of Film Censors (Central Board of Film Censors India 2018). The ordinance was updated in the 1980s to cover the regulation of analogue video. Television content, however, is regulated in accordance to guidelines laid down by the Broadcasting Content Complaints Council (BCCC), a self-regulatory body set up by the Indian Broadcasting Foundation in consultation with the Ministry of Information and Broadcasting as recently as 2011.

Under this regime, Indian broadcasters and cable carriers self-regulate by pre-censoring content at the production stage. By contrast, an arbitrary practice of censorship is imposed on imported English-language programming in order to meet 'Indian' moral standards. Thus, for example, HBO's globally popular *Game of Thrones* had major story plots edited out, visual details blurred and profane words/dialogues bleeped in the audio track and left blank in the subtitles. However, in the absence of government regulation, it is becoming apparent that some online streaming services have already begun to self-censor global content. While both Netflix and HotStar largely provide their subscription-based content uncensored, Amazon Prime Video has adopted a more stringent approach to censoring content in line with 'Indian cultural sensitivities'. Thus, although web content currently does not have formal censorship codes to adhere to, Amazon Prime Video was sued in 2018 for airing 'vulgar' and 'sexually explicit content' on their platforms (News Minute 2018). The case is currently being heard in the Delhi High Court which is awaiting the response of the Central Government. For their part, Netflix and HotStar are pushing for an industry censorship code akin to one that exists in Southeast Asian nations for Netflix, Fox and Disney. This move has been prompted by VOD companies' anticipation of the Government of India passing legislation that they fear will be onerous for the industry.

On 15 November, 2018, Netflix and HotStar came to an agreement with the Ministry of Information and broadcasting to adhere to a regime of 'self-regulation' by adopting the 'best practices internationally' and to come up with a set of sectoral guidelines (Pathak 2018). Amazon is opposing this move, as it fears that such a move could alienate its paying subscribers who have indicated a preference for uncensored imports (Srivastav 2018). Despite its formal opposition, however, it is equally clear that Amazon unilaterally adopted its own self-censorship route when it entered the Indian market. For example, an episode of the motoring show *The Grand Tour* is only 30 minutes long on Amazon Prime, while the original is actually one hour. The half-an-hour difference is the sum of cuts made to remove all references to a car made of beef (Bose 2016) Nude scenes in TV shows such as *Californication* are pixelated (Dhingra 2018). Mindful of cultural norms in India, Amazon Prime released two versions of the TV series *American Gods*: censored and uncensored. The censored version removed female frontal nudity, blurred out male genitalia and removed references to a 'holy cow' due to the animal's religious significance amongst Hindus (Arora 2017). Responding to the *Huffington Post*, Amazon has stated:

> Amazon Prime Video offers the largest selection of movies and TV shows of any OTT video service in India and give customers the choice on what to watch. We respect our customers' preferences and will comply with the regulations applicable to our service. Amazon is a responsible company and we are here to entertain the Indian customer with award-winning content from the US along with blockbusters from Indian and regional makers. We will keep Indian cultural sensitivities in mind while offering this content to customers. (Bose 2016)

Thus, as Wagman and Urquhart observe, the fact remains that *where* you access the internet says a lot about *what kind* of internet you experience (2014). Similarly, as Graeme Turner and Jinna Tay observe: 'Notwithstanding the internationalization of the media industries, these days the answer to the question "What is television?" very much depends on where you are' (2009, p. 8). Lobato points out that approaching the internet as a localized and unevenly available set of cultural experiences reminds us that internet, just like television, is always locally configured as well as globally networked (2019). This diversity of institutional forms, production cultures, advertising systems and regulatory frameworks still vary significantly between countries. In the example above, the likelihood of audience objections and/or a response from the Indian regulation system led to the adoption of self-censorship practices, proving that location determines experience.

Indigenizing the Ecosphere

In their book *Locating Television: Zones of Consumption*, Anna Pertierra and Graeme Turner argue that one can understand the localization of television by placing it within the context of the diversity that exists internationally. They situate the consumption of television within the range of structures, patterns of everyday life and industrial norms that determine the importance of location to the audience experience of television (2013). Their argument thereby provides a useful provocation for thinking about SVOD platforms in Indian households and, from a material perspective, for the framing of scholarship underway on SVOD platforms across the world. Taking into account the distinctive local infrastructural conditions, and how SVOD platforms create their ecosphere in response, emphasizes the need for socially and culturally nuanced insights into the question of 'what it means to experience SVOD platforms'. Given the materialization of its audience in the Indian market, Amazon Prime Video's platform ecosphere is evidently marked by highly segmented audience taste and profile, low-bandwidth infrastructure, heavy reliance on mobile phones, regulatory inconsistencies, prudishness and a persistent reliance on celebrity to sell content. The future intentions of regulators, the uneven purchasing power and propensity of the audience and the competing presence of major local and global players are all contingencies in the evolving strategies of Amazon Prime Video.

Amazon Prime Video, fully recognizing this distinctive configuration of content, audience, infrastructure and business norms, 'Indianizes' both its 'skin' and its internal structures to suit these market conditions. At the same time, it consistently pursues its central aim of disrupting the local media economy in order to entrench its own platform ecosystem at the technical level. In terms of product offering, the process of content adaptation to local conditions is undertaken primarily as part of the broader programme of developing the Amazon India ecosphere as a customer experience. As a business model, the underlying imperative remains to build a user base that can be locked in across a wider ecology of mutually supporting services. This ideal ecosphere, with its multiple products, business partnerships and value transfers is entirely in keeping with the model that Amazon has developed internationally. At the same time, the process of developing an actualized ecosphere in the Indian market has consistently required Amazon Prime Video to develop new strategies for negotiating distinctive and changing conditions of consumer taste, regulations and norms. Accordingly, this chapter has begun to explore the strategic evolution of Amazon Prime Video to date not only in terms of the Indian SVOD market, but also in light of the larger platform ecosphere that Amazon is seeking to develop. The evolution of the Amazon ecosphere can thus be a useful model to understand the likely pathways for other proponents of platform ecospheres, such as Apple and Jio. This is where the primary field of competition for Amazon Prime Video will emerge, alongside but nonetheless distinct from the wider proliferation of India's online video market.

References

Arora, A. (2017, May 10). Amazon Prime Video Censorship Evolves with an 'Indian Version' of American Gods. *NDTV*.

Berland, J. (2010). Cultural Technologies and the "Evolution" of Technological Cultures. In A. Herman & T. Thomas Swiss (Eds.), *The World Wide Web and Contemporary Cultural Theory* (pp. 235–258). New York: Routledge.

Bhushan, N. (2016a, December 16). Here is Why India will be a Key Battleground for Amazon and Netflix. *The Hollywood Reporter*.

Bhushan, N. (2016b, September 26). Amazon Strikes Licensing Deal with Bollywood Banner Dharma Productions for India. *The Hollywood Reporter*.

Bhushan, N. (2018, September 21). Amazon Prime Video India Boss on Peak TV, Competing with Netflix. *The Hollywood Reporter*.

Bhushan, N., & Brzeski, P. (2018, November 29). Netflix, Disney or Amazon: Who Wins the War for Streaming in India. *The Hollywood Reporter*.

Bose, A. (2016, December 16). Amazon Prime Deleted a Segment Showing a 'Beef Car', Because, Sanskar. *The Huffington Post*.

Bose, A. (2017, December 17). #Yearender2017: Stand Up That Stood Out, a Year of Progressive, Relatable Comedy. *InUth*.

Central Board of Film Censors India. (2018). *The Cinematograph Act*. Retrieved from http://cbfcindia.gov.in/html/Cinematograph/cine_act1952.PDF.

Chalaby, J. (2005). The Quiet Invention of a New Medium: Twenty Years of Transnational Television. In J. Chalaby (Ed.), *Transnational Television Worldwide: Towards a New Media Order*. London: I.B. Tauris.

Dhingra, S. (2018, November 15). After Amazon, Netflix Said to Have Agreed to Censor its Content in India. *The Print*. Retrieved from https://theprint.in/culture/after-amazon-netflix-agrees-to-censor-its-content-in-india/149976/.
Dourish P. & Bell G. (2011). *Divining a Digital Future: Mess and Mythology in Ubiquitous Computing*. Massachusetts: MIT Press.
exchange4media. (2018, June 27). Comicstaan Gets Robust Marketing Through Digital, TV and Outdoor Media. *Exchange4media*.
Farzeen, S. (2018, August 17). Comicstaan: Nishant Suri Declared Winner. *The Indian Express*.
FICCI. (2017). *Frames Report 2017*. Retrieved from https://assets.kpmg.com/content/dam/kpmg/in/pdf/2017/04/FICCI-Frames-2017.pdf.
FICCI. (2018). *Frames Report 2018*. Retrieved from http://ficci.in/spdocument/22949/FICCI-study1-frames-2018.pdf.
Financial Express. (2017, July 12). Amazon Prime Video vs Netflix Vs Hotstar: From Price to Content, Which Is the Best Video Streaming Site in India. *Financial Express*. Retrieved from https://www.financialexpress.com/photos/technology-gallery/759938/amazon-prime-video-vs-netflix-vs-hotstar-from-price-to-content-which-is-the-best-video-streaming-site-in-india/.
Ghosh, M. (2018, November 14). Amazon Launched Audible With 447% Cheaper Plan: Prime Video with Hindi Interface. *Trak.in*. Retrieved from https://trak.in/tags/business/2018/11/14/amazon-launches-audible-with-447-cheaper-plan-prime-video-with-hindi-interface/.
Gillespie, T. (2010). The Politics of Platforms. *New Media and Society, 12*(3), 347–364.
Hindustan Times. (2018, October 1). BSNL Offers Amazon Prime Video Subscription to Post Paid, Broadband Users'. *The Hindustan Times*.
Jarvey, N., & Szalai, G. (2016, December 14). Amazon Takes Video Streaming Service Global in Challenge to Netflix. *The Hollywood Reporter*.
KPMG. (2018a). *Digital Telecommunication Revolution: Innovation*. Retrieved from https://assets.kpmg.com/content/dam/kpmg/in/pdf/2018/10/digital-telecommunication-revolution-innovation.PDF.
KPMG. (2018b). *Media Ecosystems: The Walls Fall Down*. Retrieved from https://assets.kpmg.com/content/dam/kpmg/in/pdf/2018/09/Media-ecosystems-The-walls-fall-down.pdf.
Lobato, R. (2016). Introduction: The New Video Geography. In R. Lobato & J. Meese (Eds.), *Geoblocking and Global Video Culture*. Amsterdam: Institute of Network Cultures.
Lobato, R. (2019). *Netflix Nations: The Geography of Digital Distribution*. New York: New York University Press.
Lotz, A. (2017). *Portals: A Treatise on Internet-Distributed Television*. Ann Arbor: University of Michigan Press.

Lotz, A., Lobato, R., & Thomas, J. (2018). Internet Distributed Television Research: A Provocation. *Media Industries, 5*(2), 35–47.

Mukherjee, D. (2018). Architectures of Memory: Retrofitted theatres and Film Remakes in Post Liberalization India. *Wide Screen, 7*(1), 1–29.

Nath, V. S. (2017). How Big is the OTT Market Really? *Financial Express*, 6 June 2017, Retrieved from https://www.financialexpress.com/industry/the-ott-play/703996/.

Neves, J., & Sarker, B. (Eds.). (2017). *Asian Video Cultures: In the Penumbra of the Global*. Durham, NC: Duke University Press.

News Minute. (2018, November 15). Netflix, Amazon Prime Sued for Obscene Content in India. *The Newsminute*. Retrieved from https://www.thenewsminute.com/chapter/netflix-amazon-prime-sued-obscene-content-india-91579.

Pant, R. (2019). Dossier on Hotstar. *Global Internet TV Consortium*. Retrieved from https://global-internet-tv.com/india-hotstar/.

Parks, L., & Starosielski, N. (Eds.). (2015). *Signal Traffic: Critical Studies of Media Infrastructures*. Urbana: University of Illinois Press.

Pathak, A. (2018, November 15). Netflix Denies Report Saying That It Has Agreed to Censor Content in India. *The Huffington Post*.

Pertierra, A. C., & Truner, G. (2013). *Locating Television: Zones of Consumption*. London and New York: Routledge.

Ramachandaran, N. (2019). Amazon Prime Launches Original Series 'The End' with India's Akshay Kumar. *Variety*, 5 March 2019.

Raman, S. G. (2018, November 21). Amazon Prime Video Hopes to Win India's Market Through 'Great Content, Great Experience. *Scroll*. Retrieved from https://scroll.in/reel/902356/amazon-prime-video-hopes-to-win-indias-market-through-great-content-great-experience.

Rashmi, M. (2018). The Offline Media Economy: Digitally Marginalized Users of Mobile Phones. In A. Adrian Athique, V. Parthasarathi, & S. V. Srinivas (Eds.), *The Indian Media Economy, Vol. 2, Market Dynamics and Social Transactions*. New Delhi: Oxford University Press.

Sachitanant, R. (2018, October 7). Voice, Video and Vernacular: India's Internet Landscape is Changing to Tap New Users. *The Economic Times*.

Srivastav, S. (2018, September 12). Amazon India Says 'No' to Self-Censorship, Urges Other OTT Players to Follow. *Inc 42*. Retrieved from https://inc42.com/buzz/amazon-india-says-no-to-self-censorship-urges-other-ott-players-to-follow.

Steemers, J. (2014). Selling Television: Addressing Transformations in the International Distribution of Television Content. *Media Industries Journal, 1*, 44–49.

Suvarna, S. (2018, June 28). Amazon Users May Soon Buy Clothes a Character Is Wearing on a Prime Video Show. *My Smart Price*. Retrieved from https://

www.mysmartprice.com/gear/2018/06/28/amazon-india-users-may-soon-buy-clothes-character-wearing-prime-video-show/.

Szalai, G. (2016). Eros Executive Calls Netflix a "Friend," Amazon a "Tough Competitor" in India. *The Hollywood Reporter*, 6 December 2016.

The Television Post. (2018, June 1). SonyLiv JioMusic Saavn Big-Gainers in Video Music OTT Market. Retrieved from https://www.televisionpost.com/sonyliv-jiomusic-saavn-big-gainers-in-video-music-ott-market-in-q1-jana-report/

Thomas, P. (2019). Infrastructure and Platform Anxieties in India. In A. Athique & E. Emma Baulch (Eds.), *Digital Transactions in Asia*. New York: Routledge.

Thussu, D. (2007). The 'Murdochization' of News? The case of Star TV in India. *Media, Culture, and Society, 29*(4), 593–611.

Toulmin, V., & Loipendinger, M. (2005). Is It You? Recognition, Representation and Response in Relation to the Local Film. *Film History: An International Journal, 17*(1), 7–18.

TRAI. (2018). *2017–2018 Report*. Retrieved from https://www.trai.gov.in/sites/default/files/PR_No.107of2018_TSD_Aug2018_0.pdf.

Turner, G., & Tay, J. (2009). *Television Studies after TV: Understanding Television in the PostBroadcast Era*. London: Routledge.

Wagman, I., & Urquhart, P. (2014). This Content is Not Available in Your Region: Geo-blocking Culture in Canada. In D. Wershler, R. Rosemary Coombe, & M. Martin Zeilinger (Eds.), *Dynamic Fair Dealing: Creating Canadian Culture Online* (pp. 124–132). Toronto: University of Toronto Press.

Warf, B. (2013). *Global Geographies of the Internet*. Dordrecht: Springer.

Wayne, M. (2017). Netflix, Amazon, and Branded Television Content in Subscription Video On-Demand Portals. *Media, Culture & Society, 40*(5), 725–741.

Zook, M. (2006). The Geographies of the Internet. *Annual Review of Information Science and Technology, 40*, 53–58.

CHAPTER 6

Telecom and Technology Actors Repositioning Music Streaming

Christine Ithurbide

Throughout the twentieth century, the music industry in India has undergone changes in processes of production and distribution due to technological developments that have offered new opportunities. Since the 2000s, the entry of players from the information and communications technology (ICT) sector—both Indian and international—has led to important reconfigurations of the music industry. ICT companies started positioning themselves as downstream intermediaries for the distribution of musical content. In parallel, the expansion of digital infrastructure, along with cheaper mobile and data access, has facilitated the development of music streaming platforms, paving the way for a highly competitive digital music market. A growing literature has explored the industrial, legislative, technological and economic developments that have shaped India's music industry (see Manuel 1993; Zuberi 2002; Parthasarathi 2013). Recently, researchers have begun to focus on the impact of digital

C. Ithurbide (✉)
University of Paris XIII, Villetaneuse, France

A. Athique, V. Parthasarathi (eds.), *Platform Capitalism in India*,
Global Transformations in Media and Communication Research - A
Palgrave and IAMCR Series,
https://doi.org/10.1007/978-3-030-44563-8_6

technologies (Gopinath 2013; Booth 2015, 2017). Internationally, the digitalization of music has prompted researchers to question attendant changes in the music industries, especially regarding industrial reconfiguration and copyright issues (Anderson 2014; Hesmondhalgh 2009; Hesmondhalgh and Meier 2018; Leyshon 2014; Pratt 2016; Vaidhyanathan 2001).

This chapter explores processes of "platformization" in the music industry in India by analysing the evolving relationships between musical creation, music companies and labels, and considers the role of new intermediaries in the digital music economy. I argue that the multiplication of music platforms in India, available essentially via mobile and smartphones, is the visible part of deeper reconfigurations of the industry in the digital context. The displacement from the study of music platforms to the "platformization" of music enables us a focus not only on a new object (the music platforms), but also upon the multiples forces (historical and recent, local and global, public and private driven) that are shaping the music digital space. It enables me to unbox what typically appears as a catchall and sanitized notion of "platform", anchored into the global discourse on creative industries and deeply rooted into the neoliberal approach of culture (Combès and Petit 2015). Discourses on creative industries typically argue for a redefinition of the relationship between cultural products and services by emphasizing the technological remediation of their distribution. This agenda has been institutionalized by major organizations such as UNESCO, thereby legitimating the entry of information and communications technology companies into key segments of the economy for cultural goods and content. Hence, behind the development of music digital platforms, lies the expanding role and strategy of players from the ICT sector.

Who are the different ICT players involved? How precisely do they contribute to the reshaping of the music landscape? Are the same power struggles observed internationally also at play in India between ICT actors and historical actors of the music industry? A fundamental question arises, regarding the logics that underlie processes of "platformization" and how they may differ from older processes of industrialization of music. In this chapter, I refer to the analytical framework proposed by Pierre Moeglin, which highlights three distinctive and interdependent features constituting industrialization processes: technologization, rationalization and ideologization (1998). In this respect, I ask to what extent is the process of "platformization" representing the continuation of those three features at the heart of the industrialization of music? Technologization, closely associated with the development of the industrial society, is linked to the principle of substitution of capital for work and bears the mark of attempts to automate living work (Moeglin 2016). Rationalization in the Weberian sense, is not limited to the organization of work through managing and planning (1963). It also concerns the economy (yield and profitability) as well as the law. The desire to rationalize processes of production and dissemination of cultural products by technologies comes from the uncertainty linked to the "symbolic nature" of cultural products (Caves 2000; Bouquillion 2010). Ideologization should thus be understood in reference to Habermas' critique of technology and science as "ideology" closely associated with capitalist production (1970). More specifically, in the context of "communication society", ideologization aims at standardizing behaviour and promote economic adjustment (Combès 2004).

After outlining the evolution of the recorded music sector in India and its logics of industrialization, this chapter examines how the restructuring of the music industry is linked to the entry of Indian telecom operators (Vodafone, Bharti-Airtel, Reliance Jio) and global tech giants (Google, Apple, Facebook, Amazon). I will discuss the evolution of content and economic models in music platform business in order to illustrate both the emergence of a highly competitive market and the reinforcement of older commoditization processes, whereby music is produced as a by-product of other goods and services. In conclusion, I will discuss the challenges related to the diversification of musical content and the transfer of value for creators. My methodology will combine empirical material, including semi-structured interviews conducted with a diversity of players from the music industry in Delhi and Mumbai in 2018, document analysis of publications by the Government of India and its ministries and annual industry reports and articles from the economic and professional press. My analytical focus is the organizational structure of the music industry and the trajectories of Indian and transnational players, their strategies, relations and collaborations with each other.

Music Industry in India: Contextualization and Industrialization Process

The process of industrialization of music in India has always operated in parallel with larger technological changes, with the arrival of digital music being only the most recent example. From the beginning of the twentieth century until the 1960s, the music industry was effectively held by a single company, Gramophone & Typewriter, Ltd., a global business whose corporate roots lay in America, that came to operate, evolve and consolidate in British India initially based out of Calcutta (Parthasarathi 2013). This effective monopoly ended with the entry of new players in the 1970s, starting with Polydor and Indian Record Company (INRECO). The music market diversified in the 1980s with T-Series and again in the 1990s, with the entry of Sony Music (1997), Universal Music (1999) a new major Indian company, Times Music (1998). Originally, the Gramophone Company, Polydor or Sony were electronic good manufacturing companies primarily interested in selling gramophones and records players. As Hesmondhalgh explains in his macro-historical approach, the technological changes that have marked the evolution of the cultural industries have always been driven by the economic interests of major consumer-electric goods companies who have been manufacturing media supports for cultural content and whose economy is based on the development and production of systems and devices made increasingly obsolete (2013).

For a long time, the consumer market for the music industry in India was confined to an urban elite, since record players were expensive and unavailable to the masses. The arrival of the audio cassette in the mid-1980s decentralized and diversified the consumer base by making playback technology more accessible, and this was reflected in the emergence of regional commercial music and the sale of cheap cassettes (Manuel 1993). The cassette industry rapidly developed by drawing on untapped demand and the resources of the unorganized sector:

> Entrepreneurs would go the electronic market in Lajpat Nagar Delhi, borrow some money in the morning, produce a large number of K7 during the day, and go back in the evening with the K7 in exchange of the money they had borrow. If the MP of the original song cost INR 45, 90 the K7 for the same song would cost INR 18. The K7s (resulting from piracy) were then distributed for cheap on the wholesale markets in Delhi and Mumbai. (Churamani, interview 2018)

This comment shows how the industrialization of music in India has been inextricably intertwined with formal and informal production and distribution channels. The industries of the formal sector started losing money because of administration cost and so on. Film producers would sign with the organized music companies but would often not receive royalties because those companies were losing money. Hence, the relationship between film producers and music companies evolved towards a flat fee system. Instead of waiting for royalties, music companies paid money upfront to the producer to close the deal. Producers were then happy, as they had their money. Given their heavy sunk costs, film producers started to look forward to this amount of prepaid money and there was no question about composers' rights and so on. This arrangement was essentially a contract for service between music companies (responsible for paying royalties) and film producers (who commissioned the music content).

The liberalization of the Indian economy from the late 1980s onwards had numerous consequences for the music landscape. Restrictions on foreign equity ownership were relaxed, which encouraged the inflow of foreign direct investment (FDI) into this sector. International majors began to develop their presence in the India market, especially Sony Music, Universal Music Group, Time Warner (USA) and EMI (UK). However, they had to adapt to a sector overwhelmingly led by film music and also fragmented into regional language product markets dominated by domestic companies. This led initially to alliances between the major international players and local companies. Sony Music Entertainment is the largest and oldest foreign-owned label in India thanks to its acquisition of Bollywood film music and regional repertoires. Today, it is still controlling an estimated 25% of India's music market (Hu 2017). Universal Music group is the leader for international music, focusing on marketing western and other International repertoire (Hu 2017). Most of the international majors have diversified their operations into related media sectors, such as film production, broadcasting and retailing operations, to the extent that music revenue typically accounts for a minority share of their total revenue (Mukharjee 2002). Significantly, as Arpita Mukherjee explains, the entry of global players changed the existing distribution and marketing system and expedited the growth and absorption of new technologies (Mukharjee 2002, p. 36)

The early liberalization period was marked by the arrival of digital sound recording in India, due to the lifting of import duties and restrictions. These technological developments, along with the arrival of digital audio production software, remediated processes of composition and recording and, consequently, the working lives of recording studios and musicians (see Booth 2017). For instance, digital synthesizers removed the need for orchestras and pushed those musicians to find opportunities outside the studio system. New technologies also made small scale home studios affordable. Subsequently, the new possibilities offered by the development of internet and social networks (Facebook, Instagram, YouTube) in the late 2000s further transformed the production process, creating both opportunities and problems. Digital music gained popularity at the user level with the mobile phone boom in the first half of the 2000s, when recorded songs turned into a wide range of telephonic functions especially ring tones and ring-back tones. Now, almost anyone with basic recording equipment could make music and digitally distribute it to a wide audience, the remaining challenge for artists was the question of monetization. While digital technologies have dramatically changed the creation and production phases of music, the impact on the distribution and dissemination phases has also been significant. Suresh Thangiah, former manager at Times Music explains:

> Organization structures have changed completely with the shift in medium from physical to digital media—content delivery, content marketing methods are different and the functions/profile of employees has changed significantly. While once we had big physical sales teams etc., we now have content delivery, digital marketing and sales teams. The artists themselves are putting great effort into developing and managing their fans on Facebook, their twitter accounts, Instagram. (Interview)

Extending the changes brought about by cassettes and CD players, mobile phones have become the primary medium for consuming music today. This transition to digital music was accelerated by the lowering cost of mobile phones, manufactured mainly in China, and subscription charges falling sharply, making digital music affordable for a larger part of the population. A major inflection point came with the launch of a new telephone operator, Reliance Jio, in September 2015 offering free 4G data services and fostering a dramatic increase in the number of mobile users (Khan 2017). The subsequent launch of low-cost smartphones by Jio and Airtel in 2017 (retailing at less than 30$) further enabled deeper penetration of internet services and digital media content (EY 2018, p. 105). Reliance Jio benefited from the official Digital India policy, which aims to transform India into a digital society and a knowledge-based economy through massive investments in infrastructure expansion, including 4G and 5G networks. A diverse range of digital music, from Bollywood to international and indie, became readily accessible in geographically isolated districts and larger metropolitan areas. Regional musical producers also gained access to a wider consumer market furnished by networks of migrant workers (Kumar 2015).

The reconfiguration of recording studios with the arrival of digital sounds and programming software represented a shift in the technologization of creation and production processes. In the subsequent distribution and dissemination phases of digitalization, we have seen a process of rationalization across the whole chain of activity, with the emergence of professionals (art managers, music publisher), services (design, marketing, investment) and a departmentalization within music companies (production, marketing, licensing, sales) in line with global formats. The ideological conviction is that, as with developments of digital technologies more broadly, the music industry will adopt more sophisticated methods of production and distribution. However, it should be recalled that in a country where almost half of GDP and more than three quarters of employment are based on the informal economy, the music digital sector cannot be understood in terms of managerial organization (ILO 2017). The informal ethos remains prevalent in the transaction patterns of all industries, signifying greater flexibility in business relationships and greater responsiveness in the production process (Amelot and Kennedy 2010). The reality remains that signed contracts are rare in India's creative industries, typically substituted by oral agreements, and formal and informal systems are inseparable at all levels of creation, production and distribution. Thus, although streaming platforms are taken to represent the culmination of processes of technologization, rationalization and ideologization in the music industry, this cannot erase the fact that the economic frameworks of the music industry are still deeply anchored within informal systems.

From Telecom Operators to Technology Players

Since the 2000s, we have witnessed the entry of players from the telecommunication and information industries downstream of the music sector. This has profoundly transformed the music industry and its distribution infrastructure, along with the roles of various intermediaries and stakeholders involved in the creation, distribution and consumption of music. It has created uncertainties about the business models of the industry and increased complexity in the distribution of revenues (Huang 2014). Initially, these changes were driven by the arrival of telecom operators such as Airtel, Vodafone, Idea and Tata Docomo, who offered a range of services, including ringtones and mobile radio streaming services, bundled with their subscription packages. These offerings quickly positioned them as key players in the digital music industry, to the point that, in 2009, Bharti Airtel's deputy CEO, Sanjay Kapoor, claimed that Airtel had become "the biggest music company of India" with revenues higher than those of the oldest Indian music label Saregama (Pahwa 2009). Airtel aggregates and sells music from many Indian labels and music companies, including Saregama and T-Series, and also from film companies such as Yash Raj Films. This new scenario saw major music companies enter into various agreements with telecommunications companies, whose services enabled them to monetize their catalogues of Hindi and regional music built up over decades (Booth 2017). As they expanded their activity into digital music, however, telecom companies operating in India founded their own music platforms: Vodafone India launched Vodafone Music (2013), followed by Bharti Airtel with the Wynk music app (2015), Idea Cellular with Idea Music Lounge and Reliance Jio with Jio Music (2017).

The main music streaming platforms that developed outside the telecom industry were Hungama (2000) and Gaana (2010), both owned by domestic media and Internet companies, (respectively, Hungama Digital Media Entertainment and Times Internet). There was also the start-up Dhingana founded by twin brothers and Bollywood fans Swapnil and Shenal Shinde in 2007. Dhingana primarily relied upon US-Indian venture capital, before being acquired by US-based social jukebox Rdio in 2014 (Mishra 2013). Saavn, an Indian-focused music streaming platform headquartered in New York, was also driven by international venture capital (variously, Indian [Bertelsmann India Investments], US [Tiger Global, Liberty Media, Senvest Management LLC, Mousse Partners], UK [Steadview Capital] and Hong Kong [Quilvest]) (Verma 2015). In March 2018, Reliance Industries signed a deal to merge JioMusic with Saavn, a combination seen as a threat by competitors. Popular e-ticketing platform BookMyShow also launched its own music platform, Jukebox, in 2017, with the aim to become a "360-degree entertainment destination" to quote Aditya Kuber, Associate Vice President-Audio Entertainment, BookMyShow (Kala 2017). A few months earlier, BookMyShow acquired the tech platform Nfusion to pursue the development of its audio entertainment offerings. This move occurred in a context where one of BookMyShow's main competitors, Insider.in, previously owned by the entertainment company Only Much Louder (OML), had been acquired by India's leading e-money platform Paytm, allowing it to become a serious challenger in the event ticketing business (Mukherjee and Pahwa 2017).

The development of "indigenous" music streaming platform, although often backed up by foreign investments, highlights the increasing size and significance of internet and e-commerce companies operating downstream of the music industry. At the same time, Indian platforms quickly found themselves in competition with major international players seeking to position themselves in a promising music market of 480 million internet users. Apple Music arrived first (2015), followed by Google Play Music (2016), Amazon Music (2018) and Spotify (2019). Like the telco companies, Apple, Google and Amazon use music content as a "call product" to sell their other services or products. Unlike Indian music platforms, the major international player in digital music, Swedish platform Spotify, draws its revenues primarily from paying subscribers. Nonetheless, in a context where international music represents less than 20% of the domestic Indian market, transnational players have had to Indianize their catalogue through expensive licence acquisitions, as we will see in the next section. It is also important to note that the largest platform for music continues to be YouTube, whose business model differs significantly from the telecom companies and music platform companies, as it remains largely based on user-generated content (UGC). Since its 2008 launch in India, YouTube has become the catch-all platform for UGC and free consumption of TV and film, music, earning it an audience of 180 million. More than a third of the entire Indian internet user base of 460 million visit the platform each month. Consequently, YouTube is where the vast majority of digital music consumption takes place (Peto 2017).

The development of international streaming platforms has also benefited from a favourable legislative framework, more specifically a regulatory policy in favour of foreign investment. While many countries, such as Canada and European Union countries, implemented restrictions on the entry of foreign ownership in their domestic markets with the development of internet-based services, in India, a contrary choice was made to attract foreign funding in the media and entertainment (M&E) sector (Mattelart 2005; Mukharjee 2002). More recently, as part of the Make in India programme, further liberalization and tariff relaxation has been promoted as a growth-driver for the M&E sector (Make in India 2018). Through facilitating business opportunities for foreign players and FDI, India aims to position itself as a destination for manufacturing and services, primarily in order to create additional employment opportunities and ensure an orderly growth in the sector and a diversity of players. This stance positions India on the side of free trade proponents, who commonly argue that liberalization of M&E markets fosters foreign investment, encourages adoption of new technologies and lead to a more competitive domestic industry (Bouquillion and Ithurbide forthcoming). Certainly, the music market structure that has been emerging over the past two decades has seen a diversification of its players, both Indian and international.

There are two broad categories of players: the historical cultural industry players and the ICT players. The former are historical players of the music industry, encompassing music companies (Saregama, Indian Record Company—INRECO, Times Music, Venus Music, Zee Music Company), young labels (Azadi Records, Strumm, Kadak Apple Records), film music rights owners, such as Yash Raj or T-Series. Their activity is essentially based on the creation, production and sale of musical content. They remain powerful players, due to their copyright assets, but their distribution has increasingly become dependent upon digital platforms which are owned and operated by the second category of players. This latter category of players brings together the internet, telecommunications and consumer electronics industries, whose main activity and expertise is not based on music. In this context, music distribution is part of a larger diversification of their main activities, and music offerings are designed to draw more consumers into their main and more profitable network service activity. In the case of the global tech giants, these are unquestionably much more important economic and financial entities than the historical players of the music industry. The activities of these ICT players has steadily evolved from the distribution of musical content into production, thereby appropriating an increasingly important part of the activities and incomes of the first category of players (Bouquillion et al. 2013). Similarly, the main music platforms developed in India have been either directly created by Indian Telco providers (Jio Music, Airtel-Wink) or by internet and e-commerce companies, both Indian based (e.g. Hungama, Gaana-Times, Jukebox) and international (e.g. YouTube, Amazon Music Prime, Google Play Music).

Market Structure of Music Platforms

While telecom and ICT players have made important contributions to the development of the music market, they have also repositioned power relations within the industry. In terms of content, digital music platforms have to build their catalogue by acquiring music from music and film companies who are the copyright holders. To obtain a licence, platforms must pay global minimum guarantee, generally of 1–3 years, and agree per-stream revenues with the music labels. The latest entrant Amazon Music pursued a blistering acquisition policy, signing with the five major Indian companies in two months and, more significantly, with the Indian Performing Right Society (IPRS) to gain access to more than a million titles across multiple languages, eras and genres of Indian music. This suite of deals was described by IPRS as "one the biggest of its nature in the digital content publishing in India" (Elias 2018). Through such deals, music companies, labels and publishing houses have been able to compensate for the loss of CD sales, with the acquisition of their content by the largest streaming services offering them minimum guarantees, and sometimes an advance, on their revenues. According to an International Federation of the Phonographic Industry (IFPI) report, streaming revenues from digital music now amount to over 91% of the Indian recorded music industry revenues (2017).

However, according to Nikhil Pahwa, there are two key problems: the first is a lack of standardization in licensing deals, which enables labels and copyright societies to hold power over multiple platforms, while the second is exclusivity of licensing, where one player corners the rights to a particular music catalogue (2014). In the former case, a lack of standardization prevents start-ups from licensing music easily. In the latter case, international players such as Amazon and Netflix have been insisting on exclusive content deal with production houses (Jha 2017). T-Series had granted exclusivity rights to Hungama to stream songs from its catalogue on its mobile app for several years (Balanarayan 2014). Spotify has already been criticized for pursuing exclusivity deals during the first two weeks of artists' new album release and for directly licensing artists and paying them advances, as a music label would do. These practices have created frictions with international majors and contributed to delay Spotify licensing in India (Ingham 2018). Nonetheless, Apple Music has been acquiring a large volume of exclusive content (Bhatia 2018).

Two major trends have emerged in the acquisition strategies of music platforms. The first is the regionalization of catalogues in a context where small towns are increasingly connected to digital platforms. This has been achieved through the acquisition of a diverse range of regional music across film and non-film genres. A second trend is the production of original content by the streaming platforms, with Saavn and Gaana being among the first platforms to launch their own original content in 2017, followed by Jukebox. By doing so, they differentiate their offering in a very competitive market. Between September and October 2017, Gaana Bollywood's top five tracks generated 27 million views, while Gaana Originals top six tracks came close with 20 million streams. Saavn and Jukebox also began investing in the production of original music, distribution and management of artists, essentially from the independent scene. This strategy, however, is not adopted by all players in the platforms, as declared by Steve Boom Amazon Music Vice President: "Labels really play an important role in the world and it's not in our interest to replace them" (2017). Nonetheless, there are also advantages for artists as they benefit from streaming companies' ability to leverage their algorithms to ensure that their music reaches relevant audiences (Salman 2017).

The feature that stands out across the platforms is their rationalization of the distribution of music. First of all, there is an in-built curation of their offerings into regional languages and also into musical genres (Bollywood, Rock, *Ghazals*, Devotional, Hip Hop) and sub-genres (Upbeat Bollywood, Bollywood Love, Bollywood Workout, Soft Rock, Hark Rock, Hindi Rock, Folk Rock etc.). GPS localization through users' smartphones has enabled features such as "local favourites", which selects popular music from the immediate locality of the consumer, or a "Hot 50" list of the most trending hits from your city. Algorithms are also used for planning the organization of artist tours, where managers can draw on platform user data to map the largest concentrations of listeners. Streaming platform data is also used to understand more broadly consumer profiles and behaviour in order to suggest targeted music content. This also enables the streaming platforms to sell higher volumes of ad spaces to clients seeking particular audience profiles. This evolution towards a predominant function and tacit acceptance of digital technologies as tools of monitoring, modelling and exploiting music consumers of musical content has produced little debate in the industry so far. Thus there is an ideological paradigm fostered by the adoption of digital technologies, one that disregards issues such as data privacy or "filter bubble" effects for the consumer.

This technological and commercial experimentation has triggered uncertainties about sustainable and profitable business models for music industry players. Currently, there are three models for streaming platforms: (1) free music streaming financed by advertising and by investors, (2) bundled telecom offers and (3) premium paid subscriptions without advertising. The first model, free music streaming, is financed by advertising and by venture capital investors. For example, in 2015, Saavn announced $100 million in investments, including new international investors, including Quilvest, a Hong-Kong-based investment fund, and Lion Tree Advisor, New York (Shashidhar 2017). In 2016, the Chinese largest smartphone maker Xiaomi provided $25 million investment to Hungama. In February 2018, Gaana received $115 million from the internet giant Tencent (ToI 2018). The second model, used by Telecoms operators, provides their customers with access to unlimited music streaming from the platform catalogues, but not download rights. Jio Music, however, goes further by offering free streaming and downloads to all Jio customers. Thus, the volume of music data is much higher on Jio Music. According to estimates from MediaNama, for one hour a day listening over for a month, 4572 MB are consumed on average on Jio Music against 900 MB on Gaana. This reflects the importance of data consumption in this model, as an underlying profit source for telephone operators. The third model of "Premium" services, with monthly or yearly paid ad-free subscriptions is only really seen on international platforms (such as Apple Music, Amazon Music). Elsewhere, the trend has been the "Freemium" model, which combines limited free streaming with paid access to the latest catalogue. This reflects the interest of music companies seeking to impose limitations on free consumption and to encourage more users to pay.

These business models all reflect interdependency between markets for music and telecoms, and between content and data markets. Thus, even if Amazon Prime Music India is not profitable on the basis of subscriptions, it aims first and foremost to draw users into the larger e-commerce platform which is the real source of profits. Thus, musical content is a loss-leader for their e-commerce business, as well as being an important source of consumer data for guiding operations across other service domains (e-commerce, video, fashion). For Atul Churamani, control is in the hands of platforms who have different interests from those of the music and label companies (interview). At the time of physical business, music shops only interest was to sell the music, Churamani explains: "Today with digital platforms as the shop, it is the shop that determine the price of the album or song, not the label and their agenda is to get the highest number of people on the platform to sell spaces to advertisers and attract venture capital. So they don't mind pushing the price of the song down or even give music for free, because the highest number of subscribers they have, the more they will strike deals with advertisers and investors". Suresh

Thangiah has another perspective, explaining that "while it is true that not everyone has the opportunity to sit at the table of negotiation with the major platforms, a number of agreements are being reached regarding the amount of payment, periodicity of reports, etc. As a start-up (Label Strumm), we had limited bargaining power with the platforms. However, we find that by aligning ourselves with what digital music services want we can achieve results" (interview).

There are important differences between the fortunes of labels that arise from scale. For the smaller labels, the payout-per-stream could be a fraction of what is offered to the major players. Consequently, more and more smaller labels are approaching the music digital platforms through aggregators, such as Believe Digital, who combine the catalogues of smaller labels to achieve scale and better deals. A former employee of Sony Music explained that some labels and music companies charge exorbitant minimum guarantee fees from streaming platforms when renewing the rights exploitation licences. However, for the platforms, revenues from song downloads are fairly low, typically not even 50% of the minimum guarantee amount (Pahwa 2014). For the labels, there is also diversification of licence rights (for website, mobile apps etc.) which, combined, become a greater source of income. The larger point is that sources of revenue other than music consumption are indispensable to streaming platform models, and from this we can assume that the amount trickling down to the artists (musicians, composers, lyricists) is even more negligible. The attendant question is how much of the money raised by new ICT players, through music selling, data sharing or ad revenues, is being put back on content production business? Whereas historical musical players primarily reinvested profits in music events and content production, the profits of ICT players are invested in advertising, technology, partner ventures and expansion of their sales force and consumer acquisition strategies.

Clearly, with the platformization of India's music market, new power relations have emerged between historical players of the music industries and the ICT players, and also amongst each category of players. While Gaana and Saavn have operated at a loss in terms of music revenues, they have been sustained by adds, venture capitalist funding and larger corporate backing (Huang 2014). At the same time, we can assume that the aim of players like Amazon and YouTube is not to make profit out of music but to incorporate users into their wider commercial offerings, and to monetize user meta-data and analytics. In such highly competitive market, many players may not be able to survive and will be facing two choices: to raise more money to stay in the competition or to sell. Times Internet Limited opted for the first option and infused fresh capital of INR 2.48 billion into Gaana in February 2018 (Peermohamed 2018). Other Indian music streaming platforms have already folded, such as Dhingana and Flipkart's online music store Flyte which lasted only one year after its creation. Processes of merger and acquisition has already begun, with examples such as the acquisition of Saavn by Reliance Jio, prompting Airtel to tie up with Amazon. Amidst this larger setting, the whole digital music market is becoming a play within an oligopoly game.

Genre Diversity and Creator Revenues

A number of challenges have arisen as streaming platforms have established themselves as the structuring element of the music industries. Among these, the preservation of genre diversity and the remuneration of creators have received particular attention. The 2005 UNESCO Convention on the Protection and Promotion of the Diversity of Cultural Expressions was intended to protect and foster national musical creation and production. Yet, the development of internet-based music platforms to date appears to have escaped most national policies. The debate has finally been reopened on the regulation of digital content markets in favour of guaranteeing local music genres and diversity. The consequences of the platformization of the music industry on this diversity of musical genres are not necessarily consensual among the players of the Indian industry. Compared to other countries, the question of the protection of domestic musical genres from foreign competition has been quite marginalized in the Indian national debate. Indeed, there is no real competition with American or Anglophone music as the market remains focused on Indian music both in Hindi and in other regional languages. Hence, there is no minimum quotas for domestic music on radio as observed in other countries. Most of the actors interviewed were against the setting up quotas, which were perceived as unnecessary constraints. Even the players who felt that the diversity of music genre had diminished stated that they did not believe that such top-down regulation, if it was passed by the government, could be implemented in the music industry.

In India, while Bollywood music still captures up to 95% of the physical market, its share of streaming in services is only 60%, which is leaving more room for international, Indipop and regional repertoires (Hu 2017). Prashan Agarwal, Chief Operating Officer of Gaana, explained that international music is the fastest growing category on its platform. Artists and small labels confirmed during interviews that platforms allowed marginal music genres (jazz, blues, funk, electro) to be made accessible. Thus, both international and independent music appear to be the biggest beneficiaries of music streaming platforms. However, others players argued that, with the switch from analogue to digital, the diversity of music had been greatly diminished. “That’s because music platforms are in a race for subscribers and focus on mass content”, says Strumm Entertainment’s Thangiah. “Many of the smaller musical genres that have worked well in the CD era are now ignored in the digital music space—this includes Indian classical music, devotional music, ghazals, etc.” (interview). The rationalization of music listening through algorithms also tends to channel listeners into musical genres they already know and like, instead of opening them to other music experiences. This consequence of algorithmic guidance, widely known as the “filter bubble”, highlights the risks of trapping consumers within homogeneous bubbles of content and preventing them to grow their musical awareness and learning (Pariser 2011). Diversity, as an appeal strategy, can “serve as a lure for an organization of production and distribution that pushes the opposite to the standardization of behavior and consumption” (Benhamou 2006, p. 254). Hence, we must look beyond the diversity of the platforms’ musical genre offer at the shopfront and consider the low consumption diversity of individual consumers (Joux 2016).

In regard to the evolution of intellectual property rights and, more specifically, creators’ copyright and remuneration, international players have been putting increasing pressure in India to enforce the Berne and WIPO conventions. The remuneration of creative talent and transfer of value seems to remain a blind spot of Indian digital music market, despite a significant amendment to the Copyright Act in 2012. Previously, as music was essentially created as part of a commission for a film, composers, writers or singers were paid a fixed price for their creation and their rights belonged to the film producer, considered as the first owner of song. The Indian Copyright Act, originally passed in 1957, did not call into question the convention that the first ownership of the rights belongs to the film producer of film. It was not until the rise of mobile phones and the success of ringback tunes that artists started to claim their share of the revenue generated from their creation. This long-running contest resulted in an amendment to the Copyright Act in 2012 that designated the composer and authors as the first owners of rights and beneficiaries of royalties that cannot be transferred. There are many limitations to this amendment, however. First of all, many problems in enforcement remain, especially because of the lack of clarity on the distribution of profits between artists, composers and the other rights owners (music companies or film producers).

A former employee of Sony Music explained that "after the 2012 Amendment, the contracts signed with artists were modified accordingly. Officially, an artists couldn't assign his rights in perpetuity but in reality nothing much changed" (interview). This highlights the continuing domination of industrial hierarchies over the law and the inherent difficulty of copyright enforcement a system where formal and informal contracts are tightly interwoven. In addition, pressure continues to be put on artists to accept fixed-price work contracts by adding an exception clause in which they renounce their royalties. Manojna Yeluri, lawyer and founder of the organization Artistik License, which advises artists on their rights and contracts, explains that the 2012 Amendment mainly concerned Bollywood film music composers. It did not really spread throughout the music industry. Few artists really claim their new rights for three reasons: (1) a lack of knowledge of their rights, (2) the fact that these questions are not talked about in the schools of music and (3) because young artists have no bargaining power over labels or platforms (Yeluri, interview 2018). Over the same period, the sale of physical formats has been almost totally replaced by streaming and downloads on platforms, and the price per song for creators has dropped dramatically. Musicians who were interviewed tended to feel this price drop was justified because of the greater reach provided by the digital platform compared to CD and the opportunity to diversity their sources of income.

For their part, platforms are prepared to put content online for free in order to increase their number of views, and hence advertising revenue. It is primarily labels and record companies who denounce a dangerous model that has fostered a generation that believes music is for free, as Neeraj Kalyan, president of T-Series explained (interview). Discussions about putting in place sustainable revenue models for music streaming platforms are struggling to progress in a context of increasingly imbalanced power relations between platforms, telecoms providers and music companies. As in the case of the ring tones affair in the late 1990 leading to the Copyright Act Amendment of 2012, only the mobilization of artists for their rights and a fresh decision from the Court of Justice could lead to effective regulations on the price of online musical content. In the context of a liberalized economy expected to operate through self-regulation, there is little expectation of government action to regulate the price of content or the relationship between vastly different kinds of players. Consequently, the proliferation and consolidation of streaming platforms reinforces the importance of physical venues for performances and concerts, especially in urban centres, which are now the main source of income for recording artists.

Conclusion

This study of the platformization of India's music industry has emphasized the "inter-sectoral relations" with other industries and, specifically, over the course of three decades, with consumer electronics, then information technology, and now telecommunications. I have noted the presence and significance of transnational firms and their role in introducing technological disruptions. Currently, it is mainly ICT and telecoms companies that are reshaping India's musical industry, as is the case globally (Hesmondhalgh and Meier 2018). The same power struggles observed at global scale are at play in India, with ICT actors increasingly capturing historical music companies. All of the dedicated music companies are now in some form of collaboration or dependency with ICT players who are expanding into cultural content as a loss leader for their main offering. Indian streaming platforms (Saavn, Gaana) are in competition with their international counterparts (Spotify), but also with historical players of the music industry (T-Series, Sony), and the wider interests of super-platforms (Apple, Amazon, Jio). Musical production is clearly evolving towards a concentration of interests, and this has implications for the diversity of musical genres and the realization of creator's revenue. Despite a strengthening of the legal protection of artists' copyright with the 2012 Amendment of the Copyright Act, issues of regulatory implementation and enforcement remain a concern. In an essentially self-regulating market, only a minority of (typically smaller) players are in favour of more stringent legislation for the giants of the internet and e-commerce and a fairer remuneration of creators. In the absence of coherent cultural policies and state regulation in India, one can only wonder about the likely future of cultural industries that are being left in the hands of the major actors of the ICT sector, including Google, Apple and Amazon, who have acquired dominant positions over end-user access to cultural products

Acknowledgements The author would like to thank all the artists and music professionals interviewed for their time. Special thanks are due to Kenneth Hopkins, Mae Mariyam Thomas and Emmanuelle de Decker, for our passionate and fruitful discussions and for recommendations to several industry professionals during this fieldwork.

Interviews

Blaise Fernandes, *Indian Music Industry* (IMI), 24 November 2017, Mumbai; Samron Jude, Musician, 1 February 2018, Mumbai; Atul Churamani, *Turnkey Music & Publishing*, 2 February 2018, Mumbai; Achille Forler, Ex CEO *Universal Music*, 20 February 2018, Mumbai; Neeraj Kalyan, *T-series*, 23 February 2018, Delhi; Manojna Yeluri, *Artistik License*, 28 February 2018, New Delhi; Suresh Thangiah, *Strumm Entertainment*, 12 April 2018, Mumbai; Dhruv Anand, *Anand & Anand*, 24 April 2018, New Delhi; Karan Malhotra, Music Composer and Producer, 26 April 2018, Mumbai; Ex-employee, *Sony Music India*, 4 May 2018, Mumbai; Tejas Menon, *Kaddak Apple Record*, 12 May 2018, Mumbai.

Funding

The author received financial support for her research from the Laboratory of Information and Communication Sciences (LabSIC) and the Laboratory of Excellence Cultural Industries and Artistic Creation (LabEx ICCA), Paris 13 University.

References

Amelot, X., & Kennedy, L. (2010). Dynamique Économique et Recompositions Territoriales, Une Industrie Traditionnelle Locale De l'Inde Du Sud Face À La Mondialisation. *Annales de Géographie, 1–2*(671–672), 137–155.

Anderson, T. (2014). *Popular Music in a Digital Music Economy: Problems and Practices for an Emerging Service Industry*. New York, NY: Routledge.

Balanarayan, N. T. (2014, May 15). End of Exclusivity: T-Series Songs Now Available on Saavn Mobile App. *Medianama*.

Benhamou, F. (2006). *Les Dérèglements De L'exception Culturelle*. Paris: Le Seuil.

Bhatia, A. (2018, August 26). As Apple Music Starts Composing Its India Song, It Bets Big on Independent Musicians, Indie Bands. *Indian Express*.

Booth, G. (2015). Copyright Law and the Changing Economic Value of Popular Music in India. *Ethnomusicology, 59*(2), 262–287.

Booth, G. (2017). A Long Tail in the Digital Age: Music Commerce and the Mobile Platform in India. *Asian Music, 48*(1), Winter/Spring 2017, pp. 85–113.

Bouquillion, P. (2010). Industries, économie créatives et technologies d'information et de commusssnication. *ICT & Société, 4*(2). https://doi.org/10.4000/ticetsociete.876.
Bouquillion, P., Miège, B., & Moeglin, P. (2013). *L'industrialisation Des Biens Symboliques. Les Industries Créatives En Regard Des Industries Culturelles.* Grenoble: Presses Universitaires de Grenoble.
Bouquillion, P., & Ithurbide, C. (forthcoming). La globalisation culturelle et les nouveaux enjeux d'hégémonie à l'heure des plateformes: le cas indien. *Réseaux*, Special issue « Globalisation de la culture et circulation des biens culturels ».
Caves, R. (2000). *Creative Industries: Contracts between Art and Commerce.* Cambridge, MA: Harvard University Press.
Combès, Y. (2004). Penser les Mutations des Télé-Services Info Communicationnels: Approches et Perspectives. In *Sciences De L'information et de la Communication.* Université Charles-De-Gaulle Lille 3.
Combès, Y., & Petit, L. (2015). The Emergence of Creativity in Digital Thematic Platforms: A Comparative Study in the Areas of Education and Patrimony. *Les Enjeux de l'Information et de la Communication, 16*(3B), 43–55.
Elias, J. (2018, March 12). Amazon Prime Music Gets Access to Millions of Indian Musical Works. *PCMag.*
FICCI—EY. (2018). *Re-imagining India's Media & Entertainment Sector.* Ernst & Young LPP.
Gopinath, S. (2013). *Ringtone Dialectic: Economy and Cultural Form.* Cambridge: MIT Press.
Habermas, J. (1970). Technology and Science as "Ideology". In *Toward a Rational Society.* Boston: Beacon Press.
Hesmondhalgh, D. (2009). The Digitalisation of Music. In A. C. Pratt & P. Jeffcut (Eds.), *Creativity, Innovation and the Cultural Economy* (pp. 57–73). London: Routledge.
Hesmondhalgh, D. (2013). *The cultural industries.* (3rd ed.). London: Sage.
Hesmondhalgh, D., & Meier, L. (2018). What the Digitalisation of Music Tells Us about Capitalism, Culture and the Power of the Information Technology Sector. *Information, Communication & Society, 21*, 11.
Hu, C. (2017, September 23). How India, The Global Music Industry's Sleeping Giant, is Finally Waking Up. *Forbes.*
Huang, M. (2014, November 18). Methodology: Access to Music through the Mobile. Centre for Internet and Society.
Ingham, T. (2018, June 15). The Major Labels Could Block Spotify's Expansion into India Due to Direct Licensing Fallout. *Music Business World.*
International Federation of the Phonographic Industry (IFPI). (2017). *Global Music Report.*
International Labour Organization (ILO). (2017). *India Labour Market Update.* ILO Country Office for India.

Jha, L. (2017, February 24). Netflix, Amazon Give Ailing Bollywood Production Houses a New Lease of Life. *Livemint.*

Joux, A. (2016). La Régulation Des Industries Culturelles a L'heure d'Internet et les Enjeux Pour la Diversité Culturelle: Le Cas des Quotas Radiophoniques Français. *Global Media Journal—Canadian Edition, 9*(1), 37–50.

Kala, S. (2017, September 7). BookMyShow Launches Music Streaming and Digital Radio with Jukebox. *Telecomtalk.info.*

Khan, D. (2017, June 1). India's Monthly Wireless Data Usage Rose to 1.3 Bn GB in March, Courtesy Reliance Jio. *Economic Times.*

Kumar, A. (2015). *Provincialising Bollywood: Bhojpuri Cinema and the Vernacularisation of North Indian Media.* PhD thesis. University of Glasgow, Glasgow, Scotland.

Leyshon, A. (2014). *Reformatted: Code, Networks, and the Transformation of the Music Industry.* Oxford: Oxford University Press.

Manuel, P. (1993). *Cassette Culture: Popular Music and Technology in North India.* Chicago, IL: University of Chicago Press.

Mattelart, T. (2005). *Diversité Culturelle et Mondialisation.* Paris, France: La Découverte.

Mishra, P. (2013). Rdio Acquires India's Troubled Music Streaming Startup Dhingana to Push for Global Expansion. *Techcrunch.com.*

Moeglin, P. (1998). *L'Industrialisation de la formation. État de la question.* Paris, CNDP.

Moeglin, P. (2016). *Industrialiser l'éducation. Anthologie commentée (1913–2012).* Presses universitaires de Vincennes.

Mukharjee, A. (2002). *India's Trade Potential in Audio-Visual Services and the GATS.* Working Paper 81. Indian Council for Research on International Economic Relations.

Mukherjee, R., & Pahwa, N. (2017, July 13). MediaNama's Take on PayTM Buying Event Ticketing Platform Insider.in for Rs 35 Crore. *Medianama.*

Pahwa, N. (2009, May 11). Airtel Claims to be India's Largest Music Company; We Do the Math. *Medianama.*

Pahwa, N. (2014, February 14). Dhingana Shuts Down. *Medianama.*

Parthasarathi, V. (2013). The Evolution of an Early Media Enterprise: The Gramophone Company in India, 1898–1912. In R. Sundaram (Ed.), *No Limits; Media Studies from India.* New Delhi: Oxford University Press.

Pariser, E. (2011). *The filter bubble. What The Internet Is Hiding From You.* New York: Penguin Press.

Peermohamed. (2018, February 23). Times Internet Infuses Rs 2.48 Bn into Gaana to Battle Amazon Prime Music. *Business Standards.*

Peto, E. (2017, July 12). Interim Economy: An Introduction to India's Digital Music Industry. *Medianama.*

Pratt, A. (2016). Music Rights: Towards a Material Geography of Musical Practices in the 'Digital Age'. In B. Hracs, M. Seman, & T. E. Virani (Eds.), *The Production and Consumption of Music in the Digital Age* (pp. 206–222). New York: Routledge.

Salman, S. H. (2017, November 27). Saavn, Gaana Tie Up with Independent Artists to Produce, Market Original Music. *Livemint.*

Shashidhar, K. J. (2017, November 22). Streaming Service Saavn Gets Two New Strategic Investors on Board. *Medianama.*

Times of India. (2018, February 28). Tencent Leads $115 Million Funding in Music Streaming Service Gaana. *Times of India.*

Vaidhyanathan, S. (2001). *Copyrights and Copywrongs: The Rise of Intellectual Property and How it Threatens Creativity.* New York: New York University Press.

Verma, S. (2015, July 8). Tiger Global, Others Invest $100 Million in Saavn. *Livemint.*

Weber, M. (1963). *Le Savant et le Politique.* Paris: UGE.

Zuberi, N. (2002). Indian Song: Popular Music Genres Since Economic Liberalization. In D. David Hesmondhalgh & K. Keith Negus (Eds.), *Popular Music Studies* (pp. 238–250). London: Arnold Publications.

CHAPTER 7

Industrial and Financial Structures of Over-the-Tops (OTTs) in India

Philippe Bouquillion

The purpose of this chapter is to bring out the challenges of deploying over-the-top (OTT) offers in the audio-visual sector in India. To delimit its scope, a first precision must be provided about the notion of OTTs and a second clarification must relate to the components of the audio-visual field that will be addressed. First, OTTs operate over telecommunications networks, and therefore enable them to operate over national regulatory frameworks, especially Broadcasting Acts. Being important consumers of bandwidth, OTTs have typically conflicted with telecommunications operators, sometimes even leading to their streaming being blocked. But by the end of 2010, in many countries, including to a certain extent India, the different actors involved seemed to have reached to a level of consensus. Second, in this chapter we focus on "professionally" produced audio-visual OTT suppliers, that is to say, commercially produced content variously remunerated by the OTT platform, and therefore not user-generated content (UGC) audio-visual content.

P. Bouquillion (✉)
University of Paris XIII, Villetaneuse, France
e-mail: p.bouquillion@free.fr

A. Athique, V. Parthasarathi (eds.), *Platform Capitalism in India*, Global Transformations in Media and Communication Research - A Palgrave and IAMCR Series,
https://doi.org/10.1007/978-3-030-44563-8_7

How has Indian capitalism in the audio-visual cultural industries deployed OTTs? This question is at the heart of the chapter. Our hypothesis is that, as an instance of industrial movement, OTTs can also be apprehended from the point of view of the insertion of capitalist logics within the existing media industries. Before being able to support this hypothesis, it is necessary to specify how we will consider the relationship of cultural industries to capitalism and what we mean by such an "insertion" within capitalism. We will be inspired by an approach of the political economy of communication (PEC) where scholars have put forward a specific conception of capitalism. This differs from other approaches such as that of the creative industries and economy in which capitalism is viewed in a broader sense (such as Throsby 2000; Caves 2000). Capitalism is then extended to the entire economy and many authors emphasize the deepening of the market and financial dimensions of the economy. In contrast, in PEC, capitalism is conceived as the superior sphere of the economy, a restricted sphere in which power, the ability to define major orientations and also profits are concentrated.

One stream of scholars in PEC have found theoretical reference in the works of Fernand Braudel. Although not a scholar of the creative industries, his work allows us to engage with the differences, if not oppositions, between capitalism and market economy. I distinguish these two registers of the economy, one being considered superior and the other as inferior. The activities of capitalism are accessible only to a very small number of actors, who alone have the information, the know-how, and the financial and logistical capacities necessary to carry out large-scale operations (Braudel 1979, p. 493) The risks involved are considerable; but the potential profits, because of the absence of a competitive market situation, are just as important. Thus, the reference to Braudel also allows us to analyse transnationalization since capitalism as we envisage is built on a global scale, that of the world economy. Thus, Braudelian scholars of PEC have considered the culture industries developing in a capitalist logic. Moreover, these industries today are seen to lie at the heart of capitalism, perhaps even one of its privileged domains.

Focusing on the insertion of the cultural industries in capitalism helps to underline that these activities, because of their specificities, can escape the market economy—understood in the Braudelian sense as activities regulated by effective competition and low rates of profit. Cultural industries, or at least some part of them, are the most speculative or the most powerful belonging to the higher sphere of the economy, capitalism, where dominant positions and power struggles are extremely strong. The initial observation of PEC scholars, especially Miège (1984, 1989), is that capitalism is constantly seeking to find new spaces for the valuation of capital. For this, it must extend to areas previously occupied in whole or in part by non-market institutions, or create new spaces of production. Thus, considering the integration of culture industries into capitalism underlines how the transformation occurring in these industries are permanent, various, and difficult to predict.

Of course, the reflection on the insertion of cultural industries into capitalism has been renewed from the 2000s, when the deployment of digital technology gradually unfolded. Thanks to the deployment of digital technology with all the new tools, devices and services that they constitute, new spaces for capitalism developed. No other social space has offered in these last decades so many opportunities to capitalism. The question that arises since the beginning of the 2000s is: whether, with the deployment of digital technology, cultural industries are always favoured and considered as an activity at the heart of capitalism? Or if, on the contrary, they are put at the service of the industries of communication, which would then have become one of the main sectors of contemporary capitalism?

It has to be recalled that the culture and communication industries are two very different sets of industries although in strong interaction. The cultural industries are activities that relate to the industrialized production of content with a large symbolic dimension: namely book, information press, recorded music, audio-visual and video games. The turnover of these companies is mainly and directly coming from such productions and contents. On the other hand, communication industries gather a heterogeneous set of activities, ranging from telecommunications, consumer goods, web industries and software. They therefore include the tech giants (Google, Apple, Facebook, Amazon, Microsoft), which have in common their wider dealings with transport, storage and processing of data. In other words, unlike cultural industries, the core business of communication industries is not in the creation and production of cultural content, even though for the past two decades, they have increasingly entered into the economy of cultural productions. The size and the economic and financial power of these actors are also very different. The biggest players in the cultural industries are much less powerful than the major players in the communication industries. Later, we will give quantitative data on active industrial players in India showing this great disparity.

OTTs being one of the main vectors of digitization in the audio-visual sector, one of the questions asked in this chapter deals with the relationship between the players in content and those in the communication industries in the audio-visual sector during the 2010s. Is this relationship the same as that between the players in content and actors in the communication industries observed in the press and in recorded music in the 2000s? Dealing with cultural products enabled the communication industries to assert themselves against their competitors, as we will discuss later in the Indian case. PEC has two main advantages in order to analyse the issues of OTTs in India. First, it allows to articulate a reflection on the links between OTT market dynamics and the dynamics of capitalism, without necessarily considering that competitive dynamics and insertion capitalism go together. Second, thanks to the concept of world economy (Braudel 1979), it is possible to think the insertion of the OTT in transnational industrial and financial relations. A world economy is "a part of the planet, economically autonomous, capable for the most part of self-sufficiency and to which its links and internal trade confer a certain organic unity" (Braudel 1979, p. 12). The world economy is organized around a centre from which the exchange of capital, goods and workers is organized. Trade in the world economy is built in favour of the centre, while the rest of the world economy is made up of different concentric circles less and less favoured as they are far from the centre. This Braudelian approach does not oppose the research referring to the notion of "platform capitalism" (Srnicek 2016; Sundarajan 2016). Rather, it helps to reorient and clarify the meaning of these proposals in relation to two central ideas.

Thus, on the one hand, we insist on the fact that pure and perfect competition is not the rule in the higher spheres of capitalism, while on the other hand we can consider that transnational exchanges are structured by powerful power relations. One of the objectives of this contribution is to identify the new balance of power created by the deployment of OTTs, both between the various types of industrial actors and between the territories participating in transnational exchanges.

OTTs as a Market Regulation or an Insertion of Capitalism

This subtitle refers to the Braudelian problematic that distinguishes market economy and capitalism, as recalled earlier. If the second option is confirmed, it will be appropriate to characterize the strategies of capitalism at the end of 2010 in India in OTT. Are these strategies comparable to those at work previously since the beginning of 2000 when the dispersion of digital technology began? Or can we observe specificities related to the particularities of OTTs or the Indian case? Our hypothesis is that the deployment of OTTs accentuates the insertion of these industries into capitalism but in a quite specific way. In particular we presume that OTTs are offering a new opportunity for the actors in the cultural industries to control for their benefit the articulation between cultural contents and the digital without being vassalized by the actors of the communication industries. The links between the deployment of OTTs and the integration of the Indian culture and communication industries into capitalism can be assessed on three levels: (1) OTTs offering new spaces for the valuation of capital, (2) OTTs offering opportunities for industrial actors to renew their stakes and (3) the display of oligopolistic tendencies in the overall OTT market. Regarding the first level, thanks to the development of OTTs, a new sub-segment within audio-visual offers got created and contributed to the emergence of new areas for the valuation of capital. In a very short time, the OTT market grew in turnover, in users, and in the "quantity" of use, measured in viewing hours.

It is difficult to evaluate precisely the size of the OTT market since few quantitative data are available, and much of this being disputed. Figures tend to reflect the interests of certain actors who have an interest in presenting an optimistic vision of their activity. Both advertising and subscription revenues grew during 2017, by 34% and 262% respectively (Ernst & Young 2019, p. 108). Viewership of online videos online grew by 25% from 2017 with regional consumption driving this growth, albeit this includes viewership of UGCs (Ernst & Young 2019, p. 112). These figures concern a larger universe than our immediate analysis, as they include all digital services, including for instance music streaming. But this growth is also uneven due to uneven levels of broadband penetration beyond the top eight cities, which led to average time per user coming down. Similarly, the percentage of consumers who pay is abysmally low, some 5% and 1% for video and audio respectively (Ernst & Young 2019, p. 120). This perhaps explains why the offer on digital audio-visual platforms are not in itself profitable, as for most OTT platforms—video, news or audio—the cost of content and customer acquisition continues to be higher than the revenues earned per customer—despite advertising rates being at much higher levels than in traditional media" (Ernst & Young 2019, p. 13).

The industrial stakes of OTTs are not limited to the direct earnings they generate. Although not attaining breakeven point, the overall momentum in the consumption of a host of online services (social networks, music streaming, etc.) has pushed household spending and advertising expenditures in favour of digital media. This explains the growth rate in digital media, of which OTTs are a dynamics component, being double that of the average for the entire media and entertainment economy (Ernst & Young 2019, p. 10). Thus, OTTs seem to play a vital role in the larger movement of digitization and consequently, in the incremental expansion of capitalism in the Indian culture and communication industries. In our second level of analysis of capitalist integration and the expansion of the Indian culture and communication industries catalysed by OTTs, we look at the four categories of industrial actors in this space: historical audio-visual players, global OTT actors, players from the global communication industries, and domestic telecommunication operators. In laying this out, we note how each type of industrial actors in the OTT space tends to extract value differently.

Many of actors in the television and film business have developed OTT offers. The most important are: Hotstar, subsidiary of the TV network, StarIndia, now belonging to Disney; Eros Now, a subsidiary of Eros International, one of the largest in television and film production; Voot, a joint venture between the US media group Viacom and TV18, controlled by India's Reliance Industries; ALTBalaji, a subsidiary of Balaji Telefilms, an Indian producer and distributor of television and film content; Zee5, belonging to Zee Entertainment, part of an Indian conglomerate present in various media industries; HOOQ, a joint venture between Sony Pictures, Warner Bros. and Singtel; Viu, a subsidiary of a Hong Kong group active in Information Communication Technology (ICT), PCCW. Dominant among the former are Hotstar, SonyLiv and Zee5, the OTT subsidiaries of the leading multi-lingual broadcast networks in India. Through their OTT subsidiaries, they seek to retain their broadcast audience and their advertisers (in the latter case by integrating their ad sales across OTT and linear platforms) (Ernst & Young 2019, p. 24). The principal market for content being in Indian languages is an asset for the other historical audio-visual actor as well—film producers. The consumption of films on OTTs is clearly dominated by Eros, one of the oldest cinema production and distribution companies, with a market share of 69% in 2017 (Ernst & Young 2018, p. 92).

The business of content production has benefited from the high demand generated by the profusion of rivalling OTT players. This profusion has compelled OTT players to distinguish their original offerings, though they often are obliged to offer non-exclusive content. Thus, new entrants with no catalogues purchase rights of existing content while also produce or commission original content, this latter category having grown by 1200 hours in 2018 (Ernst & Young 2019, p. 12). OTTs have positively impacted the wider sphere of the historical audio-visual economy. For one, the acquisition cost of broadcast rights has increased. The separate negotiation of OTTs has benefited content producers. "Instead of bundling satellite and internet rights for television broadcasters, producers now see greater monetization in dealing with OTT platforms separately for digital rights" (Ernst & Young 2019, p. 87). Nevertheless, content production directly linked to OTTs is still limited; for instance, in cinema it represents only 10% of revenues (Ernst & Young 2019, p. 76). For the OTTs, however, this part of revenue is growing fast; in turn, the demand spurred by them has increased the price of relevant and quality content, that is, content directed at the Indian market.

The second category of industrial actors in the OTT space are the new transnational entities in the cultural industries, which are valued mainly through content, particularly through subscriptions. The main player here is Netflix, which entered India in January 2016 by offering its transnational catalogue at acceptable prices. Netflix India reached profitability in its first year of operations (Economic Times 2018). Contrary to its initial strategy, the company furthered adapted both its pricing and its content to the specificities of the Indian market. Reed Hastings, Netflix's CEO, declared: "We will go from expanding beyond English into Hindi and then into many more languages, more pricing options, more bundling, all of those things are possible' (ibid.). However, contrary to the situation in Europe, Netflix has not become the dominant OTT offering in India. This can be explained by the high subscription price, relative to incomes, and the importance of the possession of the rights of diffusion of contents produced in India and for an Indian audience.

The third category of industrial actors in the OTT space are global players in the communication industries, which for now is mainly Amazon. For Amazon, OTTs are a joint product, part of a bundle services led by its e-commerce offerings. They can thus afford to offer lower tariff than their content-centric OTT rivals, which explains Amazon Prime's annual tariff of INR 999 being far more appealing that the monthly tariff of INR 500 by Netflix. The Indian telecom operators constitute the fourth category of industrial actors. This highly oligopolistic market is comprised of Reliance Jio, a recent entrant in the telecom space owned India's large conglomerate Reliance Industries; Bharti Airtel, the first mover in the mobile telecom business 25 years ago; and, Vodafone India, owned by the British Vodafone Plc. Their importance stems from two factors: mobile phones being the main platform in India for accessing OTT content; and their ability to offer gratis a basic package of audio-visual content as part of their connection and data services. Among these three competitors, the conglomerate power of Reliance Jio enabled it to slash data tariffs, thereby making OTT content widely affordable. This enabled JIO to simultaneously garner a large share in the market of mobile telecom in general and of OTTs in particular.

This brings is to the third level of analysis regarding the integration of the Indian culture and communication industries into capitalism catalysed by OTTs. Despite the profusion of OTT offers by industrial actors with different bents, market development on the whole has been accompanied by oligopolistic tendencies. We emphasize two aspects here: the complex industrial alliances around the OTT, and the role of the OTT in the consolidation within the telecommunications sector. The various OTT players are connected by relationships of both collaboration and competition. A situation of "coopetition" has been set up, which while not new has found a new development with "platformatization". To a certain extent, these players form a "system". This means that their relationships are not only based, and probably not primarily, on market competition but result from agreements that are either explicit (contractual) or implicit. The games between these different actors are complex and these relationships can also be unstable. The more implicit agreements are regarding their editorial strategies or their pricing strategies in order to limit frontal competition, especially between actors whose core business is different, such as content producers, broadcasters and telecommunication operators.

Similarly, players exchange rights of access to content (to more or less original content), easier access to networks and access to subscribers. Players of very different sizes are involved in these competitions/collaborations. Thus, content players, as the film producer Eros International, may appear small in terms of their turnover or market capitalization compared to other players, including the communication industries players, but they can stay in the game. This situation of coopetition is not unique to India. However, in India, these relationships take a specific turn notably due to the need for OTT platforms to offer Indian content, the insufficient broadband penetration, the huge pool of subscribers of the Indian telecom operators, and the centrality of mobile tools in the consumption of OTT platforms.

As a result, telecommunication operators are at the heart of these networks in India, and not global OTT players like Netflix and Amazon. In fact, at the end of the 2010s, three coopetition networks are in place in a more or less stable way. The most important and first to be formed is around Reliance Jio, the first among telcos to develop OTT platforms. JIO is now associated with Eros Now, Hotstar, ALTBalaji, and Zee5. The second network is built around Airtel with Eros Now, HOOQ and SonyLiv, Zee5 and two global players, Netflix and Amazon Prime. The third set combines Vodafone with Amazon Prime and Netflix, as well as with Eros Now, ALTBalaji and HOOQ. It is difficult to know all aspects of these agreements because of industrial secrecy. However, Ernst & Young have estimated the total paid by telcos for content of all types to which they allow access: "The amount telcos paid for syndication was around INR 3.5 to 4 billion in 2018 [...] Telco content deals were both fixed-fee/minimum guarantee deals as well as cost-per-stream deals" (2019, p. 120).

Reliance Jio has many assets in hand to conclude such agreements. Having a financially powerful owner, its industrial agreements can be coupled with a capitalistic partnership, such that one reinforces the other. For instance, in 2018 "Jio's parent, Reliance Industries Limited (RIL), acquired a 24.9% stake in Balaji Telefilms, the parent of the OTT player ALTBalaji" (Khan 2018). RIL also bought a 5% stake in Eros, "after which Eros Now's multi-lingual library was made available on Jio TV and Jio Cinema" (Mitter). Other partnerships relate specifically to content production services. For example, Viacom entered a multi-picture deal with Netflix (Ernst & Young 2019, p. 89). Netflix and Amazon entered into numerous contracts with Indian content providers to obtain exclusive content. Although such a strategy is not specific to India it gains importance due to the role of local language content in the OTT market. Moreover, the informal economy of production in India, together with the low commissioning costs compared to other countries, allow global OTT players to obtain content at easier terms. We recall that in Braudel's thinking, the non-respect of the rules, brigandage and piracy are not considered characteristics of a pre-capitalist economy but are at the heart of capitalism since they allow the balance of power to develop without legal constraints.

Finally, oligopolistic tendencies have been considerably reinforced through Indian telecom giants which have reconfigured OTT offers. The inflexion point was when Reliance JIO drastically reduced its tariffs, combined with offering low-cost smartphones, since "Jio launched its INR 1,500 smartphone, and Airtel announced a smartphone priced around INR 2,000–2,500" (Ernst & Young 2018, p. 105). Thus, Jio's subscription offers included both telecom access and free OTT content. Rival telecom operators had to adapt to their strategies. As a result, operators' expenses increased while revenues were constrained by lower prices. Faced with these pressures, industrial concentration has strengthened, as Bharti Airtel admitted:

> The fiscal year 2017–2018 was a transformational year for the telecom industry. Because of the brutal price war, there was an unprecedented consolidation from 8 operators to only 3 private operators in the market. This price war also led to a rapid shift in consumer behaviour from voice to entertainment that led to explosion of data usage and ultimately, massive network investments. (Bharti Airtel, Annual Report 2017–2018, p. 14)

Concluding this first section of the paper, we emphasize that the organization of the OTT market obeys more to a Braudelian capitalist logic than to a logic of free market and free competition. Although unprofitable today, the OTT market is being built as a new area of capital valuation. Capital is valued differently according to the sectorial affiliations of the industrial players who find different interests in the OTT business. Thus, the OTT market forms a system structured by agreements between actors. Among other things, OTTs offer rest at the heart of recent reorganization in the telecommunications sector. It concentrated strongly.

OTTs: A New Balance of Power Between Territories Participating in Transnational Exchanges?

Under this heading, it is now necessary to examine to what extent the deployment of OTTs in India can be read according to the concept of world economy of culture and communication. The cultural and communication industries, especially the film and television industries, are articulated in various ways on a transnational scale. The idea of economy-world suggests these articulations are crossed by relations of force and domination. Braudel's world economy forms an "economic whole" with three characteristics: it occupies a given geographical space; it has a centre; and every world economy is divided into successive zones "less and less favoured as one moves away from one's triumphant centre". (Braudel 1985, p. 94) Inspired by Braudel, Wallerstein (2002) and Mattelart (1992), we can consider the world economy of culture and communication being structured and hierarchized in different concentric circles. The peripheral areas are "exploited" for the benefit of the centre, in particular for the benefit of dominant Anglo-Saxon actors.

These articulations and these relations of domination are both industrial and financial. On the industrial perspective, according to PEC, trading conditions are very unequal. Works produced in the centre are bought in the peripheries while the exchanges in the other direction are very small. On the financial level, the world economy of communication also refers to the domination of major US financial players on others. This domination is itself linked to the rise in the shareholding of industrial players of large investment funds (as, for instance, the Vanguard Group or BlackRock), present in the capital of many industrial groups around the world. In addition, the complex and multiple influences of the two major global credit rating agencies, Standard & Poor's and Moody's, both US, and some very large investment banks, including Merrill Lynch, Morgan Stanley and Goldman & Sachs, significantly strengthens this dominance. The orientation they give greatly affect the ability of industrial players to raise funds. Not only do they have difficulty raising funds, but the badly evaluated players also have to devote a significant portion of their income to dividend distributions and buybacks of their own shares in order to support their share price. As a result, from the point of view of digital deployment, financialization has greatly favoured the actors of the communication industries compared to those of the cultural industries. Do these theoretical constructions shed light on the situation prevailing in India, at the financial as well at the industrial levels?

Firstly, on the financial level, in many ways, the situation of OTTs in India can be interpreted in terms of the world economy, that is, closely related to the capital of the centre of the world economy, American capital and the major US players in the financial sphere. We will therefore examine here to which extent OTT players active in India are financialized and whether the shareholding of these actors is mainly foreign, especially American, or Indian. Before entering into the specifics of OTTs' financial dimension in India, it should be remembered that India's openness to transnational financial exchanges is relatively recent. Various economic and financial liberalization measures have been taken since 1991, facilitating both privatization and increasing openness to foreign capital in various economic sectors, including the cultural and communication industries. In 2016, a new impetus was given to this liberalization movement. On June 20, 2016, the government announced a reform of the rules applicable to foreign investments. In various sectors, foreign ownership thresholds have been high, or 100% ownership has been allowed, while authorization procedures have been simplified and relaxed. The acquisition of distributors of television channels, whether broadcast by cable, satellite or mobile phone, may however be done without this approval (Bouissou 2016). The legal opening does not mean, however, that foreign financiers are rushing to invest. In most cases, the investment limits have been achieved, and the sectors implicated by OTTs are not necessarily at the forefront of foreign direct investment (FDI).

Indeed, the cultural industries (information-broadcasting, including print media) are only the 15th sector concerned with foreign investments with, in 2018, $8.38 billion, or 2% of total FDI this year. Thus, the transformation of foreign direct investment rules has not drastically changed the capital position of Indian OTT players. The presence of the financial interests of the centre of the world economy in the ownership of the OTT actors in India is contrasted according to the actors and the sectors. Table 7.1 summarizes the financial performance in terms of market capitalization and turnover of the main players in the market for OTT audiovisual platforms offering "professional" content (and not UGC). The first column gives the name of the platform and that of the parent companies. The second column contains the market capitalization of the parent company or subsidiary offering the platform when the company is listed on the stock exchange. The third column contains the turnover. The platforms are ranked in descending order of market capitalization.

Several lessons can be drawn from this table. First lesson, it shows that the presence of foreign interests in the OTT market is massive. Of the 13 OTT actors included in this table, eight are foreign players, four are Indian and one actor is almost equally controlled by Indian and American interests. Some of those foreign industrial players have established subsidiaries sometimes for a long time in India, as Walt Disney (through Fox's audiovisual assets in India) or Viacom. The presence of American players is important, four platforms are under American control and one is half

Table 7.1 The financial dimension of OTT platforms. (Data source: Economic Times 2019)

Name of the subsidiary OTT and of the parent companies	*Market capitalization*	*Revenue*	*Shareholding details*
Amazon Prime Video/Amazon	(Amazon) $886.7 billion (August 17, 2019)	(Amazon) $252.8 billion (FY 2018)	The company is controlled by US shareholders.
Hotstar (StarIndia)/Walt Disney	(Walt Disney) $240 billion (August 15, 2019)	(Walt Disney) $67.7 billion (FY 2018)	The company is controlled by US shareholders.
Netflix	(Netflix) $132.57 billion (August 17, 2019)	(Netflix) $17.6 billion (FY 2018)	The company is controlled by US shareholders.
Reliance Jio/ Reliance Industries	(Reliance Industries) $113.6 billion (August 17, 2019)	(Reliance Industries) $85.43 billion (FY 2019)	The company is controlled by Indian shareholders.
Sony Liv/Sony Corporation	$69.5 billion (August 17, 2019)	$81.4 billion (FY 2019)	The company is controlled by Japanese shareholders.
HOOQ / Singtel&Warner Bros&Sony Pictures	(Singtel) $37.4 billion (August 17, 2019)	(Singtel) $12.2 billion (FY 2019)	HOOQ is a joint venture between Singtel (85%), Warner Bros (7.5%) and Sony Pictures (7.5%).
Airtel Wynck/ Bharti Airtel	(Bharti Airtel) $25.9 billion (August 17, 2019)	(Bharti Airtel) $11.4 billion (FY 2019)	The company is controlled by Indian shareholders.
Voot/Viacom18/ Reliance Industries/Viacom	(Viacom) $10.3 billion (August 17, 2019)	(Viacom) $12.8 billion (FY 2018)	Voot is owned by Viacom18, which belongs to Reliance Industries (51%), and to Viacom (49%), the American entertainment player.

(*continued*)

Table 7.1 (continued)

Name of the subsidiary OTT and of the parent companies	*Market capitalization*	*Revenue*	*Shareholding details*
Zee5/Zee Entertainment	(Zee Entertainment) $4.6 billion (August 17, 2019)	(Zee Entertainment) $11.4 billion (FY 2019)	This company was until mid-2019 majority-controlled by Indian interests and in particular by the Essel Group and its founder. The foreign interests became dominant with 47% of the share owned by foreign institutions and 12.36% by foreign promoters.
Viu/PCCW	(PCCW) $4.2 billion (August 17, 2019)	(PCCW) $4.5 billion (FY 2019)	PCCW is a player from Hong Kong active in ICT
Vodafone Idea	(Vodafone Idea) $2.5 billion (August 17, 2019)	(Vodafone Idea) $5.9 billion (FY 2019)	Company created by the merger between Vodafone and Idea Cellular in August 2018. Foreign promoters own 53.57% of the company and foreign institutions, 15.67%.
Eros Now/Eros International	$120.4 million (August 17, 2019)	$270.1 million (FY 2019)	The company is controlled by Indian shareholders.
ALTBalaji/Balaji Telefilms	$69.4 million (August 17, 2019)	$55.4 million (FY 2019)	The company is controlled by Indian shareholders.

American. However, this presence is not exclusive. Asian interest is also present, with players from Hong Kong, Singapore, Japan and of course India. Finally, a British actor is also to count. Thus, the classic scheme of the world economy with a single financial centre, and of course an American one, corresponds only partially to the reality of the Indian OTT market. In this respect, this situation is not specific to the OTT or to India but corresponds to a central geopolitical trend in recent years, with the rise in power at the industrial and financial levels of the Asian players.

Second lesson, these foreign players are among the most financially powerful. Apart from Amazon, one of the largest market capitalizations in the world, there is also Walt Disney, the world's leading market capitalization among cultural industry players, as well as Netflix. The latter benefits from a particular financial situation with a capitalization disproportionate to its profits. However, this does not mean that these powerful players are able to crush their competitors especially the Indian competitors. Because they are global players, they have to think about their investments on a transnational scale and not just on the Indian scale.

Third lesson, in comparison with the main global actors, the players active in the OTT whose shareholding is mainly Indian have a much lower financial performance. Similarly, again the centrality of telecommunications operators must be emphasized. Their "financial size" is larger than that of Indian-owned audio-visual actors, but it is smaller than that of the major transnational players with OTT affiliates in India. Reliance Industries, active through Reliance Jio but also through majority or minority holdings in other companies (Balaji Telefilms, Viacom18, Eros International) and Bharti Airtel are the most powerful Indian operators of the OTT. On the other hand, the financial size of the historical audiovisual players held by Indian interests and present in the OTT is rather weak, even very weak in comparison with those of their competitors. The market capitalizations of Eros International and even more of Balaji Telefilms are very small. The rise of Reliance Industries within their capital can therefore be interpreted as an attempt to seal the industrial alliances by financial partnerships but also as an Indianization of OTT capitalism vis-à-vis foreign interests. The only player with an international financial footprint, Zee Entertainment, came under foreign majority control in 2019.

Fourth lesson, it would be interesting to further investigate the transnational stakes of certain alliances. Is there a link between Reliance Industries' presence in Balaji Telefilms' shareholding and the strategy of this firm in order to propose OTT services abroad, in particular to the Indian diaspora? Moreover, does the presence of strong American industrial interests active in the field of content industries (Disney, Viacom, Warner) to the capital of OTT actors in India lead these actors to bet especially on American content and especially on blockbusters to assert their offer in the Indian market?

These questions can be addressed in the following subsection, which is dedicated to the industrial aspects of the integration of the Indian OTT into the world economy of culture and communication. We have just observed that at the financial level, the schemes proposed by PEC and in particular that of the world economy apply partially. American interests are very present but many other foreign interests are present while the Indian interests thanks to the telecommunications operators are also powerful and are not under the dependence of the American actors, those of the centre of the economy-world. What about on the industrial level? Secondly, on the industrial level, the question that now arises is whether foreign content, in particular American content, dominates the Indian market of OTT audio-visual platforms. Do the Indian OTT platforms function as relays for distributing content produced in the centre of the world economy? Or is another perspective emerging thanks to the deployment of SVOD OTT audio-visual platforms?

Before attempting to provide answers to this question, it should be remembered that prior to the deployment of SVOD platforms, and still today, on conventional modes of content distribution, whether film or television content, foreign content is poorly represented while Indian content, made in India, and in Hindi or in regional languages, are very dominant. Linguistic fragmentation into different regional languages is a very important factor in the economics of cultural industries in India. The question is not only the attachment of Indians to "Indian" content but their attachment to content produced in their particular mother tongue (see Athique et al. 2018). Thus, for instance, in 1991, when News Corporation expanded its Asian business to India with the creation of Star India, now one of India's largest television player, Rupert Murdoch's group relied on the importation of American content to seduce Indian viewers. It was a failure and the group was forced to produce and broadcast Indian content and to "Indianize" the entire team including the most senior officials. Other foreign players that have established in India, including Viacom or Sony, have also produced and broadcast Indian content in various Indian languages. Do platforms change the game? In other words, is the presence in India of platforms global actors as well as the creation of platforms by the actors formerly installed in India but held by foreign interests like Star India, will lead to a reversal of the trend, to favour American and global content at the expense of Indian content? It would be necessary to conduct a study of both the content available on the platforms and their users to be able to answer precisely these questions. In addition, the situation could change over time. The development of these platforms only dates back from the second half of 2010s.

Similarly, it is difficult to assess to what extent the Indian situation presents specificities. In other countries, situations are contrasted both from the point of view of the balance of power between domestic and foreign actors and the penetration of global content. In addition, empirical work is lacking. However, some elements can be underlined. In China, American actors in the cultural and communication industries and their contents have great difficulties to penetrate with bans of certain offers or drastic quotas. The aim is to protect the Chinese market, which in very strong growth, from foreign competitors, and to reserve it for Chinese players. Thanks to this protectionist policy some of them (Baidu, Alibaba, Tencent, etc.) have already reached a significant size compared to the global American players. The Chinese situation is therefore very different from that of India. In Latin America, an area with important domestic actors in the audio-visual industries, the OTT market (counting only that of TV series and films) in 2018 would amount to $3.3 billion. Netflix is in a very dominant position with 65% of market share (Broadband TV News 2019). Brazil and to a lesser extent Mexico are the two most important markets in Latin America. There is still no published data on the place of global content in Latin American audio-visual platforms. On the other hand, in most of these countries, despite the existence of domestic cultural industries, the presence of foreign cultural productions is often very strong. For instance, in Brazil, domestic films only accounted for 16.5% of the theatrical market in 2016, according to the Agencia Nacional do Cinema (Ancine 2019).

These examples show that apart from strict protectionist measures, neither the existence of powerful domestic cultural industries nor policies of subsidies to national content are sufficient to avoid the domination of American actors and content in these geographical areas of the so-called emerging countries. In the Indian case, it is difficult to appreciate the influence and their evolution over time of the various factors contributing to favour or disadvantage global content consumption: the offer of global content and its structuring character, access fees for consumers to these contents, socio-cultural factors and the role of global content in the phenomena of distinction for the members of certain social groups and so on. However, already, two important trends are present in the strategies of the actors of the platforms. They derogate from the scenario of domination of American content.

First, all foreign players are developing intense Indianization policies for their content offer. Our interviews and expertise confirm this trend which is particularly related to the linguistic and cultural fragmentation of India: "Apart from Bollywood films, streaming platforms are also focusing on regional content" (Ernst & Young 2019, p. 87). Strategies differentiated according to the subspaces must be conducted: "Many investors realized the heterogeneity of India and have created multiple strategies to target India and Bharat and the different strata within them. There is not going to be a single market strategy, and companies adapted to the fact that global strategies do not always work in India" (Ernst & Young 2019, p. 87). Even the largest global players are pursuing such a strategy: "Amazon and Netflix have both commissioned in excess of ten originals as well from India and are expected to spend over INR 10 billion" (Ernst & Young 2019, p. 123). However, it is true that most of their content is American.

The second trend is the development of Indian content exports through platforms. Most active platform players in India are looking to expand their services overseas and offer their Indian content. OTT distribution could thus be substituted for other vectors, in particular cable and satellite. For instance, "ZEE is planning to pull the plug on its linear television service in Europe, Australia, Fiji and a few other overseas markets and offer content only via the video OTT service, Zee5" (Ernst & Young 2019, p. 36). Similarly, "Star India had discontinued distribution of television channels in Canada and the US and has been offering content only through its video on-demand player, Hotstar" (Ernst & Young 2019, p. 36). Global players, and especially Netflix, have a very special strategy in order to produce transnational content. Indeed, Netflix content is never thought of for distribution in a single national context but, when it comes to non-US content, the aim is of course to be attractive in the country of production, but also to be popular seen elsewhere. As our surveys indicate, Netflix's algorithms classify the various types of scenarios and storytelling as well as actors and directors according to their potential for transnationalization. It should not be surprising, then, that content made for one country may be successful elsewhere, as shown by the example of *Sacred Games*: "Two of every three viewers of Netflix's Sacred Games were from outside India" (Ernst & Young 2019, p. 124). This example shows that the actors of the centre of the world economy are trying not only to disseminate the contents of the centre in the peripheries, but also to exploit the resources available in the peripheries to produce content. Indeed, the peripheries offer high-quality but low-paid "talent". Thus, India has become for the transnational audio-visual players, a space of creatives.

To sum up, the second section of this paper questioned the various forms of transnationalization of audio-visual actors and content related to the development of OTT. The central question concerned the interpretation of these forms of transnationalization. Can they be considered as the exploitation of the periphery of the world economy by its US centre? We have seen that American interests are very present in the shareholding of OTT players in India. These actors have been active in India generally for a long time, long before the emergence of the OTT, but they find there a new vector of development in India. Nevertheless, actors from other geographical areas are also present illustrating the fact that the world economy is moving from a single, American centre to a plurality of centres, especially Asian. Indian actors, especially those in telecommunications, are also powerful players able to offer an alternative to the exploitation of the periphery by the centre. Similarly, in terms of content, the EPC schemas, describing a dominance of US content on domestic content, hardly apply, either before the OTT or with the OTT. It is still difficult to assess whether this is an Indian exception to the situations prevailing internationally. Anyway, the extent of Indian content production strategies by Indian and foreign OTT actors indicates how India has become a space of creative re s for the audio-visual industries. Moreover, public policies help: "to give impetus to co-productions and collaboration between Indian and overseas filmmakers, the Indian Government has entered into co-production treaties with various countries such as China, Canada, France, Germany, Brazil, Italy, New Zealand and the UK" (Ernst & Young 2018, p. 23).

Conclusion

In considering some of the trends at work in OTT audio-visual platforms, it is apparent that the dynamics of capitalism are strong within these activities. In many respects, one can observe the continuation of earlier movements: new areas of capital development are created; the nature of competition in television is oligopolistic, content production and volume of telecommunications is increasing; transnational players, especially American ones, occupy dominant positions. Similarly, larger players in the communication industries have entered the OTT platforms either in the logic of joint products or to accompany the transformation of their former core businesses. Thus, in many ways OTT platforms operate in a capitalist logic as defined by researchers in the political economy of communication. These platforms have increased the capitalist dimension in the diverse sectors involved in OTT. However, the deployment of OTTs is also marked by specificities compared to other movements of articulation between cultural industries and communication industries in the digital environment. Platform operators are generally obliged to produce original content and/or to have exclusive rights over content. Moreover, one of the specificities of the Indian case is that the most attractive content is always Indian content, especially in Hindi or regional languages. As a consequence of these factors, media industry players have managed to maintain their position vis-à-vis the players in the communication industries, including the largest ones, such as Amazon.

References

Ancine. (2019). Market Data: Cinema. Retrieved December 22, 2019, from https://www.ancine.gov.br/en/market-data/cinema.

Athique, A., Parthasarathi, V., & Srinivas, S. V. (Eds.). (2018). *The Indian Media Economy, Volume II: Market Dynamics and Social Transactions.* New Delhi: Oxford University Press.

Bouissou, J. (2016, June 21). L'Inde s'ouvre un peu plus aux sociétés étrangères. *Le Monde.*

Braudel, F. (1979). *Le Temps Du Monde: Civilisation Matérielle, Économie et Capitalisme, XVe-XVIIIe siècle, Vol. 3.* Paris: Armand Colin.

Braudel, F. (1985). *La Dynamique du Capitalisme.* Paris: Flammarion.

Broadband TV News. (2019, April 1). LatAm to Add 24 Million SVOD Subscriptions. Retrieved April 3, 2019, from https://www.broadbandtvnews.com/2019/04/01/latam-to-add-24-million-svod-subscriptions/.

Caves, R. (2000). *Creative Industries: Contracts between Art and Commerce.* Harvard University Press.

Economic Times. (2018, October 30). Netflix India Makes Profit in its 1st Year.

Economic Times. (2019). Market Data. Retrieved from https://economictimes.indiatimes.com/vodafone-idea-ltd/shareholding/companyid-3154.cms and https://economictimes.indiatimes.com/zee-entertainment-enterprises-ltd/shareholding/companyid-11769.cms.

Ernst & Young-FICCI. (2018, April 14). Re-imagining India's M&E Sector. Retrieved from https://www.ey.com/Publication/vwLUAssets/ey-re-imagining-indias-me-sector-march-2018/%24File/ey-re-imagining-indias-me-sector-march-2018.pdf.

Ernst & Young-FICCI. (2019). *A Billion Screens of Opportunity: India's Media & Entertainment.* Mumbai: FICCI.

Khan, D. (2018, January 25). Reliance Jio Inks Content Deal with ALTBalaji to Counter Airtel. *Economic Times.*

Mattelart, A. (1992). *La Communication-Monde*. Paris: La Découverte.

Miège, B. (1984). Postface à la seconde edition. In A. Huet, J. Ion, A. Lefebvre, B. Miège, & R. Péron (Eds.), *Capitalisme et Industries Culturelles* (pp. 199–214). Grenoble: Presses Universitaires de Grenoble.

Miège, B. (1989). *La Société Conquise par la Communication, Vol. 1*. Grenoble: Presses Universitaire de Grenoble.

Srnicek, N. (2016). *Platform Capitalism*. Cambridge: Polity Press.

Sundarajan, A. (2016). *The Sharing Economy: The End of Employment and the Rise of Crowd-based Capitalism*. Cambridge, MA: The MIT Press.

Throsby, D. (2000). *Economics and Culture*. Cambridge: Cambridge University Press.

Wallerstein, I. (2002). *Le Capitalisme Historique*. Paris: La Découverte & Syros.

PART III

Platform Workers

CHAPTER 8

Journalistic Practices and Algorithmic Governance

M. Shuaib Mohamed Haneef and Aquil Ahmad Khan

Digital newsrooms are experiencing continual shifts in their everyday practices through successive phases of technological remediation. With the arrival of a platform ecology, newsrooms are getting reconfigured at professional, discursive and spatial levels. The ecology of the digital newsroom thus requires us to examine the production and consumption of news from an institutional perspective in the context of the increased use of mobile devices and algorithmic processes to produce, package and distribute news content (Asp 2014; Napoli 2014). This technological reconfiguration has ushered in a paradigmatic shift in journalistic practices in India (Anderson 2012; Örnebring 2010). It can be argued that journalistic labour has received a fillip due to the material and discursive intervention of algorithms that provide a point of departure in the everyday practices of journalism. The norms of algorithms and the reflexivity of humans mutually constitute a set of disjunctive and coalescing forces that modulate the labour process and professional ethos in the business of

M. S. M. Haneef (✉) • A. A. Khan
Pondicherry University, Puducherry, India
e-mail: shuaib.emc@pondiuni.edu.in

A. Athique, V. Parthasarathi (eds.), *Platform Capitalism in India*, Global Transformations in Media and Communication Research - A Palgrave and IAMCR Series,
https://doi.org/10.1007/978-3-030-44563-8_8

journalism. The reshaping of journalists, labour and news production by algorithms is likely to constitute news as an algorithmic commodity. Fuchs (2012) and Fisher (2015) have nonetheless raised concerns that algorithms will effectively hide the labour process of journalists. Thus, while it is sanguine to argue that news is now co-produced by journalists and algorithms, this new assemblage is constitutive of power relations wherein algorithms are poised to incrementally discipline and reconfigure journalistic functions.

Our study used qualitative research design to understand emergent journalistic practices in two digital news websites, namely Ippodhu and DoolNews, as well as the Tamil-language edition of the digital portal, Oneindia. Oneindia portal, initially known as www.indiainfo.com, produces news in four South Indian languages (Tamil, Kannada, Malayalam, Telugu) besides Hindi, which is widely spoken in North India. The present workforce comprises 25 journalists, including their technical team, in addition to freelance content writers. The Oneindia desk headquartered in Bangalore uploads stories and produces graphics and data-based reports. DoolNews is a Malayalam-language digital news outlet set up in 2009 and headquartered in Kozhikode, Kerala. DoolNews has a team of 23 journalists who produce content, using cameras and other basic audiovisual technologies. Ippodhu is a small independent media outlet launched in 2015 catering to a Tamil-language audience Its team comprises of an editor, subeditor, principal correspondent and two journalists in addition to the marketing team. Ippodhu provides content on various platforms including mobile apps, a Facebook page, YouTube channel, Twitter feed as well as on its own website. In our research, face-to-face in-depth interviews and telephone interviews were conducted with editors and journalists of all three organisations in order to elicit information on journalists' perceptions of their work practices in the digital ecosystem. Interviews were transcribed and coded deductively to organise the data into themes and categories drawing on the concepts of free labour, affective labour and audience as economic capital.

Automation and Algorithmic Thinking in Journalism

Digital technologies have reinvigorated the news industry in India, and revitalised and expanded the profession of journalism. All facets of journalism have undergone marked changes, raising the question of what constitutes journalism today and who should be counted as a journalist (Carlson

2015). Legacy media organisations began integrating digital technologies into their workflow practices, thus paving the way for the emergence of digital forms of journalism that are distinct from the traditional canons and practices of news production and distribution. The rise of user-generated content throughout the platform ecosystem in India has also engendered a proliferation of citizen journalism for a digital public. At the same time, non-profit news start-ups "are proliferating, collaborating, and becoming a significant part of the emerging media ecology" (Konieczna and Robinson 2014, p. 969). The news start-ups are invariably "digital native media" companies that were born and grown entirely online or on digital platform (Wu 2016).

Contemporary journalism, in legacy and start-ups, is thus imbued with computational journalism, a practice that uses algorithms and codes to find and tell stories (Diakopoulos 2014; Coddington 2015). The mathematical precision of computational thinking that algorithms and software advance and the prescience of human thinking are the two logics that define news production, distribution and consumption in the refashioned news media ecology (Wing 2008). At the same time, the ubiquitous presence of digital technologies has entangled news producers in a crossover between human labour and technological process. With new techniques, non-profit and digital news websites aim for a revised journalist-audience relationship, wherein citizens are considered to be digital prosumers involved in the co-production of news (Toffler 1981). In addition to user-generated content, many news organisations have pursued the automation of the news making process in order to bolster the productivity, and bottom line, of their newsrooms.

Digital Journalism and Labour

Digital journalism start-ups in India are proliferating, though many of them have not yet found a sustainable business model (Aneez et al. 2016). Although critical theorists have started addressing labour studies in the digital age, labour discourse has been sidelined historically in Media Studies (Frayssé and O'Neil 2015). Mosco also described labour as a blindspot of western communication studies (2006). Likewise, Parthasarathi has argued that work and labour are perhaps the most neglected scholarship in the field of media economy (2018). Amidst the growing discussion of industrial transformation, there is still scant consideration given to the rank and file in news organisations and their changing contributions to the news industry (Hardt and Brennen 1995). At the international level, however, major contributions to labour studies are now emerging from several media scholars, directed towards organisational policy, creative class, immaterial labour, knowledge labour, conditions of labour in the changing digital industry scenarios and in the context of digital capitalism Deuze 2007; Florida 2002; Fuchs 2014; Hardt and Negri 2000; Lazzarato 1996; Mosco and McKercher 2009; Scholz 2012).

The digitisation of the news industry has witnessed "deep changes in labour markets" resulting in cost-cutting (Frayssé and O'Neil 2015). Journalists have been recast as remunerated digital labourers working alongside prosumers involved in free labour (Toffler 1981). On the flip side, the integration of technologies into the newsroom and automation of news production have raised concerns whether technologies would bolster or displace human beings, news credibility and their productivity (David 2015; Soule 1977; Susskind and Susskind 2015). The perceived inherent power associated with journalists in democratic societies is increasingly being challenged by the arrival of social media, algorithms, artificial intelligence (AI) and other disruptive communication technologies (Anderson 2011). Platforms and tools such as Facebook, Twitter, WhatsApp and so on overshadow the distribution process of traditional news industry publishers (Bell et al. 2017) All these rapid changes, occurring as part of convergence, posit that the news industry is at the cusp of transitions and asking for human resources with different skill sets primarily founded in digital ways of handling journalism. Thus, Lanier has argued that technologies do not displace human labour but only reorder it (2014).

The use of social media and the rise of algorithm-based journalism has changed the professional routines of journalists by causing them to engage in multi-skilling. Multi-skilling has caused an increase in workload and a never-ending deadline pressure for reporters. At the same time, the explosive commercialisation of the Internet, especially social media, heralds free labour with the increasing concentration of user-generated content (Terranova 2000). The user-generated content constitutes involuntary coordination or autonomic labour that does not go through a market or monetary system but eventually valourises the social value into financial earnings. As a result, social media spaces and websites become social automaton factory and value is produced in the networked economy (ibid.). The value produced may not be a boomer but it constitutes tiny parts in the long tail of the economies of digital native websites. The rise in the use of messaging apps by individuals and groups has jolted the mainstream media and journalists working within. The will of the political class to delegitimise the mainstream media (Ninan 2019) and generate its own stream of content through social media has redirected the work practices of journalists towards acceding to popular demands.

Against this backdrop, the tasks of a journalist would now include inferring comments posted by citizens, combing through databases to produce stories, ensuring a considerable following in social media, tweeting and so on. It is now more a question of how journalists leverage technologies to execute a multitude of tasks. Further, the coming of technologies has made journalists reconsider their core skills that define their journalistic labour, which is an amalgamation of human labour, watering-down of values and machine-driven algorithmic journalistic labour. In a networked collaboration, journalists aim to form huge collectives and communities of audiences. Users invest hours of their time rendering free service consuming content, which in itself is a viable productive facet of immaterial labour (Lazzarato 1996). On both ends, time thus becomes a crucial material metric that defines the complex form of labour involved in journalistic production. Fuchs has argued that "the secret of Facebook's profits is that it mobilizes billion hours of users' work time (at the level of values) that is unpaid (at the level of prices)" (2012, pp. 714–716). As for time, journalists invest in reflexive time, synchronic time and diachronic time (Siapera and Iliadi 2015). Reflexive time refers to time journalists invest in to monitor their social media accounts; responding to users and their comments is referred to as synchronic time and diachronic time refers to community building activities by journalists. The efforts of journalists in maintaining networks thus constitute surplus value, which is accumulated in the form of social capital in turn valourised by social media platforms.

Another contemporary approach towards studying labour emerges from Actor-Network Theory (Lewis and Westlund 2015), which collects human and non-human actants such as technologies, automated tools and human inputs in an assemblage. Journalists as well as citizens involve themselves in immaterial labour to produce information (Lazzarato 1996). Immaterial labour, for Lazzarato, has two components namely "informational", which deals with skills and know-how journalists need to have to perform their tasks, and "cultural", which leads to the production of cultural standards. Hardt and Negri (2000) defined affective labour as one which involves production of collective subjectivities through networking and human contact. Extending the notion of affective labour to journalism, one could argue how the labour of production is actualised through social media and other digital spaces. Thus a news product is not to be evaluated based on how much time a journalist spends or invests in producing it but it is to be determined by the affective publics and rhizomatic connections the journalist produces through his/her news reports (Papacharissi 2015).

Algorithms and Bots and Multi-skilled Digital Journalism

With the advancement of technology, Aljazairi has claimed that human journalists will be replaced by nonhuman journalists very soon as editors have been replaced by software editing programmes (2016). As today's journalism is more about generating volumes of articles, the role of ro(bots) in journalism is going to be key to news industry. Though journalistic community is very fearful about the introduction of robot, James Kotecki, the Head of Communications at Automated Insights (AI)—an American-based technology company, claimed that he is not aware of any single job that technology has replaced. Nonetheless, in an algorithmic environment, programmers and data analysts are also producing news stories apart from trained journalists. Bots are used to produce bespoken stories based on users' inputs and feedback. In this case, some of the public interest stories are not decided by expert journalists rather than by real-time web analytics. Traditionally, journalists of print media attempted to ignore audience feedback fearing it would affect their news judgement (Aljazairi 2016; Beam 1995). However, the rise of digital platforms and real-time analytics has instituted audience feedback in the reckoning of news production. The use of algorithms not only enables journalists to track users to know what content they access but also informs journalists on what news is to be given. Algorithms are being used to extract social value from the economic asset of Big Data (Just and Latzer 2017). The widespread use of algorithms in almost every Internet application illustrates their acknowledgement and relevance for the digital era (Anderson 2013; Gillespie 2014; Mager 2012; Pasquale 2015). Algorithms as software, and as a structure, institution or an actor, increasingly govern the news industry. Algorithms govern the everyday practices of news production through their material affordances and their interlacing of software, journalists and users.

The onset of multi-platform publishing also requires that journalists are proficient in technical as well as journalistic information gathering and writing skills. Engaging in a multitude of tasks, journalists at the three outlets, produce multimodal stories using mobile phones and other technologies. Typing was earlier considered to be a technical skill that journalists did not have to deal with. However, Suhail, the editor of DoolNews, said that in changed conditions under informational capitalism, journalists are required to multi-task:

> It was not the task of journalists to type, check or proof read the content but gradually changed. But today if journalists know graphic, camera and designing it is an additional credit.... But we expect journalists to be doing multi-tasking. (Interview)

The small team of journalists at DoolNews collects stories from different beats and at the same time churn out more stories to attract larger audience. Suhail expressed that the emphasis on quantity has resulted in downsizing employees and simultaneously in scaling up the responsibilities of a journalist:

> Instead of appointing four or five journalists in different sections, they are now appointing two or three people who can work in all the sections. Thereby the number of employees is reduced, without compromising on the product. (Interview)

Every journalist at DoolNews takes upon himself/herself the responsibility of producing stories as well as editing them for fear of getting most of the content brusquely snipped by editors. The senior correspondent, Shafeeq, said that the editor would have no understanding of the background of the story:

> When the footage of our shot is given to an editor, without our supervision most of its contents are likely to get destroyed. Because the editor doesn't know about the background of the news footage they are editing...the outcome will not be what the reporter might have foreseen. So, in this context, the role of multitasking will be of great use. (Interview)

The journalist also outlined the downside of multitasking as attention is divided between technical skills and information gathering. However, he added that mojo (mobile journalism), has eliminated the need for paying attention to technical details:

> When I went to the field as both the reporter and cameraman, I have to adjust the frame, focus, have to check the audio … while controlling all these, we can't seriously follow the content in the bytes … I think for mojo, there isn't much importance given for perfect framing and other things … But, I am personally a guy who gives importance to visual aesthetics. (Interview)

While journalists have a propensity to handling mobile phones and shooting photos, they are of the view that a dedicated team must be in place to handle videos so that visual aesthetics and sound are taken care of. One of the respondents said that except in emergency situations such as breaking news stories, cameramen should be designated to produce videos. News production cannot be rigidly compartmentalised in a digital economy. The flexible labour practices ushered in by technologies and the extensive labour process of digital news websites and portals are homologous with post-Fordist regimes of flexible accumulation (Compton and Benedetti 2010). DoolNews and Ippodhu use WordPress-enabled Content Management System (CMS). Every journalist in the newsroom has been assigned user credentials to facilitate uploading of news stories. Some of the tasks such as adding editors or new tabs in the CMS are restricted to the admin operating the CMS.

Oneindia, on the other hand, uses Java framework and has a dedicated team of developers to monitor and upload stories in its web portal. However, journalists at its desk have been equipped to handle the portal to ensure that news stories do not wait in the absence of technical persons or during contingencies. Oneindia, being a larger portal, ensures that its technical team does not engage in news production activities. Stating that journalists are from different educational background, a couple of them being engineers, the editor of Oneindia said its desk team consists of engineers who generate news reports. This reflects how journalists with the tag of journalism degree do not have dominance with respect to the production and distribution of content (Aneez et al. 2016). Swetha, a journalist working for Oneindia, opined that a journalist those days relied completely on memory to recollect knowledge about historical events and contemporary moments. Today, individual memory of recollecting events finds its alterity in Google search engines and other digital tools:

> Today, one does not have to depend on memory. We appreciate if someone can recollect 15 years of political history in India or in Tamil Nadu. But, one can access Google and get all the information. (Interview)

The recognition of technical skills of journalists and their ability to produce cultural public good has stretched the production cycle in newsrooms from producing content to distributing it in social media and other channels. With this, multi-skilling has become ineluctable for a journalist in digitally run websites. The current times in digital journalism witnesses the convergence of disparate and diversified newsrooms into an organic site where all media modalities and their functions coalesce.

Social Media and Collaborative Storytelling

Since the digital transitions, social media have taken centre stage impinging daily routines and journalistic roles in digital news start-ups and native news outlets. In the converged news media environment, the coming of social media has changed the relationship between journalists, audience and news organisations significantly. As a result, daily practices of digital journalists are getting restructured and reordered with audience participating in news production through citizen journalism (Jönsson and Örnebring 2011). Further, social media platforms such as Facebook, YouTube, Twitter, Instagram and the messaging app WhatsApp afford horizontal distribution of news stories in contrast to the vertical flow of content to readers favoured by traditional journalism.

All journalists at Oneindia desk are required to have an account in social media such as Facebook and Twitter. The editor of the Tamil edition of the portal said that a journalist who does not use social media is detached from the information world. He stated that virality determines the popularity of news indicating that journalists need to find news stories in and tell stories through social media. Thus, the task of the desk journalists at Oneindia encompasses investing time in keeping a close vigil on trending stories and identifying news reports with human interest value from social media that are later developed into elaborate stories for publication in its news portal. As part of the routine, the team at desk monitors emerging posts and tweets by following the pages of potential newsmakers including politicians and celebrities. Stating that news is not viral, rather virality is news, Arivalagan, the editor of the Tamil edition of Oneindia portal, added:

> Some of the best news reports, short and long, are published by users in social media ... Our desk sources stories that have human interest values from social media pages. They also visit PM's page as information is first released in one's individual pages and accounts ... Journalists need to know the importance of speed and judgement while selecting stories from social media and publishing them online. (Interview)

On the other hand, journalists at DoolNews use less of Twitter for news distribution. According to the editor of DoolNews, Suhail, Twitter is an elite medium and it is mostly used to get updates about celebrities that audience is curious to know.

The social media strategies of Ippodhu for news production and distribution stand out in stark contrast. The digital media outlet has a daily offering of 30-minute live discussion through Facebook live on socially and politically relevant topics. Experts from different fields are invited to talk on contemporary issues and they offer their expertise free acting in the best interest of the community. These programmes are later shared on its official website. At DoolNews, social media are considered to be important sources of regional and local news. The editor of DoolNews said that digitally native websites have stopped depending on national and mainstream news websites for content as the focus has shifted from international and national stories to regional and local stories. More stories are generated from social media compared to field reporting. The editor expressed:

> Presently, social media is the biggest provider of news. Two or three years ago, most of the online media followed a pattern. They copy news stories from national websites and other leading newspapers. Now ...we generally don't go through other national websites because mainly, we are showing local regional news. For us, social media is the main news source. (Interview)

Shafeeq, a senior correspondent at DoolNews, mentioned that the organisation is still translating stories from national websites. He said that DoolNews has a specific social media team where currently one person is involved in monitoring social media pages. That does not remove journalists from following their social media accounts or relieve them from monitoring analytics. On the other hand, journalists have to verify the authenticity of news stories that they intend to publish, localise and rework on. While social media consists of stories, mostly written by independent authors and self-made citizen journalists, they are also the breeding ground for fake news. This puts a heavy burden on journalists to sift fake news from real content. Consequently, the social media engagement of journalists includes publishing and promoting their own stories, sourcing story ideas and also exercising caution and using tools to check if a certain news is authentic or not:

> We get around 100 news stories. Sometimes, we go on reports seen on social media after checking their authenticity. We check the credibility by identifying reliable resources, if possible, we try to collect photographs. (Interview)

Overdependence on social media would have journalists erring yet they cannot divorce themselves from using them. On the other hand, social media have intensified the labour practices of journalists. Interestingly, this has given rise to new digital start-ups only to detect fake news. The editor of Oneindia admits that social media produce a deluge of ingenious and equally fake and misleading content. The senior correspondent of DoolNews said: "We didn't have any technique to check the authenticity of the news. In such cases, we must be vigilant if the news is from social media" (interview). The use of social media is woven around immediacy, which has become the overwhelming priority among online digital journalism. Immediacy in the backdrop of digital ecology redefines the labour practices of journalists who co-opt varied skills such as reporting, editing, scanning through social media pages of celebrities and politicians, monitoring for user feedback and so on. Such an unfailing immediacy would refrain journalists from reflecting on issues and events as they would not have time to work on specific stories eventually producing "churnalism" (Davies 2008). As the senior correspondent of DoolNews put it, journalists at DoolNews use WhatsApp more than Facebook. Shafeeq also said that when DoolNews realised that Facebook alters algorithms for its monetary ends, the digital news outlet preferred WhatsApp to Facebook:

> Facebook changes their algorithm and they are interested in commercial purpose. They reduce the reach on normal post and increase the reach of sponsored ads. They change the algorithm to earn money from us. So, we use WhatsApp widely to overcome it. (Interview)

Audience as Capital

Traditional journalism fashioned a direct correlation between content production and journalistic values. It naturally followed that content produced by journalists, adhering to journalistic values, added to the advertising revenue. In other words, the cultural capital embodied in content production and management of legacy media houses contributed to the economic capital operationalised as revenue generated. By contrast, Ippodhu declares that it practises independent journalism on the grounds that it provides opportunity to readers in the process of news production through social media. Readers are encouraged to produce content in the form of news stories, opinion pieces, photographs or videos. The use of social media has given rise to appropriating stories and story ideas of users resulting in increased unpaid free labour. Journalists at DoolNews and Oneindia have the additional responsibility of monitoring social media pages for trending stories and stories that audience provide through their perspectives. None of the three digital news outlets would consider the cultural capital that they accrue through the mode of production aided by audience participation as free labour. The editor of Ippodhu, Peer, argued that the website is provisioning technology and space to users in order to promote democratic media. He says:

> Yeah, particularly our mobile app is designed in such way that audiences can contribute. It's a participatory journalism exercise, where audiences can contribute on an hourly basis. They can keep writing, they take picture and post on the app, so it's quite interactive and it is easy to use. (Interview)

The participation of users helps Ippodhu, DoolNews and Oneindia in generating traffic while at the same time, some of the comments posted by readers inadvertently become the content or issue to be broached upon for other readers. In both ways, the digital news outlets benefit out of free labour that users render. As a journalist with more than 15 years of experience, the editor of Ippodhu, brings his editorial judgement to bear upon the relevance of user-generated content before choosing them for new story ideas. DoolNews and Oneindia allow journalists to pick news stories from social media according to immediacy and news values. Apart from human selection, algorithms undergirding social media impel readers to produce content and participate in society through sharing and responding to posts. The meeting of algorithms and human journalist underscores the interplay of machines and humans in journalistic processes.

The social value and community-building accomplished through user-generated content form part of affective labour, where journalists and users intermingle in larger spatial economies. On the other hand, experts also contribute their knowledge to Ippodhu and DoolNews through news programmes. Experts invited by Ippodhu to participate in live video discussions are not paid. As Ippodhu editor put it, they render their services realising the motto of independent journalism that the news outlet promotes. This illustrates that all three news outlets rely on a steady stream of content flowing from users, otherwise termed as unpaid contributions. What is produced as news as a public good gets converted into a private property when the traffic data of programmes produced through free and voluntary labour are valourised and monetised, let alone Ippodhu and DoolNews are not bent on raking profits. Unlike Ippodhu, freelancing is not considered free labour at DoolNews. Shafeeq, the senior correspondent at DoolNews, said:

> We also accept freelance stories with payment. Dool has freelancers working on particular subjects like land issues, gender issues and other issues. Some of them are social activists also as they know more about the subject. (Interview)

DoolNews also sources news stories from users. The senior correspondent said: "We are giving a chance for people involved in protest to report their own news. There is a possibility of turning them in(to) reporters and we are utilising the chance" (interview).

Interplay of Algorithmic and Editorial Judgements

The combination of algorithms of Facebook, Twitter's impenetrable application programming interfaces (APIs), and similarly that of Google layered with the interface of WordPress and other software, including ones used by journalists to write and file stories, constitutes the assemblage of algorithms of journalistic practices at Ippodhu, DoolNews and Oneindia. In the digital era, the sustenance of a news website is determined by traffic along with content. To succeed consistently in this race, news organisations have to use different technological innovations and digital arsenals available such as (messenger) bots, automated applications, analytical tools and many more. Google Analytics and Facebook are widely being used by all three news outlets to gauge real time data of visitors and all other details related to user activities. However, Ippodhu, in principle, does not want to have any truck with Google AdSense. Journalists at Oneindia have been trained to take cues from Google Analytics to examine the performance of a news report.

However, selection of news stories is not solely determined by algorithms. News stories that are algorithmically signalled to be attracting considerable audience are also tempered with editorial judgements for their propriety and relevance. When the desk notices that a story purported to do well, a presupposition derived from editorial judgement, has not garnered adequate hits, editors of Oneindia advise desk journalists to "repair" the news stories. Stories are thus not killed but are tweaked to deliver better results in subsequent hours. The headline or the lead paragraph or sometimes the entire content is dressed up as newsworthy stories after they are treated with search engine optimisation techniques. The editorial judgement prevails but the role of Google Analytics in shoring up the news report for better desired results cannot be ruled out. He said: "Judgment is a challenging task. Even if a story does not do good, we will find out how to repair it or explore it further". The labour process here instantiates the intermixing of human and non-human actants, as postulated by the actor-network theory, referred to as ANT, in producing news and sharing it through a distributed environment (Latour 1987). This makes the work of journalists at Oneindia particularly time consuming, having to write headlines for the same story more than once or working with the same report to suit requirements spelt out by analytics.

At Ippodhu, a couple of journalists go to the field to report on socially relevant and political stories whereas others aggregate and curate news content within the office. Ippodhu as an independent digital news platform is an evolving digital news media with a considerable audience following. However, the editor would like to gain popularity and increase user base in future to be able to reach out to advertisers. He bets it on analytics that determines the number of page views, bounce-off rate and time spent viewing an article, among others (Napoli 2014). Peer, the editor of Ippodhu, said that it helps the website in identifying the audience. He uses metrics thrown up by analytics to convince advertisers to buy spaces in the website:

> We have not grown to the extent of growing our numbers to the advertisers …. We have grown up to that we are growing slowly may be two years we will be there … Every editorial meeting we discuss that …you know, why

> we are not being appreciated on this particular news. We do keep record of what is happening, how many people are getting engaged, why not they are getting engaged, how much time they are spending ... all these data we derive from Google analytics and we take it very seriously. (Interview)

DoolNews maintains that journalists have the technological know-how related to web analytics. However, he said that DoolNews does not depend on metrics-based journalism, nor does it want to task journalists with tracking analytics. He felt that analytics data can obscure and botch up quality journalism that it stands for. Thus, editorial judgement of selecting or reporting news stories remains unaffected while a separate team handling analytics uses the data as a baseline to fine-tune content. The editor said that DoolNews always draws its audience through its content and not through its technologies. Apparently, this aligns with the long tail theory of Anderson (2004) by which DoolNews caters to minority tastes and offers greater choices to them. Analytics as a non-human actor in the networked labour at DoolNews still intersects with the judgement of human journalists. However, its role in determining the newsworthiness of stories published is far from predominant:

> In online platforms performance of a news story can be analysed. But sometimes it is confusing and difficult to infer the response of audience. For example, in rural Journalism we take so much effort go to the location stay there and collect news and we learn that specific significant news might not necessarily be even read by them, and they might switch only to the top stories. So in Dool more than the metrics we focus on target audience let it be even a small community, we make sure that a certain section do regularly read our news. We don't give the burden of the analytics to the journalist because it affects the quality. (Interview)

Further, the editor of DoolNews said that tracking analytics amounts to intruding into one's privacy and underscored that ethical journalism should desist from monitoring one's private activities and producing journalistic content accordingly. However, Suhail does not rule out the possibility of incorporating technologies into newsroom practices in future thus illustrating that journalistic practices are emergent and marked by fluidity:

> Since our policies are contingent on delivering news ethically, we do not want to peek into the private spheres of a reader's life as to what s/he likes and deliver customised content by taking cues from analytics or algo-

> rithms ... This is our stand till now but tomorrow the technologies may change ... but we will be transparent in our moves. We already built an audience who are concerned about privacy, which cannot be altered suddenly. (Interview)

The senior correspondent at DoolNews explained that analytics helps in knowing the audience and its preferences better. The agenda is set by the audience and journalists produce what the audience is keen to read. He also said that algorithmic inferences of what the audience would want to read, depending on quantitative data such as number of visits and time spent, are sacrilegious metrics that do not delve into qualitative aspects of the preferences of the audience. The correspondent expressed that editorial judgement is untenable without integrating analytics data into journalism. Shafeeq referred to a meticulously produced investigative report that met with less popularity as opposed to curated entertainment stories attracting huge audience, since

> [i]f we understand what draws people's attention to a topic or its sub-topic, we'll be getting advantage out of it...But at the same time, certain things which analytics give us ... are to be taken seriously and critically. As journalists, we'll be doing our job sincerely by visiting places ... and when we finally make a report on a news story, within 15 minutes a copied material from other source will be a big hit. (Interview)

The responsibilities of the desk team involve accessing software to get information about analytics apart from their regular task of editing stories and giving headlines. Field reporters are fed with this data to produce follow up stories that receive good hits. Sandeep, chief visualiser of Ippodhu explains:

> Those who are working in the desk analyse this data, each and every time they observe which news is read by more number of people. And we try to give follow up stories related to that particular news. So, analytics is done regularly by people on desk. (Interview)

Likewise, Suhail, the editor of DoolNews, pointed out that many media houses shut down holding on to traditional editorial judgement practices and when they failed to realise the salience of new ways of doing journalism apparently including analytics/algorithms. DoolNews altered its strategy from presenting only hyperlocal stories of social and political relevance to paying heed to analytics and publishing stories on entertainment:

> Many media houses, which came recently finally had to shut down. Even Dool, as well. It was saved because there was a change in its strategy. Dool was political at first … But it got registered as a company with having more public interest news. (Interview)

To recapitulate, journalists use a range of digital technologies, tools, apps and social media to produce and deliver news stories. Engaging in a multitude of tasks, journalists in the three outlets produce multimodal stories using mobile phones and other technologies. In a post-Fordist sense, multiskilling has resulted in journalists enjoying their freedom and at the same time has caused newsrooms to shrink with a few journalists in digitally born news websites carrying out multiple tasks. Notably, the use of social media channels such as Facebook, Twitter, YouTube and WhatsApp among others have shaped the journalistic practices at the three outlets. Social media have become the quintessential component in contemporary journalism while one cannot negate the extended labour process they have ushered in for journalists. Analytical tools used by journalists in the three news outlets provide granular and detailed data regarding the shifting trends in news consumption, which become resourceful in strategising the construction and dissemination of news stories. Thus journalism, in today's context, is characterised by a socio-technical formation wherein the exercise of news production is performed by a combination of human (journalists, citizens, etc.) and non-human actors (technologies, algorithm/analytics, etc.) collectively and collaboratively.

Journalistic Practices and Algorithmic Governance

The onset of new media technologies has made the role of a journalist more inclusive pointing to multi-tasking journalistic practices in the digital age. As a result, strait-jacketed classifications of journalists based on their designations and responsibilities are getting erased. What is acknowledged today are the broadening capabilities of a professional journalist to produce information by engaging with social media, analytics, messenger apps, CMS tools and so on. One of the commonalities that Oneindia, DoolNews and Ippodhu share is that all three news organisations outsource a part of their work to freelancers. Further, using social media, they have resorted to transferring some of the burden of creating content to users (Briziarelli 2011). The unpaid labour of users and the user-generated content has had a cascading effect on journalists resulting in layoffs, shrinking editorials and the birth of new digitally native websites. Field reporting for Oneindia is taken care of by freelance content writers. On the contrary, journalists at DoolNews and Ippodhu produce news as well as engage in multi-tasking. Ippodhu does not rely on news agencies but generates its own reports as well as curates stories from other digital sources.

The two news websites and the news portal illustrate that journalists, apart from carrying out institutionalised traditional canons of newsroom practices, have also become content curators and aggregators. While this does not signal the outright collapse of traditional principles, outsourcing of writing news stories of the day by Oneindia bears out that that the digital labour of journalists has altered the institutional scope of the digitally native news industry. Oneindia is founded on the principle of generating content that will in turn beget advertising revenues. The ideologies of DoolNews and Ippodhu are not to get fixated on huge profits but function as alternative news outlets in digital format. Further, they are supported by the funding agency Independent and Public Spirited Media Foundation (IPSMF) on conditions that the two websites would focus on publishing stories of public interest.

DoolNews, Ippodhu and Oneindia use Google Analytics to identify its specific audiences visiting its website. While DoolNews presented that they would like to put editorial judgement before algorithms, the editor accepted that they were open to changes. All three news outlets also derive users' data from social media pages also. All three news outlets focus on producing cultural goods, which are later valourised. All journalists keep tabs on stories that perform well and that do not. Journalists at DoolNews experience precarious conditions as one is not certain which stories would perform. While decisions are made to remove some of the non-performing stories, it does not mean that editorial agency is overshadowed by analytics; rather human intelligence is tempered with technological inputs.

Work does not take place in a specific geographic environment as the spatial nature of the labour process is exacerbated through digital tools used in newsrooms. In this context, labour must be understood in spatial terms where the emphasis is on "spatial economies". The three news outlets have their presence in social media sites such as Facebook, Twitter,

WhatsApp and YouTube. The news outlets have integrated social media extensively into journalistic practices. This negates the idea of newsroom space while multiplying spatial possibilities for news production and distribution across different media and digital tools. Interestingly, the faraway and the nearby, the disparate and the homologous spaces are thrown together in producing affective news spaces. The spatial economies can also be explained by field reporting at Oneindia largely outsourced to freelancers from all over the world. DoolNews publishes articles written by activists and experts. When they are embedded in social media, they acquire a degree of profusion through sharing, collocation and collaboration. The labour thus becomes recursive in which journalists and audience as humans and algorithms, Big Data and digital technologies as non-humans assemble (Latour 2005).

Readers of all three news outlets produce content in the form of news stories, opinion pieces, photographs or videos, apart from sharing and liking, all of which constitute free labour. The editor of Ippodhu said that the news outlet is an independent news media space designed to promote democratic media where people can express their ideas freely. However, looking at it through the lens of Christian Fuch's concept of immaterial labour, readers come across as prosumers. By the logic of prosumption, users are consumers and are also the consumed or they become commodities (Smythe 1981). The labour put in by users and journalists is black-boxed in an environment of impenetrable codes, files and algorithms. All three digital news outlets subsist on the collaborative labour of journalists and users, a combination of waged labour and free labour. Benkler terms the social and collaborative production as commons-based peer production wherein contributors are not compensated (2006). It is also a combination of market production and commons-based peer production in that journalists are paid incentives for performing their tasks while users are encouraged to be part of news production without any financial reward. Free labour performed by users in this context, is part of social-technical assemblages (Terranova 2000).

While co-creation of content by journalists and users might have altered journalistic work, we tend to overlook the precariousness of journalistic work on the one hand and users on the other. The technology such as Facebook is a private property on which users build public goods which are again converted into private good for monetisation. Algorithms of Facebook thus aid in the proliferation of free labour. It is the algorithm of Facebook that journalists work with to collect individuals together and create communities for their news stories. Social media are thus marked by affective (Hardt and Negri 2000) and emotional labour (Hochschild 2003). The affective labour of Ippodhu, DoolNews and Oneindia journalists presuppose their investment of time and effort in building communities on social media. The artillery of technologies used in journalistic practices—which includes software, analytics and other tools founded on algorithms—is driving the automation of labour. Nonetheless, to say that journalists set their fundamental qualities aside and simply succumb to the designs of analytics or algorithms is perhaps little too trite. Advancing a more optimistic ontology, research studies need to recognise the combined capacities of human subjects and algorithmic governance used in the production, distribution and consumption of digital news content.

References

Aljazairi, S. (2016). Robot Journalism: Threat or an Opportunity. Retrieved October 13, 2018, from http://oru.diva-portal.org/smash/record.jsf?pid=diva2%3A938024&dswid=1735.

Anderson, C. W. (2004). The Long Tail. *Wired, 12*(10), 170–177.

Anderson, C. W. (2011). Blowing Up the Newsroom: Ethnography in an Age of Distributed Journalism. *Making Online News, 2*, 151–160.

Anderson, C. W. (2012). What's the Best Model for a Digital News Business? *Columbia Journalism Review, 51*(3), 40–41.

Anderson, C. W. (2013). Towards a Sociology of Computational and Algorithmic Journalism. *New Media & Society, 15*(7), 1005–1021.

Aneez, Z., Chattapadhyay, S., Parthasarathi, V., & Nielsen, R. K. (2016). Digital Transition of Newspapers in India: Dainik Jagran, Hindustan Times, and Malayala Manorama. Reuters Institute for the Study of Journalism. Retrieved January 11, 2019, from https://reutersinstitute.politics.ox.ac.uk/sites/default/files/2017-04/Indian%20Newspapers%27%20Digital%20Transition.pdf.

Asp, K. (2014). News Media Logic in a New Institutional Perspective. *Journalism Studies, 15*(3), 256–270.

Beam, R. A. (1995). How Newspapers Use Readership Research. *Newspaper Research Journal, 16*(2), 28–38.

Bell, E. J., Owen, T., Brown, P. D., Hauka, C., & Rashidian, N. (2017). The Platform Press: How Silicon Valley Reengineered Journalism. Tow Center for Digital Journalism, Columbia University. Retrieved January 18, 2019, from https://academiccommons.columbia.edu/doi/10.7916/D8R216ZZ.

Benkler, Y. (2006). *The Wealth of Networks: How Social Production Transforms Markets and Freedom*. New Haven and London: Yale University Press.

Briziarelli, M. (2011). Neoliberalism as a State-Centric Class Project: The Italian Case. *Continuum, 25*(1), 5–17.
Carlson, M. (2015). The Robotic Reporter: Automated Journalism and the Redefinition of Labor, Compositional Forms, and Journalistic Authority. *Digital Journalism, 3*(3), 416–431.
Coddington, M. (2015). Clarifying Journalism's Quantitative Turn: A Typology for Evaluating Data Journalism, Computational Journalism, and Computer-Assisted Reporting. *Digital Journalism, 3*(3), 331–348.
Compton, J. R., & Benedetti, P. (2010). Labour, New Media and the Institutional Restructuring of Journalism. *Journalism Studies, 11*(4), 487–499.
David, H. (2015). Why are There Still So Many Jobs? The History and Future of Workplace Automation. *Journal of Economic Perspectives, 29*(3), 3–30.
Davies, N. (2008). *Flat Earth News*. London: Chatto and Windus.
Deuze, M. (2007). Convergence Culture in the Creative Industries. *International Journal of Cultural Studies, 10*(2), 243–263.
Diakopoulos, N. (2014). Algorithmic-Accountability: The Investigation of Black Boxes. Tow Center for Digital Journalism. Tow Center for Digital Journalism, Columbia University. Retrieved November 20, 2018, from https://www.cjr.org/tow_center_reports/algorithmic_accountability_on_the_investigation_of_black_boxes.php.
Fisher, E. (2015). 'You Media': Audiencing as Marketing in Social Media. *Media, Culture & Society, 37*(1), 50–67.
Florida, R. (2002). The Economic Geography of Talent. *Annals of the Association of American Geographers, 92*(4), 743–755.
Fraysse, O., & O'Neil, M. (2015). Introduction: Hacked in the USA: Prosumption and Digital Labour. In O. Frayssé & M. O'Neil (Eds.), *Digital Labour and Prosumer Capitalism: The US Matrix*. London: Palgrave Macmillan.
Fuchs, C. (2012). The Political Economy of Privacy on Facebook. *Television & New Media, 13*(2), 139–159.
Fuchs, C. (2014). *Digital Labour and Karl Marx*. New York and London: Routledge.
Gillespie, T. (2014). The Relevance of Algorithms. In T. Gillespie, P. Boczkowski, & K. Foot (Eds.), *Media Technologies: Essays on Communication, Materiality, and Society*. Cambridge, MA: The MIT Press.
Hardt, H., & Brennen, B. (Eds.). (1995). *Newsworkers: Toward a History of the Rank and File*. Minneapolis and London: University of Minnesota Press.
Hardt, M., & Negri, A. (2000). *Empire*. Cambridge, MA: Harvard University Press.
Hochschild, A. R. (2003). *The Commercialization of Intimate Life: Notes From Home And Work*. Berkeley; Los Angeles; and London: University of California Press.
Jönsson, A. M., & Örnebring, H. (2011). User-Generated Content and the News: Empowerment of Citizens or Interactive Illusion? *Journalism Practice, 5*(2), 127–144.

Just, N., & Latzer, M. (2017). Governance by Algorithms: Reality Construction by Algorithmic Selection on the Internet. *Media, Culture & Society, 39*(2), 238–258.

Konieczna, M., & Robinson, S. (2014). Emerging News Non-profits: A Case Study for Rebuilding Community Trust? *Journalism, 15*(8), 968–986.

Lanier, J. (2014). *Who Owns the Future?* New York: Simon and Schuster.

Latour, B. (1987). *Science in Action: How to Follow Scientists and Engineers Through Society*. Cambridge, MA: Harvard University Press.

Latour, B. (2005). *Reassembling the Social: An Introduction to Actor-Network-Theory*. Oxford: Oxford University Press.

Lazzarato, M. (1996). Immaterial Labor. In P. Virno & M. Hardt (Eds.), *Radical Thought in Italy: A Potentia Lpolitics* (pp. 133–148). London: University of Minnesota Press.

Lewis, S. C., & Westlund, O. (2015). Actors, Actants, Audiences, and Activities in Cross-Media News Work: A Matrix and a Research Agenda. *Digital Journalism, 3*(1), 19–37.

Mager, A. (2012). Algorithmic Ideology: How Capitalist Society Shapes Search Engines. *Information, Communication & Society, 15*(5), 769–787.

Mosco, V. (2006). Knowledge and Media Workers in the Global Economy: Antimonies of Outsourcing. *Social Identities, 12*(6), 771–790.

Mosco, V., & McKercher, C. (2009). *The Laboring of Communication: Will Knowledge Workers of the World Unite?* New York: Rowman & Littlefield Publisher, Inc.

Napoli, P. M. (2014). Automated Media: An Institutional Theory Perspective on Algorithmic Media Production and Consumption. *Communication Theory, 24*(3), 340–360.

Ninan, S. (2019, June 7). How India's Media Landscape Changed Over Five Years. Retrieved January 5, 2019, from https://www.theindiaforum.in/article/how-indias-media-landscape-changed-over-five-years.

Örnebring, H. (2010). Technology and Journalism-as-Labour: Historical Perspectives. *Journalism, 11*(1), 57–74.

Papacharissi, Z. (2015). *Affective Publics: Sentiment, Technology, and Politics*. New York: Oxford University Press.

Parthasarathi, V. (2018). Labour Conditionalities. In A. Athique, V. Parthasarathi, & S. V. Srinivas (Eds.), *The Indian Media Economy Vol. 2: Market Dynamics and Social Transactions* (pp. 99–111). New Delhi: Oxford University Press.

Pasquale, F. (2015). *The Black Box Society: The Secret Algorithms that Control Money and Information*. Cambridge, MA: Harvard University Press.

Scholz, T. (Ed.). (2012). *Digital Labor: The Internet as Playground and Factory*. New York and London: Routledge.

Siapera, E., & Iliadi, I. (2015). Twitter, Journalism and Affective Labour. Sur le journalisme, About Journalism. *Sobre jornalismo, 4*(1), 76–89.

Smythe, D. W. (1981). On the Audience Commodity and Its Work. In *Media and Cultural Studies: Keyworks* (pp. 230–256). London: Wiley-Blackwell.
Soule, G. H. (1977). *What Automation Does to Human Beings*. Ayer Co Publisher.
Susskind, R. E., & Susskind, D. (2015). *The Future of the Professions: How Technology will Transform the Work of Human Experts*. Oxford: Oxford University Press.
Terranova, T. (2000). Free Labor: Producing Culture for the Digital Economy. *Social Text, 18*(2), 33–58.
Toffler, A. (1981). *The Third Wave*. New York: Bantam Books.
Wing, J. M. (2008). Computational Thinking and Thinking about Computing. *Philosophical Transactions of the Royal Society of London A: Mathematical, Physical and Engineering Sciences, 366*(1881), 3717–3725.
Wu, L. (2016). Did You Get the Buzz? Are Digital Native Media Becoming Mainstream? *ISOJ Journal, 6*(1), 131–149.

CHAPTER 9

Inequalities in Ride-Hailing Platforms

Ravinder Kumar Verma, P. Vigneswara Ilavarasan, and Arpan Kumar Kar

The business models of the emerging digital economy supposedly provide equal opportunities to all stakeholders in the market. Contrary to this, we argue in this chapter that structural inequalities exist in digital economy interactions. Using the case of ride-hailing platforms (RHPs) Uber and Ola in New Delhi, India, we show that the projected symbiotic relationships between the RHP, the drivers, and the customers are not equally beneficial. Specifically, our study focuses on the rating mechanisms that constitute algorithmic governance within RHP platforms. Our study uses data collected through qualitative interviews with RHP drivers in New Delhi and a sample of the drivers' rating data. The study finds that drivers bear the brunt of consequences within the rating systems. The algorithm appears to replicate traditional critiques of the interactions between workers and employers under capitalism. The mechanism of discipline via the rating systems exerts considerable power over the drivers, but not their customers. We argue that limited resources and unequal power biases in

R. K. Verma (✉) • P. Vigneswara Ilavarasan • A. K. Kar
Indian Institute of Technology Delhi, New Delhi, India
e-mail: ravinderkv1@gmail.com

A. Athique, V. Parthasarathi (eds.), *Platform Capitalism in India*, Global Transformations in Media and Communication Research - A Palgrave and IAMCR Series,
https://doi.org/10.1007/978-3-030-44563-8_9

the digital economy favour the platform operators and customers differently from platform workers.

Ride-hailing platforms (RHPs) have transformed the way taxi services are offered. RHPs have adopted a lean business model with limited or no ownership of assets, by mobilizing human and other physical resources on a large scale to deliver their services. The major players are Ola and Uber in India who are providing daily 3.65 million rides and have more than 1 million drivers (Shrivastava 2019). They have changed the way people book taxis, the technology involved, number of customers and drivers, and precipitated changes in regulations. The ride-haling ecosystem involves the following stakeholders: customers, drivers, platform operators, government, banking institutions, technology partners, and vehicle manufacturers. RHPs, under the ethos of the emerging digital economy, claim to offer equal opportunity for stakeholders. Customers enjoy greater choice, convenience, and access to taxis. RHPs claim to be enabling employment opportunities, along with freedom and choices for drivers. During the initial phase of RHPs, drivers were able to earn more than Rs. 100,000 ($1413.68) per month in India, and many drivers joined RHPs to gain a higher income.

Initially, both drivers and customers were offered substantial incentives by the RHPs. However, as the market has grown, these incentives and offers are being decreased or removed (Ravikumar et al. 2019). As academic research begins to focus upon the maturing phase of RHPs, different perspectives are emerging. Some studies suggest that drivers are exploited and are not able to earn the minimum wage, while other studies suggest that both employment opportunities and automobile sales have increased in certain urban centres. The present study focuses upon algorithmic governance of RHPS, through the reciprocal rating systems used by the RHPs. In the RHP rating system, the customer gives a rating to the driver post trip, and the driver gives a rating to the customer. Drivers are expected to maintain a minimum rating to continue working for the platform, and higher ratings accrue better work allocations. Driver ratings by customers are thus used as inputs for algorithmic governance of the available drivers. The ratings of customers given by drivers are also supposedly used for allotting ride allocations and access to priority services. Alongside the mutual ratings of drivers and customers, the RHP algorithms also employ other parameters, such as availability of taxis, geographical area, number of ride requests in play, and traffic conditions to determine ride allocation.

Digital Platforms, Digital Labour, and Interactions

Digital platforms are intermediaries that connect two or more individuals or groups and enable the online transaction of services between them. The platforms may or may not charge fees for enabling the transaction. The platforms typically use automated data collection and analysis processes to determine the prices, markets, products, and respond to customers. These forms of "platform capitalism" are considered to be a new mode of organizing markets through digital infrastructure and data (Srnicek 2017). Digital platforms have transformed service delivery in many areas like hospitality, mobility, education, social media, and public service (Martin 2016). In terms of capitalization, digital platforms have surpassed the growth of many traditional industries in recent years (Leismann et al. 2013; Matzler and Kathan 2015). In the attendant platform economy, digital labour can be both paid and unpaid, and can be categorized into cloud work and gig work (Heeks 2017). The former is web-based and can be done from any place via the internet, while the latter is tied to a particular location, time, and person. The taxi drivers associated with RHP platforms thus fall under the gig work category, where digital platforms are supported by a flexible, lean, and cost-effective digital labour market (Schmidt 2017).

In this respect, the digital economy is often criticized for extending the exploitative aspects of capitalism, through the casualization of labour, lack of transparency, and unequal sharing of resources. The regulatory ambiguities of digitally mediated operations have also led to charges of tax avoidance, unfair competition, and risk transfers to stakeholders (Martin 2016). Although the digital economy encourages an entrepreneurial environment, individual freedom and work choices, there are many concerns related to a lack of fair work standards and unequal distribution of profits. In the platform economy as a whole, providers of digital labour have mixed experiences of the automated market conditions (Friedman 2014). In many cases, the controlling mechanisms of the digital economy have stripped way the bargaining power of digital labour, resulting in more extensive and arbitrary control over the working conditions of digital labour. Competition among the providers of digital labour is shifting their income standards to a lower level. While negotiating with the fulfilment of immediate needs, and diminishing returns per task, the future sustainability of digital labour appears to be at risk (Malhotra and Van Alstyne 2014). Thus, arguably, the present form of the digital economy is biased towards the operators of digital platforms rather than the producers of goods and services (Graham and Hjorth 2017).

In essence, digital platforms follow variants of a "lean" business model, where there is no direct hiring of employees or ownership of assets. RHPs address their drivers as "partners", and provide no/ limited contracts or liabilities for them, unlike more traditional contractual arrangements between employers and employees (Rosenblat and Stark 2016). At the same time, digital platforms have standardized their business processes around mechanisms where price coordination is attuned to demand and supply in real time (Blal et al. 2018). These processes of optimization operate alongside the algorithmic standardization of their logistical operations. Thus, this business model fosters both cost reduction and faster expansion of the market (Hahn and Metcalfe 2017). Consequently, the following factors are critical for the success of RHPs: increasing the networks of the customers and drivers, effective customer support services, and building the trust of stakeholders (Belk 2014) and retention (Kumar et al. 2018). Consumer loyalty towards platform services is influenced by satisfaction and service quality (Cheng et al. 2018, p. 58; Bijarnia et al. 2020). However, an increasing number of transactions in the digital economy poses a challenge to maintain service quality. Through the use of algorithms, platforms have shifted the burden of service quality standardization to their stakeholders. In the case of RHPs, this is primarily achieved through peer to peer ratings. Here, managerial quality control is replaced by algorithm based instructions for the management of drivers (Gandini 2019; Schmidt 2017). Consequently, the inclusion and exclusion of service providers and recipients in the digital economy are determined by the inputs of ratings, feedback, and work history. The standardization of operations via algorithmic governance leads to disparities of equality between digital labour and customers, and to the compartmentalization of production and consumption from the cognition of individuals and society. In some instances, there is moral injury inflicted, where the algorithmic processes of platform businesses conceal the logics of their operations from their users, workers and the wider society (Hill 2019).

Ride-Hailing Platforms (RHPs) in Delhi

The significant players in ride-hailing space are Ola and Uber in India. Ola started its operation in 2010–2011 and is present in 110 cities. Uber has operations in India since 2013 and it is currently operating in 40 cities. Before the arrival of RHP in India, taxi services were offered by licensed "black and yellow" (*kaali-peeli*) taxis, and by few "radio taxi" operators such as Meru and Mega cabs. There are no road side hailing taxis in New Delhi. Customers were thus dependent on neighbourhood taxi stands, or radio taxi services. New taxi regulations were introduced in Delhi to recognize radio taxis, under the Radio Taxi Scheme in 2006, Economic Radio Taxi Scheme 2010, and City Taxi Scheme 2015. The latter regulations also recognized digital platforms in transportation services (Transport-Dept 2015). In New Delhi, the transportation sector is regulated by the Delhi transport department under the Motor Vehicles Act 1988. The government exercises its control on the number of taxis in operation in the city, location of operations, taxi permits, and calculation of fares. They also regulate parameters such as vehicle age, mechanical condition, and fuel used, and ensure the compulsory instalment of devices like electric meter, global positioning system (GPS), security button, and fire extinguisher.

The advent of RHPs provided doorstep taxi services, where customers can book taxis using their smartphone application (app). The RHP app calculates the approximate fare and connects the customer with a nearby matching taxi. If the driver accepts the ride request, he then moves towards the rider's pick-up location using the GPS instructions enabled in the RHP app. The controlling mechanisms differ fundamentally between traditional taxi players and RHP taxis, which are based upon peer review of service quality, digital records of trips, and dynamic pricing in real-time. After reaching the customer's pick-up location, the driver starts the ride [in the case of Ola ride, by asking the one-time password (OTP) shared with the customer, the driver puts the OTP in the app to start the trip]. After reaching the drop location, the RHP app indicates the arrival and trip completion function appears in the app that shows due fare. The payment can be made in online and offline modes. After the trip completion, a rating option pops up in the app of the driver and the customer. Algorithmic taxi controls have now become a multi-polar mechanism under the ambit of ride-hailing platforms (RHPs), the state transportation department, and central government regulations.

Rating System in RHPs

RHPs have a reciprocal rating system where, after the completion of the ride, the customer rates the driver and the driver rates the customer. Above this, the RHP operators offer customer care support and in-app support for both drivers and customers. RHP driver rating systems have different specifications: In case of Ola, customers have up to five stars rating options for the drivers. They can also opt for a compliment from among a list that includes pre-defined options like "polite and professional driver", "on-time pick-up", "comfortable feature-rich car", "driver familiar with the route", and "value for money", or "my reason is not listed", with an option to add any other reason/comment in the given space. In case of Uber, customers can give up to five stars, and they can add complements (badges) like "six-star service", "expert navigation", "great attitude", "neat and clean", "great conversation", "hero", "great amenities", or they can write another compliment. In the case of Ola, only cumulative star ratings of drivers are visible to other customers while booking. In the case of Uber, along with the star ratings, a detailed rating of the driver is visible, which includes ratings, the number of trips completed, six stars received by the customers, duration of the association with the RHP, badges received and comments. To rate the customer, in both Ola and Uber, drivers can choose out of five stars and comment about the customer. An example of an Uber driver's ratings is presented in Table 9.1.

In this sample Uber driver rating, out of the total lifetime trips of 1317, a total of 662 trips were rated by the customers. Around 50% of the customers gave a rating to the driver. Besides ratings, the driver received 12 comments and 58 badges, which includes following badges: 436 stars badge, 9 great attitude badge, 3 hero badge, 3 neat and clean badge. The RHP provides online and offline training to the drivers on service delivery instructions. Training involves instructions for the driving behaviour, reaching the pickup location on time; wishing and opening the gate for the customers, keeping the luggage, maintaining a clean car and keeping the air conditioner in a good condition.

Table 9.1 Sample ratings of an Uber driver

Number of stars given by the customers	*Percentage of customers (%)*
5	86
4	8
3	2
2	1
1	3

Digital Records: Algorithmic Management

Algorithmic management goes beyond the digitalization of taxi services. Data inputs include customer details, feedback about drivers and customers, taxi movements, speed of taxis, type of taxis, records of taxis, documentation of drivers' registration, information on routes, real-time traffic records, pick-up and drop location, real-time information of demand and availability of cabs. The RHPs use these data points to manage their operations. To maintain the service quality and standards, RHPs use the digital records of the ratings and feedbacks as inputs to improve service delivery for the drivers and customers. These ratings and feedback are acting as the inputs for the algorithmic system for the drivers, and it decides the amount and frequency of work, type of customers (low- or high-rated customers), and service type of ride requests. Similarly, for the customers, the algorithmic system will decide and allocate a taxi with a low- or high-rated driver in less or more duration of time. The rating records of the drivers influenced the work they received. If a driver has good ratings, then the driver receives a good number of rides requests. One of the drivers mentioned that

> the ratings influence the number of rides received by me. Now I have low ratings, and I was not receiving as many ride requests as I used to receive previously. To get a good number of ride requests, I need to drive properly for the next 3–4 months to improve my ratings. (Interview)

The number of algorithmic inputs to decide the service rules/standards is higher for drivers than customers. If drivers have good driving behaviour and fewer cancellations, then that results in good ratings. Overall the ratings that a driver gets is decided by the customers, and the company policies, and it is influenced by factors including cancellation of rides, complaints, and diversity in service delivery (Uberinsights 2019). Drivers need to maintain a minimum rating to receive a specific type of service request. Many times the ride-hailing online applications fail to judge the real conditions well. The algorithmic errors or biases often result in inconvenience for the drivers. There are times when there is a mismatch between the drivers' data and that of the RHP. These differences in the data and errors in the software make the driver suffer. One of the drivers mentioned:

> I dropped a passenger by driving 15 km, whereas the RHP app was showing only 5 km of the distance between the pickup and drop location. RHP app calculated fare for 5 km, which was around Rs. 114 ($1.59), whereas that should be around Rs. 300–350 ($4.18–4.88). (Interview)

Even after raising a complaint with the RHP, the driver had to bear the loss in this case. In many such cases, the company fails to empathize with the driver's situation, sometimes leading to monetary loss and state of dissatisfaction towards the work. The issues seem to be more in the shared cab services where more than one passenger can book the same taxi. Each of the commuters might get picked and dropped in different locations and pay different fares. In shared services, the drivers and customers do not have much control over the ride allocations. The app allocates the taxis and routes. Once the driver accepts the ride request, the app takes over. The probability of a mismatch with the real conditions remains high, often because of location marker errors and poor coverage of mobile phones and the practical inability of following multiple instructions while driving:

> The app [RHP] accepted a share ride request and cab was moving with other share passengers. After reaching the destination of customers, the app [RHP] was showing that I have dropped three share customers instead of two and deducted money from my account. However, I did not receive any money from the invisible passenger, but I had to pay the commission to the company [RHP]. (Interview)

This driver mentioned that he complained about the incidence to the RHP, but the RHP apparently told him that profit and loss is a part of the business and drivers ought to deal with their losses. Many times, drivers also have to deal with the insensitive behaviour of the customers. One driver mentioned:

> We are supposed to pick and drop the customers based on the location mentioned in the app. The same is not possible always, for instance, customers call the cab inside the narrow streets and it is tough to get inside such narrow streets. Customers keep telling that they kept the location of their house doorstep. (Interview)

The GPS location tracker is not always able to comprehend cab movement feasibility. To quote a driver: "if we get stuck in a street and cause damage to the taxi, we have to bear the losses." RHP taxis also have to pay an entry fee to enter some locations, like state boundaries and airports. If there is a mismatch between the customer location and the one that the app is indicating, the driver ends up paying the stipulated amount. Another kind of monetary loss for the driver is when the customer books on cash payment and later cancels. This matters when the driver has already paid to access the location. A driver narrated:

> I entered the terminal 1 of the New Delhi airport by paying an entry fee of Rs. 150 ($2.09). When I called the customer, then the customer replied that he was standing at terminal 2. I told the customer that the location of the pickup is terminal 1, then the customer cancelled the ride. I have to pay the entry fee from my pocket as the company did not receive any money, then they [RHP] will not pay to us. (Interview)

Ownership of Resources

In theory, driver ownership of resources (as the means of production) acts as a buffer to absorb the shocks of inequalities in the digital economy. Thus, the patterns of resource ownership aspect become critical to understanding power relations in the digital economy. In our research, we found various types of resource ownership amongst RHP drivers, including the following:

1. The driver owns the taxi and gets the net income after deducting RHP commission and taxi maintenance cost.
2. RHP owns the taxi and provides it to one driver on rent. The driver pays a daily rent (around Rs. 1000 ($14.01), depending on the taxi type) to RHP, RHP commission and bears the fuel cost. Uber lets the drivers have an option to convert the taxi in their name after three years.
3. RHP owns the taxi, provides it on rent and multiple drivers use same taxi. One driver takes a cab from RHP on daily rent and two or more drivers are driving the cab on a shared basis. In this category, the cab is running for 24 hours and cost to the drivers are daily rent, fuel cost, and RHP commission.
4. A third-party vendor owns the taxi and hires a driver. The driver gets a monthly salary and the owner takes care of taxi-related expenses.

Based on the nature of resource ownership, ratings have a different impact upon drivers. A higher grade of resource ownership makes the driver more accountable for its ratings. In contrast, where resources are owned by the RHP or a third party drivers are less worried about their ratings and work relations. We were told:

> It is not profitable to hire a driver to drive for the company [RHP]. A salaried driver is not/less worried about the work, even if he does not work, then also he will get a salary in the month-end. Also, a hired driver would not go to those places where chances of getting rides are higher. (Interview)

On the other hand, higher grade of ownership can potentially work in favour of the driver, since it provides flexibility in terms of income opportunities and time resource management. If the driver owns a taxi and other liabilities related to payment of the loan and rent are low, then he can potentially be in a better position to negotiate with other aspects of life like family and health. To quote a driver:

> I am the owner of this taxi, and I do not have to pay any loan to the bank. I am working for 10–12 hours starting at 8 am, and I return by 7–8 pm. I am spending time with my family, children, and I do not bother about completing the incentive target. (Interview)

Resource ownership becomes a significant factor in calculating the potential work stress for a driver working with the RHPs. This is important, since frequent incidents causing stress and monetary loss drain a driver's resources and energy and lead to job dissatisfaction. One of the drivers mentioned:

> I am working with the app [the RHP] for the last three years. Once I repay the taxi loan, then I will convert this taxi into a private car and will leave this driving profession. (Interview)

In the ride-hailing ecosystem, the platforms operators initial focus was on increasing the number of drivers and customers. Thus, this driver also noted that he was dissatisfied with the RHP due to their reduction of incentives and increases in the number of taxis, which forced drivers to work for longer hours to achieve their income targets. Systematically, the increasing number of drivers and their investment in vehicles via financing has impelled a power shift towards RHPs and customers. Another driver mentioned that he needs to complete 48 trips in four days to get an incentive, "[T]oday is the last day to complete my incentive target, and I need to work for longer hours, else my whole incentive will go away."

Power Relations in the RHP Ecosystem

RHPs require drivers and customers to regulate the service quality through instigating a reciprocal mechanism between the rating system and incentives regime. However, the drivers, whom RHPs refer to as "business partners", claimed that while customers concerns are listened to, those of driver-partners are not, since

> [n]ow, many taxis are working with the company [RHP], and the company [RHP] will not be hurt if some of the cabs stopped working. However, our interest is at the stake as we have to repay the bank loan and earn a living. (Interview)

Though RHP claims to provide a minimum business guarantee to drivers, with increasing number of drivers, the dependency on RHP has created an environment of unequal bargaining power between the drivers, RHP and customers. A driver lamented:

> [C]ompany [RHP] will not do anything to customers but reduce our incentives and keep penalty on us. Company [RHP] should put a penalty on customers for their misbehaviour. But RHP representatives are saying, how we can track the customers? In some cases, when customers are not paying ride fare. After making a complaint against such a customer, even then, the company [RHP] will not do anything. (Interview)

In New Delhi, many drivers are migrating on a daily and weekly basis from neighbouring states like Uttar Pradesh, Haryana, Rajasthan, and Punjab. These migrant drivers tend to have lesser resources than New-Delhi-based drivers. New Delhi drivers have opportunities to work simultaneously with other firms or can shift to a regular job, which offers them more bargaining power. Migrant drivers have limited choices and are dependent on the RHP system. The growing contingent of migrant labour has also shifted the power balance towards RHPs and customers. One driver said:

> I migrated from Uttar Pradesh and living along with other drivers in a rented room in Delhi. I borrowed money to pay for a taxi. Now I have financial liabilities for repayment of taxi and support my family. My native place has no employment. I must work here. Though I like the app [RHP] driving, which enables me to earn. (Interview)

The differences in driver's ratings are also an institutional cause of inequalities. Lower-rated drivers receive delayed ride requests, often from low-rated customers, while high-rated drivers get access to high-rated customers and more frequent ride offers. One driver said that when he has low ratings, "I need to move to different locations to get the ride requests". Another driver with a rating of 4.84 said: "I am receiving the rides request in advance (before completing the existing trip), and sometimes I do not have time to eat food, and I need to sign out from the app [RHP] to eat food." The relationship between ratings and work exacerbates inequalities during peak hours, and in surcharge zones, where bargaining power accrues to high-rated drivers rather than low-rated drivers.

The use of online portals to raise grievances is prominently oriented towards customers. The details of errant drivers are often revealed by customers in public forums (such as social media platforms). In the case of Ola, a total of 7098 complaints were registered online, out of which 120 got resolved, and most of those complaints were filed by the customers (Consumercomplaints.in 2019). The RHPs appear to treat the grievances of customers and drivers on an unequal basis. Based on customer complaints, drivers are penalized by monetary deductions, reduced work and the blocking of drivers' accounts. To remain on RHP platforms, drivers need to maintain at least four star ratings, which is just one star less than the highest possible. Below that level, a driver's account will be deactivated. This treatment of drivers causes them to question their agency within the ride-haling ecosystem:

> Company [RHP] is putting all kinds of restrictions on drivers. Now we caught in the web, what kind of business partners we are? If the company [RHP] is not able to resolve our issues. Drivers are listening to both customers and the company [RHP]. What else can we do? We have to work. (Interview)

Ratings influence the drivers' position and perception about the relations with the customers and RHP. Drivers feel that they are dependent on the customer feedback. To quote: "Yes, rating influences us; we always remain in fear that company [RHP] can remove us." Concerns about ratings make drivers nervous about raising any of their own concerns. RHPs provide instructions to drivers about problem behaviours by customers, like smoking in the taxi, using abusive language, and not settling fares before starting a shared ride. However, raising their concerns about such behaviours by customers remains difficult for drivers:

> The feedback system made us dependent on the customers. The moment customers entered the cab and we remain in fear. Despite our good service, customers give fewer ratings. What is our fault? In some cases, customers misbehave and make the wrong complaint against me, then company [RHP] penalizes me. (Interview)

Drivers fear that customers can file false complaints against them and a lack of responsiveness by the RHPs can leave the drivers frustrated. One of the drivers told us:

> Once a customer filed a wrong complained against me. Then I received a call from the company [RHP] to know about the incidence. Then I told the whole incidence then RHP executive told me to continue driving and behave properly without keeping any penalty on me. Despite the wrong complaint, RHP cannot do anything to the customer. (Interview)

The RHP operators' response to the drivers' grievances and the inability of RHP to control customer behaviours puts drivers in a weaker position. The biased redress process leads to dissatisfaction. The drivers' dissatisfaction results in the attrition of drivers or the joining of other RHPs (Variyar and Sachdev 2019). A driver shared the following account:

> My previous RHP put penalties on me and deduct money from my account. They [RHP] are not responding properly and I was not able to understand why they are doing so. Therefore, I left that company [RHP], and my current ride-hailing platform has a transparent payment system. (Interview)

Drivers invariably give higher ratings to the customers because they believe that customers ratings are very important for them. Most of the drivers said that they always give high ratings to customers. To quote a driver: "Even if a customer misbehaves, I am giving five stars to them. We are driving with the company to get work and earn our living." The impact of instances of dissatisfaction is felt differently through reciprocal ratings by drivers and customers. If the driver receives lower ratings from customers, then that will reduce the driver's overall rating, negatively impacting their ride offers. In case of the customers, however, low ratings from the drivers have little or no impact upon their access to the service. One of the drivers expressed his dissatisfaction with some of the ratings he had received from the customers and was angry about the rating system, saying: "Why should I give five stars to customers when they are giving fewer ratings to me?"

Regulation, Inclusion, and Exclusion

In India, regulatory institutions are different across issues relating to labour, transportation, and consumer grievances. RHPs are registered as a technology company and drivers are designated as partners of the firm. Due to this configuration, public transportation laws do apply to drivers, but not to the RHPs. Critically, there are no labour-related regulatory obligations for the RHPs, and the service conditions of drivers are primarily determined by their algorithmic instructions. Consequently, the working conditions RHP drivers are not regulated by labour laws, despite the RHP effectively controlling their labour through algorithmic management. RHP algorithms determine the number and type of rides a driver can take, who can enter the platform and the payments received. Further, the rating system is a quality mechanism for managerial control over drivers. If a driver's rating falls below a certain point, then an automatic training session is started by the app. Without completing that session, a driver cannot drive for the RHP. Despite not being considered as employers, RHPs also manage drivers' behaviour through their training of drivers. RHPs have details of driver's account, their movements, trips, records of driving pattern and duration spent in the RHP system. The digitalization of services makes it difficult for a deactivated driver to leave RHP and re-join later using a similar license or documents. Other than documented identity, RHP drivers are also required to prove their identity using face recognition technology. If a driver's account is deactivated due to a complaint or low rating, the driver needs to visit RHP office to receive further training or a warning.

In the digital economy, peer to peer ratings enable the service quality and building trust in the system through discipline and control mechanisms. RHP, through ratings controlling the drivers and customers' inclusion and exclusion. RHPs have more control over the drivers than the customers. RHP control leads to the experience of inclusion and exclusion by the drivers, not by the customers. In the case of drivers, when ratings fall below a standard, then the driver will be removed from the platform. In terms of control, RHP imposed penalties on drivers, reduce their ratings, reduce their work, and give rewards to higher-rated drivers. RHP driver mentioned that "based on the customer ratings and feedback, we are receiving work. Now my rating is good and receiving ride requests before completing the existing trip. Previously advanced ride request was stopped and started again after improvement in ratings." Ratings influence the amount of work and kind of work received by digital labour and subsequent continuance in the platforms. Drivers need to maintain a minimum of 4.7-star ratings to be eligible to deliver specific services like prime and rental services. One of the drivers was saying that to improve his ratings, he needs to work correctly for the next three months: "I have to drive without cancelling the rides and take a greater number of rides to improve my ratings to receive a prime ride request."

The relations between the drivers' ratings and work they received also determine their incentives. According to a driver there are two targets to meet in a week—four days' duration from Monday to Thursday to complete 40 trips to get an incentive of Rs. 1500 ($20.98) and a duration of three days from Friday to Sunday to complete 44 trips to receive an incentive of Rs. 1800 ($25.17). The high or low ratings of drivers determine work allocation, and thus the capacity to achieve their targets. Ride allocation also depends upon the kind and quality of cars owned by the drivers. RHPs favour new taxis compared to old taxis and taxis owned by them. One driver mentioned that "company gives more ride requests to new taxis compare to the old taxis". Another driver added: "Suppose, if two taxis are standing. Then ride request will come first on company taxi rather than another driver taxi [out of those two taxies, one taxi belong to RHP and other is of driver]." These strategies serve the RHP's interests but work against a group of drivers. The ratings determine the exclusion from the exclusion. Once a driver excluded, then it is difficult to reregister with the same driving license without intervention by the RHP. Some drivers were driving using other's accounts as their accounts are blocked.

Drivers are not allowed to offer prime services when their ratings fall below 4.7 stars, unlike the customers. However, one of the drivers mentioned that ratings have little effect on his business. When his rating reduced to 4.64, RHP stopped particular services like prime and rental, he is unaware of why he is not getting prime and rental bookings which he used to receive in the past. The exclusion of drivers to offer a particular type of taxi service further excludes them from achieving their incentive targets. The cancellation of rides leads to loss for both drivers and customers. However, the effective penalty is higher for the drivers compared to the customers. Drivers need to bear the physical, psychological, and financial loss in the cancellation of rides. To control their drivers' behaviour, RHPs allow only a limited number of cancellations by drivers, around 10% of the total rides. Thus, if we consider the incentive target, then drivers need to complete around 10–12 rides a day, from RHP10% cancellations relaxation to a driver account to one ride. Drivers drive for 3–5 km on an average to reach the customers' pickup locations. Customers can cancel the ride within 5 minutes of booking without any cancellation fee. In many cases, the driver does not receive any compensation. In contrast, the driver accepted the ride, prepared mentally to have a trip, already started towards the customer's pick-up location, and covered some distance but receive no money if a customer cancels the ride. One of the drivers mentioned:

> I was about to reach the pickup location of the customer; then the customer cancelled the ride. In that case, the company [RHP] will not give anything to me. To receive the cancellation fee, I need to reach the pick up location and wait there before cancellation. Platform [RHP] even take their commission from the cancellation fee. In the cancellation fee of Rs. 42 ($0.59) out of which they (RHP) keep Rs. 11 ($0.15) with them and give Rs. 31 ($0.43) to the driver.

In some cases, customers cancel the rides after five minutes, on the basis that the driver has exceeded the estimated arrival time. In such cases, RHPs waive the cancellation fee for customers. This also leads to RHPs reducing the drivers' ratings and/or penalizing them or suspending their accounts. The drivers do get a chance to prove themselves not guilty, by giving their reason for the delay and requesting the removal imposed penalties. One driver mentioned an incidence, where the RHP imposed a penalty on him because a customer claimed that the driver exceeded the estimated arrival time. The driver raised the concern with the RHP, who checked their records to establish that the driver's cab was stuck in a traffic jam, and then removed the penalty. However, drivers do not always get an opportunity to relay their grievances. In most cases, algorithmic governance determines their income, completion of incentive targets, digital records and freedom of work. These controlling mechanisms thereby separate the human elements from the responsibility of management and reduce human services to a set of data standards for algorithmic inputs.

Lessons for the Digital Economy

The digital economy in India is flourishing in different sectors like e-commerce, education, mobility, public sector, and hospitality. The Indian economy is facing challenges of decreasing the growth of employment in the organized sector decreasing GDP growth rate (GoI 2019a). The majority of the jobs are supported by the unorganized sector (GoI 2018). The unorganized sector jobs lack economic stability with no or little social security measures. The state of micro, small, and medium enterprises (MSMEs), which have a significant share of employment (RBI 2019), is worrisome with declining growth or rampant closing of MSMEs (Kandavel 2018). The variation in the minimum wages in India for different kinds of jobs (GoI 2019b) leaves more significant space for the digital economy to exploit the labour. In the above economic background, the digital economy has created jobs in the market, but the quality of these jobs is questionable. We might argue, however, that digital economy firms are still in an initial stage, and struggling to achieve their breakeven point (ET-Rise 2019). To sustain their operations, massive funding has to be raised from private markets. Nonetheless, in the initial disruption of the existing market, good incentives were offered to attract the customers and drivers. These incentives, however, have proved not be a perennial feature of ongoing business strategies. Consequently, the gradual removal of incentives has reduced the income of drivers as the market becomes established. By providing only limited or no incentives for the drivers and customers, the RHPs are re-focusing on profits or, at least, reducing their operating losses (ET-Rise 2019).

The differences in the laws in developed and developing countries lead to a different digital economy ecosystem. In India, where the state transportation department documents the taxis, drivers need to abide by the regulations to register with the RHP. In the West, regulations permit private cars to operate with the RHP. In India, the car should be registered as a commercial vehicle with yellow number plate and have an emergency button inside the taxi, a GPS, and a taxi meter (Vigneswara Ilavarasan et al. 2018). Recently the Indian government has allowed private driving license for RHP drivers (Das 2018). The limited resources ownership (Erickson 2018), strict control over the drivers and differential treatment to the customers have resulted in unequal space to the drivers. In India, many RHP drivers are the first-time drivers and migrants from poor economic background. The unequal treatment is hurting the drivers' interests, despite that drivers continue with RHPs due to limited employment opportunities elsewhere. As a consequence of algorithmic governance, drivers give ratings to all the customers and are mostly higher ratings. However, around 50% of the customers are rating the drivers. To improve the rating, drivers need to work more as only half of customers are rating. The drivers have an evident and ongoing fear of exclusion, a sense of limited inclusion, and feeling of dependency.

Thus, it seems clear that algorithmic management in the digital economy puts the burden on the drivers. This burden on the drivers is further amplified due to differential resource ownerships (Erickson 2018; Varma 2017). The customers do not share the drivers' imperatives deliver the desired quality services, negotiate road traffic conditions, manage number of work hours, maintain drivers' logs in the app, account for number of kilometres driven, absorb losses from time spent stuck on congested roads, idle time without ride requests, fluctuating cost of fuel in the car, calculating amount of money earned as profits, amount of money paid as commission to RHP and taxi documentations and so on. The experience of taxi arrival is far different for drivers and customers, which means the apparent congruence of rating systems is misleading. The ignorance of customers regarding the physical logistics of taxi movement, margins and operational processes while giving ratings to drivers often leads to biased inputs in the algorithmic evaluation of drivers' services. Our conclusions are that these digital economy inequalities are a direct result of platforms policies and the environment of operations. This is not to say that the previous transport economy was not similarly marked by more or less institutionalised inequalities. The emergence of RHP operators in Delhi has clearly brought changes in both the travel behaviour of the customers and the driving behaviour of the drivers. However, these changes have been largely favourable for the customers at the expense of RHP drivers. Based on the insights gained from the research, we provide our conclusions under the following points: algorithmic management, resource, power relations, institutions and control:

1. Algorithmic discipline has transformed the relationships between consumers, RHP, and drivers. The inputs received by the algorithmic system determine a system where drivers have the limited voice, and drivers are dissatisfied with algorithmic errors and responses from their RHP. The difference between the algorithmic system and reality result in unfavourable conditions for drivers.

2. The ownership of resources creates inequalities, where drivers with limited financial liabilities are in a better position to deal with risks and losses. Resource ownership also influences the freedom of drivers to manage their time and physical resources. The bargaining power further of drivers is also limited by factors like migration and other employment opportunities.
3. The standardization of service delivery through the ratings mechanism creates a power imbalance between drivers and customers. Ratings have no or limited consequences for the customers, whereas drivers are dependent on the ratings. In the RHP ecosystem, power relations are enforced by real-time data and individualised regulatory mechanisms, and the interactions between the RHP, customers, and drivers indicate unequal relations and voices.
4. There are multiple institutional arrangements for drivers, but only limited regulation of RHP operators. Previously existing taxi systems in New Delhi maintain by multiple regulatory bodies for the regulation of labour, taxis, grievances, training, incumbent taxis, and travel agencies. The lack of regulations for RHPs provides them with operational freedom, but it increases the regulatory burden and economic dependency of their drivers.

Within the RHP ecosystem, the inequalities between multiple actors results in unequal resources, agency, and levels of control. Despite their technological innovations, RHPs are appear to be recreating traditional inequalities within the digital economy. Despite the presence of such inequalities, people continue to join the digital economy due to limited options and means. Nonetheless, we hope that operators of digital platforms may use these findings to fashion a more representative environment, and to bridge the gap between algorithmic governance and human workers. Similarly, in setting policy directions, the government should consider how reducing these inequalities should be balanced with efficiency, accountability, and the interests of stakeholders and investors in the platform economy.

Acknowledgements We thank the audiences and jury at the International Conference on Digital Economy at IIM Raipur, 2019, where the initial version of this chapter was presented. We are thankful to the Cities Programme organized by the Centre for the Implementation of Public Policies Promoting Equity and Growth (CIPPEC) for funding the project.

References

Blal, I., Singal, M., & Templin, J. (2018). Airbnb's effect on hotel sales growth. *International Journal of Hospitality Management*, 73(July 2017), 85–92. https://doi.org/10.1016/j.ijhm.2018.02.006.

Bijarnia S., Vigneswara Ilavarasan P., Kar, A.K. (2020). Comparing SERVQUAL for Transportation Services in the Sharing Economy for Emerging Markets: Insights from Twitter Analytics. In: Rana N. et al. (eds) Digital and Social Media Marketing. Advances in Theory and Practice of Emerging Markets. Springer, Cham. https://doi.org/10.1007/978-3-030-24374-6_9.

Cheng, X., Fu, S., & de Vreede, G. J. (2018). A mixed method investigation of sharing economy driven car-hailing services: Online and offline perspectives. *International Journal of Information Management, 41*(10), 57–64. https://doi.org/10.1016/j.ijinfomgt.2018.03.005.

Consumercomplaints.in. (2019). Ola Cabs/ANI Technologies Customer Care. Retrieved December 4, 2019, from https://www.consumercomplaints.in/ola-cabs-ani-technologies-b106650.

Das, M. (2018, April 18). Now, Cabbies can Drive with Regular Licence. Retrieved November 2, 2019, from https://www.thehindubusinessline.com/economy/now-cabbies-can-drive-with-regular-licence/article23590172.ece.

Erickson, A. (2018, March 20). India's Uber Drivers Went on Strike because They're Making $3 a Day. *The Washington Post.*

ET-Rise. (2019, February 1). Ola Halves Losses, Revenue Up 61%. *Economic Times.*

Gandini, A. (2019). Labour Process Theory and the Gig Economy. *Human Relations, 72*(6), 24–25.

Gerald Friedman. (2014). Workers without employers: shadow corporations and the rise of the gig economy. *Review of Keynesian Economics, 2*(2), 171–188.

GoI. (2018). *Economic Survey 2017–2018 Volume II.* New Delhi: Government of India.

GoI. (2019a). *Economic Survey 2018–2019 Volume II.* New Delhi: Government of India.

GoI. (2019b). Minimum Wages Order, Pub. L. No. File No. 1/36 (1)/2019-LS-II, 10 (2019). Government of India, New Delhi.

Graham, M., & Hjorth, I. (2017). Digital Labour and Development: Impacts of Global Digital Labour Platforms and the Gig Economy on Worker Livelihoods. *Transfer: European Review of Labour and Research, 23*(2), 135–162.

Hahn, R., & Metcalfe, R. (2017). The Ridesharing Revolution: Economic Survey and Synthesis. Oxford University Press, IV (More Equal by Design: Economic design responses to inequality), 1–19. Retrieved from https://www.brookings.edu/wp-content/uploads/2017/01/ridesharing-oup-1117-v6-brookings1.pdf.

Heeks, R. (2017). Digital Economy and Digital Labour Terminology: Making Sense of the "Gig Economy", "Online Labour", "Crowd Work", "Microwork", "Platform Labour", etc. *Development Informatics. Working Paper 70.*

Hill, D. W. (2019). The Injuries of Platform Logistics. *Media Culture and Society, 42*(4), 521–536. https://doi.org/10.1177/0163443719861840.

Kandavel, S. (2018, June 8). What Revival? Close to 50,000 MSMEs Shut Up Shop in Tamil Nadu in Past Year. *The Hindu.*

Kumar, V., Lahiri, A., & Dogan, O. B. (2018). A strategic framework for a profitable business model in the sharing economy. *Industrial Marketing Management*, 69(February 2018), 147–160. https://doi.org/10.1016/j.indmarman.2017.08.021.

Leismann, K., Schmitt, M., Rohn, H., & Baedeker, C. (2013). Collaborative Consumption: Towards a Resource-Saving Consumption Culture. *Resources, 2*(3), 184–203.

Malhotra, A., & Van Alstyne, M. (2014). The Dark Side of the Sharing Economy and How to Lighten It. *Communications of the ACM, 57*(11), 24–27.

Martin, C. J. (2016). The Sharing Economy: A Pathway to Sustainability or a Nightmarish Form of Neoliberal Capitalism? *Ecological Economics, 121*, 149–159.

Matzler, K., & Kathan, W. (2015). Adapting to the Sharing Economy. *MIT Sloan Management Review, 56*(2), 71–77.

Ravikumar, S. S., Shah, A., & Kalra, A. (2019). As Uber Gears Up for IPO, Many Indian Drivers Talk of Shattered Dreams. *Reuters.* Retrieved October 22, 2019, from https://in.reuters.com/article/uber-ipo-india-drivers/as-uber-gears-up-for-ipo-many-indian-drivers-talk-of-shattered-dreams-idINKCN1SE0OR.

Reserve Bank of India (RBI). (2019). Report of the Expert Committee on Micro, Small and Medium Enterprises. Retrieved December 12, 2019, from https://rbidocs.rbi.org.in/rdocs//PublicationReport/Pdfs/MSMES24062019465CF8CB30594AC29A7A010E8A2A034C.PDF.

Rosenblat, A., & Stark, L. (2016). Algorithmic Labor and Information Asymmetries: A Case Study of Uber's Drivers. *International Journal of Communication, 10*, 3758–3784.

Russell Belk, (2014). You are what you can access: Sharing and collaborative consumption online. *Journal of Business Research, 67*(8), 1595–1600

Schmidt, FA (2017). Digital Labour Markets in the Platform Economy: Mapping the Political Challenges of Crowd Work and Gig Work. Bonn: Friedrich-Ebert-Stiftung.

Shrivastava, A. (2019, October 22). Hail No More! Ola, Uber's Ride Growth Slows to a Crawl. *Economic Times.*

Srnicek, N. (2017). *Platform Capitalism.* Cambridge: Polity.

Transport-Dept. (2015). City Taxi Scheme-2015. Delhi. Retrieved October 22, 2019, from http://transport.delhi.gov.in/sites/default/files/All-PDF/City%2BTaxi%2BScheme.pdf.

Uberinsights. (2019). Hack Your Ratings. Retrieved October 21, 2019, from https://uberinsights.in/.

Variyar, M., & Sachdev, A. (2019). Ola, Uber Face Severe Shortfall of Drivers and Cars. Retrieved December 4, 2019, from https://www.cnbctv18.com/economy/ola-uber-supply-crunch-drivers-sees-vehicles-seized-lending-falls-50-4676761.htm.

Varma, S. (2017). Section of Ola, Uber Drivers on Strike in Delhi, No Major Impact. Retrieved October 22, 2019, from https://www.ndtv.com/delhi-news/ola-uber-drivers-might-go-off-road-today-1682631.

Vigneswara Ilavarasan, P., Verma, R. K., & Kar, A. K. (2018). Sharing Economy Platforms as Enablers of Urban Transport in the Global South: Case of Digital Taxi Aggregators in New Delhi, India. In *Urban Transport in the Sharing Economy Era Collaborative Cities* (pp. 128–158). CIPPEC. Retrieved from http://www.cippec.org/wp-content/uploads/2018/09/UrbanTransport-completo-web_CIPPEC.pdf.

PART IV

Platform Politics

CHAPTER 10

Aadhaar: Platform over Troubled Waters

Pawan Singh

The chapter offers a critical account of Aadhaar as an identity authentication platform and its evolving narrative in relation to its deployment by banking, telecom and other private entities in India. The sources for this chapter include the B.N. Srikrishna Committee Report on data protection, Personal Data Protection draft bill, statements made by various members of the Parliament (MPs) in the Rajya Sabha during the passage of the Aadhaar Amendment Bill 2019 and media reports. I will begin by providing an overview of the Aadhaar privacy debate from 2012 to 2018, paying attention to the petitions filed in support of Aadhaar's use by the private sector. I will subsequently examine the positions of pro-Aadhaar groups, who which see Aadhaar data as a kind of "new oil" that can fuel economic growth through digital innovation. These countervailing positions represent efforts to manage the crises of legibility and credibility in order to rationalise the use of Aadhaar through the language of constitutional values, social progress and nationalism. These debates allow us to identify the key values that have emerged from the contestations around data protection in India, and which may prove vital to salvaging the

P. Singh (✉)
Australia India Institute, Carlton, VIC, Australia
e-mail: pawan.singh@deakin.edu.au

A. Athique, V. Parthasarathi (eds.), *Platform Capitalism in India*, Global Transformations in Media and Communication Research - A Palgrave and IAMCR Series,
https://doi.org/10.1007/978-3-030-44563-8_10

Aadhaar project, addressing other crises of confidence and ensuring the protection of citizen data shared across public and private contexts of the platform economy.

The 2009 launch of Aadhaar, the Indian government's biometric identity project, ushered in a new regime of identification, especially for the economically marginalised populations, who were previously understood to be invisible, outside the legitimacy of a valid identity (UIDAI 2010). The project was implemented as a voluntary scheme for the poor to enable their access to welfare in a corruption-free, transparent manner directly using their fingerprints and other biometric markers. Over a period of time from 2012 onwards, Aadhaar became embroiled in legal challenges pertaining to its potential for creating a surveillance state through possible violations of the right to privacy, an affordance that was at the time yet to be codified in the law as a fundamental right. The 2012 challenge by a retired Karnataka judge filed in the Supreme Court of India led to two landmark decisions: the first came in 2017, codifying privacy to be a fundamental right subject to certain limitations guaranteed by the Indian Constitution, also called the Puttaswamy judgement (Supreme Court of India 2017). The other followed in 2018 by the same court that upheld the constitutional validity of Aadhaar as mandatory for access to welfare schemes by the poor while exempting the non-welfare uses of Aadhaar authentication (banking, mobile communications) except taxation from mandatory submission (Supreme Court of India 2018). The non-welfare uses, as discussed in subsequent sections, pertains to Aadhaar's use as an identity verification platform by private companies that sought to leverage data collection under Aadhaar to grow their businesses.

The period between 2012 and 2018 is particularly instructive in considering Aadhaar as an identity authentication platform beleaguered by legal and activist challenges on grounds of privacy and various other adverse outcomes of welfare exclusion and fraud based on implementation practices on the ground (Khera 2019). This chapter examines the nexus of Aadhaar with ongoing questions around data privacy, identification and data-driven economic growth that define the core of contestations around Aadhaar's status as a state-managed authentication platform and its orientation towards use by India's private sector. With a view to advance a critical discussion on India's flourishing digital platform economy, this chapter discusses how platform capitalism intersects with another key formation shaped by data-driven commodification processes (Srnicek 2017) or what others call surveillance capitalism (Zuboff 2019).

Aadhaar's promise of unique identification and linkage to databases of services led to public warnings by legal activists and experts around the onset of a surveillance state, a prospect bolstered by the use of Aadhaar by private corporations. The Indian Supreme Court'sS 2018 ruling on the constitutional validity of Aadhaar legitimised its mandatory use by the Indian state for welfare (Section 7 of the Aadhaar Act 2016) but also struck down Section 57 of the Act, disallowing private players to use biometric identification for their services. This was deemed to be a partial victory by pro-privacy groups, who were concerned with Aadhaar's non-welfare uses, which would effectively place Indian residents' data in the hands of private entities in order for the latter to monetise and profit from it. Prior to the Aadhaar verdict, majority of banks and mobile phone communication companies had already linked citizens Aadhaar numbers with their services between 2013 and 2018 when Aadhaar's mandatory use had remained an unsettled question. Despite the Indian Supreme Court's 2018 ruling preventing Aadhaar verification by banks and telecom companies, many continued the electronic-know your customer (e-KYC) using Aadhaar in violation of the court's order (Software Freedom Law Center 2018). In July 2019, the Aadhaar and Other Laws (Amendment Bill), 2019 was passed by the Lok Sabha (Lower House of the Indian Parliament) to allow the voluntary use of Aadhaar by banks and telecom operators for purposes of customer verification (Economic Times 2019). It was passed in the Rajya Sabha (Upper House) on 8th July 2019. Of particular salience was the amendment's emphasis on addressing privacy and data security concerns, given that India's data protection laws remain under development.

In that respect, it is important to account for the Indian private sector's vested interest in Aadhaar (literally, "foundation") as a verification platform underpinning the pursuit of India's digital economy. Based on an analysis of legal verdicts, activist documentation, media stories and data protection policy frameworks, I will argue that the growth of India's digital platform economy through the proposed voluntary use of Aadhaar verification has necessitated the management of two kinds of interrelated crises pertaining to legibility and credibility. The crisis of legibility concerns the inevitable framing of digital platform capitalism as surveillance capitalism given Aadhaar's integration of user identification through a centralised state-owned platform. Aadhaar faced a crisis of legibility as a surveillance tool 2012 onwards leading up to the 2017 Puttaswamy judgement declaring privacy to be a fundamental right guaranteed by the Indian

Constitution, and the 2018 decision that upheld mandatory Aadhaar for welfare but not for non-welfare, private sector uses. The crisis of legibility surrounding Aadhaar became more acute given the absence of a data protection legislative framework, which gave way to an attendant crisis of credibility—the key concern surrounding data privacy and user trust. The management of these two crises required mitigation of the framing of India's growing digital platform economy as a surveillance capitalist enterprise by highlighting the potential of data-driven innovation in the delivery of services of the empowerment of Indian citizens.

To this end, policymakers, government officials, experts and industry leaders mobilised an affective-regulatory apparatus of policy coupling the urgent need for data protection with the nationalist framing of citizen data as a national resource that can deliver user empowerment through the growth of digital economy. Data in this formulation has been framed inherently as an economic resource that can advance collective social good, which takes priority over individual privacy. Various developments in the Aadhaar privacy debate offer the broader context for situating the twin crises of legibility and credibility facing the growth of India's digital platform businesses that seek to leverage Aadhaar for access to user data managed by the Unique Identification Authority of India (UIDAI). These developments include the 2017 Puttaswamy decision, the 2018 Supreme Court judgement and importantly, the report and draft bill on data protection submitted by the expert committee headed by Justice B.N. Srikrishna in 2018 (Committee of Experts 2018a). While the draft Personal Data Protection Bill, 2018 lays out the various digital rights as well as protocols regarding data storage, transfer and transmission, the report recognised the need to protect individual data privacy but in the context of the accompanying objective of facilitating the growth of India's digital economy (Committee of Experts 2018b). Similarly, media statements by India's leading industrialists have also likened data to a national resource, a matter of sovereignty in economic terms. Pro-Aadhaar groups, which include government officials, policymakers and the private sector, have consistently maintained that data-driven innovation through the digital economy can empower Indians through socioeconomic progress. Clearly, Aadhaar as a verification platform offers a bridge across these disparate services to facilitate the identification of potential customers based on their data.

Aadhaar Legal Challenges 2012–2018: The Crisis of Legibility

In 2012, Aadhaar was challenged by a retired judge from Karnataka, Justice K.S. Puttaswamy, who filed a petition in the Indian Supreme Court claiming that Aadhaar violated the constitutional right to privacy. Meanwhile, as Aadhaar went from a voluntary scheme to a mandatory one, for not just subsidised cooking gas cylinders but also banking and mobile phone communications, various other challenges followed in the highest court. These pertained to issues of exclusion of beneficiaries, mandatory linkage, Aadhaar's passage as a money bill and its linkage to the Personal Account Number (PAN), which is an income tax identity card (Chaturvedi 2017; Bhuyan 2018). In 2016, the Aadhaar (Targeted Delivery of Financial and other Subsidies, Benefits and Services) Act was passed as a money bill in the Lok Sabha without debate in the Rajya Sabha to provide legislative backing to Aadhaar. A money bill pertains to flows of moneys into and out of the Consolidated Fund of India. In 2017, a nine-judge bench of the Indian Supreme Court declared privacy to be a fundamental right subject to exceptions of national security among others (Supreme Court of India 2017). Then the 2018 judgement by a five-judge bench of the same court ruled mandatory Aadhaar legitimate for welfare but overruled such a requirement for non-welfare purposes, or the private sector.

Petitioners opposing the Aadhaar project had been vocal in media coverage of the legal case, raising the spectre of the unique identification scheme's surveillance potential and data security flaws (Jyothish 2017; Ramanathan 2017, 2018). As the government changed at the Centre in 2014, Modi, who had vehemently opposed the project when it was in the Opposition, met with Nandan Nilekani once the former became the Prime Minister and sought greater enrolment in Aadhaar (Dhoot and Rajshekhar 2014). When Aadhaar began its mandatory incursion into people's lives who, before the 2018 judgement, had been required to link it to their mobile phone connections and bank accounts, the identification project's coercive aspects became a subject of public hardship inflicted by the scheme originally meant to empower people. As a result, the dominant story of Aadhaar was framed in media as a clash between the Indian government seeking to empower marginalised citizens through socioeconomic rights and affordances and pro-privacy groups, including activists, lawyers and advocates, who saw the danger of a national biometric identification project that would hollow out the Indian Constitution (Firstpost 2018). This battle represented the main crisis of legibility for Aadhaar, whose official position as a technology of social good came to be overshadowed by its potential for citizen surveillance through biometric id's linkage to public programmes as well as private services. The 2018 Supreme Court ruling that Aadhaar's mandatory use in welfare did not violate citizen privacy in part moved towards a resolution of this crisis. The ruling also struck down Section 57 of the Aadhaar Act 2016, which allowed Aadhaar's use by private companies to deliver their services. The Court further observed the need for a data protection bill to be passed to secure citizen data in India.

However, the more "subversive" aspects of the private interests attempting to cash in on a state-managed identification scheme received coverage in niche media outlets. A 2018 story in the *Huffington Post* reported the international technology business interests in integrating Aadhaar with their product platforms. These included Microsoft (whose founder Bill Gates publicly endorsed and praised Aadhaar), which uses Aadhaar in a new version of Skype, Amazon, which also uses Aadhaar in some cases for a quicker resolution to customer complaints of missing packages, and Facebook, which has prompted users to log in with the same name as their Aadhaar card, supposedly in order to build in an Aadhaar functionality (Blumenthal and Sathe 2018). Such embedding of Aadhaar in communication, commercial and social connection services under the ruse of authentication instantiates a logic that Adrian Athique terms the "integrated commodity form", which consolidates distinct media forms seeking to deliver content, entertainment and sociability to the user, and as the obverse, to deliver audiences to media corporations, who can monetise the data flow (2019). The proposed use of Aadhaar by global communication and media technology behemoths seeks to integrate biometric sign-in as a credential validation technology in their platforms in order to minimise the time taken to verify. Amazon's digital wallet, Amazon Pay, has rolled out the know-your-customer (KYC) using Aadhaar as one of the options, which is cheaper and quicker than other documents such as passport, driver's licence or voter ID (Gill 2019).

While according to the Indian Supreme Court's 2018 order, Aadhaar's use by private sector cannot be mandatory, its voluntary use as an alternative isn't necessarily against the law. Aadhaar as a verification platform that may connect diverse communication and commercial online services on a voluntary basis illustrates how Aadhaar's credential authentication serves another key integrating function within the integrated commodity economy. Surveillance is not so much an end result or the banal scandal of compromised user privacy; rather it is built into the interactive processes through which communication technology companies stage the indisputable requirement to authenticate their subscriber. The need to "know your customer" and validate their credentials combines a sound business practice with the potential for access to data. Such an integration of biometric identity with online credential sign-ins may not be pervasive in its current iteration. However, with the passage of the Aadhaar and Other Laws (Amendment) Bill 2019, the list of communication technology and fintech enterprises wanting a piece of the Aadhaar pie is likely to grow. Among the supporters and keen drivers of Aadhaar in the Supreme Court was not just the Indian government. An entire coterie of private interests offered their support to Aadhaar in a legal petition filed in the Indian Supreme Court from 2017 onwards. Aria Thaker's story "The New Oil: Aadhaar's Mixing of Public Risk and Private Profit", published in the 2018 issue of the culture and politics magazine *The Caravan*, uncovers the strategic intimacies among various private stakeholders who had served in their official capacity in the design and architecture of Aadhaar and the UIDAI, which manages Aadhaar.

Thaker highlights the role of one particular company, OnGrid, that joined various others in the Supreme Court to argue in favour of Aadhaar's use to continue unchanged because their businesses had developed entirely as a result of the biometric scheme (2018). OnGrid describes itself as the "trust platform of India", which uses a consent-based system for verification and background checks of blue-collar employees such as handymen, electricians, plumbers and others. It uses an India Stack application programming interface (API) enabled by Aadhaar while also gathering information about employees from numerous sources. OnGrid's co-founder Piyush Peshwani held a managerial position at UIDAI, which had employed several executives of Khosla Labs—a business incubator and investment firm that joined the petition supporting Aadhaar's continued use. Other co-petitioners supporting Aadhaar included the bicycle-sharing company Yulu, the authentication services firm, Transaction Analysts and the Digital Lenders Association of India, a group of financial start-ups. Together, they formed the "Coalition for Aadhaar" and claimed in their petition:

> There are several persons and businesses who depend on the Aadhaar system in the same manner as the Applicants therein, and a society comprising many such businesses who are dependent upon the Aadhaar system is being formed. (Thaker 2018: 6)

Various companies such as Paytm, OlaCabs, Flipkart and PhonePe and the user agencies licensed by the UIDAI also joined with petition with contributions ranging from Rs. 10 lakhs ($14,464) up to Rs. 20 lakhs ($28,931). Thaker further reports her conversation with Rachita Taneja of the Mozilla Foundation, who suggested that Aadhaar's use by private companies would enable user data collection without their consent or in cases where a consent-model exists, it would be difficult to establish whether consent was communicated meaningfully to the customer or subscriber. The intricate network of associations among Khosla Labs, UIDAI and other private actors playing a key role in the deployment of biometric technology for a government programme suggests a "revolving door"—the phenomenon of individuals using experience, knowledge and clout gained in public service in pursuit of profit for private companies (ibid.: 12). Another group called iSPIRT—the Indian Software Products Industry Round Table is a think-tank and an industry group for businesses that rely on Aadhaar—developed India Stack, a set of APIs that facilitate the use of Aadhaar by other platforms. While not a private firm, iSPIRT represents private technology industry interests enlists volunteers for its work for a compensation of $55,000. The volunteers, too, have held prominent position in the UIDAI as chief system-architect and technology advisors, marketing and demand generation professionals, chief product managers and biometric architects. Thaker further cites a 2017 Privacy International report on financial technology in India to explain the level of influence exerted by private interests on Aadhaar who do not have to operate transparently or be accountable in terms of the right to information legislation (2018).

Scholarly analyses of Aadhaar have been critically engaged with multiple primary concerns of surveillance of subjects (Henne 2019; Khera 2019), identity and political subjecthood/citizenship (Shukla 2010; Rao 2013; Nair 2018; Cohen 2019), and issues of governance, datafication and marketisation of rights (Chaudhari and König 2017; Rao and Nair 2019). Research on privacy concerns of Aadhaar have also offered valuable ethnographic insights about data-privacy trade-off as well as perceptions of technology's credibility in terms of agents and means of information collection (Srinivasan et al. 2018). The mandatory uses of Aadhaar have been critiqued for undesirable outcomes of exclusion of legitimate beneficiaries despite Aadhaar compliance, faulty design of biometric technology and fading fingerprints, corruption owing to offline practices by the ration dealer and legal arguments in the Supreme Court (Scroll 2018). The scheme's voluntary use through the proposed amendment passed earlier this year by the Indian government remains to be understood with greater attention to conflicts of interests, influence of the private sector on data policies in India given their role in UIDAI, and whether Aadhaar can legitimately serve the purpose of socioeconomic empowerment both via its welfare delivery in the public and by streamlining of various services in the private sector.

One reason for Aadhaar's apprehension by the narrative of mass surveillance is owing to the crisis of legibility despite there being evidence of the scheme's overall success (Banerjee 2016). The State of Aadhaar Report 2017–2018, based on a survey in rural parts of four states in India, also reports general greater overall approval of Aadhaar by subscribers and improvement in financial inclusion aside from areas that need urgent attention (Government of India 2018). However, Aadhaar represents a datafication of populations in developing societies (Taylor and Broeders 2015) and, materially, an audacious reconfiguration of residents' identities and rights in an unprecedented manner. Thus, the crisis of legibility it faces marks a necessary stage in its status as an authentication technology that seeks, not only to uniquely but succinctly know its subjects but also to pervade their lives towards its foundational promise of socioeconomic transformation. This crisis also prefigures and frames, in part, Aadhaar's perceived potential for driving the growth of platform capitalism in India. While the deployment of Aadhaar in the private sector continues to be contested, given the yet-to-be passed data protection bill, the imperative of legibility has, in part, been sanctioned by the Indian Supreme Court's 2018 verdict legitimising Aadhaar's raison d'être for welfare. With the passage of the Aadhaar and Other Laws (Amendment) Bill 2019 in the Indian Parliament, various pro-Aadhaar groups have been engaged in eliding the obvious crisis of credibility that has emerged from mandatory biometrics in the absence of a data protection law.

The Aadhaar and Other Laws (Amendment) Bill 2019: The Crisis of Credibility

It is important to consider, then, how various stakeholders are engaged in addressing the crisis of credibility. Much of the media and scholarly writings on Aadhaar have been concerned with the question of individual identity and privacy in the context of an emergent data protection legislation. However, there is an equally urgent need for the institutions seeking to administer that identity through Aadhaar as a platform to ensure their own identities as service-providers inspires trust on an ongoing basis. The evolution of Aadhaar debate concerning its use by the private sector faces this dilemma or what I call a "crisis of credibility". Given that the Supreme Court of India struck down Section 57 of the Aadhaar Act 2016, effectively preventing the use of Aadhaar by hopeful private actors whose business potential resided in leveraging Aadhaar's authentication platform, the urgent task at hand for them is to manage and avert this crisis from escalating.

Ashish Bhardwaj and Anand Mishra from the School of Banking and Finance at Jindal Global Law University point out the concerns of India's fintech sector arising from the Supreme Court's ruling, mainly pertaining to the time and cost of establishing user identity (2019). They suggest that while establishing customer identity is central to their business, their users should also have trust in the digital identity system. Another aspect of the crisis of credibility concerns a kind of image problem for Aadhaar, or a clear understanding of what Aadhaar means to different stakeholders and demographics. For the poor, it is an identity verification mechanism, which sometimes functions against their interests by excluding them. Their struggles with Aadhaar have been brought to public attention by development economist Reetika Khera, who describes Aadhaar as a solution looking for a problem, and legal scholar Usha Ramanathan, who calls it a marketing scheme by Nandan Nilekani, who has pitched Aadhaar to various constituency as a solution to their diverse problems (Ramnath and Assisi 2018). As journalists N.S. Ramnath and Charles Assisi point out, Aadhaar is not a solution to any problem by itself, which it is often taken to be (2018). Rather, Aadhaar, which was built as a platform to allow for innovations from above and below, is a Lego block, "one piece in a larger system, not a solution by itself, but something that can accelerate a solution" (ibid.: 86). The Lego block metaphor suggests that Aadhaar as a platform is not intended as a solution to India's complex social problems but as a mechanism to improve the government's capacity to build solutions and implement them on the ground. Despite this immanent view of Aadhaar as just a block in a larger system, its pervasive uptake and transformational effect in public and private service delivery have shaped the crisis of trust that has arisen in the absence of a data protection law in India.

Aadhaar's second life post the Supreme Court's judgement began with the Aadhaar and Other Laws (Amendment) Bill 2019 passed by the Indian Parliament in July 2019 through the amendment of the Telegraph Act 1885 and the Prevention of Money Laundering Act 2002. The Bill provides the voluntary use for Aadhaar by banks and mobile communication provides to authenticate user credentials. In the Rajya Sabha, Ravi Shankar Prasad, Indian Minister for Electronics and Information Technology (MeiTY), stated that informed consent of the customer was necessary for authentication while further observing that the system with its 256-bit encryption for bank transactions and 2048-bit encryption for Aadhaar data (virtually unbreakable in the minster's view) is absolutely sound and secure (Rajya Sabha TV 2019). During the Rajya Sabha proceedings, MPs from the Congress and Aam Aadmi Party (AAP) objected on grounds of data protection concerns and possibilities of Aadhaar data leakage. Another MP of the Indian National Congress (INC) from West Bengal opposed the Aadhaar Amendment Bill by defining what Aadhaar is not or ought not be: a singular identity for one nation, mandatory or exclusive, certification of identity's truth, a tool of exclusion or data collection, a tool of surveillance and for use by private agencies. Further observing that it is only meant for government services, subsidies, benefits and welfare, he questioned why a data protection act was not passed before Aadhaar was implemented. However, these objections were countered with the reiteration of the voluntary nature of the amendment and quality of encryption that secures data and the emphasis on injunction by law against storage of Aadhaar data by telecommunication providers. A violation of this injunction would incur a fine of Rs. 1 crore ($144,370.00).

Further objections were raised on how the amendment bill would further go against the spirit of the Indian Supreme Court judgement of 2018 that dispensed with such use of Aadhaar by the private sector. Statements made by other MPs in the Parliament including Prashant Nanda of the Biju Janata Dal (Orissa) extolled the virtues of Aadhaar for improving the welfare of farmers in the country and seconded the claim made by Ravi Shankar Prasad that about 1.23 billion Indians approved of Aadhaar. Ashwini Vaishnaw, an MP of the ruling BJP, cited various statistics pertaining to correction of identity records—4.23 billion connections of liquefied petroleum gas (LPG), 2.98 billion ration cards—owing to Aadhaar's implementation to clean out corrupt practices of fraudulent identity documents. He further quoted the triple constitutional test laid down regarding Aadhaar's use by the Indian Supreme Court and taken up in the Justice Srikrishna Committee's recommendations on data protection in its report: (1) Aadhaar should be backed by law, (2) a legitimate state interest in implementing Aadhaar for a scheme and (3) proportionality or the steps taken by state to implement Aadhaar ought to be proportional to the purpose of such implementation. Asserting that Aadhaar is purpose-blind, that is, it only authenticates a person as a yes/no response and does not collect, share, store or transmit data about the purpose of authentication, the MP remained emphatic about the security of data under Aadhaar. The data security standards described by Vaishnaw sound more reasonable than previous defences of Aadhaar's data security by the former Attorney General of India in the Supreme Court during Aadhaar hearings, with the claim that Aadhaar was secured in a complex with 13-feet-high and 5-feet-thick walls (Jain 2018).

While most defences of the amendment bill underscored the benefits to the poor, approval by majority of Indian citizens and its design features of encryption, its use by private sector in violation of the Supreme Court judgement was only addressed by members opposing the bill. Aadhaar has also suffered a number of data breaches brought public's attention by journalists, think-tanks and other advocates. Rachna Khaira of *the Tribune* newspaper reported in January 2018 that access to Aadhaar data through a login and password could be purchased for Rs. 500 ($7), which could provide Aadhaar details of a billion subscribers, including name, phone numbers, addresses and email. For another Rs. 300 ($4.31), the report goes on, software could be purchased to print the Aadhaar card of a subscriber (Khaira 2018). These services were purchased from an anonymous source from the popular messaging service WhatsApp. The UIDAI rubbished the exposé, asserting that the biometric data was not breached, and initiated police action against the journalist. Similarly, in 2017, the think-tank Centre for Internet and Society (CIS) reported the publishing of Aadhaar details on four government websites, an investigation that was again dismissed by the UIDAI, which asked CIS for an explanation (Livemint 2017). The most problematic misuse of Aadhaar was by the mobile communication operator Airtel, which used Aadhaar numbers of its mobile subscribers to reroute their LPG subsidy benefits from their personal bank accounts into bank accounts opened by Airtel without the subscribers' consent. The telecom operator was fined Rs. 2.5 crores ($360,166) and its e-KYC licence was suspended.

Despite these data breaches, the UIDAI has maintained that its biometric database is secure and has never been breached, a claim that is true given that biometric data contained in the Central Identities Data Repository (CIDR), which manages and stores data collected during Aadhaar enrolment, has not been reported to be breached. These data breaches do represent a real crisis of credibility for Aadhaar and the UIDAI, however, a fundamental lack of clarity about what specific data is private and cannot be leaked and what data may be ambiguously public or private (such as Aadhaar number and demographic details) has remained largely unclear (Legally India 2017). Insofar as the biometric data, the most sensitive information, remains secure and unhackable, Aadhaar and the UIDAI's credibility would withstand scrutiny.

A Free and Fair Digital Economy

As I have previously noted, the most prominent piece of the credibility puzzle for Aadhaar is India's data protection bill, which has been under consultation with the Justice B.N. Srikrishna Committee, a group of legal and technology experts appointed by the government in 2017 to formulate India's data protection legislation. The Justice Srikrishna Committee released its report on India's data protection bill in October 2018. The report entitled, "A Free and Fair Digital Economy: Protecting Privacy, Empowering Indians" lays out the framework for personal data protections rules in India and contextualises them within the broader constitutional framework of India that upholds common good and social progress as goals the state must pursue (Committee of Experts 2018a, b). The report also recognises the right to privacy laid down in the Puttaswamy judgement while tying the need for data protection to the unlocking of the limitless potential of the digital economy. Couching its objectives in constitutional terms, the report suggests that there is no conflict between the individual right to privacy and data protection and the social interest served by the digital economy. Instead, they both "serve a common constitutional objective" pertaining to the "protection of individual autonomy and consequent harm prevention" and the creation of real choice for citizens (p. 8). By wedding the larger objective of common, public good (as also identified by the Supreme Court of India in its 2018 judgement on Aadhaar) to the language of rights—privacy, individual autonomy, self-determination—the report positions rights *not* as individual affordances but as being constitutive of the common good of a free and fair digital economy.

The proposed compatibility among data protection, rights and digital economy in the report prioritises the importance of serving public good through data that may be harnessed as a national resource simultaneous with protecting its security, confidentiality and integrity across data systems. While India's Personal Data Protection Bill is yet to become law as of 2019, the momentum towards data protection is being reframed in part through the language of colonisation and nationalism. In January 2019, Reliance Industries chief, Mukesh Ambani urged Prime Minister Narendra Modi to act against the use of Indian citizen's data by global corporations at the Vibrant Gujarat Summit. Likening such use as a form of data colonisation, Ambani invoked Gandhi's struggle against political colonisation to make the case for Indian citizens' data to be owned and used by Indians to advance their digital economy (Langa 2019). At the G20 Summit in Japan in 2019, Piyush Goyal, India's Commerce and Industry Minister, spoke of data sovereignty, the idea that India has a sovereign right to the data generated by Indians, which should be used for the welfare and development of their people. Opposing the Japanese Premiere Shinzo Abe's proposal of Data Free Flow with Trust (DFFT), which enables cross-border transfer of information by electronic means and its storage on foreign servers, Goyal referred to India's e-commerce policy that favours data localisation and locating computational facilities within India to ensure job creation. The principle of data sovereignty takes data to be a national resource, a form of societal commons or national asset that the government holds in trust (Agrawal 2019).

In the light of the Aadhaar and Other Laws (Amendment) Bill, 2019 passed by the Indian Parliament, the developments around a data protection legislation have emerged through the merging of the rights vocabulary with the state's developmentalist agenda. This agenda seeks to harness personal data as a national resource through the language of sovereignty that resists data colonisation by global corporations. These positions also represent attempts to mitigate the crisis of credibility surrounding Aadhaar. Aadhaar's voluntary use by banks, telecommunication operators and possibly other private companies goes against the letter of the law, as highlighted by India's Opposition parties in the Parliament. Through a subsumption of the contra-narratives of surveillance, data misuse and inadequate data protection legislation within larger nationalist registers of collective, common good and citizen empowerment through real choices in a free and fair digital economy, the use of Aadhaar as an authentication platform is likely to accelerate. However, India's pro-privacy groups including think-tanks, advocates, lawyers and activists are also just as likely to keep re-animating the crisis of credibility surrounding Aadhaar. In August 2019, Trinamool Congress MP Mahua Moitra alleged in the Lok Sabha that there was a conflict of interest in the drafting of the data protection law given the possibility that lawyers working on the bill may have private clients in the field of technology. She demanded the MeITY to make public the name of the lawyers and firms empanelled with the government, especially those drafting the data protection bill (Saha 2019). The delay in bringing the data protection bill to the Parliament in her view was due to vested interests working in the government to ensure the passage of amendments to the Aadhaar Act 2016 allowing for Aadhaar's extensive use by the private sector.

While the Government of India continues to claim that it recognises the urgent need for a robust data protection legislation, it has not addressed the concerns of pro-privacy groups, who see Aadhaar's use by the private sector—despite its voluntary nature and punitive provisions for data breaches—as leading to potential monetisation of user data without proper privacy and consent frameworks in place. Aadhaar as a platform will continue to evolve serving public interests of welfare delivery as well as business interests of a robust digital economy. The data protection bill, when it is passed, will certainly further legitimise Aadhaar's uptake, however, the UIDAI will need to ensure new values concerning information/data security in the data protection bill when it is tabled in the Parliament. Broadly, at the institutional level, it will need to ensure integrity of information through processes of data collection, storage, sharing, transfer and transmission. At the individual level, information autonomy in terms of consent, right to access and correction of data, erasure of data as well as a right to be forgotten provides the necessary bulwark against privacy harms. The draft data protection bill does lay out a framework to accommodate these new values emerging from the experience of Aadhaar's implementation in India. However, for these new formulations that encompass the scope of data protection in India to have relevance to the predicament of India's information society, ethnographic and qualitative research on privacy, consent, autonomy and data-sharing practices from a social and cultural perspective needs to inform policymaking.FundingThe research for this chapter was supported by a grant from the Toyota Foundation's "Exploring New Values for Society" scheme and the "Digital Identity Research Initiative" fellowship programme of the Indian School of Business, Hyderabad.

References

Agrawal, A. (2019, June 11). Piyush Goyal at G20: Data Is a Sovereign Asset, Free Trade Can't Justify Its Free Flow. *Medianama*.

Athique, A. (2019). Integrated Commodities in the Digital Economy. *Media, Culture and Society*, Online first. 1–17. https://doi.org/10.1177/0163443719861815.

Banerjee, S. (2016). *Aadhaar: Digital Inclusion and Public Services in India*. World Development Report, World Bank. Retrieved from http://pubdocs.worldbank.org/en/655801461250682317/WDR16-BP-Aadhaar-Paper-Banerjee.pdf.

Bhardwaj, A., & Mishra, A. (2019, March 14). Fintech Needs a Strong Identity. *Mail Today*.

Bhuyan, A. (2018, January 18). Aadhaar Isn't Just About Privacy: There Are 30 Challenges Govt. Is Facing in Supreme Court. *The Wire*.

Blumenthal, P., & Sathe, G. (2018, August 25). India's Biometric Database Is Creating a Perfect Surveillance State – And US Tech Companies Are on Board. *HuffPost*.

Chaturvedi, A. (2017, June 10). Overview of Legal Issues Around Aadhaar. *PRS India*. Retrieved from https://www.prsindia.org/theprsblog/overview-legal-issues-around-aadhaar.

Chaudhari, B., & König, L. (2017). The Aadhaar Scheme: A Cornerstone of a New Scheme in India? *Contemporary South Asia, 26*(2), 127–142.

Cohen, L. (2019). The 'Social' De-Duplicated: On the Aadhaar Platform and the Engineering of Service. *South Asia: Journal of South Asian Studies, 42*(3), 482–500.

Committee of Experts. (2018a). *A Free and Fair Digital Economy: Protecting Privacy, Empowering Indians*. Committee of Experts Under the Chairmanship of Justice B.N. Srikrishna. Retrieved from https://www.thehinducentre.com/resources/article24561547.ece/binary/Data_Protection_Committee_Report-comp.

Committee of Experts. (2018b). *A Free and Fair Digital Economy: Protecting Privacy, Empowering Indians*. Committee of Experts Under the Chairmanship of Justice B.N. Srikrishna. Retrieved from https://www.thehinducentre.com/resources/article24561526.ece/binary/Personal_Data_Protection_Bill,2018_0.

Dhoot, V., & Rajshekhar, M. (2014, July 24). Nandan Nilekani Impresses Narendra Modi & Arun Jaitley, Gets Aadhaar a Lifeline. *The Economic Times*.
Economic Times. (2019, July 4). Lok Sabha Passes Aadhaar Amendment Bill.
FP Staff. (2018, January 18). Aadhaar a Giant Electronic Leash, Will Hollow Out Constitution: Petitioner to Supreme Court. *Firstpost*. Retrieved from https://www.firstpost.com/india/aadhaar-a-giant-electronic-leash-distorts-states-relation-with-citizen-petitioner-tells-supreme-court-4307107.html.
Gill, P. (2019, January 13). This Is Why Amazon Wants Your Aadhaar Number. *Business Insider*.
Government of India. (2018). *State of Aadhaar Report*. Retrieved from https://stateofaadhaar.in/report_pages/state-of-aadhaar-report-2017-18/.
Henne, K. (2019). Surveillance in the Name of Governance: Aadhaar as a Fix for Leaking Systems in India. In B. Haggart, K. Henne, & N. Tusiklov (Eds.), *Information, Technology and Control in a Changing World: Understanding Power Structures in the 21st Century* (pp. 223–245). Cham: Palgrave Macmillan.
Jain, M. (2018, September 26). Aadhaar Data Kept Behind 13-Feet High Walls: Attorney General to SC. *Business Standard*. Retrieved from https://www.business-standard.com/article/economy-policy/aadhaar-data-kept-behind-13-feet-high-walls-attorney-general-to-sc-118032100822_1.html.
Jyothish, R. (2017, May 6). Aadhaar vs Security: Is the Biometric System a Tool for Surveillance? *Business Standard*. Retrieved from https://www.business-standard.com/article/economy-policy/aadhaar-vs-security-is-the-biometric-system-a-tool-for-surveillance-117050600183_1.html.
Khaira, R. (2018, January 4). Rs 500, 10 Minutes, and You Have Access to Billon Aadhaar Details. *The Tribune*. Retrieved from https://www.tribuneindia.com/news/nation/rs-500-10-minutes-and-you-have-access-to-billion-aadhaar-details/523361.html.
Khera, R. (Ed.). (2019). *Dissent on Aadhaar: Big Data Meets Big Brother*. Hyderabad: Orient Blackswan.
Langa, M. (2019, January 18). Mukesh Ambani Urges Modi to Take Steps Against Data Colonisation by Global Corporations. *The Hindu*. Retrieved from https://www.thehindu.com/news/national/mukesh-ambani-urges-modi-to-take-steps-against-data-colonisation/article26025076.ece?utm_campaign=socialflow&fbclid=IwAR2LWYiiPjcUGk5a61ZRtNv-4SmPc_amLF8VpsR_22f-DL8ss1pI-vxJTjc.
Legally India. (2017, March 31). Is Your Aadhaar Number Confidential? Retrieved from https://www.legallyindia.com/views/entry/is-your-aadhaar-number-confidential.
Nair, V. (2018). An Eye for an I: Recording Biometrics and Reconsidering Identity in Postcolonial India. *Contemporary South Asia, 26*(2), 143–156.
Livemint. (2017, May 19). UIDAI Puts Posers to CIS over Aadhaar Data Leak Claim. *Livemint*. Retrieved from https://www.livemint.com/Politics/

Yccoa65tKKQCt9jC68fHyJ/UIDAI-puts-posers-to-CIS-over-Aadhaar-data-leak-claim.html.

Rajya Sabha TV. (2019, July 10). In-Depth – Aadhaar Amendment Bill, Rajya Sabha TV. Retrieved from https://www.youtube.com/watch?v=etqggYER2P0.

Ramanathan, U. (2017, December 9). UID Is About Data for Surveillance, Profit, Not Serving Citizens. *Deccan Herald*. Retrieved from https://www.deccanherald.com/content/647321/uid-data-surveillance-profit-not.html.

Ramanathan, U. (2018, January 18). Aadhaar: From Compiling a Govt Database to Creating a Surveillance Society. *Hindustan Times*. Retrieved from https://www.hindustantimes.com/opinion/aadhaar-from-compiling-a-govt-database-to-creating-a-surveillance-society/story-Jj36c6tVyHJMjOhCI8vnBN.html.

Ramnath, N. S., & Assisi, C. (2018). *The Aadhaar Effect: Why the World's Largest Identity Project Matters*. New Delhi: Oxford University Press.

Rao, U. (2013). Biometric Marginality: UID and the Shaping of Homeless Identities in the City. *Economic & Political Weekly, XLVIII*(13), 71–77.

Rao, U., & Nair, V. (2019). Governing with Biometrics. *South Asia: Journal of South Asian Studies, 42*(3), 469–481.

Saha, P. (2019, August 2). Data Protection Law: Mahua Moitra Alleges Conflict of Interest Against Lawyers Working with Govt. *India Today*.

Scroll. (2018). Identity Project Archive. Retrieved from https://scroll.in/topic/38792/identity-project.

Shukla, R. (2010). Reimagining Citizenship: Debating India's Unique Identification Scheme. *Economic & Political Weekly, XLV*(2), 31–36. https://www.epw.in/journal/2010/02/insight/reimagining-citizenship-debating-indias-unique-identification-scheme.html

Software Freedom Law Center. (2018, November 27). Someone Still Asking for Aadhaar?: Let Us Know! Retrieved from https://sflc.in/someone-still-asking-aadhaar-let-us-know.

Srinivasan, J., Bailur, S., & Seshagiri, S. (2018). The Poverty of Privacy: Understanding Privacy Trade-offs from Identity Infrastructure Users in India. *International Journal of Communication, 12*, 1228–1247.

Srnicek, N. (2017). *Platform Capitalism*. Cambridge: Polity Press.

Supreme Court of India. (2017, August 24). *Justice K.S. Puttaswamy (Retd.) and Anr. vs. Union of India and Ors.* Writ Petition (Civil) No. 494 of 2012, Supreme Court of India. Retrieved from https://globalfreedomofexpression.columbia.edu/cases/puttaswamy-v-india/.

Supreme Court of India. (2018, September 26). *Justice K.S. Puttaswamy (Retd.) and Anr. vs. Union of India and Ors.* Writ Petition (Civil) No. 494 of 2012 and Connected Matters. Retrieved from https://indiankanoon.org/doc/127517806/.

Taylor, L., & Broeder, D. (2015). In the Name of Development: Power, Profit and the Datafication of the Global South. *Geoforum, 64*, 229–237.

Thaker, A. (2018, May 1). The New Oil: Aadhaar's Mixing of Public Risk and Private Profit. *The Caravan*.

Unique Identification Authority of India (UIDAI). (2010). UIDAI Strategy Overview: Creating a Unique Identity Number for Every Resident in India. Planning Commission, Govt. of India. Retrieved from https://www.prsindia.org/sites/default/files/bill_files/UIDAI_STRATEGY_OVERVIEW.pdf.

Zuboff, S. (2019). *The Age of Surveillance Capitalism: The Fight for a Human Future at the New Frontier of Power*. New York: Public Affairs.

CHAPTER 11

Political Communication on Social Media Platforms

Usha Rodrigues

Prime Minister Narendra Modi claimed a landslide victory in the 2019 national election, with his Bharatiya Janata Party (BJP) winning 303 seats, comfortably beyond the 272-seat required for a majority in the Indian Lok Sabha (lower house of parliament). As has been the recent trend, the 2019 Indian election campaign was fought on social media apps and platforms. After the 2014 national election was named the 'first social media election' in India, it was predicted that WhatsApp, a messaging app owned by Facebook, would play a significant role in the 2019 election campaign (Rodrigues 2018). During the state elections in 2018–2019, WhatsApp was increasingly being used by BJP and various opposition parties to keep in touch with their constituents. In fact, a number of political parties set up data analytics departments to analyse voter data at district and booth levels to tailor their election campaigns, and almost all regional and national leaders were using FacebookLive to connect with voters. Although

U. Rodrigues (✉)
Deakin University, Melbourne, VIC, Australia
e-mail: usha.rodrigues@deakin.edu.au

A. Athique, V. Parthasarathi (eds.), *Platform Capitalism in India*, Global Transformations in Media and Communication Research - A Palgrave and IAMCR Series,
https://doi.org/10.1007/978-3-030-44563-8_11

traditional factors such as caste- and religion-based candidate selection and voting patterns, and more contemporary issues of unemployment and farmers' unrest were significant issues in the 2019 election campaign, it was the use of social media platforms as a communication tool for political campaigning that gained further ground for parties in India.

Considering the context of an increasingly platform-driven society, where private and public communication is largely channelled through a global online platform (social and mobile) ecosystem, I discuss in this chapter how social media and mobile platforms are utilised for political communication in India and the implications for India's public sphere. I will begin by outlining how Modi and his government use social media as a means of ***direct communication*** with their followers, and the technological structural shift in the country that has enabled this online conversation between various private and public networks. The chapter will end with an analysis of the positive and negative impact of the direct communication of political messages on social media platforms in a country such as India, where the level of media and digital literacy varies dramatically.

Campaigning on Social Media Platforms

In the past decade, various social media and mobile platforms have been part of economic, interpersonal and political communication in India. It was in 2011, during the so-called Arab Spring period, that scholars and the mainstream media noted the use of social media for mass communication and mobilisation in India. The social and political movement against sitting governments in the Arab countries of Tunisia, Egypt, Yemen, Libya and Syria in 2011, were also reflected in India when a series of mass civil demonstrations were organised against corruption by those in power. The organisers of the 'India against Corruption' movement, under the leadership of Anna Hazare and Arvind Kejriwal, planned nation-wide protests and *dharnas* (sit-ins) in early 2011. 'Team Anna' demanded that the Indian central government consult with members of 'civil society' to draft a strong Lokpal (ombudsman) bill to increase accountability of those in public office. The mass protests that followed were organised by the youth, educated, professional and working class in India, who used mobile phones and social networking sites to garner support across the full spectrum of Indian society. In an inter-media agenda-setting process, the movement was cheered by the country's hundreds of 24-hour news channels and thousands of newspapers (Rodrigues 2014; Ashutosh 2012). The mainstream media responded to this so-called middle-class movement because it also represented their target audiences in the electorate (Rodrigues 2014).

Following the mass civil unrest, some in the anti-corruption movement formed a new political entity called the Aam Adami Party (AAP) to contest the idea of public probity on the political front. In 2012–2013, AAP leader Arvind Kejriwal and his party were active on social media sites such as Twitter and YouTube, and subsequently formed local government in the capital city of Delhi. However, it was the BJP and its prime ministerial candidate Narendra Modi, who best utilised social media platforms to engage with the educated, networked, middle-class Indians, including 150 million first-time voters. Although both the BJP and the Indian National Congress (INC or Congress) party extensively used YouTube as their own television channels during the 2014 national election campaign, the Congress party could not compete with the BJP's three-dimensional hologram rallies, gamification of political messages, the prime ministerial candidate's focused messages on Twitter and his Google Hangouts. The head of the BJP's information technology cell in 2014, Arvind Gupta, noted that 'with technology and social media, we have been able to create an alternative medium with which we can directly communicate with the citizens' (Goyal 2014).

In 2014, as the prime ministerial candidate, Narendra Modi had about 4 million followers for his Twitter handle @narendramodi, whereas his rival, INC president Rahul Gandhi, only had about 55,000 followers of his @rahulgandhi2020 account. As many as 56 million election-related tweets were posted during the five months of the election campaign in early 2014 (Merelli and Quartz 2014). However, an analysis of the Twitter feed showed that the Twitter conversations were concentrated amongst the elite and men, including politicians, journalists, academics, prominent social activists and professionals (Rodrigues 2015). In 2014, India had about 200 million internet users, with about 100 million users active on social media networking sites. Despite the digital divide, the mainstream media's dedicated coverage of social media conversations made the role of social media platforms one of the talking points of the election. In an inter-media agenda-setting process, the mainstream media amplified Modi's messages to mainstream media consumers (McCombs 2005; Messner and Garrison 2011). Considering the impact and potential of social media platforms to engage and organise the younger and educated middle class in India, who are also the target of many advertisers, it is not surprising that mainstream Indian news media and journalists tapped into this rich tapestry to get a sense of what mattered to this audience. In the absence of a meaningful interaction with the new prime minister, the mainstream media was left scrambling, covering his articulations on social media.

The successful use of social media platforms by Modi and BJP in the 2014 election, compelled opposition parties, both at the national and regional, level to jump on the bandwagon. During the 2019 elections, a number of party leaders and their teams used FacebookLive, WhatsApp, TikTok, YouTube, Twitter, Instagram and NaMo App to connect with their supporters. Twitter said that 396 million tweets related to the election were sent during the campaign period (Vinayak 2019). Prime Minister Modi and the BJP had made further social media inroads since their 2014 victory, using the 'inexpensive medium' to stay in touch with their base (Amit Malviya, personal communication 2018). BJP information technology cell chief Amit Malviya said his party had a clear view of the efficacy of social media as a tool for political communication. Since the 2018 state elections, INC social media head Divya Spandana and her team also gained ground on the BJP's social media strategies. Political parties sought to gather supporters' phone numbers, to give them a call on a mobile, which in turn allowed them to add the number to their database and to their local WhatsApp group. They treat these phone numbers and demographic details as important data, building a social relationship by keeping in touch with supporters during non-election periods. Experienced political journalists note that there is a two-tier communication system on social media (personal communication, 2018). Political leaders use their own personal handle to promote their policies and positive messages, while their online supporters disseminate divisive views of their party and troll those who do not agree. The parties also set up data analytics departments to analyse and target local election campaigns.

Structural Shift and the Public Sphere

Over the past two decades, India has experienced a dramatic increase in mobile-phone subscriptions. The first mobile telephone service was launched in 1995 and since then the tele-density in India had surpassed 91 per cent of the country's population of 1.35 billion in 2018 (TRAI 2019). The change in telecommunication policy from being restricted to monopolistic government corporations till the mid-1990s to private competition saw the mobile-phone subscription cross the one billion mark in 2018. Access to the internet has improved with the entry of private and international telecom service providers using 4G technology, with the average cost of data falling from $3 per gigabyte to $0.20 per gigabyte in the four years between 2014 and 2018 (Tanwar 2019). As a result, annual data usage per subscriber increased to 7.6 gigabyte in 2018, according a TRAI report. In addition, in 2019, the number of people accessing internet is expected to be around 627 million, with 87 per cent of users accessing the internet on their mobile phones, according to Kantar, an advertisement agency report (Exchange4media 2019). According to one estimate, India had about 468 million smartphone users in 2017, which was expected to double by 2022 (Shenoy 2019). Social media and mobile platforms thus offer politicians an inexpensive medium to communicate with their constituents, while the young, educated and networked citizens have become the conduit of political communication in their respective local networks.

Social media is any digital medium that enables users to communicate and interact socially. Users of social media utilise various internet and electronic services and tools to actively participate in sharing information through comments, posts, reviews and discussion via text, graphic, audio, video and animated content. 'Social media can be defined as digital multi-way channels of communication among people and between people and information resources, and which are personalised, scalable, rapid and convenient' (Katz et al. 2013: 12). This definition of a social media platform includes popular social sites, such as Facebook, YouTube and Instagram, and messaging apps, such as Twitter, WeChat and WhatsApp. One of the basic functions of a social media platform is that it allows many-to-many communication instantly. Meanwhile, the process of platformisation happens when platforms extend into the web and pull web data back into their platforms, as is the case with Facebook, Google and Apple. Helmond uses the term platformisation to refer 'to the rise of the platform as the dominant infrastructural and economic model of the social web and the consequences of the expansion of social media platforms into other spaces online' (2015: 5). As an infrastructural model, social media platforms provide a technological framework to build on, geared towards connecting to and using other websites, apps and their data. At the same time, the external data is tailored for their own databases (Helmond 2015: 8). Helmond says that the dual process is operationalised through platform-native objects such as application programming interfaces (APIs) and social plug-ins, allowing for the social platforms to expand into the web and to create data channels for collecting and formatting external web data to fit the underlying logic of its own platform.

Twitter, as an online news and social networking platform, has gained significance in political communication as a microblogging platform that allows users to post and read short multimedia messages known as tweets. Facebook is one of the most popular social networking platforms, with 2.41 billion monthly active users as of 30 June 2019 (Statista.com 2019a, b). YouTube, the biggest online video platform worldwide, has 2 billion monthly active users. More than 5 billion videos have been shared to date, and nearly 1 billion hours of videos are watched daily (YouTube.com 2019). Short messaging apps, such as WhatsApp, have become increasingly popular as an easy-to-use mobile-phone service. WhatsApp allows users to share data (text, audio, video) with individuals and groups. With more than 1.5 billion monthly active users, WhatsApp is the most popular mobile messenger app worldwide. Recently, WhatsApp confirmed that it had more than 400 million users in India (Singh 2019).WhatsApp messages are encrypted, so it is difficult to detect where a forwarded message originates from. This means that media messages can be shared between social groups without the knowledge of who first distributed the message on the service. Friends, family and acquaintances can form a group on WhatsApp and share content of interest.

One billion groups are in use on WhatsApp. Some have been formed for e-commerce reasons, while others are made up of family members or friends. Facebook, which owns WhatsApp, has noted that private messaging, ephemeral stories and conversations between small groups are the fastest growing areas of online communication (Kalogeropoulos 2019). Reuters Digital News Report 2019 also noted that in many countries people were spending less time with Facebook and more time with WhatsApp and Instagram in 2019 than in 2018 (Newman et al. 2019). This, in turn, is having an impact on social communication around news, which is becoming more private, as messaging apps continue to grow everywhere. 'WhatsApp has become a primary network for discussing and sharing news in non-Western countries' such as Brazil, Malaysia, South Africa and India (Newman 2019). Concerns about misinformation and disinformation remain high; trust in the news in general is declining (42 per cent) and trust in social media remains low at 23 per cent according to the Reuters report (Newman et al. 2019).

Modi Leads the Way

Modi is the key politician leading the structural shift to *direct communication* by developing his base of followers on social media and mobile platforms. Modi's presence on social media began in 2012. He is, in terms of his online following on global social media platforms, the second-most 'popular' politician in the world. He maintains an active presence across multiple platforms, including Twitter with 51 million followers, Facebook with 44 million likes and followers, Instagram with 30 million followers and YouTube with 433 million views of videos as on October 2019, and more than 10 million downloads of his NaMo App (as of March 2019). Modi's messages are relayed in multiple languages to connect with his range of followers across poly-linguistic India and to reach audiences abroad. For example, when Israel's Prime Minister, Benjamin Netanyahu, visited India, his meeting with Modi was reported on the latter's social media pages in English and Hebrew, with a number of staged visuals demonstrating the close relationship between the two countries and prime ministers.

Modi and his social media team have carefully crafted his online image through strategic engagement with his followers, influencers, celebrities, overseas dignitaries, movie and sports stars, and successful business people, and, at times, by engaging with and congratulating common people for their efforts to support his agenda, including as the 'Clean India' campaign. Modi launched Clean Indian on Twitter just after coming to office as the prime minister in late 2014. In 2015–2016, he posted 100 tweets related to the Clean India agenda, but he did not retweet or reply to any tweets in this time (Rodrigues and Niemann 2017). Similarly, during the three-month period following the announcement of demonetisation, Modi's Twitter account incessantly emphasised the benefits of the ban of 85 per cent of Indian currency notes. His team kept moving the Twitter conversation along during this historical event by changing the hashtag from #Indiafightscorruption to #Indiadefeatsblackmoney to #ipaydigitally (Rodrigues and Niemann 2019). During the 2019 elections, Modi and his BJP made clever use of the term 'Chowkidar' to keep the focus on nationalism, patriotism and his role as the protector of the nation. His articulations on various platforms were supported by the @PMO_India account; his cabinet ministers and government departments Twitter handles.

Studies of Modi's use of Twitter to communicate with his followers over the past five years show that his communication is a one-way process.

In what is described as 'selfie nationalism' (Rao 2018), Modi keeps his followers aware of his day-to-day activities using various social media platforms, including his NaMo App, and of his views, in his radio programmes such as *Maan Ki Baat* (what is in my heart) on the public service broadcaster. Modi's messages are almost always positive, promoting a 'digital India' agenda and various 'pradhanmantri' (prime ministerial) funding schemes. While minimising his interaction with the mainstream media, which he has branded as 'news traders' (ANI 2014), he uses celebrities and influencers to get his message across on various social media platforms. His reservations about mainstream news media stem from his years as the chief minister of Gujarat, when several national media outlets and their journalists held Modi responsible for the 2002 religious riots in Gujarat, in which hundreds of people were killed. Modi and his social media team have built his political agenda (Cobb et al. 1976) by directly conversing with the electorate. Modi's use of alternative means for communicating with the electorate has reduced the mainstream media's power to question him as prime minister, with the political discourse in the country being guided by 'political logic' rather than by 'media logic' (Stromback and Esser 2014: 245). Social media, mobile technologies and the internet have offered an alternative avenue to political leaders to gain attention to their causes and directly connect with the masses, bypassing the mainstream media. In what Chadwick (2013) refers to as a *hybrid media system*, the new media ecology has changed the relative power of actors in political and media systems, as well as the nature of political communication itself.

Political Engagement and Social Media Gratification

A number of studies have formulated a typology for gratifications that audiences seek and receive from being active on social media (Smock et al. 2011; Chen 2011; Hanson and Haridakis 2008; Lee and Ma 2012; Valeriani and Vaccari 2018). Chen's study of Twitter users found that people gratify their need to connect with other people, forming an informal camaraderie to stratify their need to belong to or to be affiliated with a community (2011: 760). Hanson and Haridakis, in their study of on-demand video-sharing site YouTube, found viewers were active participants in the distribution chain, playing an active role in the production, distribution and receipt of YouTube media content (2008). News consumers used YouTube to gain information, to enjoy light-hearted entertainment and to express themselves in the marketplace of information (Hanson and Haridakis 2008: 5). Smock et al. surveyed students to ascertain their motivation for using Facebook and found three motivations significantly predicted general use of Facebook: relaxing entertainment, expressive information sharing and social interaction (2011). Users had varied needs for using specific Facebook features, such as posts, private messages and the chat service, including seeking companionship, professional advancement, habitual pastime and escapism (Smock et al. 2011: 2326). Lee and Ma's study of factors influencing users' intention to share news on social media, showed that 'while newer users make active media selections based on gratifications, more experienced social media users may rely on habitual and ritualized modes of content sharing behaviour' (Lee and Ma 2012: 337). In their study, prior social media experience emerged as a significant predictor for intention to share news, while socialisation, status seeking and a desire to improve one's credibility were other gratifications motivating users to share news.

The gratification of being part of a group of like-minded people, being close to a political party and its leaders, a sense of connectedness with those in power and sharing and expressing views about everything that is politics, enhanced individual's status in their networks, who felt that they knew the 'truth' or the real story. In India, WhatsApp activism has become the order of the day (Harris 2019). Even before the 2019 election period, the sharing of fake news, rumours and misleading information had been linked to 46 deaths and several injuries, prompting WhatsApp to modify its policies on forwarding message in India (Gilbert and Saberin 2018). In fact, just before the election, an apparent BBC news story was circulated among WhatsApp groups predicting that the ruling BJP party would lose the election to the INC alliance. The story was attributed to the 'American spy agency CIA', 'British spy agency KGB' and 'Israeli spy agency MOSAD'. The story was, of course, 'fake news' and nowhere to be found on the BBC News network. During the 2019 election period, it was not only the various political parties and their candidates pushing their messages to thousands of local WhatsApp groups, but many of the loyalists became a conduit, spreading their party's message among friends and family. Political parties—the BJP, INC and various regional parties—not only pushed political propaganda material through social media platforms but also negative and misleading posts. The war rooms monitored and trolled those who opposed a political party and spread rumours, lies and fake news on WhatsApp (Harris 2019).

This misinformation and disinformation in byte-size packages, with crude posts, videos and memes, went viral because of the ease with which they could be shared. The reason information of obviously questionable veracity was being shared without regard for the truth was that it reinforced the beliefs sharers had about the opposition. Valenzuela et al. in their study of sharing misinformation on social media, found that, paradoxically, using social media for news could indirectly lead to the spread of misinformation because of its association with individuals' political participation or zeal:

> Using a platform for informational purposes, such as Twitter or Facebook allow, can motivate users to become more politically engaged. Increased political engagement is correlated with increased spread of content, including misinformation. (Valenzuela 2019: 14)

In the Indian case, there could be several reasons for the rapid spread of fake news, misinformation and disinformation on social media, including the perceived novelty of participants' capacity to share and forward information on their mobile phones, and a partisan urge to reinforce beliefs about the opposition. One journalist notes that his investigation of 20 WhatsApp groups revealed widespread slander, abuse and conspiracy claims directed at the Gandhi family (Purohit 2019). A cynical tendency to believe conspiracy theories amongst the population becomes amplified when it receives a slight nudge from political leaders via their official accounts. For example, on 6 May 2019, one day after Narendra Modi said that Rajiv Gandhi had died as '*bhrashtachari* number 1 (corrupt number 1)', a floodgate of conspiracy theories opened on social media platforms. It initially began with messages reiterating Modi's allegations. Then, swiftly, a more organised flood of media unleashed itself on various WhatsApp groups, including a six-minute long video that detailed how Gandhi allegedly was of Muslim lineage, rooted in Afghanistan, and that his 'real' name was 'Rajiv Khan' (Purohit 2019).

Applying Brakes on the Runaway Train

In March 2019, the Election Commission of India (ECI), an autonomous constitutional authority responsible for election administration in India, demanded that multinational technology companies, such as Facebook,

Twitter, Google, TikTok and Indian social messaging site ShareChat, ensure the integrity of the election process during the 2019 elections. The social media companies agreed and signed a voluntary code of ethics, effective 20 March until the end of the election period, 23 May (ECI 2019). The agreed code included a direct line between the ECI and the social media platforms to notify and swiftly rectify any potential violations of the Indian electoral laws. Under the agreed code, social media companies also undertook to monitor and label paid political messages broadcast on their platforms in addition to removing any images or reference to the Indian armed forces by political campaigners. The companies also volunteered to facilitate access to information regarding electoral matters, undertake education campaigns to build awareness of electoral laws and endeavour to conduct platform-specific training for ECI nodal officers (ECI 2019). At ECI's request, Facebook and Twitter took down political posters that featured an Indian Air Force pilot's photographs. Social media firms confirmed that they had taken down the accounts of thousands of people allegedly associated with political accounts. Google organised town-hall meetings to improve users', including students, journalists and the general public, digital literacy. Facebook and WhatsApp representatives confirmed that they had engaged several fact-checking partners, including Boom Live, AFP India, *India Today*, *Dainik Jagran*, Face Crescendo, Factly and NewsMobile, to identify false and misleading information on their platforms (Rodrigues 2019).

A Microsoft study found that Indian citizens were more likely to see fake news and internet hoaxes on social network platforms than the global average of internet users, as well as a rapidly increasing circulation of political information (PTI 2019). Meanwhile, the large Indian news media and its journalists have been witnessing the moving away of news audiences from their mainstream medium to social platforms. Several articles have been published by the Indian mainstream media, warning of the dangers of believing news published on social media platforms (Ghosh and Desai 2019; Purohit 2019). A number of established Hindi and English dailies with some of the largest brands and circulation in the country also took out a full-page advertisement to underscore the need for verification and the role of journalists in providing readers with credible information during the election period (Roy 2019). The advertisement 'Print Is Proof' featured a pointed editorial against the sharing of 'fake news' and 'misinformation' on social media platforms during the Indian elections. The campaign, sponsored by media outlets (including *The Hindu* group, *The*

Times of India and *Dainik Bhaskar* among others) emphasised that print newspapers were still the most reliable source of news. Raj Jain, the CEO of publishing company BCCL, told a reporter that before news was carried in their newspaper, it had to go through a rigorous process of being checked and rechecked, unlike digital news. The 'Print Is Proof' advertisement stated:

> For us, the starting point of any story is verification. But for social media, its sensation. And if a story doesn't check out, it can always be deleted. As newspapers, we have no such luxury. You see, it's hard to go back on your word when millions have a copy of it. So, we do it right. We take the time to verify all the information before we call it news. News that's backed by fact. Print is proof. (Print Is Proof 2019)

Large advertising firms agree with the print publishers' view that newsrooms have a strong verification system. Girish Agarwal, promoter director at DB Corporation Ltd., noted that the growing circulation of print media was a sign of growing trust in the medium as a credible source of news (Roy 2019). The Indian mainstream media—more than 100,000 news publications, over 850 television channels and nearly 1100 radio stations—continues to grow in extremely competitive market conditions with increasing circulation, viewership and advertisement revenue. Print readership increased to 425 million in the first quarter of 2019 and television channels reached nearly 77 per cent of households in India (John 2019). Meanwhile, FM radio is also reaching an increasing number of Indians, along with public service broadcasting network All India Radio and community radio stations, radio in India has a reach of over 90 per cent. The Indian media and entertainment sector reached took Rs. 1.67 trillion ($23.9 billion) in 2018, a growth of 13.4 per cent, according to an end-of-year Federation of Indian Chambers of Commerce and Industry report (Mukherjee 2019). Advertising revenue in India is expected to grow by over 11 per cent in 2019 on the back of the national elections and the Cricket World Cup, according to IPG Mediabrands (Laghate 2018). Although television continues to be the dominant media platform, with 39 per cent advertising spend in India, followed by print, the advertising revenue spent on digital media is projected to grow rapidly to about 21 per cent share of total advertising expenditure. The growth in advertising dollars spent on digital platforms is spurred by the increasing access to the internet and mobile-phone ownership.

Erosion of Public Trust in News and Information

The Indian media has bucked the downward trend in profitability experienced by many of their counterparts in more mature media markets in the Western countries due to increasing literacy and a growing population. However, subsequent government efforts to expand the availability of communication technologies have led to a change in the communication landscape in India. The opening of the communication industry to competition over the past two decades has resulted in more than a billion mobile-phone subscriptions, and with the recent drop in the price of mobile data, access to the internet has improved dramatically. As noted above, Indian internet access is fuelled by mobile-first, which is not only powering away in urban India, but making inroads in rural India too (Exchange4media 2019). The aspiring class is increasingly connected to the world via their mobile phones. As such, in a two-step process, internet-connected and often educated young Indians have become a conduit of political communication in their local networks, in addition to the vast media industry in India. The public sphere in India has bifurcated the function of print and broadcast mass media within a burgeoning networked society. However, there is a cost to such a rapid increase in access to data, mobile phones and an unregulated public sphere, where anyone can post and share information, verified or not. The mainstream media's verification process cannot compete with the virality of social media messages. The sharing of news and information related to politics has also led to sharing of fake news, misinformation and disinformation, where there are only miniscule checks and balances despite the efforts of the ECI, social media companies' increased monitoring and fact-checking organisations (Valenzuela et al. 2019).

Traditionally, an active and independent news media is considered to be critical for holding to account those in positions of power—that is those responsible for public good in government, corporations and executive positions. The free flow of verified news and information provided by journalism has been seen to build communities and empower people to participate in the creation of their own governments. However, over the decades, news media outlets have become profitable businesses, part of a larger entertainment industry, often running their own agenda, or the agendas of other powerful interests. In India too, journalism has generally been respected because of its association with independence from British rule. Despite its commercial ethos, the print media, which surpassed

100,000 news publications in India in 2018, has always been seen as a plurality of ideas, healthy for democracy. Following economic reforms in the early 1990s and subsequent advances in technology, television in India flourished. Today, there are 850 television channels, with more than half of them covering news. The initial heydays of broadcast media being freed from government ownership and the increase in quality and quantity of news in the 1990s and 2000s has given way to a cacophony of talking heads on television screens (Rodrigues and Ranganathan 2015). In addition, in the 2010s, politicians calling out the news media as 'news traders' and highlighting the news media's weaknesses due to a focus on profit, sensationalism and partisan reporting damaged the brand of journalism in India (Purohit 2019; Rodrigues and Ranganathan 2015).

With politics shifting to social media platforms, where the distribution of unfiltered expressions of ideas, views and news remains unregulated, audiences are enjoying the affordances provided by these social platforms. In the post-truth era, the menace of 'fake news' and misinformation on encrypted services such as WhatsApp during India's various state and national 2019 elections, has seriously eroded the public's trust in the information they consume from various sources. There is also a general distrust of news that one does not agree with. This erosion of trust stemming from social media news ironically seems to have had an impact on the credibility of mainstream journalism too (Newman et al. 2019), which is already struggling to be heard in the cacophony of media messages coming from hundreds of television channels, numerous news sites and several social networking platforms. The expansion of television had already created extremely competitive market conditions, in which most of the national television channels remained focused on a handful of news stories, with wall-to-wall coverage provided on breaking news stories, such as the release of a captured Indian pilot by Pakistan in March 2019. If television has turned politics into talking-heads screaming at each other, the social media's free-for-all is creating a public sphere where there are no limits in public discourse. The circulation of fake news, mis- and disinformation and unfiltered partisan views is creating an atmosphere of distrust all around. The improving access to mobile data and other media technologies has connected a large proportion of the Indian population to the internet, but the level of literacy, particularly media literacy, has remained questionable. Indian citizens' trust in direct, but often unverified, messages has resulted in mob lynching and deaths, leaving the news media and local law enforcement authorities helpless (Morris 2018).

References

ANI. (2014). News Traders Dance on Congress's Tune: Modi. Business Standard, April 30. https://www.business-standard.com/article/news-ani/news-tradersdance-on-congress-s-tune-modi-114043001572_1.html.

Ashutosh. (2012). *Anna: 13 Days that Awakened India*. New Delhi, India: Harper Collins.

Chadwick, A. (2013). *The Hybrid Media System: Politics and Power*. New York: Oxford University Press.

Chen, G. (2011). Tweet this: A Users and Gratifications Perspective on How Active Twitter Use Gratifies a Need to Connect with Others. *Computers in Human Behavior, 27*(2), 755–762.

Cobb, R., Ross, J. K., & Ross, M. H. (1976). Agenda Building as a Comparative Political Process. *American Political Science Review, 70*(1), 126–138.

Election Commission of India. (2019). Social Media Platforms Present Voluntary Code of Ethics for the 2019 General Election to Election Commission of India. Retrieved from https://eci.gov.in/files/file/9467-social-media-platforms-present-voluntary-code-of-ethics-for-the-2019-general-election-to-election-commission-of-india.

Exchange4media. (2019). Internet Users in India to Reach 627 Million by 2019-End: L Kantar ICUBE 2018 Report. Retrieved from https://www.exchange4media.com/digital-news/566-million-internet-users-in-india-18-annual-growth-kantar-icube-2018-report-95137.html.

Ghosh, L., & Desai, S. (2019, April 20). The War Against Fake News. *Bangalore Mirror*.

Gilbert, D., & Saberin, Z. (2018, July 18). India's Fake News Epidemic Is Killing People, and Modi's Government Has No Plan to Stop It. *Vice News*.

Goyal, M. (2014, April 7). How BJP, AAP, Congress and Their Candidates Are Using Social Media to Woo Voters. *The Economic Times*.

Hanson, G., & Haridakis, P. (2008). Youtube Users Watching and Sharing the News: A Uses and Gratifications Approach. *Journal of Electronic Publishing, 11*(3), 6.

Harris, J. (2019, April 7). Is India the Frontline in Big Tech's Assault on Democracy? *The Guardian*.

Helmond, A. (2015). The Platformization of the Web: Making Web Data Platform Ready. *Social Media + Society*. https://doi.org/10.1177/2056305115603080.

John, N. (2019, April 26). Indian Readership Survey 2019: India Today Is the Largest and Fastest Growing Magazine. *Business Today*.

Kalogeropoulos, A. (2019). Groups and Private Networks – Time Well Spent? *Digital News Report*. Retrieved from https://reutersinstitute.politics.ox.ac.uk/sites/default/files/inline-files/DNR_2019_FINAL.pdf.

Katz, J. E., Barris, M., & Jain, A. (2013). *The Social Media President: Barack Obama and the Politics of Digital Engagement*. New York: Palgrave Macmillan.
Laghate, G. (2018, December 8). Print Media Ad Growth to Accelerate in 2019. *The Economic Times*.
Lee, C. S., & Ma, L. (2012). News Sharing in Social Media: The Effect of Gratifications and Prior Experience. *Computers in Human Behavior, 28*, 331–339.
McCombs, M. (2005). A Look at Agenda Setting: Past, Present and Future. *Journalism Studies, 6*(4), 543–557.
Merelli, A., & Quartz. (2014, May 16). Modi Won the Indian Election on Twitter, Too. *The Atlantic*.
Messner, M , & Garrison, B. (2011). Study Shows Blogs Affect Traditional News Media Agenda. *Newspaper Research Journal, 32*(3), 112–126.
Morris, J. (2018, September 22). Reports of 'WhatsApp Lynchings' Fall in India After App Changes Rules on Sharing Messages. *Evening Standard*.
Mukherjee, J. (2019, March 12). Indian Media Industry to Cross $33.6 Billion by 2021: EY-FICCI Report. *Fortune India*. Retrieved from https://www.fortuneindia.com/macro/indian-media-industry-to-cross-336-billion-by-2021-ey-ficci-report/103040.
Newman, N. (2019). *Section 1: Executive Summary and Key Findings*. Reuters Digital News Report 2019 (pp. 9–32). Retrieved from https://reutersinstitute.politics.ox.ac.uk/sites/default/files/inline-files/DNR_2019_FINAL.pdf.
Newman, N., Fletcher, R., Kalogeropoulos, A., & Nielson, R. K. (2019). *Reuters Digital News Report*. Retrievd from https://reutersinstitute.politics.ox.ac.uk/sites/default/files/inline-files/DNR_2019_FINAL.pdf.
PTI. (2019, February 5). Microsoft Survey: Indians More Likely to Encounter Online Fake News. *Business Standard*.
Purohit, K. (2019, May 13). Sonia Gandhi Knew of Rajiv's Assassination Plot, Her Husband had 'Drinking Problems': WhatsApp Groups Awash with Rumours About Ex-PM. *Firstpost*.
Rao, S. (2018). Making of Selfie Nationalism: Narendra Modi, the Paradigm Shift to Social Media Governance, and Crisis of Democracy. *Journal of Communication Inquiry, 42*(2), 166–183.
Rodrigues, U. M. (2014). Social Media's Impact on Journalism: A Study of Media's Coverage of Anti-Corruption Protests in India. *Global Media Journal, 8*(1), 1–10.
Rodrigues, U. M. (2015). The Media, the Social Media and the Elections. In E. Thorsen & C. Sreedharan (Eds.), *India Election 2014: First Reflections* (pp. 114–124). Poole: Bournemouth University.
Rodrigues, U. M. (2018, November 18). Will Social Media Decide India's Next Election? *East Asia Forum*. Retrieved from https://www.eastasiaforum.org/2018/11/14/will-social-media-decide-indias-next-election/.

Rodrigues, U. M. (2019). Can India Stop the Social Media Runaway Train? Retrieved from https://www.aii.unimelb.edu.au/blog/indian-election-series/can-india-stop-the-social-media-runaway-train/.

Rodrigues, U. M., & Niemann, M. (2017). Social Media as a Platform for Incessant Political Communication: A Case Study of Modi's 'Clean India' Campaign. *International Journal of Communication, 11*, 3431–3453.

Rodrigues, U. M., & Niemann, M. (2019). Political Communication in Modi's Style: Demonetisation Campaign on Twitter. *International Journal of Media & Cultural Politics, 15*(3), 361–379.

Rodrigues, U., & Ranganathan, M. (2015). *Indian News Media: From Observer to Participant*. New Delhi: Sage Publications.

Roy, T. L. (2019, April 11). Print Is Proof: Newspapers Hit Out at Social Media with Campaign on Credibility. *Exchange4media*. Retrieved from https://www.exchange4media.com/media-print-news/print-is-proof-newspapers-hit-out-at-digital-medium-with-campaign-on-credibility-96016.html.

Shenoy, J. (2019, May 9). India to Have 859 Million Smartphone Users in 2022: ASSOCHAM-PwC. *The Times of India*. Retrieved from https://timesofindia.indiatimes.com/business/india-business/india-to-have-859-million-smartphones-users-in-2022-assocham-pwc/articleshow/69252335.cms

Singh, M. (2019, July 26). WhatsApp Reaches 400 Million Users in India, Its Biggest Market. *Techchruch*. Retrieved from https://techcrunch.com/2019/07/26/whatsapp-india-users-400-million/.

Smock, A. D., Ellison, N. B., Lampe, C., & Wohn, D. (2011). Facebook as a Toolkit: A Uses and Gratification Approach to Unbundling Feature Use. *Computers in Human Behavior, 27*(6), 2322–2329.

Statista. (2019a). Number of Monthly Active Facebook Users Worldwide as of 2nd Quarter 2019 (in Millions). Retrieved from https://www.statista.com/statistics/264810/number-of-monthly-active-facebook-users-worldwide/.

Statista. (2019b). Number of Social Network Users in India from 2015 to 2023 (in Millions). Retrieved from https://www.statista.com/statistics/278407/number-of-social-network-users-in-india/.

Stromback, J., & Esser, F. (2014). Introduction: Making Sense of the Mediatization of Politics. *Journalism Studies, 15*(3), 243–255.

Tanwar, S. (2019, August 22). Powered by 4G, Mobile Data Consumption in India Rose 56-Fold in Four Years. *Quartz India*.

TRAI. (2019). Highlight of Telecom Subscription Data as on 30th November, 2018. Retrieved from https://main.trai.gov.in/sites/default/files/PRNo05Eng18012019_0.pdf.

Valenzuela, S., Halpern, D., Katz, J. E., & Miranda, J. P. (2019). The Paradox of Participation Versus Misinformation: Social Media, Political Engagement, and the Spread of Misinformation. *Digital Journalism, 7*(6), 802–823.

Valeriani, A., & Vaccari, C. (2018). Political Talk on Mobile Instant Messaging Services: A Comparative Analysis of Germany, Italy, and the UK. *Information, Communication & Society, 21*(11), 1715–1731.

Vinayak, A. J. (2019, May 26). Twitter Captures 2019 Polls in 396 Million Tweets. *The Hindu*. Retrieved from https://www.thehindubusinessline.com/info-tech/social-media/twitter-captures-2019-polls-in-396-million-tweets/article27254990.ece.

YouTube. (2019). YouTube for Press. Retrieved from https://www.youtube.com/about/press/.

CHAPTER 12

Portfolios of Fear and Risk in Platform News

Hrishikesh Arvikar

Platform Politics and Platform News

When Noam Chomsky was asked about Russia's interference in the 2016 US elections, he noted that America has interfered in several foreign elections itself. Chomsky's pragmatic, if unpopular, observation was swiftly borne out of the Cambridge Analytica scandal, which not only implicated a number of Western governments and 'technology companies' in electoral interference, but also revealed the strategic interventions of India's major political parties within our own much-vaunted democratic process. Thus, while the centrality of social media platforms to political persuasion has given rise to new modes of everyday politics (bordering variously upon the comic, dangerous and absurd), the underlying impulse towards democratic subversion within and across state borders is nothing new in itself. More broadly, these dynamics have set the current temper of politics in a post-factual world, including in India. It is hardly surprising that, with the rise of WhatsApp as India's preferred mode of communication, a vitriolic register of politics has spread virally through news clickbaits that peddle,

H. Arvikar (✉)
University of Queensland, Brisbane, Queensland, Australia
e-mail: h.arvikar@uqconnect.edu.au

A. Athique, V. Parthasarathi (eds.), *Platform Capitalism in India*, Global Transformations in Media and Communication Research - A Palgrave and IAMCR Series,
https://doi.org/10.1007/978-3-030-44563-8_12

provoke or deny conspiracies, accusations and acts of violence. The sensory environment of platform news is a highly charged and polarized public domain that appears to have supplanted or co-opted the domain of journalism in India, long a constitutionally protected and elite profession, but now effectively channelled into the economic logics of telecoms providers and the cellular dispersal of urban street and village politics.

Paying attention to the co-evolution of a broader international phenomenon of platform politics, this chapter attempts to track two facets of the local story of platform news in India: (1) the expansion of the digital media economy and its strategic imperatives in capturing the infrastructure that provide carriage to platform news, and (2) the interaction of platform news with rise of platform politics, both in terms of resistance and in terms of tacit and even explicit participation in the expanding portfolios of fear and risk.

Standardization, Diversification and Sachetization

Several sweeping changes can be seen as India switches over to the digital media economy from its earlier forms of public communication. In the past couple of decades, we have moved from satellite to cloud and from mode to code. It seems abundantly clear that the overwhelming focus is not on content as a public good, but rather how it can be monetized, both as a unit of data and a data point of influence at every procedural calculation of the digital machinery. In terms of regulation, the Indian situation is relatively content-agnostic, but at the same time, it is identitarian divisions that bring the eyeballs and footfalls to the digital bazaar. A representational essentialism thus occupies both lanes of identity and difference, one where identity is qualified through stencils of caste, gender and religious forms of categorization, and, in the parallel track, where such plurality becomes illusorily representative as identity warps inward. In an age of superabundance, it would take us around 750 years to watch the content uploaded on YouTube in just one day. Even amongst such apparent plenitude, it is visibly clear that many forms and foci of information are being left out, missed, ignored and trivialized under this emerging market regime. It is implicitly accepted that millions of people will inevitably be left out of the digital circuit of communication. As Bratton succinctly puts it:

> One of the key games for any architecture is based on who and what is inside and/or outside. At a regional scale, who or what is not a migrant of one sort or another? But in that solidarity, there are such differences: for some, that status is a death sentence, and for others, it's a token of privilege. (Bratton 2018: 20)

Audiences are a vital component of the digital commodity logic beyond the points of access and sale (see Athique 2019: 558). Indeed, they are embedded as the drivers of today's media architecture. Ostensibly, this constitutes a 'grassroots utopia' where tastes become opinions, opinions become facts, facts become truth, leaving the conception of journalists' self-identification as instructors of audiences blowing in the wind. Even as audience mass increases, the mass audience dissipates as a mode of public address, to be replaced by bracketed niches like *Lallantop* (owned by Aroon Purie, from the *India Today* group, whose major shareholders are the Birlas). In the era of targeted advertising and individuated newsfeeds, a one-to-one correspondence is no longer necessary between editorial ideologies and brand ownership. The Foundation for Independent Journalism (FIJ) established by TheWire.in founders (Venu, Varadarajan and Bhatia) is funded by the Independent and Public-Spirited Media Foundation (IPSMF). Yet the very same organization funds *Swarajya*, a right-wing mouthpiece. TV news channel NDTV was owned by left leader Brinda Karat, Oswal and the same Rajeev Chandrashekhar (who was part-owner in a later right-wing Republic channel), along with its founders Radhika Roy and Prannoy Roy. Yet, NDTV is accused of non-disclosure of loans, leading to allegations of being bought by Reliance. *Firstpost* is now entirely owned by Reliance, as a part of its acquisition of CNN-TV18 group, which was earlier owned by Raghav Bahl.

In 2014, the Telecom Regulatory Authority of India (TRAI) was compelled to raise a red flag over media ownership patterns resulting in an inextricable nexus of politics and media patronage, which elicited this response from *Firstpost* editor R. Jaganathan:

> How do we know a media house not owned by a politician is telling the truth too? [...] Does non-ownership of media houses prevent a corporate house from influencing it? Is the advertising rupee, or indirect benefits to media editors, any less influential in the media?

With the following five points, Jaganathan sought to reassert press freedom, which was seemingly facing familiar threats, but also quietly going through fundamental revision as digitality was being ushered into the very temper of news-making:

Point 1—Bias and neutrality cannot be eliminated by any system […]
Point 2—If big media is anyway becoming unviable, how is restricting funding from new sources going to do it any good? Will neutral media be run by starving journalists?
Point 3—TRAI's recommendations will have the unhealthy effect of pushing straightforward ownership of the media into surrogacy or benami holdings. This is a move away from transparency, not towards it. […]
Point 4—The issue is competition. This is what should be facilitated, not restrictions on current ownership or market shares, which may anyway start falling in the internet age. By trying to keep people out, TRAI is actually ensuring that all media ownership will get more concentrated. […]
Point 5—What is TRAI's *locus standi* in making recommendations in areas outside telecom? Is TRAI a telecom regulator or media regulator? (Jaganathan 2014, August 13)

This posture has not aged well, particularly the last point, as we now have immensely and undeniably porous borders between telecom and media. News now operates in a digital era, where standardization, diversification and sachetization are embedded into media commodities by the economic, social and political institutions that shape their production. Standardization operates with the idea of sustenance of form, packaging and content. Thus, the vertical and horizontal mediation through scrolling of newsfeeds of Facebook, Instagram and Twitter with the editorialized air of mystery around the content ensures that the user is attracted, if not addicted, to the content and will click on it to access more information. Sample the clickbait: *We don't know about cleaning toilets, but these five things an elected member of Parliament should never do*, or *These are the tariffs India is putting on America in response to Trump's policy.* Many such stories, the origins of which lie in the click-baiting method refined by Buzzfeed, are built with arresting captions. This format was being emulated by other venturing into platform media until bigger smartphone screen, particularly or Chinese Xioami, Red Mi and Real Me forayed into the Indian market, allowing for horizontal widescreen displays on the smartphones. The technological obsolescence of a smart phone device plays an important role in formatting and reformatting reception techniques of platforms news media.

There has also been a need for content diversification, since the language and dialect that NDTV uses is centred around Delhi and its intellectual gravitas and glitterati, which is often and easily critiqued by other channels and newspaper outlets like *Dainik Bhaskar* and *Jagran* that operate in the Hindi heartland of North India. Diversification is thus enacted by providing differing perspectives on the story that all nonetheless offer allegiance to the political inclination of the news outlets and the current ruling dispensation in India. In a country which speaks hundreds of languages, rallies its faith around million gods and goddesses, part of the media diversification takes place by tapping into the diverse publics. Moving away from earlier elite and foreign educated journalists, *Lallantop*, which could best be translated as swagger, is a voice which compounds the right amount of Bollywoodized hyperbole, juggling the language of the 'rural cool' with borrowed dialects from North India small towns. The name itself has a behavioural informality of discussions of endless cups of tea which are visible at every street corner. Historically, various regional media have been owned by political parties or their leaders from Sharad Pawar's *Sakal* (Morning), Shiv Sena's *Saamna* (Confrontation) to left-inclined Telegraph in Bengal and Maran's Sun TV down south to only name a few. These mouthpieces often openly show party allegiances when social issue need to up the ante and stoke fire.

To moderate such journalism of ideological interests, there are several acts and quasi-judicial bodies which lay out norms, rules and regulations for Indian media. However, media laws in India have not caught up with ownership and distribution patterns. They are almost wilfully archaic. Up until now, media regulations are constituted as balancing acts of not hurting sentiments of one or another set of interests. In all three instances that I will consider here, NDTV, TheWire.in and *Firstpost*, the customary models of ownership patterns have been supplanted by new mechanisms of risk financing—through either loans or awards—effectively hedging across the aisles of the political spectrum. While the state grapples with formulating new media laws, it is the microfinancing in the new digital economy which leads to sachetization. The move to formalization of economy via digital transactions is far from complete, despite vigorous enforcement by the state. Nonetheless, Bill Maurer's work on mobile money suggests mobile operators 'turn towards a relatively untapped market among the world's poorest and, in the process, provide services that enhance financial access. Profitability and financial inclusion go hand in hand' and hence become useful in 'formatting the poor' (Maurer 2012: 590). India immediately rushes towards a suite of mobile money apps whose usage provides micro benefits, cross-subsidization and, above all, features which cement the position of apps in platform architecture. As Maurer predicts:

> Each story depends on a specific formatting of a market—the creation of individual people, in aggregate, in to a population and then a market segment. In the Empowerment Story, people have to first be made into 'the poor' or 'the unbanked,' among whose chief problems in life is their lack of access to financial services.... 'transaction cost[s]'... 'is a market device that formats the client and the payments space into which the client is being inserted'.... While formatting people as 'the poor', these market devices foreground mobile technologies, and 'the poor' and their mobile devices turn into a networked subject-object. (Maurer 2012: 597–598)

Similarly, news media 'formats the poor' with free news apps, where sachetization of outrage and scandal offers the meta-narrative of nation product in a byte-sized form, ostensibly serving the interests of the poor, who cannot afford to buy larger quantities of the same. NDTV or other players sachetize their news stories and diversify their audience segments, even though the composition of their news room is scarcely subject to such gender and caste inclusivity. While on one hand, the political party reaches its populace in their respective sachets facilitated by the news carrier, while the same channel continues to purvey exclusivity in its English language market. Thus, the combined strategies, diversification and sachetization widen the spectrum of the news commodity, without diversifying the mentality of news. As an aside, it is also worth mentioning that the double bind of linguistic and class divide can be noted through a mere translation. NDTV also has an elite lifestyle channel called NDTV Good Times. Good Times can be translated as *Achcha Samay or Achche Din*. Incidentally, this translation became popular with the masses as the tagline of BJP's 2014 campaign, designed by Bombay ad guru Piyush Pandey, of Ogilvy Mather.

Consolidating Stacks and Bundles

In order to understand how the three commodity logics of standardization, diversification and sachetization are built into the core infrastructure of Digital India, I will turn to examining the macrological changes brought about by the emergence of Reliance Jio as the largest phone carrier in India. Reliance has been a media and telecom player for a long time now, although Reliance's initial models of CDMA phones tanked. From around 16 middle-rung players active in India's telecom markets in 2009–2010 (of which Hutchison Essar [later Vodafone], Idea and Airtel were the leading market players), only three private players remain in 2019–2020 (Hill and Athique 2018): Airtel, Vodafone-Idea (a merger) and Reliance. This tripartite distribution of power can be considered apart from the state-held company Bharat Sanchar Nigam Limited (BSNL). For its part, BSNL, the underlying public network run by the Government of India, has been steadily selling off its reach, allowing Jio to spread rapidly across the communication layer and position itself as the national champion for 5G investment. Since the 2019 national elections BSNL has been in limbo, with its employees unpaid since the result was announced. By contrast, the 'free' data availability offered by Reliance Jio since 2015, has swiftly captured the lion's share of Indian telecom market.

Rather it seems that Reliance has moved closer to the government and its core ambitions than the company that the government actually owns. But unlike the notorious 'license Raj' era of the 1970s and 1980s, which had fairly explicit nepotistic arrangements, the affinities between the Government of India and the dominant players in telecoms only tend to reveal themselves at opportune moments. In 2016, a government allocation of bandwidth shows that Jio got around 20 MHz (more than BSNL) in Tamil Nadu. Furthermore, Reliance was advantaged by the sudden decision to usher in the 'Bill and Keep' system to replace the earlier interconnection usage charges (IUC) model, (which levied from the consumer for connecting across two different telecom service providers). As the former head of Videsh Sanchar Nigam Limited (VSNL) (later Tata), BK Syngal writes:

> There have been demands to bring in the Bill and Keep (BAK) system and do away with the interconnection usage charges (IUC) in the telecom industry. The BAK regime, it is said, will usher in consumer benefits and technology upgradation. But little has been said on why IUC should continue to remain in force ... IUC is still an acceptable model, based on the simple logic that operators need to recover the cost they have invested in developing the network. While no one can argue against the fact that competition is necessary, it cannot be generated at the expense of existing players and for the benefit of newcomers. Moreover, the Indian market dynamics are not prepared to move towards a BAK regime due to inherent asymmetries. The need of the hour is tariff rebalancing in order to make full use of technological evolution towards data, and not shortcuts such as eliminating IUC. (Syngal, B. 2018, March 9)

After Jio's entry in the market, the switch from IUC to 'bill and keep' (BAK) was not only favourable to them economically but also at the technological level, since it essentially allowed a change in calling modality from circuit-switching network calling to data transfer (as small packets of data get transferred over to connect the phone call). From the users' perspective, only Jio-to-Jio calls have the 4G Voice over Long-Term Evolution (VOLtE) mechanism, as used in Viber and WhatsApp. Hence, they clearly preferred a single device which provides more connectivity and is virtually 'free' to use, as the call is converted to free data packets. Of course, while the data packets could be assumed to be free, they are linked a host of consumer product services. Thus, along with the stacking of infrastructure, the other feature of this emergent media economy is commodity bundling. Simply put, where several media products come under one provider gateway, and where one product offers some discount or cashback upon the other, a bundle of commodities is created. With this push and pull intrinsic to the platform economy, it is the horizontal expansion across businesses that are 'integrated' so that every click, share, like, follow and subscription can be monetized (Athique 2019). What else can define these interlaced data packets than the market logics of standardization and sachetization?

In the news portfolio, like a Bollywood film regaling domestic clashes in business families, the long-running dispute between Ambani brothers has led to Jio (Mukesh Ambani's endeavour) claiming that Reliance will default on their earlier telecom company R-Com (Anil Ambani's brainchild). Beyond the operatics of sibling rivalries, the larger point is that in return for access to free data availability, Jio demands its users' fingerprints, Aadhaar IDs and customer bank details. It is no accident that it is becoming a primary instrument for baking surveillance capitalism into India's digital ecosystem. It is, in that respect, rather like Paytm, the mobile payments provider that uses Prime minister Narendra 'Modi's photograph prolifically in its advertisements and gets only marginally fined for its proven unconstitutional usages of customer data. As things stand, the increasingly centralized regime exercised by home minister Amit Shah and PM Modi ensures that these corporations can operate laissez-faire beyond constitutional bounds, even if not everyone is taken with the zeitgeist of disruption, including their competitors:

> The Cellular Operators Association of India (COAI) has called the interconnect regulation disastrous and has decided to go to the court. In a strong worded reaction, Vodafone said, 'This is yet another retrograde regulatory measure that will significantly benefit the new entrant alone while adversely affecting the rest of the industry as a whole. Unless mitigated, this decision will have serious consequences for investment in rural coverage, undermining the government's. (Singh, P. 2017, September 20)

Jio baits its integrated commodity with free data that can be used for endless consumption of ancillary products. Jio has also teamed up with five other companies to provide international connections across the world. By such means, Jio has captured the mobile consumer market with its predatory pricing in the first instance, but the monopoly ambitions of Jio spread far beyond the telecom sector. Now akin to the Foxtel device which rolls Wi-Fi internet at 4G speed, various subscriptions of fiction and non-fiction TV and platform shows and gaming into one device, Jio has introduced its new toy called 'Gigafiber', which will also provide access to films on the first day of their theatrical release, which the consumers can watch sitting at home (Bhushan, K. 2019, August 12). Reliance Jio is either present or entering in all domains of the media economy in some form or other. For example, Jio bought Saavn music app and created seven of its own apps for entertainment, and it is conducting rapid acquisitions of numerous digital platforms which create fiction (web series and films) and non-fiction (documentaries), apart from establishing its own Jio Studios. Since 2008, Reliance has loaned money to ETV and Network 18 and by the end of 2012, its holdings have made it a de facto media mogul in the classic sense.

Reliance Jio still faces resistance from other players providing interconnection points. A key requirement for this data packets to travel is through optic fibre, so even after their losses in the telecom sector—particularly after the Docomo partnership came to a standstill—the Tatas are still key players in the communication layer. Completing its first round-the-earth mapping of cable as early as 2012 with their fibre optic cables, Tatas have had invisible but nonetheless ubiquitous presence having practically covered the planet with MPLS (multi-protocol label switching), laying out the infrastructure for 'end-to-end' calling (Curtis 2012, March 12). How do these deep market layers intersect within India's emerging digital architectures, that is, within the prevailing code of production? Benjamin Bratton's explication is the hexagram architecture called the Stack. The media is very literally stacked on top of another on the smartphone as apps; it is stacked as they replace one another on-screen on TV, on multiple, simultaneous tabs on the internet. Six key locations of the Stack according to Bratton are City, Address, User, Interface, Earth and Cloud (Bratton 2016: 11).

Where they occupy intersectionality in the Indian context is the interface of the website called, unsurprisingly, India Stack. This intersection of imaginaries (social, institutional, infrastructural and political) has four layers: presence-less, paperless, cashless and consent layer. In this top-downing process, consent comes last from the API makers' point of view. They are, after all, the first layer users who enjoy an enhanced connection with government, businesses, start-ups and developers. The current catchphrase, 'Data is (Srnicek 2017: 40),' which aligns financial and infrastructure interests with blue sky data-mining, is made attractive primarily because of the presence-less and ubiquity of individuals, publics, institutions, states and global networks. Bundles, stacks and data are being brought together, as the ruling mechanism of digital economics and coercive politics. To this end, humans as resources and unwitting labour are bundled into integrated commodities priced by media markets (Athique 2019). However, this sweeping enclosure should not be heedlessly understood as a post-human hybridity of technological interaction, since

> [h]ybrid terms delay recognition and defer understanding of what requires our most audacious attention. So instead of piling on more hybrids, exceptions, and anomalies, we need a glossary for a new normal, and for its design and redesign. (Bratton 2018: 7)

The new normal is not simply aggressive investments in infrastructural monopolies, but also the hysterical imperatives for the swift on-sale of data portfolios loaded with fear and risk. This underlying dynamic of the digital infrastructure informs the process of news-making by porous yet uneven media meta-narratives, insurrectional regionalism from below, as the event line of market concentration is breached at the top.

Disrupting the Disruption

Chakravartty and Roy write about the 2014 elections and the BJP win, denoting that it is 'mediated populism' that determines the logics of our (Chakravartty and Roy 2015: 313). But, unlike European histories of fascism, India has not until now seen an efficient combination of corporatism and right-wing political parties capable of assuming control over its public sphere. While Trump and Putin can smirk about non-traceability of election-rigging as a joke, the Indian story of the nexus of media and politics has always been regarded as a serious (Department, O. J. U. S. 2019). There is no doubt, nonetheless, that is has operated with similar, unreflexive and increasing impunity. As an intrinsic part of this process, the space occupied by critical and investigative journalism has been closed down by the diarchy of corporate media infrastructure and authoritarian government. Thus: 'It is this 'apex' market that dominates everyday market discourses transmitted by the proliferation of media channels' (Parthasarathi and Athique 2019: 4). Occasionally, however, something unbundles itself and seeps through the layers of the stack.

Cobrapost, a not-for-profit organization led by Anirudh Bahal specializes in such media 'stings', typically with sensationalist and scandalous overtones. To date, Cobrapost claims to have 'exposed' numerous instance of corruption such as buying seats in the parliament, ministers demanding bribes to raise questions, black money laundering everywhere, social media movements organizing fake likes and followers, ministers lobbying for foreign firms, instances of paid and fake news across 36 major media outlets, and the siphoning of money through shell companies across the economy. Kalyani Chadha notes that when such sensational forms of provocative journalism become normalized, and when such scams are repeatedly put out in public eye, their homogenization of national dissolution 'not only creates a sort of false equivalence between scandals but also elides very real differences in their implications for the public interest'. Scandals get conflated onto one another like a clockwork set of exposes and result into what Chadha calls 'scandal fatigue' as 'viewers' check-out' (Chadha 2019: 242). What still seeps through could perhaps be seen in an example from a 2018 sting by Cobrapost where a senior member of the Paytm mobile transaction app admitted to giving away the personal information data of users from the volatile region of Kashmir to the Prime Minister's office on request.

Being remediated as blobs of code allows for the territorial conflation of Jammu into Kashmir, and for lurkers to read the affected people as either militants or veiled Pakistani interests who, by the ritualized, rehearsed, coloured definitions of the Indian right wing, are anti-India and pro-militancy. More broadly, reformatting all people as codes seems to be an essential aspect of framing people in the immediacy of an identitarian crisis imposed from the centre. In facilitating the datafication of dissenting identities, Paytm readily and routinely compromised personal data information of their online transaction customers to gain favour with the government. The illegality of such an arrangement was itself swiftly recoded, since the government can invoke sweeping concerns of national security, allowing it to plug and play with porous data systems like Aadhaar and the locative and financial accounts intrinsic to the format of digital citizenship. Via this mentality, the amended National Security Act was easily passed in the parliament, despite opposition parties calling out the BJP for making routine provisions which codify India as a 'Police State'. The dual inside-outside moment of expanding border and narrowing definitions of citizenship in digital times provides the pathway for the Indian government passing the Citizen Amendment Act in 2019, which offers sanctuary on the selective basis of religion, marking India as a sanctified technocracy where only Muslims are not welcome.

Another Cobrapost hidden-video sting shows actor Vivek Oberoi offering to propagate the schemes of PM for payment, preferably cash, amongst his fan base. Oberoi, of course, had just played the role of PM Modi in a puerile biopic, intended for release during the 2019 general election, but put on hold after a ruling from the Election Commission. Oberoi is seen in the video sting arguing that his desire to participate in the propaganda machine results from a desire to draw attention of the society towards issues of national development. He energetically refreshes the memory of the reporter about the merit of governmental schemes, while informing him that the ripple effect of his Twitter, Facebook and Instagram influence would constitute around two crore people as footfall. Routinely lacklustre celebrities like Oberoi look for capital induced activities such as election campaigning to remain in the limelight. The footprint of the somewhat-celebrity here is thus indicative of mundane political opportunism from Bollywood, which for Modi lends a viscerality to his propaganda. As a business proposition, neither film or news media break-even in terms of their investments, hence the *political* and *figurative* impact of such investments comes to the fore. Investments in what Srinivas calls 'economic externalities' are 'the unintended consequences…embedding corporate, religious and political capital into the media markets' (Srinivas 2018: 170–172). In such an environment, despite its regularized expose of errant celebrities, politicians and businessmen, Cobrapost's aesthetic of disruption remains a minor ripple in the broader currents of incitement, accommodation and impunity.

The Commodity of Fear

Around 2006–2007, in early days of monetizing SMS functions, the news media started cultivating the public opinion poll, routinely asking the people to consolidate a generic opinion. The ticker tactic rapidly moved to show the changing status of the stock market, while the letterbox format demanded more attention towards block headlines. Soon, Twitter hashtags found their own spaces and would casually reflect political favouritism of whichever party and/PR business house the news channel had aligned itself with. Hologram effects were used from general elections to the cricket world cup. As the velocity of news increased, there was insufficient time or inclination for a news channel to accommodate the panellists, who are poles apart from each other in opinion as well as location. Arnab Goswami, earlier an anchor on *Times Now*, now creator and part-owner of Republic TV on one end uses his decibel power to shut others down and caters mainly to corporate yuppies, while Ravish Kumar from NDTV India on the other speaks in a colloquial North Indian Hindustani to reach out to the heartland middle classes. Kumar does formal experiments on his show including blacking out screens to avoid the viscerality of the visual and the verbalization of bigotry-ridden arguments which are staple on other news channels. However, it is anchored in the voice of anchor sitting in media concentration of Bombay and Delhi. The former is the economic capital; the latter is the political one. For such diversification of the televisual, Akshaya Kumar identifies some key features of this current simulacrum of 'liveness' which is not live in fact, spirit or temper. He posits that the liveness-as-ontology becoming recoded by the digital as material and affect (Kumar 2015: 539). Kumar adds: 'The problem of liveness is two-fold: (1) the analytical gap between content and audiences collapses and (2) the news media works out convenient exceptionalism by which spaces away from the newsroom are further removed' (Kumar 2015: 539).

Regarding the screen affordances and presentation style of the TV news, Kumar notes: 'Space in televisual liveness is doubly constructed. The newsroom becomes the enunciative space, and the anchor sitting atop it becomes the referee for the non-enunciative space (…) the audience was thrown into an ecology in which relatively invisible class-based antagonisms were made visible to articulate scandal' (Kumar 2015: 539). Apart from Kumar's succinct observations about visual grammar, social structure of class divides, a lot changes with the inauguration of automation in the digital news form. In *Automating the News*, Diakopoulos informs us 'there's almost no facet of the news production pipeline, from information gathering to sense-making, storytelling, and distribution that is not increasingly touched by algorithms' and that 'anything lying outside the bounds of what is quantified is inaccessible to the algorithm, including information essential to making well-informed ethical decisions' (Diakopoulos 2019: 8–9). Eubanks writes eloquently of how automating 'systems' lead to inequalities. Telling the American story, she notes—'People of colour, migrants, unpopular religious groups, sexual minorities, the poor, and other oppressed and exploited populations bear a much higher burden of monitoring and tracking than advantaged groups' (Eubanks 2018: 3). More importantly, she critiques the celebration of technological potential merely because poor have access to them. She notes, 'technologies of poverty management are not neutral. They are shaped by our nation's fear of economic insecurity and hatred of the poor; they in turn shape the politics and experience of poverty' (Eubanks 2018: 3).

From local players rooted in regional politics, actors across the aisles venturing their own YouTube channels, there is an endless cycle of narratives and counter-narratives. TheWire.in carried the similar conspiratorial, at times alarming and reactionary ones. One opinion piece in *The Wire* reads—'*What If This Is Hindu Rashtra?*' Although its goal and temper are different from the right-wing automated bots', trolls' propaganda. The wire has diversified into Hindi, Urdu and Marathi languages. On this widening political spectrum, *Firstpost* made clickbaits out of the names of Jawaharlal Nehru University students—Kanhaiya Kumar, Umar Khalid, Shehla Rashid and actress and former Jawaharlal Nehru University (JNU) student Swara Bhaskar after the 9 February 2016 event organized to condemn state oppression, where allegedly anti-national sloganeering took place on JNU campus. The government argued that the slogans chanted should be brought under the definition of 'sedition', a colonial era law that charges people for inciting violence against the government through speech. The charge sheet was filed just before 2019 election, as Kumar was widely touted to win the local seat of his hometown Begusarai. In 2016, Kumar was immediately taken into custody, since he was the student union leader at the time of the protests. After Kumar securing bail and returned to campus, he made emphatic speeches, carrying the vocal charge of India's increasingly marginalized publics.

In this example, the *utterance* of what is now popularly known as the 'Azadi' (freedom) chant went viral and thereby altered its form through the data packets of the media. It became a YouTube hit after local DJ Dub Sharma turned parts of the speech given by Kumar into a rap song, which became an anthem for youth, subsequently also used in Bollywood film—*Gully Boy* (Akhtar et al. 2019), about a rapper's life in a slum in Bombay. Finally, it was appropriated by both the ruling party and the opposition for their campaign songs. Each version shows a generational loss of fidelity from slogans and meanings which in their earliest forms were raised by Pakistani feminists protesting their own government in the late 1980s. The film drops the slogans raised about caste and gender inequality, while the parties employed their own media PR management to make eliminate all the intended rebellion in the slogan song to highlight issues of 'development' and 'progress'. Automation and the subsequent virality does not of itself necessitate the exclusion of human actors, but it typically leads to such refractions of the intended message. Furthermore, as the slogan became a digital commodity, it was stacked against a vice-regal legacy of sedition and oppression, which has itself been reconstituted by Amit Shah in the age of datafication. Sedition laws have made a comeback, spurred by social media affordances and reinforced by the savvy bots that have the ability to track and trace citizen identities online as well as conveniently fake collective grassroots participation when needed (Arora 2019: 47).

Arora argues that old and new media act in concert and also reconfigure the earlier caste and class divides. Thus, media diversity does not necessarily result in political inclusion. Nor does fake news remain exclusive to the metropolis, since it finds its most virulent form in small town and grassroots moralism. Such multitudes of voices could be heard in the latest caste-ridden drama of Sakshi Mishra's marriage with her lover Ajitesh.

Most of these memes moralize her conduct of marrying out-of-caste and 'going public,' ultimately, seen as defaming her family members. With twists and turns of a bad, foamy TV soap opera, Sakshi's story is indicative of deep-seated social opprobrium. NDTV, from its national capital standpoint, reorganized the debate about bodies, taint and endogamous relations into realm of urban discursivity by giving a platform to Dalit leaders Chandrashekhar Azad and Rahul Sonpimple to reflect on caste atrocities. Elsewhere, strategies of diversification and sachetization milked the story, by foregrounding the conduct of the lower-caste boy Ajitesh smoking marijuana, or using a different name in social media profile, or the couple breaking off their engagement and then getting back together, or the court deciding their marriage is valid, or another entirely unrelated couple being abducted from the court premises the same day the court certifies the marriage. The hyperbole of the subject of the debate—*Is India more casteist than we were ever before?*—clearly exuded the rising paranoia as communal confrontation gathers pace.

Portfolios of Fear and Risk

The commodity of fear cuts across all channels, along with and not beside their political inclination, and after the advent of social media, it polarizes people across the political spectrum with a relentless velocity. As we have seen, this strategic digitality does not operate only through the right-wing inclined media which perpetuates fear and post-factual stories. It also infuses the language used by liberal left-inclined media as it demonstrates its own knee-jerk reactionary politics. Sides are readily taken. Soon after the 2019 elections, TheWire.in had several defamation cases, filed against them. Anil Ambani ('allegedly' involved in the Rafaele weapon scam) slapped 28 media houses with defamation cases, and very few would dare to bring such investigations regarding Mukesh Ambani's part of the Reliance conglomerate. Mainstream media outlets were compelled by the hedging imperatives of the democratic spectacle to be at least partly critical of Modi government during election season, but swiftly returned to their customary servility once the tally was in. As the new normal became further entrenched, eminent journalists like Punya Prasoon Bajpai, Abhisaar Sharma, Barkha Dutt and Vinod Dua had to leave their earlier media houses and move to smaller digital setups due to pragmatic changes in the editorial line of thinking.

Under the gathering clouds of automation and authoritarianism, it is obviously pertinent to give critical attention to the algorithmic logics through which clickbaits, trolls and bots have optimized hate culture and fear mongering. What has made this age of trolls both possible and permissible? Can we stare down the imposed and implied threats of automation and exclusion and take effective responsibility for the design and redesign of our new normal, rather than acceding so readily to technological determinism and fatalism, urban dystopias, resurgent feudal pasts, disorienting temporalities and cascading scales of data generation? Can we move away from ever more insistent apocalyptic visions of the future towards actually being aware of the ethical choices demanded by our present circumstances? It seems not. Amit Shah's digital scrutiny of citizenship is designed to border, order and number citizens, and asks them to reproduce documents from before 1971 to threaten the basic securities of legitimate citizenship. Yet, the rational processes have served this irrational impulse poorly. The hastily done citizenship tests on the brink of 2019 election results has shown that even the majoritarian Hindus do not have the required documents to remain in the matrix of Digital India. Currently millions of people have legitimate fears over their citizenship status. Can such portfolios of fear and risk be offset by further infrastructural or clickbait interventions?

What, then, is the news but a meta-narrative of our national anguish? Discourses of rationality in India have been paralysed in recent years by a collapsing tunnel vision. Whether it be NDTV or The Wire.in or *Firstpost*, the language is hyperventilated, every story shrill and scandalous, every reaction amplified and magnified, and every aversion or expression of outrage riddled with sentimentalism about the past and scepticism about the present. The aporia of our situation is that while fear permeates through the veins of media and society, the panacea of the market is cannot hold up as a repository of deferred hope. We do not perhaps even feel the need to default wilfully like Greece, since a majority of Indians are still not under the formal economy and thus lack capacity to 'drop out' in such style. While devastating measures like demonetization have resulted in the evident decline of GDP, India's economic pundits remain committed to their dream of achieving the status of a five trillion-dollar economy. Yet such dreams are swiftly erased by quantitative interventions that leave value perpetually unrealisable in the Global South. Only the narratives of expanding media power and technological intrusion seem to be enduring.

Thus, we can be reassured to know that Reliance will be there to provide security for the media conglomerates.

Nonetheless, fear is a commodity which media keeps investing in and thereby furthers the gathering gloom. Sara Ahmed, notes that more than hate, it is fear that leads us to violence. The diversification and, indeed, sachetization, of caste, gender and class numbering are such that majority, that is, Bahujans, are rendered as minorities, while 20 percent of the entire population, that is, Brahmins, reassert their hegemony over jobs, places, the national in politics and economic magicality and, by such means, appear determined to represent themselves as a majority, albeit one burdened its own portfolios of risk and, fear and doubt. Like risks in the bourses, India has a list of national aspirations that can be betted upon or against, just as the perpetually obscured failures of a farmer or an apartment dweller can be betted upon by others, whose own positions, big and small, are increasingly insecure. Hence the formalization of the economy by digital means amplifies the speculative interests of markets by opening opportunities to bet on the fear of others. Even as we run faster, the pace of the global race shrinks further, and those who run and those who hedge bets against must suffer the demands of enhanced velocity. We fall back on old strategies, like the Swachh Bharat—Clean India campaign—Cleaning and cleansing, purification and putrefaction, prescription and proscription—all go hand in hand. As we wash our hands with increasing desperation, India is signing up for sovereign bonds of 68,888 crores, the commodity form of a seemingly unending crisis. The state participates along with corporate entities and media to alter the technological, infrastructural, social and political imaginaries for propagating the commodity of fear. As Ahmed notes:

> It is the futurity of fear, which makes it possible that the object of fear, rather than arriving, might pass us by. (…) We might note here that fear does something; it reestablishes distance between bodies whose difference is read off the surface, as a reading that produces the surface. (Ahmed 2004: 125–126)

It is obvious that apparatus of digital technologies escalates the risks being taken and engenders new risks to be betted upon. On the platforms provided by this carriage, the spectacle-oriented psychology of media thrives on the growing portfolio of fear, stoking uncertainties which the markets can monetize further. V.G. Siddharth, the owner of Café Coffee Day (CCD), committed suicide after tremendous losses in the market, just like the farmers who have been committing suicide in droves for the past two decades of liberalization. This world on a wire, scaffolded by ever more pipes and platforms that pass through oceanic optic fibre and internet, simultaneously creates a metadata footprint that justifies India's shift to the dystopian meta-narrative demanded by authoritarian capitalism. The perennial ambitions of imposing such efficiencies on India's sachetized public consciousness inevitably founder amongst the competing logics of consolidated infrastructures and the disintegrating commodities of truth, trust and triumphalism. In such uncertain times, can the manifold termites of a crumbling democratic edifice continue to frustrate the data dumps and power-hungry stacks of technological territory? Distracted by the splintered logics of platform news, we are left to swipe socialbots, engross ourselves in the like-share-subscribe economy, re-circulate fake news and boost the bandwidth of the profits being drawn from portfolios of risk and fear.

References

Ahmed, S. (2004). Affective Economies. *Social Text, 22*(2), 117–139.

Akhtar, F., Sharma, S., Sidhwani, R., (Producers) & Akhtar, Z., (Director & Producer). (2019). Gully Boy [Motion Picture]. Retrieved from https://www.primevideo.com/detail/0I5OF8K1O8JNLUPOQ3VU3MBR5I/ref=dvm_src_ret_au_xx_s.

Arora, P. (2019). Politics of Algorithms, Indian Citizenship, and the Colonial Legacy. In A. Punathambekar & S. Mohan (Eds.), *Global Digital Cultures: Perspectives from South Asia*. Ann Arbor: University of Michigan Press.

Athique, A. (2019). Integrated Commodities in the Digital Economy. *Media, Culture and Society*, Online first. https://doi.org/10.1177/0163443719861815.

Bhushan, K. (2019, August 12). After Jio, India went from data dark to data shining: Mukesh Ambani at GigaFiber launch. http://tech.hindustantimes.com/. https://tech.hindustantimes.com/tech/news/after-jio-india-went-from-data-dark-to-data-shining-mukesh-ambani-at-gigafiber-launch-story-zOlVQB0Rk89Q96RQMbHuHJ.html.

Bratton, B. H. (2016). *The Stack: On Software and Sovereignty*. Massachusetts: MIT Press.

Bratton, B. H. (2018). *The New Normal*. Moscow: Strelka Press.

Chadha, K. (2019). Media Stings and the Normalisation of Scandal in India. In H. Tumber & S. R. Waisbord (Eds.), *The Routledge Companion to Media and Scandal*. London and New York: Routledge.

Chakravartty, P., & Roy, S. (2015). Mr. Modi Goes to Delhi: Mediated Populism and the 2014 Indian Elections. *Television & New Media, 16*(4), 311–322.

Curtis, S. (2012, March 12). *Tata Communications completes fibre optic "ring around the world." Techworld.Com.* https://www.computerworld.com/article/3550733/tata-communications-completes-fibre-optic-ring-around-the-world.html.

Department, O. J. U. S. (2019). *The Mueller Report: The U.S. Special Counsel's Report on the Investigation into Russian Interference in the 2016 Presidential Election.* La Vergne: Dreamscape Media.

Diakopoulos, N. (2019). *Automating the News: How Algorithms Are Rewriting the Media.* Cambridge, MA: Harvard University Press.

Eubanks, V. (2018). *Automating Inequality: How High-Tech Tools Profile, Police, and Punish the Poor.* Old Saybrook, CT: Tantor Media.

Hill, D., & Athique, A. (2018). *The role of offshore financial centres in Indian telecoms.* The Indian media economy - Volume 1: Industrial dynamics and cultural adaptation. Edited by Adrian Athique, Vibodh Parthasarathi and S. V. Srinivas (pp. 66–92). Janpath, New Delhi, India: Oxford University Press.

Jaganathan, R. (2014, August 13). *Trai's media ownership curbs make no sense: half of India's media may have to shut down.* http://www.firstpost.com/. https://www.firstpost.com/business/brands-business/trais-media-ownership-curbs-make-no-sense-half-of-indias-media-may-have-to-shut-down-1983763.html.

Kumar, A. (2015). The Unbearable Liveness of News Television in India. *Television & New Media, 16*(6), 538–556.

Maurer, B. (2012). Mobile Money: Communication, Consumption and Change in the Payments Space. *Journal of Development Studies, 48*(5), 589–604.

Parthasarathi, V., & Athique, A. (2019). Market Matters: Interdependencies in the Indian Media Economy. *Media, Culture and Society.* Online first. https://doi.org/10.1177/0163443719853495.

Singh, P. (2017, September 20). *Incumbents' loss is Jio's gain.* www.governancenow.com. https://www.governancenow.com/views/columns/incumbents-loss-is-reliance-jios-gain-trai-rs-sharma.

Srinivas, S. V. (2018). Embedding Processes. In A. Athique, V. Parthasarathi, & S. V. Srinivas (Eds.), *The Indian Media Economy. Vol. I. Industrial Dynamics and Cultural Adaptation* (pp. 167–176). New Delhi: Oxford University Press.

Srnicek, N. (2017). *Platform Capitalism.* Cambridge: Polity.

Syngal, B. (2018, March 9). Why telecom sector needs IUC model. www.thehindubusinessline.com. https://www.thehindubusinessline.com/opinion/why-telecom-sector-needs-iuc-model/article22223208.ece1.

PART V

Platform Cultures

CHAPTER 13

Informality in the Time of Platformization

Akshaya Kumar

In the 1980s, the emergence of the audiocassettes led to an explosion of recorded music throughout North India. Although North India is generally seen as the Hindi-speaking preponderance of India's linguistic geography, it is profoundly marked by a profusion of 'dialects' of this composite language, most of which are older than modern standard Hindi and remain closely linked to specific regions and population segments. In these various so-called dialects, 'vernacular' musical traditions blending ideas of 'folk' with more 'modern' motifs were greatly enhanced and expanded by the advent of portable media devices from the 1970s onwards. Vernacular singer-performers began to record albums in studios, in Garhwali, Haryanvi, Bhojpuri and other sub-regional languages on a large scale (see Tripathy 2012, 2018). The volume of production has kept expanding even as the recording and playback technologies have shifted from audio-cassettes, to music videos (on video compact discs [VCDs] first and digital video discs [DVDs] later) and to digital downloads for mobile phones (see Rawlley 2007). In recent years, the mobile phone has become the primary portable device on which sub-regional music videos thrive, whether the

A. Kumar (✉)
IIT Indore, Indore, India
e-mail: akshaya.kumar@iiti.ac.in

A. Athique, V. Parthasarathi (eds.), *Platform Capitalism in India*,
Global Transformations in Media and Communication Research - A
Palgrave and IAMCR Series,
https://doi.org/10.1007/978-3-030-44563-8_13

content is transferred offline on downloaded or streamed online (see Mukherjee and Singh 2017; Rashmi 2018). The larger part of the ecology of audiocassettes, discs, microSD cards and 'Chinese' mobile phones operates outside the formal economy. They constitute the thriving 'do-it-yourself' segment of media bazaars across the region, where repairing, refurbishing and re-using are the hallmarks of electronic merchandize retail. In this informal economy, the hardware is often 'dodgy' and the 'software' of recorded music—studio or elaborately edited videos of live concerts—is typically transacted without any concern for copyright whatsoever.

The eruption of vernacular media economy across North India has fundamentally altered the media production, distribution and consumption landscape. Bhojpuri media in particular has spread across the length and breadth of the country on account of labour migration. In the festival season, one may then witness numerous concert performances in the suburbs of Delhi and Mumbai, but also around other large cities of peninsular India. This complicates the 'regionality' of vernacular media, since it is shaped as much by the linguistic and cultural wealth of its 'native' region—western Bihar and eastern Uttar Pradesh—as by the traffic of personnel, imaginaries and devices (see Kumar 2016, 2018a). Vernacular media production has traditionally been based out of Delhi studios, but in the last decade, recording studios, mixing labs and various ad-hoc production facilities have mushroomed all across the Bhojpuri-speaking region. The relentlessly playful reconfiguration of regionality—with respect to the audience demography—lends Bhojpuri media in particular a curious slippery character that negotiates the national and the regional in site-specific ways. While the claim to national territory may wash ashore more often than in any other sub-regional media industry, in the suburbs of Mumbai, the artists may not deter from singing a *lavani* (an erotic performance constitutive of the Marathi *tamasha*) or addressing the audience as *uttar bhartiya* (North Indians), instead of Bhojpuri *bhaiyon* (brothers).

Informality has been the lifeblood of vernacular media economies, where freely sharing devices and copying media is routine practice (Lobato and Thomas 2015). In fact, much of the media content thriving in these economies only finds distribution through informal networks. Not only do pirated/counterfeit cassettes or discs sell cheaper to a large audience of limited means, but the practice copying itself allows pavement economies to operate outside the logics of formal retail distribution. For a retailer in a media market or a hawker on a pavement in Patna, it means not having to contact a corresponding wholesaler, who would call the Delhi-based production office to eventually receive more copies of a disc or a cassette witnessing a surge in demand. They can simply respond to the immediate demand by making more copies, without taking the undue risk of keeping extra inventory. Informality in the distribution chain invariably reflects the informal working conditions of marginal sellers as well as the purchasing power and technological access of the buyers. Informal distribution chains allow vernacular media markets to operate on the margins of larger formal markets, without having to endure the same risks of capital flow and investment, given that the financial securities required to hedge those risks tend to be unavailable to them.

In a sense, the juxtaposition of formal and informal media markets could be thought of as product-driven process versus services-driven supply. Formal products markets are guided by production infrastructures whereas informal markets are driven by the service demand from customers. In a formal product-driven market, the products are designed as per the existing knowledge of consumer demand, and then supported through the retail chain with adequate advertising push to ensure consumers will buy the media product catering to their demand. The informal markets pushing a services-driven commodity, untethered as they are to the big capital backing its retail distribution and advertising, tend to unhinge themselves from the production-end calculations of consumer demand. As a real-time *service* to the retail market, products are 'copied into' service provision on the pavements. Thus, it is important to understand that a key characteristic of informal media markets is that they are much less sensitive to the advertising-driven product differentiations which operate at the heart of capital-commodity dynamic of modern market economy. Partly, this has to do with the broken links between production and distribution ends, which renders informal markets their speculative character, outside of the sophisticated consumer analytics formal markets are increasingly saturated with.

Thus, for the informal economy, the prevailing idea is to attend to the segmented customer base instead of trying to aggregate them within a product-driven market, as formal industries tend to do. In that sense, the ethos of the informal economy both predates and informs the shopfront logics of the digital platforms that have emerged in India over the past decade. Thus, even though discourses of platform economy have become oriented to digital ecosystems, there is no reason why we cannot develop a broader account of platform economy. Accordingly, this chapter investigates the interactions between the distribution arsenal of platform economies and the informal media markets that had emerged previously as 'local' pockets of growth *outside* the centrally controlled distribution of mainstream media. A narrative of disruption prompts us to ask: How does the rise of platform economy disrupt or reorganize these informal markets? A more evolutionary perspective prompts us to ask: How do consumer formations in these informal markets inform the trajectory of platformization in India? This is also a pertinent question to ask of the business logics of digital platforms as an international phenomenon. This chapter therefore gives some critical consideration therefore as to whether we are witnessing the beginning of the end of informal media markets, or their profusion via digital domains as web connectivity penetrates deeper.

As I will establish, the live concerts where thousands gather to witness the artists perform through the night is a key site which escapes the grip of platformization. Not only are such concerts the kernel of activity within vernacular media economy, they are also a thriving site of informal exchanges that slip outside the archival aggregation, either in an ad-hoc manner at the arbitrage platforms or via algorithmic accumulation at YouTube. Delineating three somewhat distinct tendencies of archive, I discuss how the live concerts work against the distributive control of platform economies by privileging the informal performative presence over the relay of staged, orchestrated and edited media commodities. The chapter, therefore, highlights one of the central features of vernacular media that sits in a fundamental conflict with platform economies in media industries.

Arbitrage Platforms: From Audio Cassettes to Download Kiosks

Before the advent of audio cassettes, the centrepiece of media ecology in rural and semi-urban North India was the radio, or its younger cousin, the transistor. Men and women would congregate around the radio and perform domestic chores while listening to songs, news, or special programmes to address agrarian matters, or host a celebrity. All India Radio curated programmes featuring film songs as the key entertainment packages on the device. They would be old and new Hindi film songs produced in Mumbai. With the entry of audio cassettes, 'two-in-ones' offering both radio and cassette functions replaced the radio as the most desirable domestic media device. Importantly, song lists could now be curated by the owner of the cassette device, and recordable cassettes with song collections of personal favourites came into vogue. Even more importantly, cassettes allowed a large number of singers to record themselves through production studios and access diffuse media markets neglected by the major companies. This small revolution invigorated the music industry in North India, a tale well recounted in Peter Manuel's *Cassette Culture* (1993). As a modality of both production and distribution, analogue tape and audio cassettes were revolutionary. As opposed to the handful of music companies which had previously aligned their music catalogues to a mass market, an explosion of vernacular music industries in sub-regional North Indian 'dialects' ushered in a host of genres, studios, artists and audiences.

This expansion was, in many ways, akin to what is now labelled as platform capitalism. For the vernacular media, a new interlocking ecology was instantiated in which participants were drawn in and aggregated via new shopfronts (studios, retail stores, performance stages). As Manuel has narrated, political and religious campaigns would try to capture the public formed at the sites of musical performance. The chart-topping songs produced for a political or religious campaign reflected the repurposing potential of the vernacular media commodity via public spectacles of popular support. Thus, the celebrity performer became the most vital mediator across platforms and ideological tendencies in a series of informal domains. As in platform business models, transactions between expression and influence became subject to *arbitrage* by monetizing the congregations of live audiences (Tripathy 2018). The audio cassette thus constituted a platform that could replicate and repurpose the site of live performances, thereby instantiating strategic *arbitrage platforms* such as a neighbourhood *ramayan path*, *akhand jagran* or a political rally. Unlike digital platforms of the present, there was no algorithmic aggregation at the monetization end. Arbitrage without algorithms were the hotbed of sharing, the basis of communal relations and the lifeblood of informal economy. Thus, the calculation and billing of arbitrage, in a manner of speaking, was crude, manual and speculative. These platforms were, nonetheless, geared towards increasing diversity and the multidirectional growth of consumption sites, devices and retail.

The next major iteration in this trajectory of platformization, the VCD, appended the music video to the sonic data previously circulated on cassettes. The cassettes did not die out for a long while, however, and a majority of VCDs were simply direct recordings of live performances. In this ecosystem, Bhojpuri music interlocked with Garhwali, Himachali, Maithili and Haryanvi music, primarily in the Delhi studios, while the audiovisual effects overlapped with various other video-making practices, as in wedding and birthday videos, or religious and political campaigns. Yet, as another arbitrage platform, VCD, and later DVD, were further constituents of an arbitrage media economy that was not consolidated at the capital ownership end. The informal music economy operated in parallel to the practices that Adrian Athique has identified with the 'disorganized' Indian film economy of the twentieth century, prior to its remarkable consolidation in this century (2008). That is, cassettes, VCDs and DVDs nonetheless enabled enormous growth in artists, songs and performances through an economy which was interlocking in terms of flow of personnel and tendencies, but fragmented in terms of capital and control. India's 'festival season', from *Chhatth* all the way to *Holi*, would witness an annual deluge of songs and music videos flooding the market, from which a more limited stock of tunes, melodies and orchestration schemes would be repurposed from the concert stage to the film songs. The volume of content could therefore be misleading, since it only signified the flow across the interlocking arbitrage economy, in which platforms suspended in a shifting media ecosystem variously attended to the expanding consumer base of vernacular music.

While the VCDs/DVDs or cassettes required players which were often owned by a group, cheap mobile phones gradually replaced them as a more individually oriented interface for storage, recording as well as playing media files. Given the weakness or unavailability of network connectivity, the success of the 'smart' mobile phone among the working classes was primarily on account of its usage as a powerful media platform. The key site for feeding these mobile phones was the download kiosk at a mobile recharge shop (see Rashmi 2018). A vendor would typically need only 'a laptop full of songs and videos, a dongle to connect a memory card through a USB port, and some format conversion software' (Mukherjee and Singh 2017, p. 260). Mukherjee and Singh wrestle with this question with respect to the microSD cards that are central to the informal economy of download kiosks:

> At one level, memory cards are platforms that consist of hardware and software components that permit music to be recorded, stored, and played. At another level, memory cards span different emerging platform systems of audio/DVD players, mobile phones, and TV sets and become part of these

various sensory infrastructures. Memory cards reconfigure various mobile media assemblages and create an ecosystem of platforms around them … Indeed, the platform ecosystem consisting of Chinese DVD players, audio players with Pepsi or Axe cases, and iPod knock-offs that memory cards inhabit are accompanied by untaxed services, counterfeit goods, fake accessories, and unlicensed goods. Nonetheless, these informal platform ecosystems also grow and innovate just like industry platforms, albeit in different ways and through different channels. And just like digital algorithm-and-interface-based online platforms, the not-always-online or rather offline digital platforms … operate according to (informal) economic/business models, are characterized by an ecosystem/network logic, and provide spaces for users to participate and interact. (Mukherjee and Singh 2017, pp. 261–263)

Rather than determining whether the mobile phone or the microSD cards should be identified as platforms, Mukherjee and Singh argue for a platform ecosystem which may not be entirely web based. Taking their fundamental premise, that platform functions need to be understood independently of their code-centric data structure, I argue that we must also distinguish between platforms and platform economies. Thus, while I conceptualize audio cassettes, video compact discs, digital versatile discs, mobile phones and microSD cards as *arbitrage platforms*– parts of an elaborate interlocking network in which small differentials are monetized—I also argue that they are not yet integrated into a *platform economy*. The latter outcome hinges upon algorithms of aggregation and value-creation via which modalities of ordinary sharing are dis-embedded from existing social economies and re-embedded in new transactional forms built for digital systems, which render them legible as transactions with a definite footprint (see Athique et al. 2018a, b). As long as arbitrage platforms remain outside algorithmic governance, they constitute platforms which are relatively independent of a platform economy. As such, the aim of the latter is to recruit the former into algorithmic governance, or what Beller calls computational capital (Beller 2016a, 2016b). As we go along, therefore, it is important to remember that even though the platform economy produces and sets into motion surplus time, attention, labour and property, platforms are prerequisites for, rather than derivative of, the digital drive for data accumulation.

Subscription Versus Advertising

India's platform economy is driven by the desire to occupy, aggregate and control informality and its communal life, by breaking it down to individuals that can be plotted within the formal domain of computational capital. The two clinching revenue models of the platform economy in the media industry are subscription or advertising based. In the case of the former, captive, paying customers are allowed access to content exclusive to the platform. In the latter case, the content is made accessible for free, at the cost of hijacking consumer for advertising merchandize. While the former is a relatively straightforward service to paying customers, the latter is a monopoly model where the user analytics becomes the product, which is accumulated and sold to the advertisers, who then indulge in targeted advertising (see Kumar 2018b). Targeted advertising is derived from psychographic and demographic profiles append to the platform's 'knowledge'. In India, YouTube has become the pre-eminent advertising-based platform for vernacular media consumption within the online sphere. As a content platform, the repository offered by YouTube is unmatched. It is the pre-eminent platform to access all vernacular media content in Bhojpuri, Haryanvi, Santhali, Uttarakhandi, Himachali and other 'dialects' of Hindi, while also carrying most of the official Television channels and copyrighted content. It also conveys the equivalent content in the non-Hindi-speaking regions of India, as Srinivas notes in the context of Telugu language content from South India:

> YouTube's status as the *official* repository of the local media industry has come into sharp focus. Today, major Telugu language television news channels including TV9, TV5 and ABN *Andhra Jyothi*, beam live on YouTube. All major Telugu television channels upload content on their official YouTube channels. For their part, film production and packaged media (VCD/DVD/Blu-ray) distribution companies have put out hundreds of film titles on their YouTube channels. More recent titles are available in the HD versions with English subtitles. Almost all Telugu YouTube content is freely accessible from Indian IP addresses. (Srinivas 2017)

The multichannel network (MCN) architecture of YouTube has been crucial to this sponge-like absorption of entire media spectrums across the globe. Lobato explains the shift from singular videos to MCNs in YouTube's cultural-economic logic after the takeover by Google in 2006:

> The early YouTube was characterized by the promise of direct, DIY communication with a global audience, and its corporate image was that of the upstart outsider. Today, YouTube is thoroughly mainstream. Its signature innovations—revenue sharing of video advertising, automated content ID and open viewer metrics—have become the basis for a massive commercial ecosystem … Every surface of YouTube—display ads, overlays, comments, pop-ups and not least the mise-en-scene of the videos—has been opened for business in one way or another. This process has involved not only Google but a wide range of other actors, including advertising agencies, data analytics firms, digital marketing companies and spambots, as well as hundreds of thousands of non-professional producers … MCNs are intermediary firms that operate in and around YouTube's advertising infrastructure. A common business model is for MCNs to sign up a large number of popular channels to their network, then, using YouTube's content management system, to sell advertising and cross-promote their affiliated channels across this network, while also working with popular YouTube celebrities to develop them into fully fledged video brands … As well as having a commercial relationship with YouTube, which works direct with popular creators via the Partner programme, many YouTubers now sign contracts with MCNs to increase their audience and advertising income and agree to split their ad revenue with the MCN accordingly. (Lobato 2016, pp. 348–349)

While it may seem to be unchanged as a platform in terms of the screen interface, the architectural and algorithmic shift in YouTube has made fundamental changes on at least two accounts: (i) targeted advertising for the absorption of ad revenue, and (ii) privileging copyrighted content for monetization. Lobato observes that the MCNs 'aggregate ad sales across the platform, increase the quality of uploaded videos, reduce intellectual property infringements and generally make it a more appealing space for advertisers' (Lobato 2016, p. 351). The MCNs, therefore, provide 'non-professional creators with technical, promotional and advertising services in exchange for a commission (20–50% of net advertising revenues)—a classic intermediary function' (ibid.). The algorithmic scalability and ad placement offers a well-rounded platform ecosystem that helps content creators garner attention in the YouTube ocean. MCNs, as a search optimization service tailored for YouTube, provide 'advice on titles, keywords and metadata and to associate content with topical and frequently searched-for terms' (ibid., p. 356). However, they privilege specific consumer 'verticals' such as fashion, cooking and tech review channels for their cross-promotional potential and 'their clear link to specific advertising markets and demographics' (ibid., p. 357). In an advertising-based interlocking ecosystem, information markets, regulatory structures and cultural dynamics appear to interpenetrate across digital media (mobile and web-based applications) in a platform economy. One of the key ideas here is to enable, shape and commodify new forms of sociability (see Athique 2019).

In spite of the apparent promise of industry consolidation, content aggregation and distribution of ad revenues, the absence of such consumer verticals for vernacular media content, which is mainly addressed to working-class migrants, complicates the picture significantly. The consumer analytics on vernacular media content do not encourage greatly the cross-promotional design of vertical integration and cross-promotion. The intermediary function to aggregate the informal economy and include it within the formal fold thus comes up against the limitations of advertising-driven media industries. One of the key roles of platformization, after all, is aggregating *people as analytics* to be sold to advertisers. Yet, the drive to vertically integrate, standardize and control the informal economy also empowers those holding franchise relationships, even if the dynamic is heavily weighted in favour of the franchisor (Vonderau 2016). India's informal video production, which earlier revolved around audio cassettes or VCDs/DVDs, now primarily focuses on YouTube channels (Wave Music, Angle Music and Ganga Cassettes being the prime aggregators) and the offline video sharing economy. Of course, the smaller MCNs are rarely interested in setting up their own player platform, since it is expensive to build and is entirely taken care of by YouTube. Questions of exploitation and regulation are thus at the heart of the post-MCN YouTube architecture.

It is important, however, to highlight key shifts that platformization via YouTube has introduced within India's vernacular media industries. First, the MCNs work as portfolio economies, in which generic diversity of content becomes crucial as a risk mitigating tactic, even though the biggest beneficiaries of aggregation remain the major film stars (Ascher 2016). Cross-promotional interests and algorithmic recommendations ensure that users navigate the channel portfolios in trajectories that best serve the interests of YouTube. Second, MCN-led architecture does not only serve its own enclosed interests, since it strategically outmanoeuvres the erstwhile singular video design. Instead of risking one's creative work and livelihood by dumping it in the YouTube ocean as a singular entity, artists are compelled to enter a contractual arrangement with the aggregators, while consumers are compelled to follow a new mode of guided consumption. Without the navigation function of the channels, no video can thrive in the ostensibly 'free' world of YouTube. Third, YouTube is at the heart of the platformization of vernacular music economy in terms of distribution, and it unflinchingly privileges the formalization of the informal economy. Fourth, in terms of arbitrage, YouTube only sits *beside* the thriving informal economy operating as a mode of public spectacle. Thus, while it is undeniable that successive media technologies have aided the exponential rise of vernacular music, the centrality of live concerts has never conceded pre-eminence to platformization. We must therefore keep the live concerts in focus to understand the broader life of informality in the time of platformization.

The Live Concerts

Informality is not a mere object of scholarly fetish in this discussion, but a step outside the control exercised by the production-distribution structure. As most media production tends to be capital intensive, its production costs and distribution infrastructure remain in the hands of small cartels. The life of sub-regional media began as an initiative outside this control of capital and distribution, when the likes of Manoj Tiwari who sang in live concerts began to sell their often pirated cassettes to a mass audience. Shall we simply concede that these spaces outside the formal sector have come full circle be consumed by formalization via digital technology and web-based platforms? Not quite, because informality, not as a simple economic, but as a performative temperament continues to define vernacular media in general and Bhojpuri media in particular. The live concerts, in spite of the newfound glitz and mounting political and religious patronage, recall and restore direct communication between artists and their audience. It is this essential performative substance which portable media devices promise to capture as arbitrage platforms. That is why, even as online views multiply relentlessly and offline data kiosks thrive, the performative informality of the live concert continues to mobilize millions across remote villages, small towns and big cities. The performative excess triggers communitarian solidarities built around language affinities. The visceral nature of live concerts which witness thousands congregate for a nightlong feast of performative surplus are regularized encounters with the vernacular 'public' spheres operating outside the formal straitjackets.

Most of these live concerts are advertised on account of a relatively well-known singer-performer, but a whole bunch of younger singers, dancers and anchors hold the crowd's attention for the bulk of the event. Patriotic, devotional and sleazy genres are blended together with a lot of direct conversation between the anchors or singers on stage and the crowds. Unlike Bollywood extravaganzas on 'world tours' where the stage remediates the screen, the Bhojpuri live concerts are far more intimate and receptive to the crowd's mood. The life of informality in live concerts, therefore, revolves around the fact that performers submit to the unpredictability of popular vote. Instead of serving them a film or album *product*, they orient themselves towards the *service* of popular demand. The live concerts therefore invert the formal grid in which popular culture operates as an industrial formation, and repeatedly underline the fundamental alterity of vernacular mediation. The live concert is also the kernel of communal solidarity as the basis of vernacular media's success. It is the pre-eminent site where a plea is made by an artist to the people and his candidature ratified for further outgrowth.

A whole range of hereditary genres and artists (such as *Dhobi geet* and *Ahirauwa naach*), only perform in the neighbouring towns and villages. Increasingly, though, the younger generation of performers do not wish to confine themselves to hereditary genres. Unlike a few decades ago, when expertise within a genre was the most desirable attribute, the performative virtuosity to switch across genres and styles is increasingly the most desirable component of informality that thrives in concert performances (Kumar, Forthcoming). One of the key battlegrounds of such virtuosity is the duel, where performers or their teams engage in a lively contest. Prakash writes about the genre:

> *Dūgolā* (singer-duels), also known as *laykārī muqābalā* (lyrical rivalry) or *lokgīt muqābalā* ('folk' song competition), is a popular performance of the Magahi and Bhojpuri regions of north India, in which two or more singers-performers rival against each other. Like a standup comedian, the *dūgolā* performer sings, dances, cracks jokes, tells stories and often composes new song and stories impromptu during a performance. There are similar structures of performance across India with different names, such as *kobigān* in Bengal, and *ladāi*, *muqāblā*, and *akhārā* in Uttar Pradesh and Madhya Pradesh ... Because of its competitive nature, *dūgolā* inherits strong elements of sports and play. In the last ten to fifteen years, there has been a strong resurgence of this song performance tradition in the Bhojpuri and

> Magahi regions of Bihar and Uttar Pradesh, with the growing market of Bhojpuri music and cinema industry … The performance gives space to new singer-performers to emerge, as well as for older performers to return and share years of acquired experience with the audience … *Dūgolā* performers sing, dance, and freely draw from all possible sources. They often alter existing musical compositions and compose spontaneously to score points on the rival group. Performer-singers often break into a quarrel, sing insult songs, and demonstrate power and valour through masculine gestures. (Prakash 2019)

Even though many of these *dugola* recordings are available on YouTube and on DVDs with various vendors, the substance of performative virtuosity in direct conversation with crowd is lost in those arbitrage platforms. Yet, towards the end of the YouTube videos of these events, the flicker at the bottom displays phone numbers to contact the production company and artists for organizing live concerts. The patronage for such shows could vary from private patrons at a village or town gathering to a more political or religious patronage with multiple stakeholders. In that respect, the live concerts stand not in opposition but adjacent to the affordances of platformization and its attendant formalization of the media economy. They recruit platforms as advertising agents, while continuing to sit beside, fiddling with the unpredictable, ephemeral, ribaldrous and sovereign declarations of popular will—widely available but not fully recoverable in the platform economy. Therefore, the informality and unpredictability of the live concerts, which constitute the kernel of both the economic and political substance of vernacular media, challenge the structure of archival tendencies of vernacular media. The archive, after all, determines the nature of community formation and politics of accessing the common wealth (see Kumar 2018a).

Three Ideas of the Archive

As discussed above, the shift from audio cassettes and VCDs/DVDs towards mobile phones and microSD cards marked a shift from communal viewing towards more individual consumption. Even if cassettes and discs were individually owned, the devices on which they were played were often collectively owned by the migrant workers in a shared accommodation. Mobile phones, on the other hand, are largely personal devices. Even when women or teenaged boys borrow the phones shared among family members, or from their elder brothers, they very often use their own microSD cards to personalize the device. Mukherjee and Singh offer some insights:

> Despite the ease and seamlessness in streaming music, the content remains with the content providers, which is not the case with memory cards. People have a personal attachment to their microSD cards; they keep them safe from scratches, they love to talk about their content (unless some of it is censored/pornographic), and, as such, it perpetuates a personal archiving practice. These *personal archiving practices* are marked by variation in the frequency of visits to the download vendor and a preference regarding the type of uploading. (emphasis added). (Mukherjee and Singh 2017, p. 265)

However, more interesting hybrids such as Chinese-made DVD players have emerged in the interstices between communal and individual modes of media consumption. Mukherjee and Singh call them mobile media assemblages, as they play videos not just from DVDs but also from microSD cards, which means that 'DVD players no longer just support DVDs, and microSD cards do not remain exclusive to mobile phones and their users. To make the microSD card compatible with new DVD players, various cheap USB adaptors have flooded the local market' (ibid., p. 266). If we were to think of these practices in terms of their archival kernels, the audio cassette, VCD/DVD or the microSD card all encourage individual/private storage of an exclusive set of data while holding key interest in sites of communal storage, whether it be a retail vendor or a download kiosk with its laptops/desktops and their classified storage. The user, therefore, maintains both personal as well as communal archives, knowing fully well the vulnerabilities of breakdown with unreliable devices (see Larkin 2008). Cassettes, discs or cards may get corrupted as easily as the players may stop working. The first idea of the archive, therefore, is one where storage and access to material always remains unreliable and site-specific. Even though one approaches a shop as a buyer within the informal economy, the archive is constituted by two unstable pieces—both struggling with the precarity of livelihood and technology. The working-class settlements, precarious wage labour employment, the mobile shops or download kiosks, the 'makeshift' devices, the illegal economy of downloads, the tricky format conversions specific to mobile phones' storage and player types constitute a lifeworld of citizen-archive duality in which no bounding block appears stable enough to hold its ground.

The second idea of the archive pertains to YouTube, which offers a paradigm shift as long as the user has access to sufficient Internet bandwidth. YouTube offers itself as an oceanic archive, which contains nearly every vernacular music document produced. With increasing formalization of the economy, video production companies are incentivized to upload their entire portfolio so they can harvest user hits and monetise them with ad revenues. In this ever-expanding archive, access remains 'free' as long as one concedes some attention to the advertisements and navigation remains fluid, either via autoplay or on account of the rich metadata. The remaining site of instability is Internet bandwidth. If one wants to access the free archive, one must subscribe to Internet data packs or plug into broadband connections. As it turns out, cheaper data packs have indeed encouraged many more to stream videos instead of maintaining personal storage and offline consumption. Yet, the battle over the prevailing idea of archive continues. The nature of archive, it must not be forgotten, indicates the character of citizenship rights. Formalization as a drive cannot entirely continue without the formalization of labour laws, fair wage employment, reliable working-class housing and social security. YouTube's effort to appropriate the informal economy within its formal fold is thus challenged by the precarious conditions of production which prevail, and of which vernacular music is an exemplar. Most of the time, these 'not-yet' citizens cannot simply walk into a stable archive, in spite of its pretensions of free and limitless access.

The third persistent idea of the archive at work, therefore, manifests the life of informality in the time of platformization. The instability of shifting arbitrage platforms, and unstable access to platform infrastructure, alleviates any threat to the vitality of eclectic, informal, unpredictable and visceral performative virtuosity of live concerts. It is only popular memory, in all its creative remembering quite unlike objective documentation, which resembles the archive. Yet, it does not quite follow its structural and bureaucratic regulatory principles. It may be a stretch to say that the archive comes undone at the site which celebrates ephemerality, but the live concert certainly offers the kernel of an informal lifeworld in which 'unequal' migrant working-class citizens claim temporary sovereignty as a mass public. If the mainstream archive of academic history relies too heavily on public institutions, the archive of popular culture traditionally departs from the regimental control of statist narratives. In its departure, however, the informal archive of popular culture remains 'unreliable', self-contradictory and often overdetermined. If one were to grip the archive of vernacular popular culture via arbitrage platforms or the platform economy, one would be confronted by the increasingly assertive 'regional' or 'provincial' migrants, who seek a return to their cultural cache via copyrighted or counterfeit media commodities. However, if one were to focus on the live concerts as performative extravaganzas instead, one would be confronted by the tendency to set the archive *aside*.

The performative spectacles of vernacular music are not so much the site of consuming the musical composition as a product, but the pre-eminent site where the performative is *placed in service* to the popular will. If the archive crystallizes the sedimentations of time, whether or not arranged in neat classifications, the loud and full-frontal publicness of Bhojpuri live concerts in particular defies both—the gradual layering of time and the organization of generic clusters of cultural wealth. Yet, the archival play at work in the live concerts entails the assertive publicness of Bhojpuri language. After all, the step outside the legal economic stranglehold over media enabled by the trajectory of vernacular media, which I have recounted, also endorsed a step outside the public shaming and subversion of vernacular languages. The third idea of the archive, then, performatively confronts the normative assumption that Bhojpuri, among other so-called dialects, belongs in private everyday realms. The archive is, first and foremost, a public resource, even if accessing it entails certain qualifications. What the assertive emergence of Bhojpuri and other vernacular music cultures indicate, among other things, is the clinching convergence of a two-faced arbitrage: (i) the translation of private reveries into public assertions, and (ii) the takeover of women's songs into a very masculine assertion of scandalous publicness (Singh 2015). In this way, the 'hidden treasure' of private archives is reclaimed for quasi-regionalist assertions in the public realm, which is duly mounted by a variety of male 'stars' (Kumar 2016). While arbitrage platforms have enabled and sustained the growth of this public assertion, and the platform economy could stretch that support further, the individual or communal consumption of vernacular media cannot possibly compensate for the spectacular publicness of a Bhojpuri live concert.

The inclusion of the Bhojpuri archive within the platform economy therefore marks the logic of *overflow*, instead of being the ultimate destination of the energies unleashed upon the stage. Even though we know that Bhojpuri music is hardly a mere extension of folk songs, the back and forth interpenetration between a media industry and the performative directness of the live concert qualify and reframe the complicated life of informality in the time of platformization. The archive of mobile media assemblages, on the other hand, manifests across makeshift devices prone to breakdown, dodgy bandwidths and corruptible files. Yet, the latter privileges direct ownership and access while the former breaks the wall in between. Even if media transactions based on streaming or playing offer access to audiovisual artefacts which appear to be tangible, they very often reflect and store what is already lost, or on its way out. The performative assertions of the live audience restore the present more than relaying the past. Presence, in flesh and blood, cannot be captured in any substantial sense on digital platforms.

Three Ideas of Informality

This chapter has discussed three primary ideas of informality. First, in terms of legally valid transactions of authentic or counterfeit media commodities. Second, as the lifeblood of an event where the unpredictable and rustic play on performative virtuosity. Third, as an everyday condition in which work, life, livelihood and pleasure are collectively and communally implicated together, to the extent that one appears to be suspended within the crevices of formal-legal relations, not necessarily aware or concerned about the imperatives of society or law. Arbitrage platforms emerged to translate the third order of informality towards the first two. They were variously supported by a moment of enthusiasm and opportunity for creative producers as well as distributors. Whether they sought a sale price or rent on services, the arbitrage platforms helped unearth the everyday archive of cultural wealth and set it in motion as objects and services in economic circulation. This led to an unprecedented expansion of the popular archive with the interpenetration of new motifs, intersections and ambitions. YouTube in particular has harvested this relentlessly growing archive in exchange of freedom to access and stream the videos on personal devices. Thus, it would appear that the orders of informality could finally be abandoned—with the producers given the incentive of ad revenues and the viewers able to effortlessly stream content, thereby bringing it all within the formal fold. If it were that easy, YouTube would become the default popular archive for vernacular media, making other arbitrage platforms redundant.

However, this chapter has also explored a fundamental tension between the performative informality of live concerts and the distributive control of platform economy. As we have recounted, while arbitrage platforms offered a way to step outside the traditional media platforms, platform economy does not take a similarly benign look at informality. The trajectory of platformization is therefore also that of identifying new consumer demographics, whose attention could be monetized in due time. The monopolistic outreach of digital platforms is propelled by a relentless force to dis-embed, aggregate and reorganize via algorithms a new formal order of media consumption. While this certainly threatens the informal media markets, they have thrived by maintaining a curious balance. The formalization drive of the platform economy—so that capital flow and consumer attention are controlled—can certainly sit *beside*, and feed off, the live concert spectacle and its repeated affirmations of the popular mandate. It can harvest ever more hits and correlate consumer analytics to be sold to advertisers. But the assertive publicness of Bhojpuri popular culture, as with other vernacular media, is testament to the desire to untether such control over the popular archive. The mobile media assemblages or online footprints of vernacular media only constitute the leftover traces of an intensity, which earns its stripes by the virtue of various informalities.

Acknowledgement This chapter was published previously in *Media Industries Journal*, 6(2), 2019.

References

Ascher, I. (2016). *Portfolio Society: On the Capitalist Mode of Prediction*. Cambridge: MIT Press.

Athique, A. (2008). The Global Dynamics of Indian Media Piracy: Export Markets, Playback Media and the Informal Economy. *Media, Culture and Society, 30*(5), 699–717.

Athique, A. (2019). Integrated Commodities in the Digital Economy. *Media, Culture and Society*. https://doi.org/10.1177/0163443719861815.

Athique, A., Parthasarathi, V., & Srinivas, S. V. (Eds.). (2018a). *The Indian Media Economy Vol 1: Industrial Dynamics and Cultural Adaptation*. New Delhi: Oxford University Press.

Athique, A., Parthasarathi, V., & Srinivas, S. V. (Eds.). (2018b). *The Indian Media Economy Vol 2: Market Dynamics and Social Transactions*. New Delhi: Oxford University Press.

Beller, J. (2016a). Informatic Labor in the Age of Computational Capital. *Lateral: Journal of the Cultural Studies Association, 5*(1). https://doi.org/10.25158/L5.1.4.

Beller, J. (2016b). The Programmable Image of Capital: M-I-C-I′-M′ and the World Computer. *Postmodern Culture, 26*(2). https://doi.org/10.1353/pmc.2016.0005.

Kumar, A. (2016). Bhojpuri Consolidations in the Hindi Territory: Infrastructure, Aesthetics and Competing Masculinities in North India. *BioScope: South Asian Screen Studies, 7*(2), 189–206.

Kumar, A. (2018a). *Deswa*, the Film and the Movement: Taste, Industry and Representation in Bhojpuri Cinema. *Contemporary South Asia, 26*(1), 69–85.

Kumar, A. (2018b). Media Portfolios after Credit-Scoring: Attention, Prediction and Advertising in Indian Media Networks. *Postmodern Culture, 28*(2). https://doi.org/10.1353/pmc.2018.0014.

Larkin, B. (2008). *Signal and Noise: Media, Infrastructure, and Urban Culture in Nigeria*. Durham, NC: Duke University Press.

Lobato, R. (2016). The Cultural Logic of Digital Intermediaries: YouTube Multichannel Networks. *Convergence, 22*(4), 348–360.

Lobato, R., & Thomas, J. (2015). *The Informal Media Economy*. New Jersey: Wiley.

Manuel, P. (1993). *Cassette Culture: Popular Music and Technology in North India*. Chicago: University of Chicago Press.

Mukherjee, R., & Singh, A. (2017). Reconfiguring Mobile Media Assemblages: Download Cultures and Translocal Flows of Affective Platforms. *Asiascape: Digital Asia, 4*, 257–284.

Prakash, B. (2019). Cultural Labour: Conceptualizing the "Folk Performance" in India. New Delhi: Oxford University Press.

Rashmi, M. (2018). The Offline Media Economy: Digitally Marginalized Users of Mobile Phones. In A. Athique, V. Parthasarathi, & S. V. Srinivas (Eds.), *The Indian Media Economy Volume II: Market Dynamics and Social Transactions* (pp. 202–219). New Delhi: Oxford University Press.

Rawlley, V. (2007). Miss Use: A Survey of Raunchy Bhojpuri Music Album Covers. *Tasweer Ghar: A Digital Archive of South Asian Popular Visual Culture*. Retrieved from http://tasveergharindia.net/cmsdesk/essay/66/index.html.

Singh, A. (2015). Of Women, by Men: Understanding the "First Person Feminine". In Bhojpuri Folksongs. *Sociological Bulletin, 64*(2), 171–196.

Srinivas, S. V. (2017). Politics in the Age of YouTube: Degraded Images and Small Screen Revolutions. In J. Neves & B. Sarkar (Eds.), *Asian Video Cultures: In the Penumbra of the Global* (pp. 217–239). Durham, NC: Duke University Press.

Tripathy, R. (2012). Music Mania in Small-town Bihar: Emergence of Vernacular Identities. *Economic and Political Weekly, 67*(22), 58–66.

Tripathy, R. (2018). The Artist as Entrepreneur: Talent, Taste, and Risk in Haryana and Bihar. In A. Athique, V. Parthasarathi, & S. V. Srinivas (Eds.), *The Indian Media Economy Volume I: Industrial Dynamics and Cultural Adaptation* (pp. 197–213). New Delhi: Oxford University Press.

Vonderau, P. (2016). The Video Bubble: Multichannel Networks and the Transformation of YouTube. *Convergence, 22*(4), 361–375.

CHAPTER 14

Notes on the Platformization of Mainstream Hinduism

Pradip Thomas

This chapter explores the platformization of religion in India and, in particular, the predominant religion in India, Hinduism. To begin with, I would also like to add that my thoughts on this subject are to some extent provisional, given that religion and religiosity online are constantly being reshaped by technological change as well as by economic and political imperatives. In this chapter, I attempt to deal primarily with issues related to platforms that are dedicated to the provision of various services to everyday religion, and only secondarily with mega-platforms, such as Facebook, which are home to literally thousands of religious socialities. Nonetheless, in both cases, the mining and repurposing of these socialities by political parties and quasi-political (and sometimes extreme right) Hindu organizations towards partisan ends has become a point of contention in India, as it has with other faiths in other parts of the world. From an academic point of view, the relationship between online communication and religious nationalism has been the basis for a number of writings,

P. Thomas (✉)
University of Queensland, St Lucia, Australia
e-mail: pradip.thomas@uq.edu.au

A. Athique, V. Parthasarathi (eds.), *Platform Capitalism in India*, Global Transformations in Media and Communication Research - A Palgrave and IAMCR Series,
https://doi.org/10.1007/978-3-030-44563-8_14

including by Sahana Udupa and others (Bhushan 2015; Chaturvedi 2016; Kallen 1998; Udupa 2015). This chapter takes its topical focus from the role played by platforms in creating opportunities for various commodifications of Hinduism. At the same time, this chapter also makes the argument that equivalences between commodifications in and of Hinduism and other religions such as Christianity need to be eschewed in favour of a broader understanding of the specificities of mediated religious experiences and the 'apprehending' of the divine, which varies from one religion to another.

The Monetization of Religious 'Affect' in India

There is, of course, no questioning the fact that online transactions in the context of religion have increased tremendously in recent years, and that there has been a substantial and significant increase in the monetization of these transactions. In the context of Hinduism, that the majority of religious platforms and apps are, for the most part, catering primarily to the everyday devotional needs of local and diasporic Hindus, thereby extending efficiencies in the delivery of religious goods and services. At the same time, their situation in the context of the World Wide Web inevitably facilitates an increasingly virtual appreciation and experience of localized worship. Beyond supplying the material goods for pujas, platforms such as AadiShakti offer over 150 spiritual services to clients, including "astrology, face reading, palm reading, reflexology, Vaastu, yoga, reiki, past life regression, acupuncture, naturopathy, fengshui consulting, aromatherapy, crystal healing, Chinese astrology, numerology etc." (see Sharma 2016). In other words, these platforms are, in the main, product, counselling and prediction services, although they also include ritual and travel-related pilgrimage services.

Since India is a land of many 'living' religions, the fact that online transactions of religious goods and services have become monetized should not come as any surprise. However, this market and the transactional economies linked to these markets are also being shaped by the wider political project of 'making India Hindu', and this pan-Indian project has provided many opportunities, both offline and online, to further a nationalistic and 'affective' embrace of Hindu institutions, cultures and ideologies. This wider political reality was highlighted by the acceleration of obvious correspondences between political, cultural and material Hinduism during the 2019 national elections in India. The 'celebritization' of the BJP's distinct version of Hinduism, legacy media's broad capitulation to a majoritarian agenda, numerous Bollywood stars' endorsements of this agenda and its reinforcement by a sophisticated machinery of trolls, bots, clickbaits and keyboard warriors aligned to the political cause of greater Hinduism all point to ongoing investments being made in the manufacture of religious nationalism as a means of shaping and harvesting allegiances. This agenda inevitably inflects many 'ancillary' religious industries, in particular, yoga, health and well-being initiatives and religious consumer products ranging from health foods to Ayurvedic toothpaste. Tradition and the traditional, and its real and imagined correspondences with all that is 'pure and unsullied', have become widely monetized and are today the basis for multi-million industries, such as Baba Ramdev's *Patanjali* brand that claims to have incorporated Ayurveda (India's ancient medical texts and practices) into all its product lines from toothpaste to biscuits.

This market of sanctified consumer goods has also provided religious institutions and other purveyors of religion with new sources of income. Temple towns all over India are now heavily marketed online, not merely for the temple experience itself, but also for the ancillary services to be found in that town, ranging from ayurvedic massages to yoga classes and fortune telling. Many traditional ritual experts (or *Pujaris*) have exited within the precariat of modern India, before being 'saved' by the new opportunities offered by platform religion. Platforms, in this sense are playing an important role in reviving religious services and sites in a country where ownership of mobile devices and internet access is expanding exponentially. In the process, they are globalizing their material particularities and enabling a vast number of sacred sites to become part of the growing footprint of the religious tourism industry. While this phenomenon is most evident in the domain of Hinduism, there have also been smaller investments in Christian and Muslim religious tourism circuits, and the Buddhist circuit (which caters to predominantly international visitors and devotees) has also seen major investments in online promotion along with infrastructure projects in towns that have a connection with Buddha, such as Bodhgaya, Nalanda, Rajgir, Kushinagar, Sarnath, Sanchi, Ajanta Caves, Dhauli and Dharamshala (Intenrational Finance Corporation 2018).

It is clear that all the major and minor religions in India now have an online presence and there is increasing evidence that quite a substantial percentage of mobile downloads are linked to religious apps of one type or the other. This does not arguably come as a surprise given the space and place of religion in the everyday lives of Indians. In this sense the platformization of religion can be considered rather banal, given that arguably this is the latest iteration of religious mediation that has perhaps always been of a transactional kind. Platforms are just the latest in-between that is enabling such transactions. Faith has from time immemorial been mediated and the advent of technology and in particular online technologies has enabled multiple mediation. With mobile devices in particular and their imbrications in everyday life, embedded and embodied, this integration between technology and the religious experience has become more pronounced. One arguably egalitarian consequence of religious and platforms and apps is that they have the potential to democratize access to temples and deities for individuals and communities who have traditionally been denied such access, such as Dalits and lower caste Hindus. However, there is scant data available that demonstrates this effect. Given the sharpening of caste cleavages in the era of Hindutva, it is more than likely that online Hindu sacred space will reflect offline realities.

The Sacred Gaze, Hindu Space and Cyberspace

Before exploring the platformization of Hinduism further, I would like to deal with two important aspects of the relationship between platforms and religion. My concerns, broadly, relate to: (1) the established nature of 'material religion' and (2) the belief in 'non-physical sacred spaces'. Not all religions organize the material and metaphysical in the same ways. Consequently, there are underlying theological reasons why are represented/integrated differently in their manifestation within platforms, and it is also clear that not all religions have embraced platforms in their entirety. The obvious question, then, is what is it that has made Hinduism especially conducive to the success of religious platforms and platform religiosities? What strikes me as a fascinating aspect of Hinduism, is Hindu belief in the immanence of God within Hindu products, goods and services—a mercantile boon to the marketplaces of Hinduism market, but also a fundamental and distinctive belief that suggests the key relevance of ritual as *orthopraxy* (correct practice) to any understanding of Hinduism offline and that of *omnipraxy* (DIY practices) online. The acceptance of DIY practices signifies a flexibility that has contributed to the success of online Hinduism. Having said that, it is important that we acknowledge that the privatization of control over religious ritual online is by no means absolute and that major investments have been made by the religious status quo to bring online worship in line with their offline versions.

For the colonial onlookers during the era of Empire, everyday Hinduism appeared to consist primarily of idolatory and superstition, inspiring a key objective of the colonial missionary to counter the hegemonic influence of the Brahmanic order that presided over an amorphous Hinduism and replace it with the rational, text-based Christianity, and its potential to suture the rational 'wholesomeness' of the text-belief-experience triage. There were, of course, many colonial residents and visitors who did come to better understand the philosophical foundations of Hinduism and many more who became enamoured precisely with its material practices. Nonetheless, it remains significant that the colonial encounter juxtaposed India's ritual practices with a European culture that had substantially (and violently) truncated its own historical ritual practices in favour of an austere textual practice. Thus, until recently, material religion has only been sparingly associated with the Judaic religions that emphasize the primacy of the 'text' as mediator. Subsequent studies on the Orthodox and Roman Catholic traditions as well as Protestantism (in many ways being, alongside Islam, the bastion of the text) have begun to address its inherent materialism. The Eucharist, for example, is resolutely based on belief in the transformative potential of 'things' as is the role played by icons and images in the Orthodox and Roman Catholic traditions. With neo-Pentecostalism there is an overwhelming celebration of prosperity and of all material things associated with prosperity. In fact, in this tradition, the materiality of things and platforms are closely entwined since all technologies can be used for Godly purposes to further the 'Great Commission' and spread the Word of God.

Colonial scholars of Hinduism of course typically missed these points of comparison, because everyday Hinduism seemingly had little to do with a sacred text, but everything to do with innumerable rituals in which 'things' play the central role. As Diana Eck (1980, p. 3), describes it: "in the Hindu understanding, the deity is present in the image, the visual apprehension of the image is charged with religious meaning. Beholding the image is an act of worship, and through the eyes one gains the blessing of the divine". In other words, the 'sacred gaze' is all important to Hinduism. Arguably, that familiarity with the visual practice of seeing the deity in the image offline (in devotional calendars, for example) enables, online images of deities' immaterial authenticity, even if religious platforms and apps are clearly mediating such authenticities in unfamiliar ways. The expert on the role of images in religion, David Morgan describes it thus "The acts of looking at images and evoking imagery within the imagination are ritual practices that would not work as they do without imagery. Contemplation and devotion are only two aspects of many different visual practices. Spectacle, display, procession, teaching, and commemoration also serve religious ends … seeing is intermingled with other forms of activity such as reading, meditating, suffering, eating, dreaming, singing and praying" (2005, pp. 51–52). It is immediately obvious that all of these practices can be mediated by electronic means. In the context of Hinduism, the iconic power of the image is such that faith and its authenticity as mediated by online visualization has never been seriously doubted. Furthermore, the incorporation of commercial instincts and practices within everyday material renditions of Hinduism appear to readily allow for monetization by platforms through diverse transactionalities that traverse the material and spiritual needs of worshippers.

Vineetha Sinha's *Religion and Commodification*, explores the flows of religious material between the local and the global of "how these 'puja things' as commodities traverse various routes and circulate within networks created across transnational boundaries" (2011). Sinha explores how fresh flowers, prayer alters and visual representations are part of "business practices and marketing strategies" that " connect groups of makers, seller and buyers into a much wider network" and of how "local business are plugged into a global network" that operates between Tamil Nadu, India and Southeast Asian countries, inclusive of Singapore, Malaysia, Indonesia and Thailand. Sinha also explores various ways in which religious commodities are activated as religious objects and the complex nature of the ways in which such items flow through profane-sacred-profane cycles. In the context of Hindu nationalism, an interesting avenue for research will be to understand how global cultural flows of such products and their consumption have become 'charged' as it were with extra-religious 'Bhakti' for the faithful, diaspora Hindu who is keenly implicated in the project of Hindutva. Nonetheless, it is important to balance this very modern political drive for orthodoxy with the historical reality that Hinduism has always been a de-centralised religion, where there is no single 'authority' on matters of devotion. Within a multitude of interpretations and doctrines, there always scope to destabilise attempts and religious hegemony and 'authoritative' practice. As the historian

Vinay Lal puts it: "Only Hinduism can match the internet's playfulness: the religion's proverbial '330 million' gods and goddesses, a testimony to the intrinsically decentred and polyphonic nature of the faith, find correspondence in the world-wide web's billion points of origin, intersection, and dispersal" (2013).

Another point of convergence with the digital and another reason, arguably, for the efflorescence of online Hinduism is widespread belief in "non-physical sacred spaces" and places that are 'charged', as it were, with spiritual power. Scheifinger has argued, "If Hinduism accepts a non-physical space which is conceived of in spiritual terms then there is no reason why the non-physical cyberspace cannot also be recognised" (2008, p. 236). There is, in other words, no necessary 'virtualization' or dilution of the religious experience online, since this is just another window to the experiencing of the ineffable. As Scheifinger has argued in an article on 'The Jaganath Temple and Online Darshan', the administration of this famous temple in Eastern India have fully embraced the need for the temple's presence to be mediated online and that, contrary to the theorists of globalization, the 'disembedding' of the temple deity has not occurred because of its expanded presence online (2009). Thus, as Scheifinger notes: "An investigation of the availability of Jagannath's darshan online leads me to believe that the local site does not necessarily decline in importance. Jagannath does not become disembedded from the temple in Puri. Instead, as a result of Jagannath's appearance online, there is interplay between the global and the local" (2009, p. 279). By contrast, Meera Nanda's *The God Market* deals with the ways in which globalization does appear to have extended what she terms the 'rush hour of the Gods' under the aegis of the state-temple-corporate complex in India—what one might call a structural commodification of material Hinduism against the backdrop of the mainstream of Hindu nationalism (2009). Nanda's study explores the 're-ritualizations' of the Great Tradition, the reinventions of popular Hinduism and the increasing use of education and tourism as means to reinforce an all-India project of Vedic Hinduism, at the expense of more variable and localized Hindu traditions. One of the obvious challenges, then, in interpreting the remediation of Hindu religious practices via the digital screen is that our fundamental understanding of material Hinduism inevitably remains both diverse and contentious.

Platforms, Markets and Experiences

Having noted the unresolved status of the material religious practices now being 'remediated' for the digital age, I will shift to a more empirical account of religion's platform economy. There is now a burgeoning range of platforms and apps dedicated to the expanding business of online Hinduism. These range from apps that facilitate pujas in real time from a diaspora Indian's favourite temple in India (Puja: Mobile temple puja for Indian Hindu Gods, 27 Mantraa), apps that are dedicated to astrology and horoscopes (Astrotalk), that link ritual specialists to ordinary Hindus (ePuja & Shubhpuja), that offer devotional songs (2b Radio Bhakti), facilitate the download of religious 'wallpaper' for device screens (Hindu God HD Wallpaper), that support religious tourism, including travel (Kaawad Yatra Travel app), accommodation and access to temples and one stop sites such the *House of God* owned by the Times of India group (the largest media group in India) that offers access to rituals and to the religious experience from more than a hundred temples, forty-seven gurus, numerous Gods, along with a variety of other ancillary goods and services. The acquisition of *House of God* in 2017 added to the existing Times of India site *SpeakingTree.in* which specializes in spiritual wellness techniques and connecting seekers to online mendicants. It has become obvious that the big corporate houses in India now recognize growing business opportunities in this sector. The ex-CEO of Cognizant, Lakshmi Narayan, has, for example, invested in "*Harivara*, which has done more than 33,000 pujas and has a network of 3,200 priests .... *Harivara* gives priests a free mobile phone and insurance" and loans when needed (Ayyar 2017).

Ajay Mehta's first-hand account reproduced in the *New York Times* of taking part in a remotely organized Puja organized by the religious platform *Shubhpuja* highlights both its efficiency and inefficiencies (Skype contact was erratic) but also how an 'authentic' experience online can be left to the religious experts and platform owners who have made business opportunities in a market that is recession-proof (2015). To Mehta, this experience was fundamentally about ease and efficiency, that is, the availability of a service, in clear contrast with the caste- and class-based inequalities highlighted by the VIP lanes outside temples in India:

> After about an hour, Acharya Keshav told me I could sign off. As a nice Shubhpuja convenience, the acharyas would continue the next hour of the puja without me having to be present through Skype. I'd gotten my own

> prayer ceremony without needing to do much more than press a button and fill out a form—basically Uber, but for god. (Mehta 2015)

The authenticity of this mediated ritual was simply not in question (as is often the case when Christian rituals mediated online are discussed). Madhavi Mallapragada similarly describes online darshan as an example of remediation in which

> new media involve the repurposing of older media and … how the latter is refashioned to adapt to the new media environment … Digital darshan foregrounds the remediation of 'digital' as analog media forms such as photographs, iconic calendar art and books reconfigured as digital bits … Correspondingly, 'old media' imagery is purposefully used to sacralize 'new' digital representation. (Mallapragada 2010, pp. 114–115)

While it is certainly the case that religious platforms have enabled the remote experience of rituals via Skype, to me, the most intriguing aspect of this interface is not the enabling app or platform per se. but rather the fundamental opportunities that have arisen (and are being taken up) to materialize and re-materialize religion and expand and extend its commodification. In line with Campbell et al.'s study of religious apps, it would seem that such in apps in India can be broadly classified under "apps oriented around religious practice and apps embedded with religious content" (2014, p. 164). The $30–40 billion religious market in India has grown exponentially over the last decade largely due to a growth in an array of online services, including religious apps catering to the daily religious needs of devotees across the major faiths in India, specific religious services such as *Shubhpuja* that offers bespoke solutions to Hindu communities in India and the diaspora, *ePuja* and *Online Prasad* (connected to fifty temples in India and that also sells a religious brand of rudraksha, *Zevotion*) and that cater to the needs of diaspora Hindu communities, online religious markets such as *Shubhkart*, which is essentially a religious version of *Flipkart* or *Amazon* that includes fifteen categories of devotional products, ranging from Patanjali Aastha and gold and silver products, puja items, idols, *kamdhenu* cows, Vastu and gemstones, and the more ecumenical *Puja Shoppe*, which also offers *pandit* services and pujas to win court battles and prevent accidents, online marketing portals that also sell religious paraphernalia such as *shopclues.com*, *snapdeal.com*, travel portals such as *MyHolyTrip*, which caters to the growing market for religious tourism, and specialist sites that cater for the Hajj market such as *Proud Ummah*, along with agencies such as *Wave Hair* involved in the sale of secondary products such as hair extensions sourced from key temples in India. *ShubhKart* is owned by the Pittie group of companies, also involved in real estate, well-being and entertainment and a supplier of products that are available through Reliance Retail stores throughout India.

It would seem that there has been a constellation of very contemporary factors that have contributed to the expansion the online religious market in India. Apart from the fact that Hinduism's diversity and its space and place agnosticism has helped with a more or less seamless fit with platforms and apps, there is also the overt market orientation of 'soft' religious fundamentalism that aligns with the broader doctrines of economic neoliberalism. A range of manufactured fears and Hindu-nationalist aspirations—the dilution of Hinduism, the need to have faith in 'swadeshi', Made in India products, the purity of Indian products as opposed to those manufactured by foreign MNCs, the need to make India great again, the need to foreground India's religious/scientific heritage have each contributed to connectivity's and socialities online. The Supreme Court ruling that reinforced the right to use the pictures of gods and goddesses for commercial products have contributed to marketing opportunities within the God market in particular that linked to religious institutions and to the free-ranging God men and women who offer a range of religious services for adherents across rural and urban India (Press Trust of India 2015). These include Rajneesh's 'Osho' brand of ashrams and products, Sri Sri Ravi Shankar's *Art of Living* programmes and products and Baba Gurmeet Ram Rahim Singh Insan's natural, organic product range of over 150 products (also sold in 200 stores and market complexes across North India). The success of Baba Ramdev's *Patanjali* in the food and beverages market is apparently worth $1.6 billion, which does suggest that the 'ayurvedic' moment, along with the tropes of quality, purity and *swadeshi* have become an established frame for the everyday valuation of consumer products. Ramdev's recent launch of the messenger service *Kimbho* (a communication app designed to compete against WhatsApp) along with his own branded SIM card and stated plans to compete with McDonalds provides a broader reflection of a growing and loyal consumer base that will avail of services that are branded as trustworthy, authentic and 'indigenous' on the purported basis that its very modern products are grounded in tradition.

Thus, what we are seeing in India is the platformization of religious belonging as a privileged mode of sociality and connectivity on the one hand, and the establishment of religious tropes as the basis for massive exercises in consumer marketing on the other. This wider platformization, beyond the material needs of established religious practices, has been enabled by the pre-existing religious media ecosystem. Whilst all of India's major religions operate in this place, we also need to recognize the fact that the majority Hindu spectrum of this ecosystem has been perceptibly fashioned by the explicit and implicit politics of Hindutva. In Ramdev's case, platforms ventures are underpinned by religious cable television station (*Aastha*), his own celebrity marketing (including a TV serial shown on Discovery India on his life and work—*Swami Ramdev Ek Sangharsh*), a global fan base, a yoga empire, a large, national consumer goods business and a wealth of both advertiser- and consumer-based revenues. This is the Ramdev marketplace, an ecosystem that enables ambitious projects such as the *Kimbho* platform. While *Kimbho* has had some teething problems, including security-related issues, it is to be expected that this platform will enable a sociality, connectivity and interactivity that is shaped by intimate knowledge of Ramdev's religious constituency, translated in transactional terms into knowledge of their consumer behaviour, spiritual expectations and material needs. The development of *Kimbho* also aligns with the government's Digital India programme, being based on an argument that Indian programmers who have helped develop the world's major social media should now contribute to the development of 'national' platforms. Arguably, understanding *Kimbho* as a techno-cultural construct and its consequences for forms of religious sociality is as important as understanding it as a socioeconomic structure (Van Dijk 2013).

Patanjalinet, Shubhpuja and Business Based on Religious Common Sense

I would like to illustrate the socialities of the God market by focusing on two websites—Patanjali.net, which provides a shopping and consumer experience based on common-sense tradition, and the Shubhpuja, which caters explicitly to the puja and ritual needs of Hindu devotees online. The Patanjaliayurved.net online store offers products across the Patanjali consumer line, including hair products, personal products, Ayurvedic medicine, herbal solutions, along with a range of natural food and home care products. The text accompanying these products affirm 'purity' as the distinguishing feature of the Patanjali range, the naturalness and veracity of the ingredients, some that are ostensibly sourced from rare herbs cultivated in their own farms and production processes that not only follow the highest manufacturing standards but are in sync with the requirements of cultural tradition. Patanjali products tap into the 'common sense' of consumerism in present day India where there are real issues related to the 'impurity' and compromised nature of fast-moving consumer (FMCG) goods, a concern that has been exploited by Patanjali's marketing team. The nationalism-inspired climate for Made in India goods and services has certainly helped the Patanjali brand since it is seen to offer alternatives to, foreign-owned, MNC-linked products. Additionally, the major investments being made in the reinventions of tradition and the validations of the Vedic sciences have resulted in an environment in which tradition increasingly is becoming an importantly player in determining both long-term and every day consumer choices. Their website on the merits of Ayurveda suggests the Ayurvedic alternative to allopathic medicine: "Ayurveda has eight approaches to analyse ailment, called Nadi, Mootra, Mala, Jihva, Shabda, Sparsha, Druk, and Aakruti. It helps us to maintain the balance of vaak, pitta and kapha in the body .... So, why would anyone visit a doctor that frequent and pop in the not so needed medicines when *Ayurveda* comes in handy?!"(Patanjali Ayurved 2018). Clifford Geertz's (1993, p. 84) volume *Local Knowledge* includes a chapter on 'Common Sense as a Cultural System'. Common-sense fundamentally is based on people implicitly believing in the value, validity and explanatory power of cultural systems of sense making that provide the means to apprehend and neutralize the bad forces and harmonize the good in individual control over life's major and minor problems, from health to success in love. Geertz has suggested that the tonalities of common sense include the following: Its naturalness, practicalness, thinness, immethodicalness and accessableness (Geertz 1993). Patanjali products make for common-sense, value-based consumption based on Tradition since a majority of Indians believe in the efficacies of traditional medicine although, and in contrast with Geertz's belief in the immethodicalness of common sense, Patanjali has invested in the validation of the Vedic sciences and its 'scientific method' by placing it on a par with products and processes associated with Western science. Tapping into common sense while validating its products as 'scientific' positions Patanjali products within an environment that is supportive of Hinduism not merely as a religion but that is based on science, rationality and common sense.

This correspondence between science and tradition, or science as tradition is illustrated by the Shubhpuja website that makes this correspondence crystal clear. "Shubhpuja.com is a science and technology-based platform for authentic Vedic pujas, astrology, Vastu and spiritual products through educated and qualified professionals". "We believe in upholding our Vedas by catering to the customized needs of our clients … We are scientifically revolutionizing the ancient spiritual practices by preserving our customs and traditions that has been "Awarded equity-free seed fund by Department of Science and Technology, Government of India at Bombay Stock Exchange" (Shubhpuja 2018a). Covering pujas, pujas for problems, astrology, Vastu and products, including idols, gemstones, rudrakshas (prayer beads) and so on, the site offers an entirely alternative universe of practices linked to individual-cosmic reconciliations on issues related to health, business success, marriage that can all be dealt with by investments in the correct rituals. For example, the first item in the scroll down under pujas for problems is 'Black magic related'. There are four items listed black magic, evil eye, possessed by spirits and *vashikaran* (negativity), and the pujas are meant to bring about planetary alignment and, thus, harmony in the lives of individuals. The pujas are expensive—ranging from Rs. 10,000–15,000, and the priestly class remain prominent in overseeing these rituals: "We will send you a qualified Indian Brahman trained in Hindu Shastras to conduct puja at Devotees preferred location (home, office etc.) and time (or muhurat time suggested by Shubhpuja)"—thus suggesting that the 'disintermediation' of Brahmans as ritual experts online has not occurred to the extent that it has in Islam and Christianity where Mullahs and priests, to some extent, compete with online experts.

Among the many spiritual products for sale, there are six different varieties of rudrakshas that are described as 'tears of Shiva', very much like the anointed products sold by Christian televangelists. However, the rudrakshas are graded and the prices depend on their potency to achieve benefits to the wearer. The benefits of wearing a 1 MukhiRudraksha include the following:

- The wearer enjoys all the Worldly Comforts and all his material desires get fulfilled yet he is not bound by them.
- Attainment of very high level of Spiritual Consciousness and Mental Peace, Attainment of Nirvana.

- One Mukhi Rudraksha pacifies the malefic effects of planet SUN and makes the individual charismatic and radiant like the Divine Surya.
- As per Ancient Vedic Texts, this Rudraksha is said to be very beneficial in curing Headache, Right Eye problems & diseases of Liver, Bowels, Heart Diseases, Bone Pains etc.
- This Rudraksha renders a person the power to Concentrate, Increased Confidence, Leadership qualities and Prosperity.
- A person wearing One Mukhi Rudraksha is able to lead a Healthier, Wealthier and Happier Life by the blessings of Lord Shiva. (Shubhpuja 2018b)

While rudrakshas have been used as an aid to prayer in a variety of religious traditions, organizations like Shubhpuja have used the tropes of purity, the authentic incantation of mantras, its consecrated nature and immanence to validate *their* rudrarakshas as the most authentic and powerful. There is however the need to locate such religious products within a rudraksha economy based on buyers and sellers, ritual specialists, rudraksha experts within the larger, Hindu economy. Arguably, these specialist puja and product websites are involved in the competitive marketing of this product particularly aimed primarily at diaspora Hindus who are comfortable with personalized forms of religious piety that involve engagements with religious commodities from rudhrakshas to idols of favourite Gods. In this sense, religious platforms such as Shubhpuja are like any other retail platform except that their primary products are of a religious kind. Pattana Kitsiara's (2010) study of the commodification of an amulet in Thailand in the 1980s as an example of commodity fetishism, highlights the roles played by men in authority to invest a new holy pillar shrine with power and invest an amulet with appropriate power to ward off the evil eye. Linked to the deities Chatukham Rammathep and a pillar consecrated by the Wat Mahathat Maha Worawihan, Nakhon Si Thammarat, eighty million units of this amulet were manufactured and sold. Kitisara using Marxian logics has argued that "…commodity is a key factor organizing the social life in the capitalist society. People' s social relation is determined by market mechanism through dominant means of exchange such as money and commodities. However, the amulet, as an inanimate object worshipped for its supposed magical powers, assumes its fetish form through both religio-cultural processes and market economy institutions" (Kitsiara 2010, pp. 577–578).

I have tried to illustrate the fact that the religious platform economy in India rides on the common sense of Ayurveda and the Vedic sciences although this is backed up by major economic institutions and validated by the State. While it is the case that religious platforms and apps in India are an emerging sector with little evidence of market domination or vertical integration as of yet, the rewards stemming from the platformization of religion are only now being recognized by the corporate sector. Apart from the *Times of India* group and its major investments in digital products and platforms through Times Internet, Shemaroo Entertainment Ltd., which is a large provider of content for television and online services, owns 2500 hours of multi-faith content and that launched three religious apps in 2018—HariOm, Bhakti and Ibaadat (Press Trust of India 2018) and Baba Ramdev, there have not been major investments from established corporate houses and this has enabled a number of start-ups to explore a range of religious services. While it is certainly the case that the established players will use their market share and ownership of multiple platforms to exploit what Mark Andrejevic has described as 'affective economics', which is 'a means of thinking about the commercial logic of customization in which marketers seek to manage consumers not only via the collection of demographic and behavioural information, but also by tapping into a dominant feeling-tone or "sentiment", and selling this on to advertisers for targeted advertising' (2011, p. 606). It would seem the case, that at least for the moment, that for many of the smaller players, primary incomes are tied to selling products rather than from advertising.

Platform Hinduism: Some Lines for Enquiry

Although, for the most part religious platforms in India cater to the diversity of Hindu practices and the everyday needs of the faithful, they can also be used to mobilize around specific politics, as the platform distribution of posts on lynchings by 'gaurakshaks' (cow protectors) and mobilizations by the Hindu right reveal, The linkages between the platformization of religion and viral politics and actions remains a grey area and more research is required to understand the 'crossover' effects between the two. There are already dedicated apps available from explicitly Hindu nationalist groups, such as the Vishwa Hindu Parishad and the Bajrang Dal, although arguably the bulk of online incitement is found on 'mainstream' social media such as Facebook, Instagram and, notoriously, on the Facebook-owned cellular messenging service WhatsApp. WhatsApp has 250 million users in

India, making it a vital market for the global ambitions of the platform and the default interpersonal communication mode for much of India). This is by no means a fringe practice. During the 2017 elections in Uttar Pradesh, India's most populous and political bell-weather state, 6000 WhatsApp groups were created by the ruling BJP for targeted messaging to their followers. Arguably, this is where the platformization of religion becomes the most problematic, appearing to converge readily with populist politics and communal tensions. Given the targeted circulations of WhatsApp groups, these are also prolific channels for 'fake news' aimed at nurturing explicitly anti-secular religious socialities. There are also specific platforms that counter the hegemony of Hindutva, including a very specific Dalit presence on platforms, although it is unclear as to the extent to which these sites offer clearly alternatives modes of platform Hinduism or whether they make a difference during electoral cycles. Vindu Goel in an article in the *New York Times*, describes the ease with which WhatsApp groups can be formed and their potential to act as a conduit for fundamentalist content:

> WhatsApp has several features that make it a potential tinderbox for misinformation and misuse. Users can remain anonymous, identified only by a phone number. Groups, which are capped at 256 members, are easy to set up by adding the phone numbers of contacts. People tend to belong to multiple groups, so they often get exposed to the same messages repeatedly. When messages are forwarded, there is no hint of where they originated. And everything is encrypted, making it impossible for law enforcement officials or even WhatsApp to view what's being said without looking at the phone's screen. (Goel 2018)

Although the Indian authorities have made efforts to monitor and contain violence and unrest spreading through the platform media, there are others such as the chief minister of Tripura, Biplab Kumar Deb, who uses these very platforms to peddle outlandish claims to the faithful, including his claim that the internet was an Indian invention perfected by ancient kings to get battle updates during the era of the Mahabharata! One of the issues that can be explored in the study of religious platforms is whether the profusion of online religious experiences, socialities and interventions have begun to irrevocably shape the fabric of Hindu religiosity in India or whether, in the case of India, we simply have to deal with this broader question from the perspective of multiple religions. Let me conclude in this respect by raising a few issues that related to the platformization of religion in India. (1) There is also the need for studies that explore religious platforms from within a broad understanding of continuities. While I would argue that platforms offer innovative and creative ways to amplify religious affect, they are inevitably being built upon historically diverse, multi-media, multi-communication traditions. Thus we must ask: 'What are platforms doing to reinforce this tradition, or are they undermining it', 'what do platforms do differently and how do older systems legitimize their 'authority' in the context of disruptive platforms?' (2) Due to the evident and intensifying tie-ups between religious platforms and the wider commercial economy, there is a need for a textured, political economy of platform religion in India and its micro, meso and macro market manifestations. (3) Finally, there is need to interrogate the religious sociabilities being created on platforms and apps and their affective links to implicit and/or partisan politics. In a material world, these are all matters of religion, and they remain so in the era of platforms.

References

Andrejevic, M. (2011). The Work that Affective Economics Does. *Cultural Studies, 25*(4–5), 604–620.

Ayyar, R. (2017). Pujas to Pilgrimages: These Start Ups are Disrupting Spirituality. *Times of India*, 27 November.

Bhushan, S. (2015). The Power of Social Media: Emboldened Right Wing Trolls Who Are Attempting an Internet Purge. *The Caravan*, 28 September.

Campbell, H. A., Altenhofen, B., Bellar, W., & Cho, K. J. (2014). There's a Religious App for that! A Framework for Studying Religious Mobile Applications. *Mobile Media & Communications, 2*(2), 154–172.

Chaturvedi, S. (2016). *I am a Troll: Inside the Secret World of BJP's Digital Army*. New Delhi: Juggernaut.

Eck, L. D. D. (1980). Seeing the divine image in India, Spirituality & Practice. Available at https://www.spiritualityandpractice.com/books/reviews/excerpts/view/16122. Accessed July 2, 2020.

Geertz, C. (1993). *Local Knowledge*. London: Fontana Press.

Goel, V. (2018). In India, Facebook's WhatsApp Plays a Central Role in Elections. *New York Times*, 14 May.

International Finance Corporation. (2018). *Investing in the Buddhist Circuit*. Incredible India/International Finance Corporation, World Bank. Retrieved from https://www.ifc.org/wps/wcm/connect/a0b004004618b490804eb99916182e35/Buddhist+Circuit+Tourism+Strategy+Final.pdf?MOD=AJPERES.

Kallen, E. (1998). Hate on the Net: A Question of Rights/ a Question of Power. *Electronic Journal of Sociology*. Retrieved from http://www.sociology.org/content/vol003.002/kallen.html.

Kitsiara, P. (2010). Toward a Sociology of Religious Commodification. In B. S. Turner (Ed.), *The New Blackwell Companion to the Sociology of Religion* (pp. 563–583). Blackwell.

Lal, V. (2013). When Hinduism Meets the Internet. *The Times of India*, 20 June.

Mallapragada, M. (2010). Desktop Deities: Hindu Temples, Online Cultures and the Politics of Remediation. *South Asian Popular Culture, 8*(2), 109–121.

Mehta, A. (2015). Uber for God: Inside India's Religious Tech Industry. *NYMag*, 10 December. Retrieved from http://nymag.com/selectall/2015/12/uber-for-god.html.

Morgan, D. (2005). *The Visual Gaze: Religious Visual Culture in Theory and Practice*. Berkeley, Los Angeles, and London: University of California Press.

Patanjali Ayurved. (2018). Ayurveda: The New Health Mantra. Retrieved from https://www.patanjaliayurved.net/blog-detail/4/ayurveda-the-new-health-mantra.

Press Trust of India. (2015). No Hurdle in Carrying on Business by Using God, Goddesses Names: Supreme Court (2015). *PTI*, 24 July. Retrieved from https://www.financialexpress.com/industry/no-hurdle-in-carrying-business-by-using-god-goddess-names-supreme-court/106987/.

Press Trust of India. (2018). Shemaroo Entertainment Targets 5X Growth in Five Years. *PTI*, 23 July. Retrieved from https://www.financialexpress.com/industry/shemaroo-entertainment-targets-5x-growth-in-5-years/1254360/.

Scheifinger, H. (2008). Hinduism and Cyberspace. *Religion, 38*, 233–249.

Scheifinger, H. (2009). The Jaganath Temple and Online Darshan. *Journal of Contemporary Religion, 24*(3), 277–290.

Sharma, A. R. (2016). This Bengaluru-based Start-up Has Built an On-demand Marketplace for Spiritual Gurus. *Geektime*, 10 July. Retrieved from https://www.geektime.com/2016/07/10/this-bengaluru-based-startup-has-built-an-on-demand-marketplace-for-spiritual-gurus/.

Shubhpuja. (2018a). About Us. Retrieved from http://shubhpuja.com/shubhpuja/about-us/.

Shubhpuja. (2018b). One Mukhi Rudraksha. Retrieved from http://shubhpuja.com/product/one-mukhi-rudraksha/.

Sinha, V. (2011), Religion and Commodification: Merchandising 'Diasporic' Hinduism, Routledge, NY & Abingdon

Udupa, S. (2015). Archiving as History-Making: Religious Politics of Social Media in India. *Communication, Culture & Critique, 9*(2), 1–19.

Van Dijk, J. (2013). *The Culture of Connectivity: A Critical History of Social Media*. New York: Oxford University Press.

CHAPTER 15

Capitalist Platforms and Subaltern Creativity

Amit Rai

While a kind of "platform" capitalism appears to have emerged in India, its emergent hegemony is marked by contradictions at every level of its processes, throughout its logistical infrastructures and along the gradients of its sensorimotor ecologies (Srnicek 2017). Any analysis of datalogical media ecologies beyond biopolitics, or of postcolonial informal economies beyond Subaltern Studies (Clough 2018; Clough and Willse 2011; Sundaram 2015; Nixon 2019), is inevitably confronted with the historical imbrication of economic with political antagonisms and processes that confound analytic frames organized around quantifiable scale. This interpenetration of contradictions and multiplicities proceeds in non-linear and embedded timescales (Jameson 2009; Bergson 1988). It is manifested within the interstices between cognitive and technological domains, whose attributes include their different degrees of affective plasticity (see, for example, the works of Malabou 2005; Deleuze 1992a; DeLanda 1997, 2013; Massumi 2002, 2015a, b; Ash 2012, 2013; Behar 2016). Following Patricia Clough, I suggest that the datalogical mode in India concerns a certain "joining of neoliberal economy and neo-conservative governance"

A. Rai (✉)
Queen Mary University of London, London, UK
e-mail: a.rai@qmul.ac.uk

A. Athique, V. Parthasarathi (eds.), *Platform Capitalism in India*, Global Transformations in Media and Communication Research - A Palgrave and IAMCR Series,
https://doi.org/10.1007/978-3-030-44563-8_15

(Clough 2018, 12–13; see also Adey 2009). Indeed, contemporary postcolonial media analyses have been turned towards algorithms, informal networks, and Big Data, pointing to "the ways in which a beyond biopolitics is dependent on digital media and computational technologies, which also have enabled networks to undo system's thinking about the fixed relation of parts and whole or parts as constituting the whole" (ibid.). Networks, forcefully extended by proliferating platforms, have imaginatively, discursively, virtually, and actually displaced what "long had been referred to as the two levels of the social system: structure and individual, macro and micro".

Bruno Latour and his colleagues would propose that structure and individual, macro and micro levels of the system are "not essential realities but provisional terms", a "consequence of technologies used for navigating inside datasets" (Clough 2018, p. 13; see also Latour 2005; Latour et al. 2012). It is this regulated but unpredictable blurring of scales in derivative social datalogics that led Clough and her colleagues to articulate a decisive rupture in contemporary media theory, where

> the post-system orientation of the algorithm itself, meant that the algorithm's ontology is dynamic or mediatic, and that algorithms can learn from what they do, operating as they do on the indeterminacy of incomputable data. In this, "The Datalogical Turn" urged a further exploration of the relationship of digital media, computational technologies and the other-than-human agencies operating in a governance beyond biopolitics and a post-national capitalism. All through the first two decades of the twenty-first century, in critical theory, philosophy and media studies, there would be an ongoing shift in focus from media centered on and attuned to human experience to theorizing other-than-human agencies operating in protocols, code, interfaces, platforms, programming, and algorithms, all in the context of what Mark Hansen would come to refer to as the "data-fication" of twenty-first-century media. (Clough 2018, pp. 12–13)

The datalogical turn is deeply indebted to Marx's analysis of commodity fetishism, exploitation, primitive accumulation, the general intellect, production and circulation, the organic composition of capital, and relative and absolute surplus value in global processes of capitalist valorization (1973, 1976). Nonetheless, this retheorization of datalogical value opens the frame to the different social and affective dimensions of all these interpenetrating processes, at every scale, and across each of its antagonisms and durations (Boltanski and Chiapello 2018; Vercellone 2007). As Ravi Sundaram has noted, contemporary materialist analyses of Indian media ecologies have revealed "new informal networks entering the interstices of older, decaying infrastructures" (2015, p. 1). Indeed, the anomalies of a simultaneously Hindutva, patriarchal, and chauvinist nation-state and an aggressively digitized and globalized political economy have come to demarcate a field of political struggle pervaded by datalogical and value-capturing processes. Practices of piracy, hacking, workaround, *jugaad*, or general informality problematize, without overturning the normalized regimes of value, work, command, and control (Deleuze 1992b). In much of the popular discourses on informal economy agents, the *jugaadu* reappears alternatively as a figure of atavistic longing, romantic refusal, Indian essence, and civilizational disgrace (Rai 2019).

This chapter therefore examines the antagonistic relations of force, sense, and value in habitations of media embodiment, and capitalist value capture in contemporary platform ecologies in India. My analysis follows through on the strategic focus on transcalar datalogical processes in Clough's work, taking up the analysis in the context of caste and class domination and subordination in India (2010, 2018; Clough and Halley 2007; Clough and Willse 2011). Key to this datalogical ecology is the organising of attention across continually re-segmented populations and digital practices. The social organization of attention ties media flows of information and interaction to informal economies of data in unexpected but patterned ways. Who pays attention to this or that, and why? These questions are managed through, among other technologies, evolutionary algorithms of artificial learning in contemporary datalogical ecologies. Thus, attention is key to the social synthesis of value and data flows. Beginning with a consideration of attention in today's media ecologies as infrastructural to its political economy, I go on to link two antagonistic nodes, subaltern creativity and platform business models with the securitizing tendencies of the Hindutva state. If the infinite distraction of attention economies and datalogical securitization share a genealogy, in India, that genealogy necessarily passes through the distributed agency, both human and non-human of subaltern creativity. Consequently, this chapter makes a further contribution to that enfolded history (Pettman 2016).

The "New" Political Economy of Indian Datalogical Ecologies: The Problem of Attention

In 2019, the Hindutva right-wing government of Narendra Modi won a landslide victory in the national elections. The government would build on a well-established and global machinic assemblage of neo-fascism and neoliberalism, consolidating strong ties to Israel and the US, and developing elaborate networked PR strategies designed to capture attention (Beller 2012). Previously, Modi's government had actively pursued macroeconomic stability and a business-friendly regulatory framework, all the while emphasizing a chauvinist vision of the Indian nation. As Balakrishnan remarks,

> Very likely in reference to both ideology and capacity he had promised "minimum government, maximum governance." In a campaign that emphasised "development," there was focus on infrastructure and jobs. "Sabka saath, sabka vikas" [Everyone together, development for everyone] was a reference to the inclusivity that was imagined. The promise of an improvement in the lives of the people was contained in the slogan "Achche din aane wale hai" [Good times are going to come again]. Altogether, a superior economic performance was high on the campaign promise of Modi. (Balakrishnan 2019, p. 25).

The power of the slogans was at least partly due to the network effects of massive circulation of Hindutva memes (e.g. WhatsApp sharing) more generally and the strategic organization of these processes of registration and interaction. Attention in this ecology is the scarce resource controlled through recursive processes of habituation and communication.

In what way does a political ecology of attention help to pose the question of datalogical platforms better? In his study of the perception of religious experience and value, Nathaniel Barrett develops a notion of "perceptualization" as an ecological process (Barrett 2014; Ingold 2014). In research into the human and non-human ecologies of perception, the process of attention relates different orders of perception, bodily movements, flows of self-organising matter and data, technological substrates, elastic timespaces, appraisals of value, modes of freedom and control, strategies of reterritorializations, organizational habits, and short and long term memory (Manning 2013; Grosz 2005, 2013; Ash 2012, 2013; Thrift 2005, 2006). In much of this research, artistic and creative practice is tied sometimes by analogy, sometimes through ontological experiments to the process of attention. Indeed, through the contested thesis of the proliferation of an increasingly precarious "cognitariat", the creative industries and its research have also become part of a hegemonic project of global austerity, in which public, common goods are privatized and individualized. In this the aspect or moment of attention is reified or abstracted as a privatized and individualized commodity in which conscious selection becomes a scarce resource enfolded in and expressed through economic tendencies towards monopolization, oligopolization, and, in its political dimension, popular authoritarianism. The dominant question appears to be: How can attention be better entrained and primed to maximally exploit and more easily modulate the creative potential of its organizational ecology? (Massumi 2010)

In strictly economic terms, the apparent concern for macroeconomic stability in Modi's India has actually led to a situation in which the investment rate of the economy fell, and remained mostly at a level that was lower than what it was when the government assumed office in 2014. Consequently, the pursuit of macroeconomic stability a proof-positive of neoliberal imperatives has now come under incisive criticism (Balakrishnan 2019, p. 25). Criticism of the contradictory economic tendencies of the Modi era has also intersected with the emergence of Dalit, minority, feminist, queer, postcapitalist social, cultural, and political movements for justice and equality. Farmer suicides throughout rural India, queer struggles for identity, rights and visibility, and the critical formation of feminist solidarities across caste, sexuality, and class have all intensified throughout this era. Thus, I will argue that the abstract diagram that runs through both the fomalizing drive of Modi's economics and the emergence of political and social resistances of subaltern desire can be understood as a question of the affective disruptions of attention (or "crazes") inherent to the elaboration of the techno-perceptual assemblages of neoliberalism in India. It is amidst the multiple contradictions of macroeconomic stability, political realignment and reterritorialization, and the (self)organization of attention that we must understand what is new, if anything, in the implantation of the digital platform in India.

As Srnicek notes, the historical problem for capitalist firms that continues to the present day is that "old business models were not particularly well designed to extract and use data. Their method of operating was to produce a good in a factory where most of the information was lost, then to sell it, and never to learn anything about the customer or how the product was being used" (2017, p. 26). With the explosion of global logistics networks of lean production since the 1990s consumer data quickly became a new source of value, although with few exceptions early information management system remained a "lossy" model as well. It was in this context that the business model of the platform emerged, drawing on the long history of branding and the dwindling recording costs of datalogical technologies:

> Often arising out of internal needs to handle data, platforms became an efficient way to monopolise, extract, analyse, and use the increasingly large amounts of data that were being recorded … At the most general level, platforms are digital infrastructures that enable two or more groups to interact. They therefore position themselves as intermediaries that bring together different users: customers, advertisers, service providers, producers, suppliers, and even physical objects … Rather than having to build a marketplace from the ground up, a platform provides the basic infrastructure to mediate between different groups. (Srnicek 2017, pp. 26–28)

First, data is seen to be the key advantage platforms have over traditional business models, since the platform "positions itself (1) between users, and (2) as the ground upon which their activities occur, which thus gives it privileged access to record them" (Srnicek 2017, pp. 26–27). The platform proliferates in parallel an "internet of things", where platforms mediate whatever digital interaction takes place. Second, digital platforms inculcate and are reliant on "network effects", since: "the more numerous the users who use a platform, the more valuable that platform becomes for everyone else" (Srnicek 2017, p. 27). *Everyone* must be on Facebook, or how else would we socially network? The more numerous the users searching on Google, and the more they search, the better search algorithms become and the greater utility derived from Google. This generation cycle is enfolded into network effects, whereby more users beget more users, and which consequently expresses one of the central tendencies of platform capitalism: monopoly. Because of the ability to rapidly scale many platform businesses by relying on pre-existing infrastructure and cheap marginal costs there are few natural limits to growth (ibid.). Uber has grown rapidly because it does not need to build new factories, but rents more servers. Platforms deploy a range of tactics to ensure that more and more users come on board. For example, cross-subsidization: "one arm of the firm reduces the price of a service or good (even providing it for free), but another arm raises prices in order to make up for these losses (ibid., p. 28).

In the platform business model, the strategy is to attract a number of different groups, partly through fine-tuning the balance between what is paid, what is not paid, what is subsidized, and what is not subsidized, which sharply departs from the lean model's reduction of assets down to its core competencies and unloading any unprofitable ventures. The fixed rules, but often open source code, of platforms are mutually generative, enabling others to build upon them in unexpected ways. As Srincek notes, the core architecture of "Facebook has allowed developers to produce apps, companies to create pages, and users to share information in a way that brings in even more users. The same holds for Apple's App Store, which enabled the production of numerous useful apps that tied users and software developers increasingly into its ecosystem. The challenge of maintaining platforms is, in part, to revise the cross-subsidisation links and the rules of the platform in order to sustain user interest. While network effects strongly support existing platform leaders, these positions are not unassailable" (ibid.). Thus, we should also ask: in what ways does Srnicek's notion of platform capitalism enable a better posing of the twined problems of value, sense, and force in India's emergent datalogical security state? Combined with new state apparatuses and datalogical processes linked to the Aadhaar identification card, demonetization, PAN card registration, and mobile-phone security infrastructures (among other network effects of digital processes and caste and class struggle), the extractive apparatus for data in India's platform ecology is clearly implicated in the biopolitical question of "how must Hindutva society be defended?"

It is in India's Gaza, Kashmir, where what is at stake in the authoritarian control of datalogical processes of platforms as well as the gendering of occupied space have become key nodes of struggle, solidarity, and resistance (Kaul 2018). Again, the figure of the hacker has become ubiquitous in these struggles; in TV and filmic representations of the monstrous terrorist, in gaming culture, and in journalistic discourses, the hacker appears again and again, but in the shaded aspects of a kind of pharmakon—poison, cure, and scapegoat (Derrida 2004). In India, the figure of the *tapori/jugaadu* (Mazumdar 2001; Rai 2019) expresses a set of persistently untimely practices within and against neoliberal subjectivation that pushes us to question some of the well-worn themes of historical materialist and postcolonial analyses: (post)modernity, hybridity, the productive proletariat vs the parasitic lumpen, habituation and tinkering, becoming-minor, fixed-capital technologies and just-in-time production processes, the nationalist sensoria, subaltern piracy and commodity fetishism, individual creativity and collective becoming, etc. (Tronti 2010; Surie and Koduganti 2016). Thus, in order to proceed with understanding both the power and the contradictions of platform capitalism in India, there is an urgent need to specify the meaning of "subaltern creativity" within India's dialogical turn. My analysis here is indebted to the autonomist Marxist tradition of revolutionary self-organization and the postcolonial uptake of Subaltern Studies (Tronti 1980, 2010; Virno 2003; Berardi 2009, 2010; Hardt and Negri 1999, 2009; Lazzarato 2006; Toscano 2009; Wright 2002).

Jugaad as Postcolonial Platform Infrastructure: The Untimely Sensoria of Subaltern Creativity; or, the *Jugaad* of Everyday Life

In the legacy of Subaltern Studies, debated by two of its key practitioners Chatterjee and Chakrabarty: "the subaltern emerges as a figure which is no longer conceived in terms of the imagery of the essentialised other. On the contrary, the emphasis is on locating the mode of appropriation of modernity by subaltern groups. This departs from the 'postcolonial' approach or conception which invokes and harnesses the alterity of the subaltern to underscore the limit of the universal narrative of modernity" (Nixon 2019, p. 31; Chatterjee 2012; Chakrabarty 2013). Contemporary piracy ecologies, as subaltern modes of creative workarounds, affect everything today from social reproduction to bodily habituation (Rai 2019). This ubiquity is highlighted in an interview conducted in 2015 by media critic Shiva Thorat on digital *jugaad* (workaround) practices in Mumbai's Dalit communities:

Suresh, the 22-year-old second son of internal migrants from Karnataka, is a new media entrepreneur involved in intercalating datalogical processes in the contemporary sensoria of postcolonial neoliberalism: in one of his aspects, he is a mobile-phone repair-wallah. Interviewed at his local chai stall, he tells Thorat in Hindi that he lives and works in a poor, working-class neighbourhood in the northeast suburbs of the city. For Suresh (who also speaks Kannada and Marathi), mobile phones are the "future line [of work]", he acknowledges a "craze" (in English) for mobile phones; he insists that the mobile phone is where the value is and where it will be in the future; "people don't have food, but everyone needs a mobile" (interview conducted by Thorat in Hindi, all translations mine) Needless to say, this craze culture is the history of its attention.

Suresh's customers are mostly migrant day labourers from UP, Bihar, and Jharkhand, paying for talktime, data, and media in cash: 2 GB, 50 rupees, 3 GB 70 rupees, 4 GB, 100 rupees: the craze of the day. His services include everything from network provider recharge (mostly pre-paid accounts), web-banking assistance, selling and registering sim cards, content downloads, to handset repair (aided by DIY YouTube videos), and spare parts recycling; he emphatically doesn't deal in pornography; he doesn't employ people so much as he calls in favours from a dispersed network of friends and family, as he needs them. At the end of the month, his aim is not to have cash but to have increased his stock (phones, parts). His Canvas 2 phone runs on the battery-intensive Android platform; he likes the phone's big screen, it satisfies his "color craze" and his gaming craze; he hass had 20 phones in seven years. He does not share his phone with family or friends: "My own phone is private, I don't like it if someone looks into my phone" (ibid.).

Suresh performs *jugaads* (workarounds) all day, every day; *jugaad* practice, which for Suresh comes from tapori/subaltern street culture, is often necessary in a moment of urgency, but then the very infrastructure of everyday life is *jugaad*; "everyone does it, but they don't realise it's a *jugaad*. From waking to sleep it's *jugaad* all the time, [tooth]brush karna ka *jugaad*, toilet *jugaad*". In this culture of the workarounds of social reproduction and stratified labour, *jugaad* practice is only shared with close friends, and not spoken of in front of elders, "out of respect". For Suresh all new technologies pass from strange to normal, and by helping people familiarize themselves with strange technologies he feels he is doing "social work". At the time of interview, he had also, aside from his mobile repair service, opened up a private gym—"like my craze for mobiles, I had a craze for the gym, but don't know anything about running one! So I got a sponsor, and did it with some *jugaad*" (ibid.).

Suresh's *jugaad* ecology thus expresses the multiple tendencies of the sensory infrastructures of subaltern creativity within and against platform capitalism. It is untimely in Nietzsche's sense of that which is against the dominant organization of time, value, and work, for the benefit of a time to come: hacking ecologies actualize the potential of the future (1983). "Serving" Dalit consumers, he rides gradients of "craze" through their attentional processes, perceptual technogenesis from strange to normal, and across scales and durations. Here, *jugaad* is the individualising clinamen enfolded into digital media culture in India, the swerves in singular practices of hacking and piracy under the historical and collective conditions of a society structured in different forms of gender, caste, class, linguistic, and religious dominance (Lucretius 2008; Hall 1996). But the anomalous refusal of *jugaad* is also a reified aura, a desiring practice swathed in a specifically Indian steampunk romance of a quasi-mystical, atavistic, futurist, and usually coded male agency (Nietzsche 1983; Benjamin 2008; Adorno 2005, 2009; Rai 2019). As controlled and insurgent practice, *jugaad* expresses the contradictions and potentialities of Indian media ecologies at a historical moment when "new informal networks [are] entering the interstices of older, decaying infrastructures" (Sundaram 2015, p. 1).

This is the contradictory and overdetermined contexts of subaltern creativity in India's emergent platform economy. It also shows the limitations of Srnicek's analysis of platform business models when considering contexts beyond the global North: first, in postcolonial states transitioning from five-year economic plans that mixed socialist and free-market principals through the corrupt agencies of a developmentalist-state bureaucracy, there is a profoundly different, yet overlapping and interconnected history of business models between the formal and informal economy. The interzone between formal and informal economies has become the site of a key political and economic antagonism. Second, a specific style of *jugaad*, or the affects and attentional affordances of a given ecology of everyday hacking, already created the conditions for different types of platforms to proliferate. Suresh's *jugaad* ecology, rooted in the social and kinship networks that have been gradually elaborated for at least two generations, gives social substance to his claim to be able to get the specific *jugaad* to meet the customer's needs. These *jugaad* ecologies assemblage historically specific affordances, capacities, tendencies, parameters of change, forces, machines, desires, values, and material flows. These qualitative multiplicities are the attentional infrastructures of datalogical processes in India.

Sulekha as Formalizing Platform: Caste and Neoliberal Security

Enter Sulekha.com. Sulekha was founded by Satya Prabhakar and Sangeeta Kshettry as an app-enhanced web platform enabling different forms of monetizeable work/service interactions among Indians, raised its initial investment from Indigo Monsoon Group, and later, from the Palo-Alto-based venture capital firm Norwest Venture Partners, among others. In 2015, it raised $28 million; took a sharp hit in profits in 2016–2018 due to investment in upscaling and diversifying its technologies, and seems on a profit rebound (Anand 2018). It is today best known as a web-based search engine and "decision-making platform" for semi-organized, largely informal, gig-economy local services in India, aggregating databases of service providers and users which include home care, computer training, service apartments, party catering, baby-sitting, yoga lessons and auto repair (similar to Checkatrade.com in the UK). To recall Srnicek's definition, Sulekha provides the infrastructure to intermediate between different user groups, and it displays clear monopoly tendencies driven by network effects, it aims to draw in different user groups in creative ways, and it has a designed core architecture that governs, registers, rents, and mines the interaction possibilities (Srnicek 2017, p. 28). The platform biopolitics of Sulekha re-organizes need and desire as dynamic feedbacks into the mining of data. Their website boasts of "30 million Happy Users, 200,000 Verified Experts, and 200+ categories" traversing Home and Office, Home Improvement, Properties and Rentals, Education and Training, Professional Services, Travel and Transport, Health and Wellness, and Events. Sulekha app contains options for both standardized local needs (like pest control) and special requirements (catering or interior design). The emphasis on expertise and registration gives a sense of the datalogical processes involved in this re-organization of labour in *jugaad* ecologies. In a well-known media campaign designed by Ogilvy and Mather, Sulekha urged its potential customers thus: "Sulekha. Just click and get reliable service partners who understand that work doesn't happen through *jugaad*. Sulekha: Go Anti-*Jugaad*!"

What "work" does not happen through *jugaad*? Recalling Suresh's practice, *nothing* happens without *jugaad*. This seems to present a contradiction to any analysis of platform capitalism. In fact, through *jugaad* practice, potentially anything can happen (the irreducible element of chance immanent to *jugaad*), but very little can be registered and authorized by the state. There is an intolerable refusal of the formalized organization of work inherent in *jugaad* practice. The *jugaad* domain, as a counterpublic and countermemory, as a counter-actualizing vector towards the virtual (the pure potential of living labour), is also the key site of a struggle around caste and class in India (Toscano 2009). For historical and structural reasons, in a context in which 92% of all employment is in the informal economy and only around 25% of any given state are upper ("forward") caste, it is overwhelmingly Dalit communities who are involved in precarious *jugaad* processes cutting across all forms of (in) formalized work in the Hindutva security state. It pushes us to consider the sensory and historical infrastructures of datalogical habituations (qualitative and quantitative multiplicities) in postcolonial contexts of debilitation, violence, subordination, and control (Ravaisson 2008; Grosz 2013). Thus, Sulekha is "anti-*Jugaad*" precisely because it aims at nothing less than the monopolization of the role of mediator between heterogeneous services, quotidian habits, and security-crazed consumer demand across India (Adorno 2014, 2017). Sulekha is a continuation by other means of the caste and class war launched by the Hindutva state (e.g. as demonetization, as occupied exception in Kashmir) against Dalit and minority communities, and the expansion of neoliberal governmentality through the mode of digital platform habituation (Bhattacharya 2019, Coleman and Grove 2009.). The Sulekha platform can be read as an expression of the colonizing drive of capitalist command (Tronti 1980; Toscano 2009; Srnicek 2017).

Towards a New Political Ecology of Datalogical Sensoria

In India, platforms, and especially "gig mediators" such as Sulekha.com, emerge within the contexts of structures of dominance and creative resistance expressed in *jugaad* (informal, "non-productive", partially "uncommanded") socio-economic practices (Toscano 2009). *Jugaad* practice embodies a refusal of capitalist command, but each *jugaad* event is a repeated transgression of Brahmanical negation; *jugaad* networks operate through the multiple tendencies and within-and-against complicities of India's post-capitalist economy. But *jugaad*—as word, discourse, image, intensity—is already a reification, and increasingly a commodification of the preindividual, (non-)human processes of autonomous creativity; its tendencies are to individualize and quantify collective processes and intensive multiplicities, and all the more as the datalogical becomes the governing discourse of *jugaad*. The diagram of global capitalism in its datalogical mode in India has thus thrown up several key real antagonisms, intractable contradictions, and intensive becomings. As of yet, the political and economic organization of attention, attention as datalogical, remains completely interpenetrated by practices of "informal" social reproduction and forms of work. Consequently, I have tried to diagram here a transcalar *jugaad* infrastructure that undergirds the emergence of platform capitalism in India as its condition of possibility.

In a diagrammatic analysis of datalogical ecologies and subaltern practice what emerges as key sites of social and interpretative struggle are the stochastic resonances between historical and material tendencies in non-representational, and increasingly profitable feedback, their patterned but unpredictable (im)measures and (im)probabilities (Clough 2018, pp. 140–42, Lury et al. 2012). Moreover, these infrastructures all have historically specific affects, affordances, tendencies, and vectors of becoming: *jugaad* is the North Indian name of one style of self-organizing such within-and-against (in)formal infrastructures (Hardt and Negri 2009; Rai 2019; Deleuze 1988). The creative-complicit refusals and affirmations enfolded into *jugaad* practices evidence this anomalous politics (Spivak 1988; Best 1999). Indeed, the non-coinciding resonances between datalogical processes and subaltern creativity consistently highlight what Italian workerist have argued is the antagonistic "autonomy of the political" (see Tronti 1980, 2010). In the contexts of the globalized and postcolonial North, Toscano argues that

> any work that seeks to reinject the workerist method of antagonism into the current composition of social relations, into the uneven and combined development of capitalist command and political struggles, will be obliged to tackle two questions: How do we confront a situation in which capitalism's vicious rounds of accumulation by dispossession point to its continued and virulent, if contradictory, desire to emancipate itself from the working class, if not from humanity as a whole? And what does it mean to revive or prolong the methodologies and political gestures of workerism and autonomy at a time when—in many of the core capitalist economies that were always the privileged terrain of workerism—we are confronted by "a depoliticization of society that reinforces the power of dominant forces"? (Toscano 2009, p. 90)

Unlike historical conditions in which capitalist organization and habituation and datalogical infrastructures are secured by the strategic alliance between capital, white supremacy, and state monopoly of violence, in postcolonial India, where upper-caste Hindutva forces, militarized and patriarchal, have aligned with a global capitalist class committed to accumulation by dispossession, the datalogical regime of biopolitical security can always when necessary dispense entirely with the platform and its "interactive" accoutrements: in Kashmir today helicopters and drones patrol and register movement from the skies, on the ground, every 100 yards a checkpoint, all mobile-phone and Internet services summarily suspended. In this suspension of the network effect, another platform comes violently to the fore: the Hindutva nation. Especially under such conditions of occupation, *jugaad* networks operate their proliferating and contagious hacks, drawing on already existing tendencies of morphogenesis in techno-perceptual assemblages (DeLanda 2013; Simondon 2011; Deleuze and Guattari 1987; Guattari 1995). Functioning through the historical and material vectors of rumour and gossip, *jugaad* networks affirm the autonomy of subaltern politics within and against the datalogical nation-state (see Guha 1983; Jameson 2007). In what sense can we understand this postcolonial enfolding of the state of exception and occupation, its populist memification as unitary nation-platform, and the datalogical processes of post-probabilistic networks as a qualitatively different, uneven and combined, sensorium? Is it simply the untimely political ecology of our present, "acting counter to our time and thereby acting on our time and, let us hope, for the benefit of a time to come" (Nietzsche 1983, p. 60; Agamben 1998, 2005)?

In the meteoric rise of populism throughout the global North and in specific countries of the postcolonial South over the past decade what has been unintentionally problematized in everyday life is a putative tendency towards depoliticization. Yet the overt politicization of more and more elements and dynamics of everyday life, from social reproduction to food ecologies, suggests that datalogical tendencies paradoxically affect ambivalent forms of *re*-politicization. The aura of the datalogical, which resides in the radical indiscernibility of Big Data and the monopoly on artificial intelligence, has been repeatedly fractured with each new cybersecurity breach, each new state conspiracy shared on WhatsApp. Instead of establishing an order of rules that must be followed, the adaptable algorithmic architectures of datalogical processes seemingly allow rules and parameters to "adapt to one another without necessarily operating in keeping with a progressive or teleological sequence. These adaptations do not lead "to the evolution of one algorithm or the other but to a new algorithmic behavior" (Parisi 2009, p. 357; Clough 2018, p. 142). As Clough points out: Big Data does not care about "you" so much as the bits of seemingly random information that bodies generate or that they leave as a data trail; the aim is to affect or pretend novelty (Clough 2018, pp. 142–143). In

India's political contexts, the registration procedures of datalogical processes (digital trails) are continuous with the sometimes secret, sometimes foregrounded biopolitical archipelago of states of exception scattered throughout Hindutva and its diasporas. Thus, the molecular and molar reaching beyond number of adaptive platform architectures dovetails with the mobile and predictive extrajudicial force that is the threat and reality of India's neo-fascist machines.

References

Adey, P. (2009). Facing Airport Security: Affect, Biopolitics, and the Preemptive Securitisation of the Mobile Body. *Environment and Planning D: Society and Space, 27*(2), 274–295.

Adorno, T. W. (2005). *The Culture Industry: Selected Essays on Mass Culture*. London: Routledge.

Adorno, T. W. (2009). *Current of Music*. Trans. Hullot-Kentor. Cambridge: Polity Press

Adorno, T. W. (2014). *Lectures on Negative Dialectics: Fragments of a Lecture Course 1965/1966*. Hoboken, NJ: John Wiley & Sons.

Adorno, T. W. (2017). *An Introduction to Dialectics*. Hoboken, NJ: John Wiley & Sons.

Agamben, G. (1998). *Homo Sacer: Sovereign Power and Bare Life*. Trans. D. Heller-Roazen. Stanford: Stanford University Press.

Agamben G. (2005). *State of Exception*. Trans. K. Attell. London: University of Chicago Press.

Anand, J. (2018). Can Local Services Marketplace Sulekha's Pivot Help It Turn a Profit? *Techcircle.in*. Retrieved from https://www.techcircle.in/2018/03/30/can-local-services-marketplace-sulekha-s-pivot-help-it-turn-a-profit.

Ash, J. (2012). Technology, Technicity, and Emerging Practices of Temporal Sensitivity in Videogames. *Environment and Planning A, 44*, 187–203.

Ash, J. (2013). Rethinking Affective Atmospheres: Technology, Perturbation and Space Times of the Non-human. *Geoforum, 49*, 20–28.

Balakrishnan, P. (2019). Unmoved by Stability Capital Formation in the Modi Economy. *Economic and Political Weekly, 54*(30), 27 July.

Barrett, N. F. (2014). The Perception of Religious Meaning and Value: An Ecological Approach. *Religion, Brain & Behavior, 4*(2), 127–146.

Behar, K. (Ed.). (2016). *Object-Oriented Feminism*. Minneapolis: University of Minnesota Press.

Beller, J. (2012). *The Cinematic Mode of Production: Attention Economy and the Society of the Spectacle*. Lebanon, NH: University Press of New England.

Benjamin, W. (2008). *The Work of Art in the Age of Its Technological Reproducibility, and Other Writings on Media*. Cambridge, MA: Harvard University Press.

Berardi, F. (2009). *The Soul at Work: From Alienation to Autonomy*. Los Angeles: Semiotext(e).
Berardi, F. (2010). *Precarious Rhapsody: Semiocapitalism and the Pathologies of the Post-Alpha Generation*. Minor Compositions.
Bergson, H. (1988). *Matter and Memory*. New York: Zone Books.
Best, B. (1999). Postcolonialism and the Deconstructive Scenario: Representing Gayatri Spivak. *Environment and Planning D: Society and Space, 17*(4), 475–494.
Bhattacharya, S. (2019). Groundwater, Gurus, and Governmentality Seva in the Neo-liberal Development Regime in India. *Economic and Political Weekly, 54*(32), 51–59.
Boltanski, L., & Chiapello, E. (2018). *The New Spirit of Capitalism*. London: Verso.
Chakrabarty, D. (2013). Subaltern Studies in Retrospect and Reminiscence. *Economic & Political Weekly, 48*(12), 23–27.
Chatterjee, P. (2012). After Subaltern Studies. *Economic & Political Weekly, 47*(35), 44–49.
Clough, P. T. (2010). Afterword: The Future of Affect Studies. *Body & Society, 16*, 222–230.
Clough, P. T. (2018). *The User Unconscious*. Minneapolis: University of Minnesota Press.
Clough, P. T., & Halley, J. (Eds.). (2007). *The Affective Turn*. Durham, NC: Duke University Press.
Clough, P. T., & Willse, C. (Eds.). (2011). *Beyond Biopolitics: Essays on the Governance of Life and Death*. Durham, NC: Duke University Press.
Coleman, M., & Grove, K. (2009). Biopolitics, Biopower, and the Return of Sovereignty. *Environment and Planning D: Society and Space, 27*(3), 489–507.
DeLanda, M. (1997). *A Thousand Years of Nonlinear History*. Cambridge, MA: MIT Press.
DeLanda, M. (2013). *Intensive Science and Virtual Philosophy*. London: Bloomsbury Publishing.
Deleuze, G. (1988). *Spinoza: Practical Philosophy*. San Francisco: City Lights Books.
Deleuze, G. (1992a). *Expressionism in Philosophy: Spinoza*. London: Zone Books.
Deleuze, G. (1992b). Postscript on the Societies of Control. *October, 59*, 3–7.
Deleuze, G., & Guattari, F. (1987). *A Thousand Plateaus*. New York: Continuum.
Derrida, J. (2004). *Dissemination*. London: Bloomsbury.
Grosz, E. (2005). Bergson, Deleuze and the Becoming of Unbecoming. *Parallax, 11*(2), 4–13.
Grosz, E. (2013). Habit Today: Ravaisson, Bergson, Deleuze and Us. *Body & Society, 19*, 217–239.
Guattari, F. (1995). *Chaosmosis. An Ethico-Aesthetic Paradigm*. Indianapolis, IN: Indiana University Press.
Guha, R. (1983). *Elementary Aspects of Peasant Insurgency in Colonial India*. London: Oxford University Press.

Hall, S. (1996). Race, Articulation, and Societies Structured in Dominance. In *Black British Cultural Studies: A Reader* (pp. 16–60). University of Chicago Press.

Hardt, M., & Negri, A. (1999). Value and Affect. *Boundary 2, 26*(2), 77–88.

Hardt, M., & Negri, A. (2009). *Commonwealth.* Harvard University Press.

Ingold, T. (2014). Religious Perception and the Education of Attention. *Religion, Brain & Behavior, 4*(2), 156–158.

Jameson, F. (2007). *Jameson on Jameson: Conversations on Cultural Marxism.* Durham: Duke University Press.

Jameson, F. (2009). *Valences of the Dialectic.* London: Verso.

Kaul, N. (2018). India's Obsession with Kashmir: Democracy, Gender, (Anti-) Nationalism. *Feminist Review, 119*(1), 126–143.

Latour, B. (2005). *Reassembling the Social.* Oxford: Oxford University Press.

Latour, B., Jensen, P., Venturini, T., Grauwin, S., & Boullier, D. (2012). 'The Whole is Always Smaller than Its Parts'–A Digital Test of Gabriel Tardes' Monads. *The British Journal of Sociology, 63*(4), 590–615.

Lazzarato, M. (2006). Immaterial Labor. In M. Hardt & P. Virno (Eds.), *Radical Thought in Italy: A Potential Politics* (pp. 133–150). Minneapolis, MN: University of Minnesota.

Lucretius. (2008). On the Nature of the Universe. Trans. R. Melville. London: Oxford University Press.

Lury, C., Parisi, L., & Terranova, T. (2012). Introduction: The Becoming Topological of Culture. *Theory, Culture and Society, 29*(4–5), 3–35.

Malabou, C. (2005). *The Future of Hegel: Plasticity, Temporality, and Dialectic.* New York: Routledge.

Manning, E. (2013). *Always More than One: Individuations Dance.* Durham, NC: Duke University Press.

Marx, K. (1973 [1839]). *Grundrisse: Foundations of the Critique of Political Economy.* New York: Penguin.

Marx, K. (1976 [1867]). *Capital: A Critique of Political Economy, Volume I.* New York: Penguin.

Massumi, B. (2002). *Parables for the Virtual: Movement, Affect, Sensation.* Durham, NC: Duke University Press.

Massumi, B. (2010). Perception Attack: Brief on War Time. *Theory & Event, 13*(3).

Massumi, B. (2015a). *Ontopower: War, Powers, and the State of Perception.* Durham, NC: Duke University Press.

Massumi, B. (2015b). *The Power at the End of the Economy.* Durham, NC: Duke University Press.

Mazumdar, R. (2001). Figure of the 'Tapori': Language, Gesture and Cinematic City. *Economic and Political Weekly, 36*(52), 4872–4880.

Nietzsche, F. (1983). *Untimely Meditations.* London: Cambridge University Press.

Nixon, N. (2019). Debating the 'After' of Subaltern Studies. *Economic & Political Weekly, 54*(29), 27–31.

Parisi, L. (2009). Symbiotic Architecture: Prehending Digitality. *Theory, Culture and Society, 26*(2–3), 346–374.
Pettman, D. (2016). *Infinite Distraction: Paying Attention to Social Media.* Cambridge: Polity Press.
Rai, A. S. (2019). *Jugaad Time: Ecologies of Everyday Hacking in India.* Durham, NC: Duke University Press.
Ravaisson, F. (2008). *Of Habit.* London: Bloomsbury Publishing.
Simondon, G. (2011). On the Mode of Existence of Technical Objects. *Deleuze Studies, 5*(3), 407–424.
Spivak, G. (1988). Can the Subaltern Speak? In C. Nelson & L. Grossberg (Eds.), *Marxism and the Interpretation of Culture* (pp. 271–313). Champaign, IL: University of Illinois Press.
Srnicek, N. (2017). *Platform Capitalism.* Cambridge: Polity Press.
Sundaram, R. (2015). Post-Postcolonial Sensory Infrastructure. *E-Flux Journal, 63,* 1–10.
Surie, A., & Koduganti, J. (2016). The Emerging Nature of Work in Platform Economy Companies in Bengaluru, India: The Case of Uber and Ola Cab Drivers. *E-Journal of International and Comparative Labour Studies, 5*(3).
Thrift, N. (2005). From Born to Made: Technology, Biology and Space. *Transactions of the Institute of British Geographers, 30*(4), 463–476.
Thrift, N. (2006). Re-Inventing Invention: New Tendencies in Capitalist Commodification. *Economy and Society, 35,* 279–306.
Toscano, A. (2009). Chronicles of Insurrection: Tronti, Negri and the Subject of Antagonism. *Cosmos and History: The Journal of Natural and Social Philosophy, 5*(1), 76–91.
Tronti, M. (1980). The Strategy of Refusal. *Semiotext (e), 3*(3), 28–34.
Tronti, M. (2010). Workerism and Politics. *Historical Materialism, 18*(3), 186–189.
Vercellone, C. (2007). From Formal Subsumption to General Intellect: Elements for a Marxist Reading of the Thesis of Cognitive Capitalism. *Historical Materialism, 15*(1), 13–36.
Virno, P. (2003). *A Grammar of the Multitude: For an Analysis of Contemporary Forms of Life.* Los Angeles: Semiotext (e).
Wright, S. (2002). *Storming Heaven.* London: Pluto Press.

Index

A. Athique, V. Parthasarathi (eds.), *Platform Capitalism in India*, Global Transformations in Media and Communication Research - A Palgrave and IAMCR Series,
https://doi.org/10.1007/978-3-030-44563-8

D

The manufacturer's authorised representative in the EU is Springer Nature Customer Service Centre GmbH, Europaplatz 3, 69115 Heidelberg, Germany. If you have any concerns regarding our products, please contact ProductSafety@springernature.com

Printed and bound by CPI Group (UK) Ltd, Croydon, CR0 4YY

30/09/2026

02225461-0016